Late Antique Studies in Memory of Alan Cameron

Columbia Studies in the Classical Tradition

Editorial Board

Holger A. Klein (*editor*)
Kathy H. Eden, Gareth D. Williams,
Seth R. Schwartz, Deborah Steiner, and Katja M. Vogt

Series founded by

Walther Ludwig and W. V. Harris

in collaboration with

W. T. H. Jackson and Paul Oskar Kristeller

VOLUME 46

The titles published in this series are listed at *brill.com/csct*

Alan Cameron (1938–2017)
Oaxaca, 1997

Late Antique Studies in Memory of Alan Cameron

Edited by

W. V. Harris
Anne Hunnell Chen

BRILL

LEIDEN | BOSTON

Library of Congress Cataloging-in-Publication Data

Names: Harris, William V. (William Vernon), editor, author. | Hunnell Chen, Anne, editor, author. | Cameron, Alan, 1938–2017, honouree.

Title: Late antique studies in memory of Alan Cameron / edited by W.V. Harris, Anne Hunnell Chen.

Description: Leiden ; Boston : Brill, [2021] | Series: Columbia studies in the classical tradition, 0166–1302 ; volume 46 | Includes bibliographical references and index.

Identifiers: LCCN 2021005194 (print) | LCCN 2021005195 (ebook) | ISBN 9789004449367 (hardback) | ISBN 9789004452794 (ebook)

Subjects: LCSH: Civilization, Classical. | Civilization, Ancient. | History, Ancient.

Classification: LCC DE86 .L376 2021 (print) | LCC DE86 (ebook) | DDC 937/.06—dc23

LC record available at https://lccn.loc.gov/2021005194

LC ebook record available at https://lccn.loc.gov/2021005195

Typeface for the Latin, Greek, and Cyrillic scripts: "Brill". See and download: brill.com/brill-typeface.

ISSN 0166-1302
ISBN 978-900-444936-7 (hardback)
ISBN 978-900-445279-4 (ebook)

Copyright 2021 by The Trustees of Columbia University in the City of New York. Published by Koninklijke Brill NV, Leiden, The Netherlands.

Koninklijke Brill NV incorporates the imprints Brill, Brill Hes & De Graaf, Brill Nijhoff, Brill Rodopi, Brill Sense, Hotei Publishing, mentis Verlag, Verlag Ferdinand Schöningh and Wilhelm Fink Verlag.

Koninklijke Brill NV reserves the right to protect this publication against unauthorized use. Requests for re-use and/or translations must be addressed to Koninklijke Brill NV via brill.com or copyright.com.

This book is printed on acid-free paper and produced in a sustainable manner.

Contents

Preface   IX
  W. V. Harris and Anne Hunnell Chen
List of Illustrations   X
Abbreviations   XIII
Notes on Contributors   XV
A Personal Note   XIX
Publications of Alan Cameron, 1963–2020   XXI

1   Alan Cameron and the Symmachi   1
  Rita Lizzi Testa

2   *Fel Temp Reparatio* and Themistius' *Oration 1*
  The Story of an Iconic Coin and a Career-Defining Panegyric   11
  Edward Watts

3   The *Historia Augusta*
  Minimalism and the Adequacy of Evidence   23
  Michael Kulikowski

4   Ambrose Thinks with Slavery   41
  Noel Lenski

5   Rutilius Namatianus, Melania the Younger, and the Monks
  of Capraria   66
  Gavin Kelly

6   Late Antique Homeric Exegesis in The *Greek Anthology*   85
  Arianna Gullo

7   Returning to the Wandering Poets
  New Poems by Dioscoros of Aphrodite   104
  Jean-Luc Fournet

8   The Lost *Farnesianus* Manuscript
  Uncial Capitals for the Bishops of Rome   134
  Carmela Vircillo Franklin

VIII

9   Late Antiquity Between Sasanian East and Roman West
Third-Century Imperial Women as Pawns in Propaganda Warfare   168
     Anne Hunnell Chen

10   Simony and the State
Politics and Religion in the Later Roman Empire   198
     Michele Renee Salzman

11   Stenographers in Late Antiquity
Villains or Victims?   220
     Raffaella Cribiore

12   Three Questions about the Ancient Hospital   233
     W. V. Harris

13   Celebrity and Power
Circus Factions *Forty Years On*   247
     Charlotte Roueché

14   Alan Cameron and Byzantium   260
     Averil Cameron

References   277
Index   316

Preface

This volume commemorates the life and work of Alan Cameron (1938–2017), a unique figure in the scholarship of Late Antiquity whose loss is deeply felt by very wide circles of scholars and friends of all ages in the United States, the UK and elsewhere. The reader of this book will encounter many allusions to Alan's acumen, energy and originality, and also to his generosity and good humor. Averil Cameron provides an invaluable account of his scholarly progress. For a particularly sympathetic memoir the reader can turn to what Glen Bowersock wrote in the *Proceedings of the American Philosophical Society* 162 (3) (2018), 1–8.

Columbia University's Classics Department sponsored a conference on October 27 and 28, 2018, in Alan's honor, and twelve of the scholars published here gave papers on that occasion (very different papers, in some cases, from those we are publishing). Edward Watts could not be present, and W. V. Harris's paper on the hospitals was written later.

There is no pretense of thematic unity here beyond the fact that the whole collection centers on Late Antiquity. In fact, we are happy to have avoided any more specific unity of theme, since Alan himself ranged over very many themes as well as over many centuries. He went wherever insatiable curiosity led him. It seems likely therefore that a commemorative conference and a subsequent book that reflected all of Alan's interests would have been considered by many people to be impossibly incoherent; so there is nothing here about Callimachus or about the literature of the high Roman Empire.

But there is a rich table at this commemorative feast, with new texts as well as commentaries on more familiar ones, with political and social and cultural history, with numismatics, papyrology, paleography, and a little epigraphy, with some old favorites of Alan's—circus factions and the *Historia Augusta*—and finally two chapters—one about Ambrose and slavery, the other about the history of the hospital—that we hope would have piqued his interest.

It is our remaining privilege to thank everyone who has helped with this project, and in particular and above all Professor Dame Averil Cameron, who has generously advised us throughout.

W. V. Harris
Anne Hunnell Chen
New York, December 2019

Illustrations

Figures

2.1 Coin of Constantius with Fel Temp Reparatio legend and emperor on galley reverse (RIC 8.Thessalonica.170). Private collection. Photo by author 18

7.1 Poem 1. Infrared image: Jean-Luc Fournet; image processing: Fabrice Bessière, Collège de France 106

7.2 Poem 2. Infrared image: Jean-Luc Fournet; image processing: Fabrice Bessière, Collège de France 110

7.3 Poem 3. Infrared image: Jean-Luc Fournet; image processing: Fabrice Bessière, Collège de France 115

8.1 Bianchini 2:xxiii. C 4237. 18 F. Widener Library Special Collections, Harvard University 140

8.2 Bianchini 2:lvii. C 4237. 18 F. Widener Library Special Collections, Harvard University 141

8.3 Bianchini 2:lviii. C 4237. 18 F. Widener Library Special Collections, Harvard University 142

8.4 Bianchini 2:lix. C 4237. 18 F. Widener Library Special Collections, Harvard University 143

8.5 Biblioteca Apostolica Vaticana, Vaticanus latinus 3836 (*Agimundus Homiliary*, vol. 2), f. 64ʳ 158

8.6 Rome, Biblioteca Vallicelliana, B.25 II (Codex Juvenianus), f. 51ʳ. Photo by Siria Sarmiento 159

8.7 Paris, Bibliothèque nationale de France, MS 10318 (Codex Salmasianus), 262 (view 272) 160

8.8 Biblioteca Apostolica Vaticana, Vaticanus latinus 3836 (*Agimundus Homiliary*, vol. 2), f. 67ᵛ 161

8.9 Paris, Bibliothèque nationale de France, MS 10318 (Codex Salmasianus), 229 (view 239) 162

8.10 Paris, Bibliothèque nationale de France, MS 10318 (Codex Salmasianus), 156 (view 166) 163

8.11 Paris, Bibliothèque nationale de France, MS 10318 (Codex Salmasianus), 134 (view 144) 164

9.1 Galerius and Narseh engaged in equestrian combat. Arch of Galerius, Thessaloniki (B.II.20). Photo by author 174

9.2 Sardonyx cameo featuring the Sasanian King of Kings capturing Emperor Valerian. Bibliothèque nationale de France, Cabinet des médailles, inv. Babelon 360. Photo courtesy of Marie-Lan Nguyen, via Wikimedia Commons 174

ILLUSTRATIONS

XI

9.3 Rock relief of Narseh with his queen (right) and a royal child (below). Naqsh-e Rustam III. Image courtesy of Livius.org 176

9.4 Investiture relief of Ardašīr I. Naqsh-e Rajab III. Image courtesy of Livius.org 178

9.5 Rock relief of Šābuhr I. Naqsh-e Rajab I. Image courtesy of Livius.org 179

9.6 Coin of Warahrān II with his queen and heir. Photo courtesy of The British Museum; Creative Commons Attribution-NonCommercial-ShareAlike 4.0 International (CC BY-NC-SA 4.0) license 180

9.7 Medallion obverse featuring jugate busts of Philip I and his wife Otacilla, facing Philip II. Image after Gnecchi 1912, v. 2 pl. 108 181

9.8 Warahrān II flanked by family and nobles. Naqsh-e Rustam II. Image courtesy of Livius.org 182

9.9 Relief dating to the reign of Warahrān II. King receiving a flower from female figure (queen?). Tang-e Qandil. Image courtesy of Livius.org 183

9.10 Relief dating to the reign of Warahrān II. Male figure (king?) presenting a flower to a female figure (queen?). Barm-e Delak I. Image courtesy of Livius.org 183

9.11 Warahrān II defends his queen from a lion. Sar Mashhad. Ernst Herzfeld Papers, FSA A.6, Freer Gallery of Art and Arthur M. Sackler Gallery Archives. Gift of Ernst Herzfeld, 1946, Ernst Herzfeld, FSA A.6 04.GN.2780 184

9.12 Silver bowl from the reign of Narseh. Metropolitan Museum accession no. 1970.5. Photo in the public domain; CC0 1.0 Universal (CC0 1.0) 186

9.13 Capture of the Persian Harem (A.I.2). Arch of Galerius, Thessaloniki. Photo by author 188

9.14 Transport of Persian prisoners (A.II.6). Arch of Galerius, Thessaloniki. Photo by author 188

9.15 Mirrored scenes (top two panels; A.III.9–10) of Tetrarchs receiving a male Persian suppliant, while the captured Sasanian imperial family looks on. Personifications of Persian cities (third panel from top; A.III.11). Arch of Galerius, Thessaloniki. Photo by author 189

9.16 *Pompa Triumphalis* with figures of Persian women and children aboard a cart (B.III.25). Arch of Galerius, Thessaloniki. Photo by author 190

9.17 Figure of Sasanian queen among a throng of gift-bearing Persians (B.I.18). Arch of Galerius, Thessaloniki. Photo by author 191

9.18 Medallion minted in 298 at Siscia in honor of Galerius, from the Münzkabinett of the Staatliche Museen zu Berlin Collection (reg. no. 18200727). Image © 2004–2020 Lech Stępniewski, https://www.forumancientcoins.com/notinric/index.html 192

9.19 Reverse of a Bronze sestersius from Rome issued by Lucius Verus, with a seated Parthian woman with Phrygian cap and coiffed hair tucked under the cap. ANS 1965.47.2. Image in the public domain: http://numismatics.org/collection/1965.47.2?lang=en 193

9.20 Eastern captives from a column base on the Arch of Constantine's eastern face. Rome. Image courtesy of the Media Center for Art History, Department of Art History & Archaeology, © The Trustees of Columbia University 196

9.21 Coin of Parthian king Phraataces and queen Musa. Image courtesy of Classical Numismatic Group, Inc. http://www.cngcoins.com, CC BY-SA 3.0 197

Table

13.1 Eastern Empire: Inscriptions mentioning the factions (as at winter 2019) 255

Abbreviations

Papyrological sources not listed below are abbreviated in accordance with Checklist of Greek, Latin, Demotic, and Coptic Papyri, Ostraca and Tablets (http://papyri.info/docs/checklist).

AJA	*American Journal of Archaeology*
AJPh	*American Journal of Philology*
Anth. Plan.	*Anthologia Planudea*
AP	*Anthologia Palatina*
AT	*Antiquité Tardive*
BASP	*Bulletin of the American Society of Papyrologists*
BHL	Bibliotheca Hagiographica Latina
BICS	*Bulletin of the Institute of Classical Studies,* London
BL	*Berichtigungsliste der griech. Papyrusurkunden aus Ägypten* (1922–)
BMCR	*Bryn Mawr Classical Review*
BZ	*Byzantinische Zeitschrift*
CCSL	*Corpus Christianorum, series Latina* (1953–)
CIL	*Corpus Inscriptionum Latinarum*
CLA	*Codices Latini Antiquiores: A Palaeographical Guide to Latin Manuscripts Prior to the Ninth Century.* 1934–1966. 12 vols., ed. E. A. Lowe (Oxford).
CLRE	*Consuls of the Later Roman Empire*, eds. R. S. Bagnall, A. Cameron, S. R. Schwartz and K. A. Worp (Atlanta, GA, 1987)
CPh	*Classical Philology*
CQ	*Classical Quarterly*
CR	*Classical Review*
CSEL	*Corpus Scriptorum Ecclesiasticorum Latinorum* (1866–)
CTh	*Codex Theodosianus*
EFH	*Entretiens [de la Fondation Hardt] sur l'antiquité classique*
EM	*Etymologicum Magnum*
GRBS	*Greek, Roman and Byzantine Studies*
HSCPh	*Harvard Studies in Classical Philology*
ICUR	*Inscriptiones Christianae Urbis Romae*
IGLS	*Inscriptions grecques et latines de la Syrie*
ILS	H. Dessau, *Inscriptiones Latinae Selectae*
JHS	*Journal of Hellenic Studies*
JLA	*Journal of Late Antiquity*
JRA	*Journal of Roman Archaeology*

JRS	*Journal of Roman Studies*
LfgrE	*Lexikon des frühgriechischen Epos*
LGB	*Lexikon des gesamten Buchwesens*
LPR	Alan Cameron, *Last Pagans of Rome* (2011)
MEFRA	*Mélanges de l'École française de Rome: Antiquité*
MGH AA	*Monumenta Germaniae Historica Auctores Antiquissimi*
MP3 + number	Mertens-Pack3 database (http://cipl93.philo.ulg.ac.be/Cedopal/ MP3/dbsearch_en.aspx)
OLD	*Oxford Latin Dictionary*
PG	*Patrologia Graeca*
PL	*Patrologia Latina*
PLRE	*Prosopography of the Later Roman Empire* 1, ed. A. H. M. Jones et al. (Cambridge, 1970); 2 and 3, ed. J. R. Martindale (Cambridge, 1980–92)
RAC	*Reallexikon für Antike und Christentum*
RhM	*Rheinisches Museum für Philologie*
RIC	H. Mattingly, E. A. Sydenham, et al., *Roman Imperial Coinage* (1923–67); rev. edn. of vol. 1 only, C. H. V. Sutherland and R. A. G. Carson (London, 1984)
SB	F. Preisigke et al., *Sammelbuch griechischen Urkunden aus Ägypten* (Berlin, 1915–)
SC	*Sources chrétiennes*
SEG	*Supplementum Epigraphicum Graecum*
SP	*Studia Patristica*
SPP	*Studien zur Palaeographie und Papyruskunde*
TM + number	Trismegistos texts database (http://www.trismegistos.org/ index2.php)
ThGl	*Thesaurus Graecae Linguae*, ed. H. Stephanus et al.
TLL	*Thesaurus Linguae Latinae*
ZPE	*Zeitschrift für Papyrologie und Epigraphik*

Notes on Contributors

Averil Cameron
met Alan Cameron while they were both undergraduates at Oxford and they married in 1962 but later divorced. Averil Cameron taught classics, and later ancient history and Byzantine studies, at King's College London from 1965 to 1994, when she moved back to Oxford as Warden of Keble College. Her first book was *Agathias* (Oxford, 1970) and she has published widely on Late Antiquity and Byzantium, most recently *Byzantine Matters* (Princeton, 2014), *Byzantine Christianity* (London, 2017), and several publications on dialogue in Late Antiquity and Byzantium.

Anne Hunnell Chen
specializes in the art and architecture of the late antique Mediterranean and Western Asiatic worlds. Recently, she has published on the ideological use of the Tetrarchic empresses, and argued for an interculturally informed rereading of Diocletian's Palace at Split. Her latest publication explores the modern socio-political circumstances that have resulted in the marginalization of Roman archaeological information from Southeastern Europe within Anglophone scholarship. She is a former Jane and Morgan Whitney Fellow at the Metropolitan Museum of Art, and currently a Postdoctoral Associate in Pre-Modern Cultures and Civilizations at Yale University.

Raffaella Cribiore
is a professor of Classics at New York University. Her main interests are ancient education and late antiquity. Among her books are *Writing, Teachers, and Students in Graeco-Roman Egypt* (Atlanta, 1996), *Gymnastics of the Mind: Greek Education in Hellenistic and Roman Egypt* (Princeton, 2001), *The School of Libanius in Late Antique Antioch* (Princeton, 2007), *Libanius the Sophist: Rhetoric, Reality and Religion in the Fourth Century* (Ithaca, NY, 2013), and *Between City and School: Selected Orations of Libanius TTH* 65 (Liverpool, 2016).

Jean-Luc Fournet
was appointed Professor at the Collège de France in 2015, holding the Written Culture in Late Antiquity and Byzantine Papyrology Chair of Papyrology. Prior to his current position, he was a scientific member of the Institut Français d'Archéologie Orientale in Cairo (1992–1996), researcher at the CNRS (1996–2004), and Professor at the École Pratique des Hautes Études (Department of Historical and Philological Sciences) in Paris (2004–2015 and again since 2017).

He devotes much of his scholarly activity to editing new papyri and to studying the culture of Late Antiquity—particularly poetry, multilingualism, and modalities of written culture.

Carmela Vircillo Franklin

is a professor of Classics at Columbia University. She served as the Director of the American Academy in Rome (2005–10), and President of the Medieval Academy of America (2016–17). She specializes in medieval Latin texts and their material manuscript context. She is currently preparing a critical edition of the twelfth-century redaction of the papal chronicle known as the *Liber pontificalis* for the *Monumenta Germaniae Historica*, and a series of articles charting the reception of the papal chronicle from the eighth to the nineteenth centuries.

Arianna Gullo

is currently Leverhulme Early Career Fellow at the University of Newcastle, having previously held a fellowship in Byzantine Studies at Dumbarton Oaks, a lectureship in Classics at the University of Glasgow, a Newton International Fellowship at Durham University and research fellowships at Dumbarton Oaks, the University of Cincinnati, and the American Academy in Rome. Her research interests are Greek epigram, Hellenistic poetry, and late antiquity. Her first monograph—a commentary on Book 7 of the *Greek Anthology*—is forthcoming in the Edizioni della Normale.

W. V. Harris

read Greats at Oxford at the same time as Alan Cameron. He spent his teaching career at Columbia, where he co-founded both *Columbia Studies in the Classical Tradition* and the Center for the Ancient Mediterranean. He is the author of *War and Imperialism in Republican Rome, 327–70 BC* (Oxford, 1979), *Ancient Literacy* (Cambridge, MA, 1989), *Restraining Rage: the Ideology of Anger Control in Classical Antiquity* (Cambridge, MA, 2001), which received the Breasted Prize of the American Historical Association, *Dreams and Experience in Classical Antiquity* (Cambridge, MA, 2009), and *Roman Power: a Thousand Years of Empire* (Cambridge, 2016). He is now working principally on the social history of ancient healthcare.

Gavin Kelly

has been based at the Department of Classics at the University of Edinburgh since 2005 and since 2016 has held a Personal Chair in Latin Literature and Roman History. He is the author of *Ammianus Marcellinus: The Allusive Historian*

(Cambridge, 2008), and articles on Ammianus, other late antique authors, and late Roman politics. He has edited *Two Romes: Rome and Constantinople in Late Antiquity* (New York, 2012) with Lucy Grig, and *The Edinburgh Companion to Sidonius Apollinaris* (Edinburgh, 2020) with Joop van Waarden. Plans include a new translation of Ammianus (with Michael Kulikowski), an Oxford text of the same author, and a commentary on Rutilius Namatianus.

Michael Kulikowski

is Edwin Erle Sparks Professor of History and Classics at Penn State, where he has been head of the History Department since 2010. He is the author of five books and numerous articles on the later Roman Empire, Romano-barbarian relations, and Eurasian Late Antiquity, most recently *The Triumph of Empire* (Cambridge, MA, 2016) and *The Tragedy of Empire* (Cambridge, MA, 2019), which together chart the history of the Roman Empire and its Eurasian context from the reign of the early second to the mid-sixth century. He and Gavin Kelly are currently at work on a fully annotated translation of Ammianus Marcellinus for the Landmark series.

Noel Lenski

is Professor of Classics and History at Yale University. He is author of *Failure of Empire: Valens and the Roman State in the Fourth Century AD* (Berkeley, 2002) and *Constantine and the Cities: Imperial Authority and Civic Politics* (Philadelphia, 2016), both of which reflect his interest in imperial politics in Late Antiquity. He has also worked extensively on the history of ancient slavery, including his co-edited volume, with Catherine M. Cameron, *What is a Slave Society? The Practice of Slavery in Global Perspective* (Cambridge, 2018).

Rita Lizzi Testa

studied in Florence, London (King's College), and Princeton (Institute for Advanced Study). She taught at the University of Turin and is now Professor of Roman History at the University of Perugia. She has published numerous articles on the Christianization and conversion of the Roman Empire, and is the author and editor of several books on the governance of late antique towns, and on the conflict and dialogue among pagans and Christians in the Roman Empire.

Charlotte Roueché

is Professor Emerita of Digital Hellenic Studies at King's College London, whose early career was helped by Alan Cameron. She has worked extensively on inscriptions from Asia Minor and (more recently) North Africa, with a particular focus on materials from Late Antiquity. Since 2000 she has been publishing both inscriptions and literary texts online, testing out the possibilities of the new medium.

Michele Renee Salzman
is Professor of Ancient History at the University of California, Riverside. She is the author of numerous articles and books on the social and religious history of the late Roman Empire. She issued a new version in 2015 of *The Letters of Symmachus: Book 1* (including a translation with Michael Roberts) and was the principal editor of *Pagans and Christians in Late Antique Rome*, with M. Sághy and R. Lizzi Testa (New York, 2016). She has served on the board of the American Academy in Rome and of the Society for Classical Studies, as well as on numerous editorial boards.

Edward Watts
is Alkiviadis Vassiliadis Endowed Chair and Professor of History at University of California, San Diego. The author or editor of ten books, his publications discuss the cultural, political, and religious history of the Roman and Byzantine worlds from the third century BCE through the ninth century CE. His most recent books include *Hypatia of Alexandria* (Oxford, 2017) and *Mortal Republic* (New York, 2018). He is currently working on a monograph tracing Roman ideas of decline and renewal from 200 BCE through the twenty-first century and on a second book examining Roman identity from 96 until 850 CE.

A Personal Note

In Alan's memory ... what a bitter phrase! We sometimes joked about which of us would write the other's obituary. Alan was six months older than me but probably lived a healthier lifestyle, apart from his propensity for riding a bicycle at great speed around Manhattan. Even when he fell mortally ill in 2016, I like everyone else hoped that he would still be able to enjoy life for several years longer. That still seemed just about possible when I last saw him, at his Riverside Drive flat, in February 2017. I was spending the academic year in Berlin, and now sorely regret that I did not come back to New York in the summer when I knew that he was due to suffer more surgery. At least he got to see his new grandson Silas Cameron, which no doubt lifted his spirits much more than any visit from a contemporary would have done.

It is impossible to commemorate properly a friendship of more than fifty years' duration in a few sentences or a few pages. For some forty of those years, though never members of the same department at Columbia, we often collaborated, worked with the same graduate students (Alan was more easy-going, in contrast with his way of dealing with the aberrations of published scholars) and tried to help the same younger faculty members. We were both very delighted to live in New York, for all its horrendous defects. We used to share characterizations of our professional colleagues and of Columbia administrators. On uncounted occasions we enjoyed each other's hospitality (in early days some of Alan's parties were so good that the neighbours complained). It pleased each of us that in mature middle age the other found himself married to exactly the right person.

In all that time we only once disagreed sharply, and the issue was quickly resolved and forgotten. As all his friends knew, Alan practised *ataraxia* in the best Epicurean manner. But that left plenty of room for generous indignation, which might be stirred by fraudulent politicians or obtuse scholars but never by students, who were always looked on with an indulgent eye.

Others have written about Alan's scholarship. Two traits always typified him—energy and scepticism. Those of his undergraduate contemporaries who became scholars stayed, most of them, quite close to traditional classical fields, in their early years at least (Averil Cameron was the great exception). We were astonished to learn that Alan very quickly became a master of late Roman and Byzantine authors and historical problems that we scarcely knew existed. And this energy continued far into retirement; he was cut off when he could still have written so much more. And scepticism was, with him, practically physiological. He was not interested in philosophy or law, fields that reinforce a person's natural scepticism, but no one was better at seeing that another scholar's more or less pretentious edifice was a house of cards or something not much better. Arguments will continue about such subjects as the circus factions and the 'pagan' intellectuals' opposition to Christianity, but it was Alan's achievement to have re-set these and many other debates. His was truly a unique voice: he was not a classicist, not a literature scholar, not a historian, not an art-historian, but a blend of all of these. There remains an astonishing body of work—

> *quod non imber edax, non aquilo impotens*
> *possit diruere....*
>
>   *William Harris*

Publications of Alan Cameron, 1963–2020

1   **Books**

1   *Claudian: Poetry and Propaganda at the Court of Honorius* (Oxford: Clarendon Press, 1970).
2   *Porphyrius the Charioteer* (Oxford: Clarendon Press, 1973).
3   *Circus Factions: Blues and Greens at Rome and Byzantium* (Oxford: Clarendon Press, 1976).
4   *Literature and Society in the Early Byzantine World* (London: Variorum Reprints, 1985).
5   (With R. S. Bagnall, S. R. Schwartz, and K. A. Worp) *Consuls of the Later Roman Empire (284–541)* (Atlanta: Scholars Press, 1987).
6   *The Greek Anthology: from Meleager to Planudes* (Oxford: Clarendon Press, 1993).
7   (With Jacqueline Long and a contribution by L. Cherry) *Barbarians and Politics at the Court of Arcadius* (Berkeley and Los Angeles: University of California Press, 1993).
8   *Callimachus and his Critics* (Princeton: Princeton University Press, 1995).
9   *Greek Mythography in the Roman World* (Oxford and New York: Oxford University Press, 2004).
10   *The Last Pagans of Rome* (Oxford and New York: Oxford University Press, 2011).
11   *Wandering Poets and Other Essays on Late Greek Literature and Philosophy* (Oxford and New York: Oxford University Press, 2016).
12   *Studies in Late Roman Literature and History* (Bari: Edipuglia, 2016).
13   *Historical Studies in Late Roman Art and Archaeology* (Leuven: Peeters, forthcoming).

2   **Articles and Reviews**

Alan Cameron also contributed significantly to the first two volumes of the *Prosopography of the Later Roman Empire* (I, ed. A. H. M. Jones, J. R. Martindale and J. Morris [Cambridge, 1970]; II, ed. J. R. Martindale [Cambridge, 1980]). The preface to volume I states that "most of the biographies of literary persons" were owed to him. As one-time chairman of the Prosopography's supervisory committee, he co-signed the preface to volume II.

1963

1   "An Alleged Fragment of Eunapius," *CQ* n.s. 13, 232–236.
2   "Priscus of Panium and John Malalas in Suidas," *CR* n.s. 13, 264.
3   "A Vatican Manuscript of Claudian," *Scriptorium* 17, 316.

1964

4   "Literary Allusions in the *Historia Augusta*," *Hermes* 92, 363–377.
5   "Palladas and the Nikai," *JHS* 84, 54–62.
6   "The Roman Friends of Ammianus," *JRS* 54, 15–28. Reprinted in A12.
7   (Jointly with Averil Cameron) "Christianity and Tradition in the Historiography of the Late Empire," *CQ* 14, 316–328.
8   "Palladas and the Fate of Gessius," *BZ* 57, 279–292.
9   "A New Manuscript of Paulus Diaconus' *Historia Romana*," *Latomus* 23, 818–819.
10 "A Disguised Manuscript of Rufinus' Translation of Eusebius' *Ecclesiastical History*," *Scriptorium* 18, 270–271.
11 "The *follis* in Fourth Century Egypt," *Numismatic Chronicle*, seventh series 4, 135–138.

1965

12 "*Tener Unguis* (Horace, *Odes* iii.6.21f.)," *CQ* 15, 80–83.
13 "Horace, *Epistles* ii.8.87f.," *CR* 15, 11–13.
14 "Claudian and St. Jerome," *Vigiliae Christianae* 19, 111–113.
15 "Two Glosses in Aurelius Victor," *CR* 15, 21–22.
16 "A Fragment from a Lost Commentary on Virgil," *Philologus* 109, 157–159.
17 "The Fate of Pliny's *Letters* in the Late Empire," *CQ* 15, 289–298. Reprinted in A12.
18 "Eunuchs in the *Historia Augusta*," *Latomus* 24, 155–158.
19 "Wandering Poets: A Literary Movement in Byzantine Egypt," *Historia* 14, 470–509. Reprinted in A4 and in a much-revised version in A11.
20 "Palladas and Christian Polemic," *JRS* 55, 17–30. Reprinted in A4.
21 "Notes on Palladas," *CQ* 15, 215–229.
22 "Roman School Fees," *CR* 15, 257–258.
23 Review/Discussion of J. Straub, *Heidnische Geschichtsapologetik in der christlichen Spätantike* (Bonn, 1963), *JRS* 55, 240–248.
24 Review of *Bonner Historia August-Colloquium* (Bonn, 1963), *JRS* 55, 248–249.
25 Review of *Atti del colloquio patavino sulla Historia Augusta* (Rome, 1963), *JRS* 55, 249–250.
26 Review of C. Gnilka, *Studien zur Psychomachie des Prudentius* (Bonn, 1963), *JRS* 55, 308.

1966

27 (Jointly with Averil Cameron) "The *Cycle* of Agathias," *JHS* 86, 6–25.

28 (Jointly with Averil Cameron) "*Anth. Plan.*72—a Propaganda Poem from the Reign of Justin II," *BICS* 13, 101–104.

29 "Caelius on C. Antonius," *CR* 16, 17.

30 "A Biographical Note on Claudian," *Athenaeum* 44, 32–40.

31 "The Date and Identity of Macrobius," *JRS* 56, 25–38.

1967

32 "Iamblichus at Athens," *Athenaeum* 45, 143–153. Reprinted in A4.

33 "St. Augustine and Cicero," *Hermes* 95, 256.

34 "Greek Tragedy in Sixth Century Epirus," *CR* 17, 134.

35 "Pliny's *Letters* in the Late Empire—an Addendum," *CQ* 17, 421–422.

36 "*Aenus* and *aenipes*: Two Notes on Prudentius," *Philologus* 111, 147–150.

37 "A New Fragment of Eunapius," *CR* 17, 10–11.

38 "The Date of Porphyry's κατα χριστιανῶν," *CQ* 17, 382–384. Reprinted in A4.

39 "Rutilius Namatianus, St. Augustine and the Date of the *De Reditu*", *JRS* 57, 31–39.

40 "Macrobius, Avienus and Avianus," *CQ* 17, 385–395.

41 "The Treatise *De Verbo* Ascribed to Macrobius," *BICS* 14, 91–92.

42 "Tacitus and the Date of Curiatius Maternus' Death," *CR* 17, 258–261.

43 "Two Notes of the *Greek Anthology (Anth.Pal.* ix.474, 395 and 458)," *BICS* 14, 58–61.

44 "Further Thoughts on the *Cycle* of Agathias," *JHS* 87, 131.

45 "The End of the Ancient Universities," *Journal of World History/Cahiers d'histoire mondiale* 10, 653–673.

46 "The Vergilian Cliché of the Hundred Mouths in Corippus," *Philologus* 111, 308–309.

47 Review of A. Demandt, *Zeitkritik und Geschichtsbild im Werk Ammians* (Bonn, 1965), *CR* 17, 60–63.

48 Review of J. Fitz, *Ingénuus et Régalien* (Brussels, 1966), *CR* 17, 229–230.

49 Review of A. Birley, *Marcus Aurelius* (London, 1966), *CR* 17, 347–350.

1968

50 "Theodosius the Great and the Regency of Stilico," *HSCPh* 73, 247–280.

51 "Echoes of Vergil in St. Jerome's *Life* of Hilarion," *CPh* 63, 55–56.

52 "The Date of Iamblichus' Birth," *Hermes* 96, 374–376. Reprinted in A4.

53 "Celestial Consulates: a Note on the Pelagian letter *Humanae referunt*," *Journal of Theological Studies* 19, 213–215.

54 "Gratian's Repudiation of the Pontifical Robe," *JRS* 58, 96–102.

55 "The First Edition of Ovid's *Amores*," *CQ* 18, 320–333.

56   "*Anth.Plan.*72.7," *CR* 18, 21–22.

57   "Notes on Claudian's Invectives," *CQ* 18, 387–411.

58   "The *Garlands* of Meleager and Philip of Thessalonica," *GRBS* 9, 323–349.

59   "Student Rebellion at Columbia," *Oxford Magazine* (Trinity no.8), 403–404.

60   "Three Notes on the *Historia Augusta*," *CR* 18, 17–20.

61   Review of J. J. Buchanan and H. T. Davis, *Zosimus: the New History* (San Antonio, 1967), *Classical World* 62, 19.

1969

62   "The Last Days of the Academy at Athens," *Proceedings of the Cambridge Philological Society* n.s. 15, 7–29. Reprinted in A4 and A11.

63   "The Date of Zosimus' *New History*," *Philologus* 113, 106–110.

64   "Gregory of Nazianzus and Apollo," *Journal of Theological Studies* 20, 240–241.

65   (jointly with Averil Cameron) "Erinna's *Distaff*," *CQ* 19, 285–289.

66   Review of C. H. Coster, *Late Roman Studies* (Cambridge, MA, 1968), *AJPh* 90, 124–127.

67   Review of J. W. Eadie, *The Breviarium of Festus* (London, 1967), *CR* 19, 305–307.

1970

68   "*Pap. Ant.* iii.115 and the Iambic Prologue in Late Greek Poetry," *CQ* 20, 119–129. Reprinted in A4.

69   Articles "Christodorus" and "Colluthus," in N. G. L. Hammond and H. H. Scullard (eds.), *Oxford Classical Dictionary*, 2nd edition.

70   "Michael Psellus and the Date of the *Palatine Anthology*," *GRBS* 11, 339–350.

1971

71   "La fin de l'Académie," in *Le Néoplatonisme* (Colloques internationaux du Centre national de la recherche scientifique). Paris, 281–290.

72   Review/Discussion of R. Syme, *Ammianus and the Historia Augusta* (Oxford, 1968), *JRS* 61, 255–267.

73   Review of R. I. Frank, *Scholae Palatinae: the Palace Guards of the Later Roman Empire* (Rome, 1969), *CR* 21, 136–138.

1972

74   "Callimachus on Aratus' Sleepless Nights," *CR* 22, 169–170.

PUBLICATIONS OF ALAN CAMERON, 1963–2020

75 Review of P. Brown, *Religion and Society in the Age of Saint Augustine* (London, 1972), *Times Higher Education Supplement*, December 15.

76 Review of P. V. Davies, *Macrobius: the Saturnalia* (New York, 1967) and N. Marinone, *Macrobio: I Saturnali* (Turin, 1967), *CR* 22, 44–46.

77 Review of E. Pasoli (ed.), *Scriptores Historiae Augustae: Iulius Capitolinus, Opilius Macrinus* (Bologna, 1968) and E. Manni (ed.), *Trebellio Pollione, Le vite di Valeriano e di Gallieno* (Palermo, 1969), *CR* 22, 115.

1973

78 "W. W. Cruickshank," *The Pauline*, 76.

79 "Sex in the Swimming Pool," *BICS* 20, 149–150.

80 Review of A. Chastagnol, *Recherches sur l'Histoire Auguste* (Bonn, 1970), *CR* 23, 58–60.

1974

81 "Bread and Circuses: The Roman Emperor and his People." Inaugural Lecture, King's College, London.

82 "Claudian," In J. W. Binns (ed.), *Latin Literature of the Fourth Century.* London, 134–159. Reprinted in A11.

83 "Demes and Factions," *BZ* 44, 74–91.

84 "The Date of Priscian's *De laude Anastasii*," *GRBS* 15, 313–316. Reprinted in A4.

85 "Heresies and Factions," *Byzantion* 44, 92–120.

1975

86 "Δυσώνομος Βασιλίσκος (*V. Dan.Styl.* 70)," *Hermes* 103, 383.

87 "Claudian and the Ages of Rome," *Maia* 27, 47.

1976

88 "A Quotation from St. Nilus of Ancyra in an Iconodule Tract," *Journal of Theological Studies* 27, 128–131.

89 "The Authenticity of the Correspondence of St. Nilus of Ancyra," *GRBS* 17, 181–196. Reprinted in A4.

90 "Theodorus τρισέπαρχος", *GRBS* 17, 269–286. Reprinted in A4.

91 (Jointly with Averil Cameron) "Textual Notes on Corippus, *In laudem Iustini minoris*," *Latomus* 35, 404–415.

92 "Catullus 29," *Hermes* 104, 155–163.

1977

93 "Paganism and Literature in Fourth Century Rome," in *Christianisme et formes littéraires de l'antiquité tardive en occident* (= *EFH* 23). Geneva, 1–30.

94 "Some Prefects Called Julian," *Byzantion* 47, 42–64. Reprinted in A4.

1978

95 "Cyril of Scythopolis, *V.Sabae* 53: a Note on κατά in Late Greek," *Glotta* 56, 87–94.

96 "The House of Anastasius," *GRBS* 19, 259–276. Reprinted in A4.

1979

97 "The Consuls of A.D. 411–412," *BASP* 16, 175–177.

98 "Propertius I.1 and Constantine the Sicilian," *CPh* 74, 58–60.

99 "The Date of the Anonymus *De Rebus Bellicis*," in M. W. C. Hassall (ed.), *Aspects of the De Rebus Bellicis: Papers Presented to Professor E. A. Thompson* (British Archaeological Reports: International Series 63). Oxford, 1–10. Reprinted in A4.

1980

100 "The *Garland* of Philip," *GRBS* 21, 43–62.

101 "Two Notes on the *Greek Anthology*," *CPh* 75, 140–141.

102 "Poetae Novelli," *HSCPh* 84, 127–175. Reprinted in A12.

103 "Crinagoras and the Elder Julia (*AP* vi.345)," *Liverpool Classical Monthly* 5, 129–30.

104 "Circus Factions and Religious Parties: a Rejoinder," *Byzantion* 50, 336–337.

1981

105 "The Consuls of A.D. 411–412 Again," *BASP* 18, 69–72.

106 "Notes on the Erotic Art of Rufinus," *GRBS* 22, 179–186.

107 "Boethius' Father's Name," *ZPE* 44, 181–183.

108 Review of D. Page (ed.), *The Epigrams of Rufinus* (Cambridge, 1978), *Latomus* 40, 394–396.

1982

109 "The Empress and the Poet: Paganism and Poetry at the Court of Theodosius II," *Yale Classical Studies* 27, 217–289. Reprinted in A4 and in a revised version in A11.

110 "Asclepiades' Girlfriends," in H. P. Foley (ed.), *Reflections of Women in Antiquity*. London, 275–302.

111 "A Note on Ivory Carving in Fourth Century Constantinople," *AJA* 86, 126–129. Reprinted in A4 and A13.

112 (Jointly with Diane Schauer) "The Last Consul: Basilius and his Diptych," *JRS* 72, 126–145. Reprinted in A4.

PUBLICATIONS OF ALAN CAMERON, 1963–2020

113 "Strato and Rufinus," *CQ* 32, 162–173. Reprinted in A4.

114 "The Death of Vitalian," *ZPE* 48, 93–94.

115 Review of J. Flamant, *Macrobe et le néoplatonisme latin à la fin du IVᵉ siècle* (Leiden, 1977), *CPh* 77, 378–380.

116 Review of W. Barr, *Claudian's Panegyric on the Fourth Consulate of Honorius* (Liverpool, 1981), *Latomus* 41, 659–661.

1983

117 "Martial 4. 17," *CPh* 78, 45–46.

118 "Crantor and Posidonius on Atlantis," *CQ* 33, 81–91.

119 "The Epigrams of Sophronius," *CQ* 33, 284–292. Reprinted in A4.

120 (Jointly with Charlotte Innes) "Wrong Autopsy Report for the Roman Empire," Letter to the Editor, *New York Times*, 14 June.

121 "Fall of the Roman Empire: More than Lead," Letter to the Editor, *International Herald Tribune*, 20 June.

1984

122 "A New Late Antique Ivory: the Fauvel Panel," *AJA* 88, 397–402. Reprinted in A13.

123 "The Latin Revival of the Fourth Century," in W. Treadgold (ed.), *Renaissances before the Renaissance*. Stanford, 42–58 and 182–184.

124 "Probus' Praetorian Games," *GRBS* 25, 193–196. Reprinted in A12.

125 "Junior Consuls," *ZPE* 56, 159–172. Reprinted in A12.

126 "Dispelling Myths about Gays," Letter to the Editor, *Bergen Record*, 16 May.

127 "Bacchius, Dionysius and Constantine," *Phoenix* 38, 256–260.

128 "Anicius Claudius (*I.Cret.* iv. 322)," *ZPE* 57, 147–148.

129 "The *Pervigilium Veneris*," in *La poesia tardoantica: tra retorica, teologia e politica.* Messina, 209–234. Reprinted in A12.

130 Contributions to Averil Cameron and J. Herrin (eds.), *Constantinople in the Early Eighth Century: the Parastaseis Syntomoi Chronikai* (Columbia Studies in the Classical Tradition 10). Leiden.

1985

131 "The Date and Owners of the Esquiline Treasure," *AJA* 89, 135–145. Reprinted in A13.

132 "A Lousy Conjecture: Housman to Phillimore," *HSCPh* 89, 235–236.

133 "Polyonomy in the Roman Aristocracy: The Case of Petronius Probus," *JRS* 75, 164–182. Reprinted in A12.

134 "Nonius Atticus Maximus," *Epigraphica* 47, 109–110.

135 Review of R. Syme, *Historia Augusta Papers* (Oxford, 1983), *Classical Outlook* 62, 136.

136 (Jointly with R. S. Bagnall) Review of Z. Borkowski, *Alexandrie II: Inscriptions des factions à Alexandrie* (Warsaw, 1981), *BASP* 22, 75–84.

1986

137 "Martianus Capella and his First Editor," *CPh* 81, 320–328. Reprinted in A12.

138 "Pagan Ivories," in F. Paschoud (ed.), *Symmaque à l'occasion du mille six centième anniversaire du conflit de l'autel de la Victoire.* Paris, 41–64.

139 Review of R. Schieffer, *Acta Conciliorum Oecumenicorum* IV.iii,2, *Index prosopographicus et topographicus* (Berlin, 1982–4, 3 v.), *CPh* 81, 98–103.

1987

140 "Sir Thomas Moore and the Greek Anthology," in K.-L. Selig and R. Somerville (eds.), *Florilegium Columbianum: Essays in Honor of Paul Oskar Kristeller.* New York, 187–198.

141 "Earthquake 400," *Chiron* 17, 343–360.

1988

142 (Jointly with J. Long and L. Sherry) "Textual Notes on Synesius' *De Providentia*," *Byzantion* 58, 54–64.

143 "An Unknown General," *CPh* 83, 13–14. Reprinted in A13.

144 "A Misidentified Homily of Chrysostom," *Nottingham Medieval Studies* 32, 34–48.

145 "Flavius: A Nicety of Protocol," *Latomus* 47, 26–33. Reprinted in A12.

1989

146 "Biondo's Ammianus: Constantius and Hormisdas at Rome," *HSCPh* 92, 423–436. Reprinted in A12.

1990

147 "Forschungen zum Thema der 'Heidnischen Reaktion' in der Literatur seit 1943," in A. Alföldi and E. Alföldi (eds.), *Die Kontorniat-Medaillons* II: *Text.* Berlin, 63–74.

1991

148 "Isidore and Hypatia: A Note on the Editing of Mathematical Texts," *GRBS* 31, 103–127.

149 "How Thin was Philitas?," *CQ* 41, 534–538.

150 "Two Mistresses of Ptolemy Philadelphus," *GRBS* 31, 287–311.

PUBLICATIONS OF ALAN CAMERON, 1963–2020

1992

151 "Observations on the Distribution and Ownership of late Roman Silver Plate," *JRA* 5, 178–187. Reprinted in A13.

152 "Filocalus and Melania," *CPh* 87, 140–144. Reprinted in A13.

153 "Callimachus and his Critics," in *Apodosis: Essays presented to Dr. W. W. Cruickshank to Mark his Eightieth Birthday.* London, 1–9.

154 "Genre and Style in Callimachus," *Transactions of the American Philological Association* 122, 305–312.

155 Review of D. Roques, *Synésios de Cyrène et la Cyrénaique du Bas-Empire* (Paris, 1987) and *Études sur la correspondence de Synésios de Cyrène* (Brussels, 1989), *JRA* 5, 419–430.

1993

156 "On the Date of John of Gaza," *CQ* 43, 348–351.

157 "Julian and Hellenism," *Ancient World* 24, 25–29.

1994

158 "Constantine the Rhodian and the Greek Anthology," *Byzantinische Forschungen* 20, 261–267.

1995

159 "Avienus or Avienius," *ZPE* 108, 252–262. Reprinted in A12.

160 "Ancient Anagrams," *AJPh* 116, 477–484.

1996

161 "Orfitus and Constantius: A Note on Roman Gold-glasses," *JRA* 9, 295–301. Reprinted in A13.

162 Articles "Alcaeus 3," "Anthology," "Antipater 3," "Antipater 5," "Antiphilus," "Anyte," "Archias," "Argentarius 1," "Argentarius 2," "Asclepiades 2," "Constantinople," "Crinagoras," "Dioscorides 1," "Diotimus," "Epigram (Greek)," "Erycius 1," "Hedylus," "Hegesippus 3," "Honestus," "Leonidas 2," "Lollius Bassus," "Lucillius," "Meleager 2," "Mnasalces," "Nicaenetus," "Nicarchus," "Nossis," "Philippus 7," "Posidippus 2," "Simylus 1 and 2," "Zonas," in S. Hornblower and A. Spawforth (eds.), *The Oxford Classical Dictionary*, 3rd rev. edition. Oxford.

1998

163 "Black and White: A Note on Ancient Nicknames," *AJPh* 119, 113–117.

164 "Basilius, Mavortius, Asterius," in I. Sevcenko and I. Hutter (eds.), *ΑΕΤΟΣ: Studies in Honour of Cyril Mango.* Stuttgart and Leipzig, 28–39. Reprinted in A13.

165 "Consular Diptychs in their Social Context: New Eastern Evidence," *JRA* 11, 384–403.

1999
166 "The Antiquity of the Symmachi," *Historia* 48, 477–505. Reprinted in A12.
167 "Love (and Marriage) between Women," *GRBS* 39, 137–156. Reprinted in A12.
168 "The Last Pagans of Rome," in W. V. Harris (ed.), *The Transformations of Urbs Roma in Late Antiquity.* Portsmouth, RI, 109–121.

2000
169 "Claudian Revisited," in F. E. Consolino (ed.), *Letteratura e propaganda nell'occidente latino da Augusto ai regni romanobarbarici.* Rome, 127–144. Reprinted in A11.
170 "The Poet, the Bishop, and the Harlot," *GRBS* 41, 175–188. Revised version reprinted in A11.

2001
171 "The *Epitome de Caesaribus* and the *Chronicle* of Marcellinus," *CQ* 51, 324–327.
172 "Oracles and Earthquakes: A Note on the Theodosian Sibyl," in C. Sode and S. Takáks (eds.), *Novum Millennium: Studies on Byzantine History and Culture Dedicated to Paul Speck.* Aldershot, 45–52. Reprinted in A11.

2002
173 "The Funeral of Junius Bassus," *ZPE* 139, 288–292. Reprinted in A12.
174 "Petronius Probus, Aemilius Probus and the Transmission of Nepos: a Note on Late Roman Calligraphers," in J.-M. Carrié and R. Lizzi Testa (eds.), *"Humana Sapit": Études d'antiquité tardive offertes à Lellia Cracco Ruggini.* Turnhout, 121–130. Reprinted in A13.

2003
175 "A Greek Source of Ovid's *Metamorphoses*," in D. Accorinti and P. Chuvin (eds.), *Des Géants à Dionysos: Mélanges de mythologie et de poésie grecques offerts à Francis Vian.* Alessandria, 41–59.

PUBLICATIONS OF ALAN CAMERON, 1963–2020

2004

176 "Poetry and Literary Culture in Late Antiquity," in S. Swain and M. Edwards (eds.), *Approaching Late Antiquity: The Transformation from Early to Late Empire*. Oxford, 327–354. Reprinted in A11.

177 "Vergil Illustrated, between Pagans and Christians," *JRA* 17, 501–525. Reprinted in A13.

2006

178 Review of M. A. Guggisberg, *Der Schatz von Kaiseraugst. Die Neuen Funde* (Augst, 2003), *JRA* 19, 695–702. Reprinted in A13.

179 Review of U. Roberto, *Ioannis Antiocheni Fragmenta* (Berlin, 2005), *Bryn Mawr Classical Review* 2006.07.37.

2007

180 "The Probus Diptych and Christian Apologetic," in H. Amirav and B. ter Haar Romeny (eds.), *From Rome to Constantinople: Studies in Honour of Averil Cameron*. Leuven, 191–202. Reprinted in A13.

181 "The Imperial Pontifex," *HSCPh* 103, 341–384. Reprinted in A12.

182 "Poets and Pagans in Byzantine Egypt," in R. S. Bagnall (ed.), *Egypt in the Byzantine World*. Cambridge, 21–46. Revised version reprinted in A11.

2009

183 "Young Achilles in the Roman World," *JRS* 99, 1–22. Reprinted in A13.

2010

184 "The Date of the Scholia Vetustiora on Juvenal," *CQ* 60, 569–576. Reprinted in A12.

185 "Psyche and her Sisters," *Latomus* 69, 170–177. Reprinted in A12.

2011

186 "The Transmission of Cassian," *Revue d'histoire des textes* n.s. 6, 361–365. Reprinted in A12.

187 Review of S. Ratti, *Antiquus error: les ultimes feux de la résistance païenne* (Turnhout, 2010), *JRA* 24, 835–846. Reprinted in A12.

2012

188 "Nicomachus Flavianus and the Date of Ammianus's Last Books," *Athenaeum* 112, 337–358. Reprinted in A12.

189 "Anician Myths", *JRS* 102, 1–40. Reprinted in A12.

190 "Basilius and his Diptych again: Career Titles, Seats in the Colosseum, and Issues of Stylistic Dating", *JRA* 25, 501–518. Reprinted in A13.

2013

191 "The Origin, Function, and Context of Consular Diptychs", *JRS* 103, 174–207. Reprinted in A13.

192 "Hypatia: Life, Death, and Works", in D. Lauritzen and M. Tardieu (eds.), *Le Voyage des légendes: Hommages à Pierre Chuvin*, Paris, 65–82. Revised version reprinted in A11.

2014

193 "Momigliano and the *Historia Augusta*", in T. Cornell and O. Murray (eds.), *The Legacy of Arnaldo Momigliano*. London, 147–164. Reprinted in A12.

194 "*Pontifex Maximus*: from Augustus to Gratian—and Beyond," in M. Kahlos (ed.), *Emperors and the Divine*. Helsinki, 139–159. Reprinted in A12.

2015

195 "City Personifications and Consular Diptychs", *JRS* 105, 250–287. Reprinted in A13.

2016

196 "The Status of Serena and the Stilicho Diptych", *JRA* 29, 509–516. Reprinted in A13.

197 "Were Pagans Afraid to Speak their Mind in a Christian World? The Correspondence of Symmachus", in M. Salzman, M. Sághy and R. Lizzi Testa (eds.). *Pagans and Christians in Late Antique Rome*. Cambridge, 64–111. Reprinted in A12.

198 "The Date of Palladas," *ZPE* 198, 49–52.

199 "Paganism in Sixth-century Byzantium," in A11, 255–286.

200 "Palladas: New Poems, New Doubts," in A11, 91–112.

2017

201 "Presentation Diptychs or Fancy Stationery?," *JLA* 10, 300–324. Reprinted in A13.

2019

202 "Why Mythology?," in C. Hallett (ed.), *Flesheaters: An International Symposium on Roman Sarcophagi*. Ruhpolding. Reprinted in A13.

2020

203 "The Date and Purpose of Claudian's *In Rufinum*," in D. Moreau and R. Gonzalez Salinero (eds.), *Academica Libertas: Essais en l'honneur du Professor Javier Arce*. Turnhout, 265–270.

204 "Jerome and the *Historia Augusta*," *HSCPh* 111.

CHAPTER 1

Alan Cameron and the Symmachi

Rita Lizzi Testa

In May 1998, during an international conference in Arcavacata, Alan Cameron remembered: 'Two books were to change the direction of my life: Theodor Birt's great edition of Claudian (1892) and Otto Seeck's irreplaceable Symmachus (1883). Both had been unobtainable for many years, but in 1961 the section *Auctores antiquissimi* of the *Monumenta Germaniae Historica* had just been reprinted', so that he left Blackwell's bookshop staggering under the weight of both Claudian and Symmachus volumes.[1] Introducing a paper on 'Claudian Revisited', about thirty years after his book on Claudian had been published (1970), Cameron wanted to explain why then, in 1961, he decided to read all Claudian's works.[2] We can be sure, however, that he also read all Symmachus. The motivation was the same. Between taking his final examinations at Oxford and starting at Glasgow, where he was offered a teaching position, he was looking for an original subject. In 1998, he recalled that he did not want a subject of literature or history, such as was then expected of Oxford classical scholars. He 'was attracted to the borderline between Literature and History'. We can also refer to Symmachus what Cameron said of Claudian in Arcavacata: 'In Claudian my literary and historical interests came together.' And in fact, while his first lecture at the Roman Society in London in 1963 was on Claudian, his first article in the *Journal of Roman Studies* in 1964 was 'The Roman Friends of Ammianus', which directly and primarily implied Symmachus.[3] Furthermore, a feature is common to both these early contributions. Just as in that first public lecture on Claudian—which he published (apparently without many variations) only in 1974[4]—the central thesis of the monograph on Claudian was already evident, so in the article on 'The Roman Friends of Ammianus' all the major themes are already present in summary, which will return in several subsequent articles enriched with new and brilliant arguments, and later flow

---

1 Alan Cameron 2000, 128 = Alan Cameron 2016a, 134.
2 Alan also pointed out (ibid.) that it was not a professor at Oxford who urged him to read the works of Claudian and Symmachus, but Edward Gibbon. He read the Bury edition of *The Decline and Fall of the Roman Empire* together with Averil Cameron, during a holiday in the Black Forest in the summer of 1961. I thank Averil for this biographical note.
3 Alan Cameron 1964a = Alan Cameron 2016a, 189–204.
4 Alan Cameron 1974a. Cf. Alan Cameron 2016b, 113–132.

© THE TRUSTEES OF COLUMBIA UNIVERSITY IN THE CITY OF NEW YORK,
2021 | DOI:10.1163/9789004452794_002

(rich with more and more supporting details) into the various chapters of his *The Last Pagans of Rome*. It seems very clear that in 1964 Cameron had already read and annotated all the works not only of Claudian but also of Symmachus and that he was already clear how his future research would develop.

In 1963/1964 the first volume of the *PLRE* had not yet been published, but Cameron had the same needs from which prosopographical research was born: knowing the family and social connections of an author, his movements from one place to another of the Empire, the political offices he had held. All these details were necessary to really understand the problems he addressed. Demonstrating that the idea that Ammianus belonged to the so-called 'circle' of Symmachus was unfounded—an idea strongly supported by contemporary scholars of great fame, such as Alföldi, Ensslin, Thompson, Pighi and Pack— the analysis of Symm. *Ep.* IX, 110 (one of the letters lacking its addressee) is at the center of 'The Roman Friends of Ammianus'. And in addition to a new, definitive interpretation of that literary piece, Cameron showed that there had been no relationship between Ammianus and Symmachus, just as there were no relations between the historian and Praetextatus. He found in Ammianus' historical work and in other letters of Symmachus the proof of an impossible integration between some of the most famous writers of the time and the exclusive, pagan members of the senatorial aristocracy of Rome. Ammianus was a lonely historian. I wonder how much Arnaldo Momigliano himself took inspiration from Cameron's new research, when he conceived his famous article with the title 'The Lonely Historian Ammianus Marcellinus', published a decade later. In fact, Momigliano started from different assumptions, such as the identification of literary genres used to define the 'persona', in a process in which biography and autobiography were identified and ecclesiastical history supplanted secular, but came to the same result.[5]

In Cameron's first essay, moreover, two features can be identified, which would become typical of his research and constitute a main characteristic of his work: the taste in challenging current opinions, a kind of investigation that he carried out as relentlessly as a hunter pursues his prey, through the compelling logic by which new dates were set, textual interpretations corrected, and new prosopographical links traced.

In the 1976 paper given in Geneva, the question of the alleged patronage of Symmachus is embedded in a more complex set of issues. 'Wider issues are involved than the existence of a literary circle', he declared in the Introduction.[6] He had become conscious that, since most of the pagan writing

---

5 Momigliano 1974.
6 Alan Cameron 1976a, 1.

of the fourth century tended to be interpreted as part of a pagan reaction, this both presupposed and in turn had largely determined how the conflict between paganism and Christianity in late-fourth-century Rome was interpreted. Although Alföldi, Straub, and Chastagnol studied either the late Roman aristocracy or late Latin literature in terms of Christian versus pagan, none of the writers who were thought to be members of the 'circle' of Symmachus had had pagan patrons: 'Ammianus wrote very sharply of the aristocracy in general and not very tactfully of the Symmachi in particular'.[7] Claudian—for whom he could summarize the results of his volume published in 1970[8]—had been the panegyrist of the two sons of Probus and the propagandist of Stilicho, Christian patrons who highly appreciated his classicizing poetry and pagan imagery; Arusianus Messius had dedicated his collection of phrases from Vergil, Sallust, Terence, and Cicero to Olybrius and Probinus, two members of the great Christian family, the Anicii; Rutilius Namatianus wrote at least fifteen years after Symmachus' death and it was therefore impossible to count him 'even on the outermost fringes of Symmachus' circle'; Rufius Festus Avienus, author of the third Latin translation of Aratus, an *Ora Maritima*, was improperly identified with the fabulist Avianus,[9] whom Macrobius inserted among the interlocutors of his *Saturnalia*.[10]

The relationship between literature and paganism, which is the main theme of the essay, represents the *fil rouge* that holds its parts together, but it is not discussed as an interpretative model. What interests the author is to demonstrate, through explicit proofs drawn from the texts, that the pagan aristocracy of Rome did not use classical culture as a shield in the battle against Christianity, and that it was not the members of the supposed 'circle' of Symmachus but the Christians who had the monopoly of classical literature.

In the essay of 1976 there are also other topics that can only be mentioned here but which must have been the result of research already completed, but left among his files, often waiting many decades before being published, and much later taken up and treated with wider breadth in *LPR*. First, the supposed editing of classical texts, which had been attributed to the great aristocratic patrons on the basis of a few badly interpreted *subscriptiones*, overstated the modest activity that was involved; second, the relationship between pagan culture and education, which had been little studied, showed that most of the classical references in the so-called pagan authors were only evidence of a

---

7   Alan Cameron 1976a, 3.
8   Alan Cameron 1970.
9   See Alan Cameron 1967a, where he already demonstrated this.
10   Alan Cameron 1976a, 4.

school culture, shared also by Christians, since that culture was the only one available for all the ancient age; and third, bilingualism had already disappeared in the West at the end of the fourth century.

Issues such as the eventual provenance of the *Historia Augusta* from the supposed pagan circle, and the purpose of Nicomachus Flavianus Senior's *History* were also put on the table at Geneva. Cameron already resolved them by denying that the biographical collection was a *Historia adversus Christianos*, as Johannes Straub, François Paschoud, and now Bruno Bleckmann argue, the latter having identified textual relations between some late Byzantine sources and historians such as Eunapius, Olympiodorus, and Zosimus.[11] On these subjects, Cameron subsequently remained at odds with the German and Swiss/French school of Straub. Nor did the essay of 1976 lack a reference to Macrobius and the *Saturnalia*, which since 1966 had become one of Cameron' s favourite pieces, after his demonstration of the religious neutrality of that work against a solid tradition.[12] He had shown that the *Saturnalia* had been fictitiously dated to 384 by Macrobius—who actually wrote in the third decade of the fifth century and not at the end of the fourth century—because 'in so far as there was a consciously pagan literary circle in late fourth century Rome, in Macrobius' judgment at least it was a circle of Praetextatus, not a circle of Symmachus at all', and 'his death in 384 marked the end of an era'.[13] These are all central problems that since Cameron brought them up have continued to occupy generations of scholars, who have again very recently been challenged by the publication of *LPR* to resume their investigation; some problems, such as the identity of Macrobius and the dating of the *Saturnalia*, have however received very broad assent, and are unlikely to be questioned in the future.

Cameron worked on ancient texts like a scientist with his test tubes, drawing conclusions judged irrefutable from the results of many small successful experiments (the evidence of the texts). They are not always such, however. Without resuming here a discussion on the paganism of the late Roman aristocracy, I will merely mention that paganism was not a religion of the heart but of the city, and not only of Rome but of many cities of the empire, because it coincided with the main values of Roman *civilitas*.[14] Paganism remained vital for longer than Cameron imagined,[15] and appeared again publicly at difficult moments for Rome, as during Alaric's siege. There was then a 'minipagan

---

11   Bleckmann 1992, with Paschoud 1994.

12   Alan Cameron 1966.

13   Alan Cameron 1976a, 17 and 16. Marcone 2008–2009 takes the same view.

14   Brown 2011a; Brown 2011b.

15   Harris 2016a.

revival' as Cameron calls it, and as earlier in 394, not a religious but a political crisis, though again with an element of pagan religious revival. It was only in an excess of zeal, I think, that Cameron also considered as Christian men who openly declared their paganism until the middle of the fifth century, such as Volusianus, the uncle of Melania Iunior.[16] On the other hand, we must be grateful to Cameron because we now know much better the religious-cultural atmosphere of that period, having been pushed to clarify, albeit in opposition, what he claimed.[17]

Above all, his lucid analysis of texts—literary, epigraphic and even iconographic—has led him to important discoveries: for example, in connection with the real identity of the Symmachi. In 1976 he had already assembled all the main arguments, although he published his 'The Antiquity of Symmachi' only in 1999. In dialogue with the Italian school, he disavowed the idea of an equestrian origin of the Symmachi family, according to which Constantine made it *clarissima* only just before 330. Giovanni Polara had showed in 1974 why the grandfather of Quintus Aurelius Symmachus, consul 330, was not a new man,[18] as universally supposed,[19] and Cameron saw that in a commentary on the *Isagoge* of Porphyry, the Neoplatonist Elias remarked that the senator to whom Porphyry dedicated the book ca. 270, one Chysaorius, was a descendant of someone he calls the famous Symmachus, of whom was written the line 'son of Symmachus, man with many allies, ally of Rome'.[20] We are now certain that these third-century Symmachi were directly connected with the fourth-century Symmachi of Rome, linked with the best families of the Fabii Titiani, the Valerii, and the Nicomachi.[21]

Cameron's opinion about the properties of the fourth-fifth century Symmachi, however, is still controversial. The Symmachi have been considered senators of 'average wealth', because Olympiodorus records the sum that Quintus Aurelius Symmachus spent for the praetorship of his son Memmius (2000 pounds of gold) alongside those attested from other senators like Probus (4000 pounds of gold) and Maximus (1200 pounds of gold).[22] Cameron tried

---

16   Contra Lizzi Testa 2012a.

17   See in particular the chapters by Clemente, Consolino, and Agosti in Lizzi Testa 2013a.

18   Polara 1974.

19   The idea of an equestrian origin of the Symmachi family came from Seeck 1883, xli, and Seeck 1931. It was accepted, with a few changes, by Chastagnol 1960, 61n3; Chastagnol 1962, 112–114; Rougé 1961, 59; Paschoud 1965, 228; Paschoud 1967, 73n9; Arnheim 1972, 19 and 164.

20   Alan Cameron 1976a, 17–18.

21   Vera 1981, xxvii–xxviii; Vera 1986, 240n36 = Vera 2020, 119n36; Alan Cameron 1999a, 477.

22   Olymp. *Frg.* 44 (*FHG* IV, 67–68 = Phot. *Bibl. Cod.* 80).

to show that Olympiodorus did not offer concrete data. He used hyperbolic figures to amaze his Greek readers, describing the extravagance and incommensurable wealth of the great Roman aristocrats. However, Domenico Vera has verified the figures of Olympiodorus from other sources and reached the conclusion that they allow us to identify different classes of senators, because they are likely to be based on an official register where the owners were catalogued in relation to the annual revenue.[23]

While reclaiming the antiquity of their senatorial origin for the Symmachi in the paper delivered in Rome in 1999, whose title was used for the volume of 2011, Cameron portrayed Symmachus and his colleagues as a group of snobs, selfish nobles, with little or no learning, who had no desire for pagan revenge and few if any political interests.[24] However, by expanding the investigation that he conducted on the Symmachi to other families, it is possible to adopt a different approach to the more general problem of the role of the late antique Senate, a topic in which Cameron never showed particular interest. This is an issue on which wider research is still active, including on its institutional base, which the recent translation and commentary of the letters of Cassiodorus suggests extended from the fourth to the sixth century. In the fourth century the late antique Senate became central again to the destinies of the empire thanks to the new political impetus that the Constantinian reforms gave to its members. Many of them, like the Symmachi, were able to remain at the center of international relationships. They established contacts with emperors and usurpers, barbaric leaders and new Catholic religious leaders such as Ambrose, or the various bishops of Rome.[25] It is true that they did not spearhead cultural movements or pagan revivals but their cultural and political identity is not entirely as Cameron imagined it.[26]

We can expand on this further if we turn to *LPR*. The 'circle' of Symmachus could hardly be missing from this volume, and indeed chapter 10 is dedicated to 'The Real Circle of Symmachus'.[27] Precisely here, however, in bringing new arguments against the existence of such a circle, Cameron scored an amusing own goal. He quotes the phrase by which Ammianus criticized Memmius Vitrasius Orfitus, father-in-law of Q. A. Symmachus, calling him *splendore liberalium artium minus quam nobilem decuerat institutus* (Amm. 14.6.1), to prove that a man like Orfitus, a prominent and active pagan, had no literary interests

---

23 Vera 1983 = Vera 2020, 35–59; Vera 1986 = Vera 2020, 115–134.
24 Alan Cameron 1999b.
25 Brown 2012, 93–147, 291–307.
26 Lizzi Testa 2004, 387–399; Lizzi Testa 2009; Lizzi Testa 2013b; Oppedisano and La Rocca 2016; Clemente 2019; Salzman 2019a.
27 Alan Cameron 2011a, 353–398.

ALAN CAMERON AND THE SYMMACHI

and therefore there was no connection between classical culture and pagan cults.[28] Cameron does not realize, however, how much the sentence implies: for Ammianus, being noble meant being *splendore liberalium artium institutus*. And not just for Ammianus. Since the historian did not arrive in Rome until 380 and Orfitus was already dead in ca. 370, the judgment on his failure to demonstrate any kind of culture, must have circulated among the senatorial nobility. It was the common opinion of the late Roman senators of Rome, therefore, that every member of the Roman senate should be *splendore liberalium artium institutus*. Not all of them, of course, had the celebrated *eloquentia*, or were learned scholars, and in fact it is virtually Praetextatus and Probus alone who are celebrated as *docti atque eruditi*. But the strict interpretation that Cameron gives of the cultural attitude of the late antique Senate simply depends on his personal conception of culture: for him, nobody can be defined a cultured man without being *doctus atque eruditus*.

There are many original elements in this chapter in *LPR*: the comparison between Symmachus and Pliny, in particular, highlights the differences between a high imperial context in which scholars exchanged drafts of works to be read in public halls and private houses, so that they could receive criticism and comments before a wider circulation, and on the contrary a feeble late antique group of aristocrats and functionaries, for whom the gift of speeches already published was in itself a source of pride and prestige. The third paragraph is devoted to the analysis of the Symmachus' letters. We may overlook that it is intended to prove the non-existence of a literary circle, which no one would have argued in 2011, not least thanks to Cameron's previous essays. The chapter is valid in itself. Even apart from the important exegesis of single letters, the hypotheses on the stages of publication of Symmachus' correspondence are essential contributions: Symmachus himself, for Cameron, not only published Book I, but also made a selection and decided on the arrangement of the materials of all the others as far as the Book VII.[29] The editing work, which Cameron reconstructs also by verifying the use of the formulas *deos oro / deorum favor*, with respect to monotheistic choices (*deo auctore, praefat ope dei* and similar), reflects the intention of a man—whose world had changed profoundly during his lifetime—who had spent the last fifteen years cultivating his relationships, securing the career of his son and son-in-law,

---

28   Alan Cameron 1996 is a first, interesting essay on Orfitus. Cameron identifies him with the figure on the glass cup in the British Museum, where an inscription says he was happily married to Constantia (perhaps the daughter of a sister of Constantine), under the name of Hercules. On this identification, see also Lizzi Testa 2004, 46n115.

29   Alan Cameron 2011a, 370.

showing that Q. Aurelius Symmachus had not abandoned the pagan cause (hence the inclusion of an entire book of letters to Nicomachus Flavianus senior and Nicomachus Flavianus iunior) but was not the uncompromising pagan that the affair of the Altar of Victory might suggested. We must agree with Cameron on this.[30]

According to Cameron, 'not only is there no evidence of any kind that Symmachus thought it dangerous to reveal his paganism in his letters. It is clear from Bks I and II that the publication of his letters was intended positively to draw attention to it.'[31] This is the central theme of the last paper dedicated to the letters of Symmachus, given in Budapest in 2013, the day when Cameron celebrated his seventy-fifth birthday, and which has now been re-edited in the volume of his late-Roman papers published by Edipuglia. As in most of his essays, he sets out to demonstrate that a recent thesis is incorrect. In this specific case, two books by Stéfane Ratti are considered: *Antiquus Error*, to which Cameron had already dedicated a long article,[32] and *Polémiques entre paiens et Chrétiens*,[33] which the latter essay answers. Cameron wonders whether the late-fourth-century pagans were already afraid to reveal their paganism in their private letters. He tests this hypothesis by taking up each of the motivations put forward by Ratti and by means of a detailed analysis of private letters that survive from the fourth and fifth century, both pagan and Christian, he shows that Ratti is inconsistent. No reference to the Altar of Victory affair can be found in Symmachus' letters. Although this is explained in *LPR* by the claim that Symmachus personally did not feel strongly about that issue, here a different explanation is given: since it was an official subject, discussing it in letters to individuals might have been held to constitute private opposition to what was current imperial policy. I must confess to prefer the first explanation: in fact, Ambrose's letters give us a misleading perception of the affair of the Altar of Victory and the Vestals, which for Symmachus and his colleagues was simply one of many other formal submissions to court on fiscal and administrative issues.[34]

In this essay, again, we have the impression of the pleasure Cameron took in reading and translating Latin and Greek literary texts and how clever he was

---

30 On the most likely date for the initial publication of Symmachus, Book I, in the late 380s or early 390s, see Salzman 2018.

31 Alan Cameron 2016c = Alan Cameron 2016a, 223–265.

32 Ratti 2010, 52, on which Cameron 2011b.

33 Ratti 2012a.

34 Cf. Lizzi Testa 2007; Lizzi Testa 2015.

ALAN CAMERON AND THE SYMMACHI

in doing that, having been a brilliant student in London at St Paul's School.[35] Having won a scholarship to New College, Oxford in 1956, thanks to his Greek and Latin, he proceeded to win three major and highly competitive university prizes in those languages.[36]

Finally, the nineteenth chapter of *LPR* continues and expands a number of contributions on ivory diptychs, which are full of information about their origin, purpose, and relation to similar objects.[37] One of these papers, 'Pagan Ivories', was given at the Colloque genèvois sur Symmaque, published in the volume that collected the proceedings in 1986.[38] Cameron discusses the celebrated ivory diptych of the Symmachi and Nicomachi, now divided between London and Paris, which Ernst Kitzinger had linked with the 'pagan revival' of the 390s. In his revision of that hypothesis, Cameron shows that the diptych cannot be related to either of two marriages between the Symmachi and Nicomachi, and suggests on the basis of a comparison with other ivories that the diptych is funerary. Similarly in his view the so-called *Consecratio* panel in the British Museum is also funerary and not, as Lellia Cracco Ruggini suggested, a depiction of the deification of Theodosius senior, father of the Emperor Theodosius I, in 384, when Symmachus was city prefect.[39] For Cameron, the diptych has classical scenes that in one way or another portray death, mourning, rebirth, and apotheosis, and relates to Memmius, who after his father's death in 402 erected a double monument (put up on the Caelian Mount) to

---

35   Alan Cameron 2016b, x. Before passing to the class known as the 'Remove' at St Paul's School at the age of 13, he was in a small class at Colet Court Prep School with Martin L. West (later an eminent scholar, especially of ancient Greek poetry; he died on 13 July 2015). Together with Alan's younger brother, Geoffrey, they had founded a journal of astronomy. at the Martin West memorial, held at All Souls, Oxford, of which West was a fellow, Cameron produced handwritten copies of the articles that they wrote in those early years, often the result of astronomical observations made by the three boys with the large telescope that Alan had at home (I thank very much Averil Cameron for this information, which is very useful for understanding his personality: see also the portrait of Alan Cameron in Cracco Ruggini and Lizzi Testa, forthcoming).

36   After school, unable to complete his military service due to a knee problem, he spent 1956–57 as a teacher in a preparatory school.

37   Among other papers, some of his more important contributions on this subject are: Alan Cameron 1984a; Alan Cameron 1998; Alan Cameron 2007a, and more recently, with an overview, Alan Cameron 2013; Alan Cameron 2015. In 1994 the authenticity of the ivory plaque of the Symmachi in the Victoria and Albert Museum was strongly established: Kinney and Cutler 1994.

38   Alan Cameron 1986.

39   Cracco Ruggini 1977, 2010.

Symmachus and Flavianus, and distributed a set of ivory diptychs in memory of the two paladins of the old order.[40]

The main objection to this hypothesis was raised during the colloquium by Lellia Cracco Ruggini: there is no explicit evidence for the distribution of diptychs on funeral occasions, or to commemorate the death of some important relatives. Cameron worked a great deal on diptychs and made an important contribution on them as late as 2016, but it seems to me that he did not give an answer to this objection.[41] He was able to show that members of the late Roman élite commemorated the holding of certain offices by distribution of ivories, and therefore that they were not originally given only by consuls, but by any official who provided games. Nevertheless, he did not find evidence of other funerary diptychs. Since I am convinced that not even Cracco Ruggini's hypothesis is correct, this paper is a good example of Cameron's legacy.[42]

His work has always provoked intellectual challenges and this makes him a complicated author; at the same time he changed the cultural and social world of Late Antiquity by a wide range of revisionist interpretations, both small and large. Some of his hypotheses will still need to be examined by the scholars of future generations for a long time to come. This is what he wished. Even his characteristic way of presenting his hypotheses as absolute certainties was due not only to his special *usus scribendi*, but also above all to a desire to provoke critical reactions and make his research a fascinating field for future intellectual battles.

---

40 Alan Cameron 1986, 51.

41 Alan Cameron 2016d. See also Alan Cameron 2017. Alan had announced that he would produce a corpus of the diptychs with A. Cutler but it did not happen. I thank Averil Cameron very much also for this information. We look forward to the new volume containing Alan's papers on silver and ivory (Alan Cameron, forthcoming).

42 See Kinney 2008 for an art historical discourse on first-generation diptychs.

CHAPTER 2

Fel Temp Reparatio and Themistius' *Oration 1*
The Story of an Iconic Coin and a Career-Defining Panegyric

Edward Watts

The performance of a later-Roman panegyric must have been one of the strangest moments of social interaction imaginable.[1] Panegyrics were delivered regularly in almost every town an emperor, governor, or military official visited. It was seen as tremendously disrespectful for an official to refuse to listen to one and perhaps even more problematic if an impressive audience failed to turn up for it. But they were also incredibly tedious events. Panegyrics were such a routine part of the lives of emperors, imperial officials, and local notables that imperial laws had to remind governors to pretend to be interested in them.[2] In some cases, the subject of the panegyric even left before the speech had concluded.[3] The people in the audience cannot have been much more interested in the event. While the ceremonial entry of an imperial dignitary into a city would indeed be impressive, a speech delivered in an often nearly incomprehensible form of Greek or Latin was unlikely to hold the interest of an audience for very long.

While nearly everyone listening to a panegyric expected to be bored, the person delivering the panegyric sweated through the occasion with an electric mixture of excitement, nervousness, and sheer terror. This was his big chance. If his words made a good impression, he could expect a lucrative gift from the subject of the speech. Speakers who gave good panegyrics of governors received things such as endowed professorships, cash, and even the gift of grain to their

---

1 For a general survey of late antique panegyrics, with extensive bibliography, see Rees 2018.
2 Note, for example, Ulpian's comment that a proconsul who arrives in some city "should bear patiently a commendation of the city and hear without irritation the singing of his own praises, since the provincials hold that as a point of honor" (Ulpian, *Duties of Proconsul*, Book 2, quoted in Justinian's *Digest*, Book 1.16.7). For the regularity of the deliverance of such speeches, see Warmington 2012, 336–337.
3 As was the case of Valens, who left halfway through a panegyric delivered by Libanius (Libanius, *Or.* 1.144).

© THE TRUSTEES OF COLUMBIA UNIVERSITY IN THE CITY OF NEW YORK,
2021 | DOI:10.1163/9789004452794_003

fellow citizens.[4] If their speech went over poorly, however, the best a speaker could hope for was to be ignored. At worst, he might lose his job.[5]

The stakes were even higher if the addressee was an emperor. Governors were important people in the empire, but they controlled a very limited set of resources for a finite period of time. The emperor controlled unimaginably vast resources for as long as he lived. Emperors, of course, heard more panegyrics than anyone in the empire and therefore were much harder to impress than a random governor—but the rewards for making a good impression on an emperor could be immense. This made it essential that the speaker say precisely the right thing in precisely the right way. If he had any hope of making a positive impression, though, the speaker also needed to say what the emperor wanted to hear in a way that was unique and notably different from what tens or even hundreds of speakers had done before. His speech needed both to make the same points as these other speakers and do it in a novel way.

This was the task that confronted a young philosopher named Themistius when the emperor Constantius II passed near to the city of Ancyra sometime early in the year 348.[6] Themistius was working, apparently as a teacher of both

---

4   Among the many examples of this are: Libanius, *Or.* 1.74 (Professorship in Constantinople from Constantius); Libanius, *Ep.* 175 (on his student Bassus delivering panegyrics in exchange for money or the promise of a position); Eunapius, *VS* 492 (Constans giving Prohaeresius' fellow citizens in Athens a gift of grain).

5   Philostratus (*VS* 622–3) describes Caracalla depriving Philiscus of an exemption from public services because of the way in which he delivered orations.

6   The dating of this speech has usually been determined by references to Constantius' Persian campaigns, with it placed between the siege of Nisibis in 346 and the battle at Singara in the summer of 348 (Heather and Moncur 2001, 69–70; Vanderspoel 1995, 74–76). Alex Skinner (2015) has argued for a date of 342, largely on the basis of a short reference to imperial clemency at *Or.* 1.14b, but, unlike later Themistian speeches that strongly emphasize recent or impending imperial actions or policy changes (e.g. *Or.* 3 [on the elevation of the Constantinopolitan Senate], *Or.* 5 [on Jovian's religious toleration policy] or *Orr.* 14–16 [on Theodosius's evolving Gothic policies]), *Oration* 1 makes only passing mention of this action of imperial clemency. Given his later tendencies, Themistius' lack of emphasis on Constantius' action suggests that it was a memorable past action but not something particularly current when the speech was delivered. As this chapter will argue, the references to the FEL TEMP REPARATIO coinage suggests that the speech must have been given following the first minting of those coins in 348. Unlike Vanderspoel (1995, 76), I am not persuaded that the exclusion of a mention of Constans in the speech precludes a date after the issue of the coins. Die studies suggest that those coins first appeared in early 348 in the East, following a set of issues commemorating Constantius' silver jubilee year of 347. The classic study on these coins is Kent 1967, although note also the earlier study of Mattingly (1933) and the recent work of Bagnall and Bransbourg (2019). Kent speculates that the FEL TEMP REPARATIO series appeared in conjunction with Rome's Natalis Urbis on April 21 (1967, 84). If this is correct, Oration 1 must have been composed soon after the coins first appeared.

rhetoric and philosophy, either in Ancyra itself or in the city of Nicomedia, but he desperately wanted to move back to his home city, the rapidly growing new capital of Constantinople.[7] When he won the chance to address the emperor, he then saw in this an opportunity to get a transfer from the schools of Asia Minor to those of Constantinople. Constantius, however, was a difficult emperor to impress. Although he was just thirty-one years old, Constantius had celebrated his twentieth year in power in 347 and had been listening to panegyrics since he was ten years old. When Constantius sat down to listen to Themistius' speech, it is unlikely that the emperor thought this would be anything more than another rather perfunctory recitation of a standard list of his virtues and achievements.

Themistius, however, wanted to prepare a panegyric that did more than simply repeat the bromides that Constantius had heard many, many times before. Themistius was an eloquent speaker, but so were many of the other figures who had praised the emperor in the previous two decades. Themistius, however, was also a philosopher who came to be recognized as the fourth century's foremost commentator on the works of Aristotle. In antiquity, this title brought with it a certain status. Ancient philosophers were seen by many as devotees of truth whose clear judgment could not be clouded by the desire for worldly honors or material rewards. If they rose to speak philosophically about a politician or a policy, they could claim that they did so only out of the purest motives.[8] What a philosopher said then had an added weight because of the wisdom they claimed.

A philosopher could speak publicly about things other than philosophy and, when he or she did so, their status as a philosopher was often not invoked. The earliest surviving speech of Themistius, for example, shows him adopting the tone of a teacher of rhetoric as he interviewed for a teaching position in the city of Nicomedia.[9] Themistius could perform quite well in this way and may even have been chosen to address Constantius in 348 because of his skill as a conventional rhetorician, but he made the fateful decision not to do so. Themistius resolved to claim his status as a philosopher and use this status to offer Constantius a powerfully original panegyric quite unlike anything the emperor had heard before.

---

7   On Themistius' background and interests at this moment see *Or.* 24.302d as well as the discussion of Watts 2015, 74–75.

8   A point that Themistius makes prominently in *Oration* 1.1a and which Constantius repeats to the Senate when Themistius is adlected to it in 355 (*Demagoria Constantii* 20c). For discussion, see Heather and Moncur 2001, 4–5.

9   This is Themistius, *Oration* 24.

Themistius made the originality of his approach clear from the outset. The speech begins with Themistius asserting to Constantius that:

> Now, for the first time, there comes on the scene for you both an independent speech and a truthful praise giver, and there is no word, however insignificant, that he would utter of his own free will for which he shall not render account to philosophy.[10]
>
> *Or.* 1.1a

Themistius made two significant claims here. First, he makes it clear that, as a philosopher, he cannot lie. Second, Themistius emphasizes that no one has ever before given Constantius this sort of honest and independent praise.

Themistius then continues. The speech will focus only on Constantius' moral worth, the "single spiritual quality" which Themistius sees as animating his entire regime. This is more important than "all of [Constantius'] possessions," but it has also been wholly neglected by the "average praise givers" whose panegyrics focus on things like "the size of the empire and the number of its subjects, the invincible phalanxes of infantry, troops of horse and great wealth of arms" (*Or.* 1.2a). It is also missed by the more skillful rhetoricians who "touch upon your crown, your cloak, your inviolate belt, and your glittering robe" as well as the fact that Constantius possesses a body "from the third generation of royalty" (*Or.* 1.2b).

Unlike his less insightful contemporaries, Themistius promises the emperor that he will speak not about his body and his material possessions but his soul. This is the natural thing with which a philosopher concerned himself but it is also "quite something that is more difficult to perceive than the body" (*Or.* 1.2c). One cannot see the virtue of a man's soul with his eyes, but one can, Themistius continues, see it manifested in his actions. Just as the creations of God reveal his nature, so too do the king's actions "demonstrate royal virtue to those who can progress from the deeds to the doer" (*Or.* 1.3a). This is, moreover, a task that only Themistius can perform. While many men can offer flattery that pepper their descriptions of Constantius' actions with empty praise, "only philosophers are witnesses to virtue" (*Or.* 1.3d). This means that Themistius alone can decode how the things Constantius achieved offer precise evidence of the virtues of his soul.

---

10   All translations of *Oration* 1 follow those of Heather and Moncur 2001 with some occasional adaptations for clarity.

FEL TEMP REPARATIO AND THEMISTIUS' ORATION 1

The philosopher had then promised Constantius a compellingly original panegyric that packaged his achievements in a novel way and offered a unique interpretation of them that only Themistius could provide. But Themistius also faced a real problem. Most panegyrists gave similar speeches because they drew upon similar raw materials. While we do not know for sure how it was communicated to speakers what achievements they were supposed to mention and how they were supposed to speak about them, it does seem, however, that members of the imperial court may have suggested certain topics in advance.[11] If a military engagement had just ended in an imperial victory or a peace treaty, panegyrists seem to have known what to say about that event and how to describe its significance.[12] If the emperor had just unveiled a new domestic policy, panegyrists apparently spoke about it too.[13] This ensured that all speeches, even those given by less skilled orators in random cities, at least said things that reinforced what the court wanted people to think about their emperor. The emperor, his courtiers, and those traveling with him may expect to be bored—but they would not be offended.

Themistius, however, had promised to do something radically different in his speech that would go beyond the praises of the empire's material wealth, the army's power, and the emperor's noble lineage—the very material that any imperial briefing would have contained. This meant that Themistius' speech would need to draw upon material that Constantius had not yet approved for inclusion in speeches.[14] There was a danger in doing this. A speaker whose panegyric wandered off into uncharted territory certainly could be spectacularly original, but he could not be entirely sure how his new ideas would be received. The speech might be a triumph—but it could also be a disaster.

---

11   For a general discussion of how much guidance may have been offered and how this may have been communicated in advance of a speech, see Nixon and Rogers 1994, 29–31. Note, too, Sabbah 1984, 363–388; Rees 2018, 214.

12   For examples of this, see Themistius' *Orations* 14, 15, and 16 on Theodosius' evolving responses to the Gothic situation in the Balkans between 379 and 382. For discussion, see Watts 2015, 173–177.

13   Perhaps the best examples of this are *Pan. Lat.* VI (7) 2.2, a speech that perhaps debuts Constantine's claim of ancestry from Claudius Gothicus, and Themistius' *Oration* 5, which previews Jovian's policy of religious toleration.

14   It is almost certain that imperial officials gave some direction to artists and authors working to convey representations of imperial achievements and character across all media. There was, however, an interpretative challenge that went along with transforming an image designed to be interacted with visually (like a coin or portrait) into one described textually. An orator working off of a visual rendering then ran the risk of misinterpreting the artist's intention and, therefore, misreading the imperial direction.

Because Themistius had never met Constantius and could not know for sure what the emperor would want to hear about himself, he needed to be creative in finding material others had not that would reflect the emperor's own ideas about who he was and what he had achieved. In short, he needed to find a trace of the emperor's self-image that no speaker had yet touched upon.

It is here that Themistius turned to an unlikely source for information about how Constantius saw himself. Whereas panegyrists often fashioned their portraits of the emperor around material found in texts, Themistius decided to use a physical object that captured new and different traces of Constantius' imperial identity. He turned to a coin that the emperor and his brother had recently issued. To appreciate the genius of Themistius' choice, we have to quickly digress into a brief history of fourth-century Roman numismatics.

In 294, Diocletian and his co-emperors began a reform of the monetary system designed to replicate the trimetallic coinage of the high empire. Their new system was based on the aureus, a gold coin weighing 1/60 of a Roman pound, the argenteus, a high purity silver coin weighing 1/96 of a pound, and a lower value 4 percent silver-coated bronze coin 26 mm in diameter and weighing 10 grams called the nummus. Small, lower-value billon and bronze coins then rounded out the system.[15] The tariffing of each coin was based on notional denarii, with the aureus likely trading at 1000 denarii, the argenteus at 50 denarii, the nummus at 12.5 denarii, and the small billon coins at 1–5 denarii, depending on their size.[16]

As the fourth century progressed, this system broke down. The gold coin, the famous solidus, was reduced in around 320 to 4.5 grams but otherwise held its purity and weight until the eleventh century. The silver coins became smaller and less common so that, by the end of the fourth century, they weighed around 2 grams and circulated primarily in the West. The silver content and size of the nummus, however, both rapidly collapsed. By the end of the reign of Constantine in 337, these once robust and weighty coins measured less than 20 mm, weighed less than 2 grams, and averaged around 1 percent silver.[17] Not surprisingly, they also collapsed in value. Whereas 96 nummi purchased a gold coin in 301, 240 did the same in 323. By 341, one needed to exchange 11,000 of these bronze coins for a gold solidus.

---

15   See Harl 1996, 158–167; Bagnall and Bransbourg 2019, §2.

16   Bagnall and Bransbourg 2019, §2. On tariffing of coinage, see Estiot 2012, 548–550. On the gold value, see Carlà 2009, 45–54.

17   These figures follow Harl 1996 with some updating based on the figures of Bagnall and Bransbourg 2019, §2.

FEL TEMP REPARATIO AND THEMISTIUS' ORATION 1

Constantius and his brother Constans decided to fix this situation by stabilizing the value of the bronze coinage in conjunction with the celebration of Rome's 1100th birthday in 348. The coin issue that resulted involved two bronze denominations. The highest value coin was 2–2.5 percent silver and averaged 23 mm and almost 6 grams. The lower value coin was 1.5 percent silver and measured 21 mm and 4.25 grams. A third, smaller coin was soon issued that was less than 20 mm, weighed 2.68 grams, and had a miniscule 0.2 perent silver content.[18] But these coins were nevertheless beautifully crafted by skilled engravers and, crucially, bore the reverse legend FEL TEMP REPARATIO, probably an abbreviated form of *Felicitatis Temporum Reparatio* or the Restoration of the Good Fortune of the Ages. This legend had never before appeared in this form, though nine emperors ranging from Antoninus Pius to Diocletian had all issued coins labeled either FELICITAS TEMPORUM or FELICIA TEMPORA over the past 200 years.[19] One of these previous examples stands out, however. In 148/9, at the time of the 900th anniversary of Rome's founding, the emperor Antoninus Pius had issued a gold aureus, a bronze sestertius, and a dupondius with the legend TEMPORUM FELICITAS COS IIII, a coin that marked it as the beginning of a new age of prosperity and happiness in his fourth consulship.[20] Now, as Rome entered its twelfth century, Constantius and his brother Constans could claim to be restoring this golden age in two new coin denominations that would also address the collapse in the value of Rome's billon coinage.

The coins themselves had a distinctive iconography. On the reverse of the smaller coin was a phoenix standing atop a platform, a symbol of imperial rebirth in the new century.[21] More intriguing, though, was the reverse of the first issues of the largest coin. (Figure 2.1) This showed the emperor in a galley,

---

18 These particular figures are based on Bagnall and Bransbourg 2019, §2, and describe the initial batch of FEL TEMP coins issued between 348 and 352.

19 These include *RIC* 3.Antoninus.857, a sestertius from 148/9 with the legend TEMPORUM FELICITAS COS IIII; *RIC* 3.Commodus.209, a denarius from 190 with legend TEMP FEL PM TR P XV COS VI; *RIC* 4a.Geta.95, a denarius with legend FELICITAS TEMPOR; *RIC* 4a.Caracalla.233a, a denarius with the legend FELICITAS TEMPORA; *RIC* 4b.Macrinus.59, a denarius with legend FELICITAS TEMPORUM; RIC4b.Elagabalus.150, a denarius with legend TEMPORUM FELICITAS and *RIC*.4b.Elagabalus.188, a denarius with legend FELICITAS TEMPORUM; *RIC* 5b.Probus.104, a billon radiate with legend TEMPO-R FELICI; *RIC* 5b.Julian of Pannonia.2, a billon radiate of 284/5 with the legend FELICI-TAS TEMPORUM; and *RIC* 5b.Diocletian.189, a quinarius with legend FELICIA TEMPORA.

20 This is *RIC* 3.Antoninus.185 (aureus), 857 (sestertius), and 859 (dupondius). The reverse shows two young boys in cornucopias, an image perhaps intended to commemorate the birth of two princes to Antoninus' successor Marcus Aurelius.

21 E.g., *RIC* 8.Siscia.228.

FIGURE 2.1
Coin of Constantius with Fel Temp Reparatio legend and emperor on galley reverse (RIC 8.Thessalonica.170)
PRIVATE COLLECTION. PHOTO BY AUTHOR

holding an orb in his left hand and a standard with a Chi-Rho in his right.[22] A phoenix sat at the front of the ship and, in the rear, was Victory steering the ship forward. This scene is extremely busy—most Roman coins contain perhaps one or two figures and symbols—but is also quite pregnant with meaning. The phoenix is, again, a symbol of imperial renewal. The orb held by the emperor is both an abstract symbol of imperial control over the world and a very tangible representation of an element of the imperial insignia carried by the court on ceremonial occasions. The military standard with this Chi-Rho similarly captures the symbolic Christian military power Constantius claims to wield and a real, physical component of the ceremonial objects that distinguished the imperial court. The presence of Victory is also self-explanatory. Victoria was one of the most common elements in later Roman coinage. Even the galley itself had symbolic meaning. It seems to have been a metaphor for the ship of state and had appeared on earlier coins bearing the legend Felicitas, including one of Elagabalus that read FELICITAS TEMP.[23] The larger value FEL TEMP REPARATIO coin then placed traces of the emperor's real, physical presence in a symbolic space that showed how Constantius' reign embodied the concepts of imperial renewal, military victory, and successful state stewardship. This coin was, in short, an object carefully designed to offer a physical representation of the new age that Constantius and his brother promised to bring in Rome's 1200th year.

---

22 E.g., *RIC* 8.Thessaloniki.108.
23 E.g., *RIC* 2.Hadrian.209–10 (denarii) and 705–6 (sestertii) each with the legend FELICI-TATI AUG COS III PP SC. For the Elagabalus coin, see *RIC* 4b.Elagabalus.188.

FEL TEMP REPARATIO AND THEMISTIUS' ORATION 1   19

Themistius' speech suggests strongly that he is drawing upon this coin for his innovative portrait of the emperor. In fact, on two occasions Themistius even openly compares the process of discerning Constantius' character to handling a coin. Near the oration's outset, Themistius says that he has identified in Constantius the virtue of *philanthropia*, a virtue unique to a good king. This is a virtue, Themistius says, that is easily observed in the emperor and it is one that can be expressed in a simple word that Themistius will give to the emperor "like a coin" (*Or.* 1.4b). Themistius returns to a metaphor of the coin as a vessel encapsulating the virtue of the emperor a page later. There he asserts that each category of being has virtues particular to themselves. A dog has canine virtues, a horse equine virtues, and a king a virtue:

> which is peculiar to a king and is royal beyond all others, to which the rest are linked as if leading to a single peak. Since, if we investigate this on its own as if turning over a coin, we would not find anything that displays the royal character more precisely than that which we call courage.
>
> *Or.* 1.5c–d

The obverse of the coin then displays the image of the emperor while the reverse offers a distillation of his character.

Metaphors of coinage are common in *Oration* 1 but they are otherwise rare in Themistius' corpus. While there are two allusions to coins within a page of each other in *Oration* 1, there are only eight other references to coins in the over 400 pages of surviving Themistian speeches. Only two of these use coins as a mechanism to determine imperial character, and one of those two comes from a speech from 373 that reproduces verbatim the passage above.[24] This was, then, anything but a stock metaphor that Themistius used.

Even more telling is Themistius' heavy use of nautical imagery in *Oration* 1. While nautical references are again quite rare in the rest of Themistius' corpus, they appear frequently in *Oration* 1.[25] The transition from the introduction to the body of the oration begins with the statement "my speech has successfully come to anchor at an image" of God's creation (*Or.* 1.3a). More powerful is

---

24   The other references are *Or.* 2.39b (which refers to money on a table); *Or.* 11.146d (which quotes Or. 1.5c–d); *Or.* 15.192a (a mention of how the image of the character of an emperor can be seen through coins), *Or.* 20.261d (referring to student fees given to teachers), *Or.* 23.286c (title of false sophist loses value like a bronze coin), and *Or.* 23.297c (a sophist selling his wares for money); *Or.* 26.323d (a notion of money as a kind of common property); *Or.* 33.367b (extended passage speaking about inflation and bronze coinage).

25   The notion of a sovereign as a helmsmen of the ship of state that appears often in *Oration* 1, recurs only in a passage of *Oration* 11 that copies content from *Oration* 1, as well as *Or.* 15 194d–195a and, more obliquely, *Or.* 16.212a.

the repeated use of a metaphor of the emperor as the individual manning the ship of state. In the same initial transitional paragraph as the anchor reference, Themistius speaks of how all kings "steered by the same helm" (*Or.* 1.3c). Three pages later he writes about how the mildness of the king makes it possible for "not only merchants and sailors but also for all men to sail through their lives in safety, whether one has embarked on a large vessel or a tiny boat. One takes the rudder while the other makes do with a rower's cushion" (*Or.* 1.7a) And, at the conclusion of the speech, Themistius speaks of how Constantius is so unlike other young men who "are borne by their emotions like ships without ballast" but Constantius, "being steered by intelligence, forces the billows of youth to grow calm ... because of his virtue" (*Or.* 1.17a).

All of these mentions are interesting, but they bear only a passing similarity to the FEL TEMP reverses. They are also not tied directly to policies or actions that Themistius would be expected to mention. Themistius does, however, use nautical imagery like those on the FEL TEMP coins to explain how two incidents that Constantius most certainly did expect to hear about in a panegyric illustrate his personal philosophical virtue. The first of these concerns some sort of judicial reform that the emperor had recently enacted that appears to have removed the death sentence from either a specific individual or a category of crimes.[26] While the specific details of the reform have been lost to us, it is clear that Themistius understood that the action needed to be mentioned in the panegyric. He describes this as a sign of Constantius' *philanthropia* because he encouraged virtue in his subjects by distinguishing the honorable from those who do wrong. But, even in treating those who do wrong, Themistius makes clear that Constantius inclined towards honor rather than vengeance. His actions were always calibrated to the type of person they touched, just as, Themistius says, "in a ship, the helmsman does not have equal care for the sailor and the passenger" (*Or.* 1.14a).

Themistius offers a much longer and more powerful nautical metaphor when discussing a recent successful confrontation that Constantius had with Persia. In 346, the emperor's army advanced on the forces of the Sasanian king Šābuhr II and compelled the King of Kings to withdraw his forces from Roman territory. This major victory for the emperor would certainly have appeared among the items Themistius was encouraged to speak about in the panegyric (if, indeed, he received any guidance at all from the emperor's associates), but

---

26 For discussion see Portmann 1988, 133, 261 n3; Heather and Moncur 2001, 92 n136. Vanderspoel 1995, 81 n43 doubts that this refers to a specific incident.

FEL TEMP REPARATIO AND THEMISTIUS' ORATION 1

Themistius here, too, decided to use the event as an indication of the deeper virtue of the emperor. Themistius suggests that the Persian king Šābuhr:

> does not understand what is the only advantage of proximity, which is to entrust the steering oar of his mind to one who is nearby and knows how to steer, and to lash his ship [i.e. the Persian Empire] to the great vessel [i.e. the Roman Empire]. For in my view, this is better than to put to sea on a small pinnacle without steering gear or other equipment, and to fight to the finish with a great and strong trireme carrying many soldiers, many oarsmen, and many marines, and a helmsman reared at the tiller from his infant clothes.
>
> *Or.* 1.12.a–b

This approximates the image of the emperor clad in military garb, holding a military standard, and standing in a galley shown on the FEL TEMP REPARATIO coin. Themistius had appropriated the very imagery of a powerful sovereign ushering in a new age of happiness that appeared on the coins that Constantius himself had issued. This speech is, in a sense, an instance where an author takes a material trace of the image of the emperor, packages it, and then presents his reception of that trace to the emperor in person. The images of the emperor and his character that found their way onto the obverse and reverse of the FEL TEMP coins had now returned to their source, but Themistius had also reinterpreted them so that Constantius understood himself in a completely new way. And Themistius' gamble succeeded dramatically. Following this speech, Themistius received an imperial appointment in the capital, became Constantius' most important mouthpiece for the rest of his reign, and set off on a career in which he would remain the foremost imperial propagandist of the middle decades of the fourth century. Never again would he have to resort to the interpretation of a coin to make an impression on an emperor.

Acknowlegdements

It is a great honor to be asked to contribute a chapter to a volume celebrating the life and scholarship of Alan Cameron. Alan was many things—a tremendous scholar, an engaging conversationalist, and the generous mentor to young scholars. But one of the things that most distinguished his work was a remarkable and almost unparalleled ability to bring together textual scholarship, historical context, and material evidence to frame new, exciting, and sometimes groundbreaking interpretations of late antique literary texts. This chapter tries to do something similar by using numismatic evidence to reconstruct the context that led to the composition of the panegyric that defined the career of the late antique philosopher Themistius. It is perhaps a small contribution, but it is one driven by my great enthusiasm for the approaches taken by Alan Cameron's scholarship and by the conversations about this sort of scholarship we once had.

CHAPTER 3

The *Historia Augusta*

Minimalism and the Adequacy of Evidence

Michael Kulikowski

Argument over the date and nature of the *Historia Augusta* is eternal, or so it seems. It has inspired vast displays of erudition, much nonsense, even madness, sometimes all at once.[1] The worst of this sort of thing has come to dominate the Historia Augusta Colloquia, once hosted at Bonn but peripatetic since 1990, and since the mid-1980s centering on the rebel senator Nicomachus Flavianus and the *Annales* he is said to have written.[2] These *Annales* are attested only once, in an inscription put up by Flavianus' grandson when his forebear's memory was rehabilitated. Though, or perhaps because, nothing is known about them save their mere existence, they are imagined as a literary masterpiece that influenced nearly every extant historical work of Late Antiquity, in both Latin and Greek, and on into the Byzantine period.[3] It was François Paschoud who really fastened on the titanic impact of Flavianus several decades ago, though their role as a possible source had been kicked around in continental scholarship since the 1940s.[4] Dominant since the 1990s, the edifice of Flavianic speculation has grown ever more baroque, particularly at the hands of Stéphane Ratti.[5] It has also deformed the Budé editions

---

1   As Alan Cameron put it, "no sensible person wants to get involved in the problems of the *HA*" (2016a, 137).

2   *CIL* 6: 1783 = *ILS* 2948, of 431/2. Earlier, while Flavianus was still alive, the husband of his granddaughter, Memmius Symmachus, honored him as *historicus dissertissimus, CIL* 6:1782 = *ILS* 2947. Hedrick 2000 is a careful, if not always persuasive, examination of *ILS* 2948 and its context.

3   It is worth stressing that absolutely nothing but modern speculation suggests these *Annales* were "un'opera indubbiamente complessa" (Baldini 2002, 14). In fact, we know so little that they might as easily have covered just Republican and not imperial history: Matthews 1975, 231; Barnes 1976; *pace* Schlumberger 1985, aprioristic and not even remotely definitive, despite its totemic role in *Flavianforschung*.

4   Especially "Nicomaque Flavien et la connexion byzantine," a 1994 piece from *Antiquité Tardive* reprinted in Paschoud 2006, 293–316, though see also many of the other articles compiled in the same volume.

5   Ratti 2007 is the *fons et origo*, but see all the many articles collected in Ratti 2010 with their ever more dogmatic iterations in Ratti 2012a; Ratti 2016a. *Flavianforschung* is a miasmic swamp, to be sure, but one must in fairness acknowledge that it takes one sort of credulity to

---

© THE TRUSTEES OF COLUMBIA UNIVERSITY IN THE CITY OF NEW YORK,
2021 | DOI:10.1163/9789004452794_004

of Zosimus, some of the fourth-century epitomators, and the *Historia Augusta* itself: the high philological and text-critical standard of many of these volumes is compromised by the fallacious historiographical frame.[6] Alan Cameron offered a comprehensive demolition of this fantasy text in his *Last Pagans of Rome*.[7] Though it has failed to have the slightest impact on the Flavianus industry, it remains a masterly demonstration of how working from first principles and refusing gratuitous speculation can separate the known from the probable, the unknowable from the fictitious.[8] One major insight, produced by this exercise and since expanded in an *opus postumum*, was to show that Jerome's life of the monk Hilarion depends upon the life of the emperor Probus in the *Historia Augusta*, rather than the reverse.[9] As we shall see, this demonstration is definitive and has major consequences for how we understand and interpret one of the fourth century's most controverted literary products. In the following pages, I aim to show what constitutes adequate evidence for establishing chronological *termini* for the *Historia Augusta*, why the historiographic legacy

---

    believe that Flavianus' lost *Annales* influenced the anonymous author of the *Historia Augusta* as well as the whole historiography of later centuries, or even that Nicomachus Flavianus junior wrote the *Historia Augusta* on the basis of his father's *Annales* (as does, e.g., Festy 2007 following Hartke 1940, 165–168) and an entirely different sort to believe that Flavianus wrote the *Historia Augusta* himself: even among the Flavianic true believers, Ratti's assertions have found no adherents however often he restates them ('m.E. nicht überzeugend': Zinsli 2014, 96n251; ibid. 95–98 is a good summary of where various scholars stand on the Flavianus question, though see the disobliging review of Paschoud 2017). Paschoud 2018, xxxii–xxxviii, is a dismissal of Ratti as effective as anything in Cameron.

6   Paschoud 1971–1989 (Zosimus), is rightly esteemed. The Budé *Historia Augusta* volumes (Bertrand-Dagenbach 1993; Callu 1992; Paschoud 1996; Paschoud 2001; Paschoud 2011; Paschoud 2018; Ratti 2000; Turcan 1993) are useful complements to Hohl's standard edition. Festy 1999a, the Budé *Epitome de Caesaribus*, is to be avoided on text-critical as well as historical grounds.

7   Alan Cameron 2011a, 627–690.

8   The effectiveness of Cameron's arguments seems to me proven by the total refusal of Ratti 2012a, 179–187, and 2016a, 179–188 to engage with them in chapters ostensibly devoted to doing so. (Perhaps the enthusiasm Ratti evidences for Jérôme Carcopino—much given to magical reasoning as a form of *Quellenforschung*—at 2012a, 80, tells its own story.) Rather than address serious critiques, Ratti and others (e.g., Nardelli 2016) respond to any and all criticism of the Flavianus thesis either by citing an alleged "Anglo-Saxon" inability to read "austere" work in French, German, or Italian or by attributing skepticism to undue deference to *doxa* and authority. These *savants* seem, rather touchingly, not to realize that in the Anglophone academy (in its distinct American, Canadian, British and Antipodean variants) one is not obliged to pay constant, unquestioning homage to the *Lehre* of one's teacher or academic patron. In consequence, they (e.g., Ratti 2016b) waste thousands of words on trivial and incompetent work like Rohrbacher 2015 and deploy against it the same "arguments" with which they dismiss proper scholarship. (Or, perhaps, and to borrow a *démonstration Rattifiée*, linguistic impediments forestall their recognizing any such distinction?)

9   Alan Cameron 2011a, 761–772; Alan Cameron 2020.

THE HISTORIA AUGUSTA   25

obliges us to take a minimalist approach to any conclusions we draw from the text, and where this leaves our prospects for new insights into it.

To date, the fairest, most succinct, and yet still comprehensive introduction to the *Historia Augusta* remains that of one of the Bonner Colloquia's earliest participants, André Chastagnol, in the monographic introduction to his facing-page translation of the whole text.[10] For a reader of the present chapter, Chastagnol will provide a fuller, thoroughly annotated account of the evidence for date and place of composition. The *Historia Augusta* is a long series of imperial biographies, 550 pages in Ernst Hohl's standard Teubner, purporting to be the work of six different authors writing under Diocletian and Constantine. Until 1889, this self-presentation was taken at face value, but in that year, Hermann Dessau detonated a mine under the scholarly consensus in a long and elegant article in *Hermes* that he followed up with two further pieces in the same journal.[11] Dessau showed that both multiple authorship and early fourth-century date were impostures. He had been working on the then nascent *Prosopographia Imperii Romani*, covering the first three imperial centuries, and it was the multitude of otherwise unattested names in the *Historia Augusta* that first stirred his suspicions. A great many of these reflect not the nomenclature of the second or third century, but rather the polyonymous elites of the later fourth century: Toxotius, Ragonius, Faltonius, and so on.[12]

But that is only the beginning of the evidence against the text's purported identity: anachronisms and absurdities abound. An author writing under Diocletian could not have written about the descent of Constantine from Claudius Gothicus since that fiction was invented only in the year 310.[13] An author writing under Constantius I (*Aur.* 44.5) cannot have had a father

---

10   Chastagnol 1994, ix–clxxviii. This is also a good introduction to the vast bibliography on
      the *Historia Augusta*, reprised here only where essential. See Paschoud 2014 for Casaubon,
      Saumaise, and the early modern scholarship on the text.

11   Dessau 1889, 1892, 1894 (this last on the manuscript tradition). Because so many of his
      conclusions have, since the early 1970s, finally been absorbed into the *communis opinio*,
      Dessau is less read than he should be: all three articles are masterpieces of Wilhelmine
      philology and *Quellenforschung*.

12   Dessau 1889, 348–359. Alan Cameron 1999b, followed by Thomson 2012, 55, argued that
      the names are insufficient evidence to prove anachronism, as a family might have been
      prominent fifty or more years before we see it attested. While strictly speaking this is
      true, the sheer preponderance of names suggesting the later fourth century can really
      only be explained away by special pleading. Syme 1968, 165–175 and Syme 1971a, 1–16 are
      particularly good on the false names (there is nothing in Syme 1971b that cannot be found
      elsewhere in his huge bibliography). Christol 2014 demonstrates that not every individual
      instance of skepticism is justified.

13   In *Pan. Lat.* 7.2; 8.2. Dessau 1889, 340–344, with a lengthy exploration of the myth at Syme
      1983, 63–79. Its use in the *Historia Augusta* does not exclude a date after the extinction of
      the dynasty, as Stern 1953 alleges in order to postulate a Constantinian date.

who was on friendly terms with Diocletian during the great tetrarch's retirement (*Aur.* 43.2). An author writing under Constantine, by contrast, could not have written biographies of the usurper Maxentius and the rival Augustus Licinius (as claimed at *Hel.* 36.5) without losing his head. Other anachronisms accumulate just as rapidly: Maximinus I could not have had a Gothic father and Alanic mother in the early third century, only after 376, or better still 382 (*Maxim.* 1.5).[14] *Sortes Vergilianae* are unattested until the later fourth century.[15]

And then there is the evidence of the sources used. Whether or not the *Historia Augusta* used the *Enmannsche Kaisergeschichte* (the postulate of which is another miracle of nineteenth-century *Quellenforschung*),[16] it certainly used one of the works that disclose the *Kaisergeschichte*'s existence, namely the *Caesares* of Aurelius Victor; moreover, it almost certainly uses another one of those works, the *Breviarium* of Eutropius.[17] The former wrote in 360/1, the latter in 370. Cumulatively, Dessau's evidence for single authorship and a late fourth-century date was overwhelming, although the response to his proof was not uniformly positive. The titans of German philology—Mommsen, of course, but also Seeck and Peter and Hirschfeld—swooped in and we now know a great deal about the evolution of their debates in correspondence and not merely in published articles.[18] Mommsen, followed by Peter and later, in part, by Hirschfeld, tried to save as much as possible of the traditional approach by positing later fourth-century redactors of an originally Constantinian text. But Ernst Hohl, who would produce the edition of the text on which we still rely, accepted more or less completely the argument put forward by Dessau.[19] In France and especially in Italy, Dessau's reception was spotty when not hostile, and Anglophone scholars ignored the whole debate until the 1920s, when Norman Baynes adopted Dessau's proofs for single authorship, but postulated

---

14   Dessau 1889, 359–360.

15   Dessau 1892, 582–583, though note the absolutely convincing argument of Ekbom 2013 that the phrase, and perhaps the idea, of *sortes vergilianae* are one of the many inventions of the *Historia Augusta* itself, based on the well-known use of Virgil and Homer in *centones* and of Homer, at least, in vaticination.

16   Enmann 1884. Rather surprisingly, he never returned to the topic or pronounced on Dessau's seminal article, though see Gilliam 1980 for a fascinating biographical exploration.

17   Dessau 1889, 363. Comparison of *Sev.* 18.5 with Aurelius Victor, *Caes.* 20.1; 20.10–30 is dispositive, as even Momigliano 1954 recognized. That of *Marc.* 16.13–18.2 with Eutropius, *Brev.* 8.11–14 is very nearly so, but leaves open a tiny window for doubt.

18   Mommsen 1890; Peter 1892; Seeck 1890, 1894; Hirschfeld 1913, 887–891, with Den Hengst 2002, arguing for the importance of Wölfflin to the debate, and Brandt 2010 for the scholarly correspondence.

19   Inter alia, Hohl 1911, 1912, 1914, 1916, 1920.

THE HISTORIA AUGUSTA

27

a Julianic date of composition, as Hirschfeld had posited a Gratianic one.[20] In the interwar and immediately postwar decades, driven first by the work of Andreas Alföldi in the 20s and 30s, and then also by Johannes Straub, the basics of the Dessau thesis were accepted as the norm, first in Germany, then in the wider circle of Western scholars who participated in the Bonner Colloquia.[21]

Nowadays, the basic types of proof for single authorship and late-fourth-century date remain those that were laid out by Dessau, but the evidence for each such type has increased exponentially. Thus, the many contradictory claims for the relationship among the six ostensible authors have been exhaustively documented,[22] as have scores of anachronisms. To take only the most glaring and consequential: the title *Alamannicus* is not attested until 328, for the then-caesar Constantinus. It cannot have been borne by Caracalla (*Carac.* 10.6), any more than Probus could have been acclaimed *Francicus* (*Prob.* 11.9). The *largitionales* of *Car.* 20.2 did not exist till the 320s when Constantine created the post of *comes sacrarum largitionum*.[23] *Quadr. tyr.* 15.5–6 speaks of *Thraciae* in the plural, another post-Constantinian usage. *Aur.* 13.1 mentions a prefect of the *annona* at Alexandria, a post that existed only after the foundation of Constantinople. The urban prefect did not hold the rank of *vir inlustris* till 368/369.[24] *Trig. tyr.* 18.5 speaks of a regional prefecture

---

20   Baynes 1926; for the French and Italian reception, with special attention to the hostility of De Sanctis to the Dessau theory, see Chastagnol 1994, xxii–xxiv.

21   See especially Alföldi 1937, 1942–1943, 1952, 1967; Straub 1952, 1963; several of the works reprinted in Straub 1972, with Kolb 1998 and the commentary of Kulikowski, forthcoming. Note that this search for pagan *Tendenzen* was equally appealing on the far side of the Iron Curtain: Johne 1976. Syme 1983, 109–130, was much the best argument against an apologetic, still less a pagan apologetic *Tendenz*, prior to Alan Cameron 2011a, 743–782.

22   Thomson 2012, 20–25.

23   The term *magister militiae* (*Aur.* 11.2, 17.2, 18.1; *Prob.* 11.7) is also Constantinian, as is *aerarium* when used of the imperial treasury rather than *fiscus* (*Hadr.* 6.5). Several other potential anachronisms laid out by Chastagnol 1994, cxvi–cxviii, and identified by various post-Dessau writers, are less immediately probative, e.g. Severus Alexander's tax on prostitutes or the election of suffect consuls, inasmuch as they could just possibly have been invented without being allusions to known events. Again, the author might have invented the name Furius Placidus (*Aur.* 15.4) without knowing that this was the name of an actual consul of 343.

24   Another anachronism that has long been thought decisive is the *iudiciale carpentum* used by the urban prefect in the preface of the *Vita Aureliani*. However, Fabio Guidetti has shown in as yet unpublished research that the objections of Symmachus, *Rel.* 4, long held to provide a *terminus post quem* of 382 are not to the prefect's use of an official vehicle, but to the number of horses that drew it. With that demonstration, the relevance of Symmachus to the *Historia Augusta* falls away. (Note that Bruggisser 1991, 1996 had already sounded a note of caution.)

of Illyricum and the Galliae: regional prefectures did not exist until very late in the reign of Constantius.[25]

Textual allusions to recent historical events are more problematic than are glaring anachronisms, because their identification, and the degree of precision needed to assert such an identification, is inevitably subjective. The legal material in the life of Alexander Severus, for example, reflects laws and norms of the later fourth century, not the third, but attempts to link it with specific material from the *Codex Theodosianus* cannot be considered definitive.[26] Likewise, the criticism of child emperors might well allude to the sons and successors of Theodosius, but could also apply to Valentinian II and Gratian.[27] That said, one *vaticinium ex eventu* seems rather definitive. The *Vita Probi* (24.1–3) confidently predicts the 'flight' of the emperor's descendants to northern Italy, specifically Verona, and their future and continued distinction in the Senate—certainly a nod to the egregious nepotist Petronius Probus.[28] Many other such historical allusions exist, but none are quite as obviously significant.[29]

To sum up the basic framework before turning to the issue of precise date, the *Historia Augusta* arrived at the Renaissance through a very narrow line of transmission, with two Carolingian witnesses to a single defective archetype, itself probably also Carolingian.[30] The work opens with the Life of Hadrian. Some have suspected missing lives of Nerva and Trajan, but there is no evidence for them.[31] The lives of Hadrian, Pius, Marcus Aurelius, Lucius Verus, Commodus, Pertinax, Didius Julianus, Septimius Severus, and Caracalla rest on a third-century source in the manner of Suetonius. The Life of Antoninus Pius is the most straightforward and Suetonian of the nine and probably gives the best indication of what this source looked like. However, many of these nine

---

25   Dessau 1892, 588–589; Vogler 1979, 110–144; Barnes 1987; Cuq had already grasped the larger problem in 1903. The conjuncture of Illyrican and Gallic prefectures occurred historically only very briefly, during the ascendancy of Ausonius at the court of Gratian.

26   See Liebs 1980; Liebs 1983 reaches similar conclusions about the monetary measures attributed to the short-lived emperor Tacitus.

27   Alan Cameron 2011a, 750–753. Hartke 1951 is a difficult and ultimately puzzling exploration of this theme.

28   Dessau 1889, 355–358, and more insistently, Dessau 1892, 561–562. It might, but need not, also be a reference to Probus' sons' joint consulship of 395: Alan Cameron 2011a, 772–778.

29   Chastagnol 1994, cxiv–cxviii gives a considered and sober list.

30   Ballou 1914 was the first comprehensive study, though Patzig 1904 was the first to recognize that there were two separate textual traditions, rather than a single one based on BAV Pal. lat. 899, known as *P*. At present, Marshall 1983 remains basically sound, and Callu 1985 is probably the best introduction to the manuscripts currently available, though now superseded by Stover 2020.

31   Dessau, 1892, 579 already believed it impossible for the work to have begun as it now does in its original shape.

THE HISTORIA AUGUSTA 29

biographies have been heavily abridged and then supplemented, either with pure invention or by reference to a second source. Syme famously postulated the existence of "Ignotus, the Good Biographer" whose abridged work was spiced up with salacious tidbits from the consular biographer Marius Maximus, memorably deprecated by Ammianus for his triviality.[32] Other scholars have simply attributed the nine authentic lives to Maximus himself.[33] The evidence for two badly conjoined base texts is strongest in the Life of Hadrian, which suggests that the contradictions and disjunctures of tone and judgment could be the work of an author not yet secure in his manner of abridging a single source. The question requires further study.[34]

Regardless, the nine primary lives are bulked out by secondary lives of the caesars Aelius and Geta and the usurpers Avidius Cassius, Pescennius Niger, and Clodius Albinus. All authentic details in these five *vitae* derive from the nine primary lives of this section. Although all modern editions print both primary lives and these subordinate *vitae* in chronological order of their subjects, the manuscripts in fact transmit several lives of caesars and usurpers out of order.[35] After the primary and secondary lives of the first section, a middle group includes lives of Macrinus, Diadumenianus, Elagabalus, Severus Alexander, Maximinus, the Gordians, and Maximus (Pupienus) and Balbinus, after which there is a lacuna, with the text picking up with a truncated Life of Valerian. The six intermediate lives are attributed to Aelius Lampridius and Julius Capitolinus and are based primarily on Herodian, when they are not based on wholesale authorial invention.[36] Whether the lacuna that swallows

---

32 Syme 1968, 89–93; 1971a, 30–134. Barnes 1978, 98–107 is the best statement of the case and the whole of that volume, because hyper-minimalist in its conclusions, remains a fair statement of the work's sources.

33 Birley 2003; Paschoud 1999b restates his consistent disbelief in the use of Maximus, to which Den Hengst 2007 is a rather effective answer.

34 As Syme 1983, 214 reluctantly conceded, with Benario 1980 offering complementary evidence; cf. Fündling 2006, 102–118, 120–127, after which the question still requires further study.

35 Stover 2020 argues convincingly that a new edition of the *Historia Augusta* is necessary and must print the lives in the manuscript order that reflects severe damage to the hyparchetype. Thomson 2012, 89–102, likewise lays out the evidence for the manuscript order of the lives without, however, proving that this says anything about the sequence in which lives were composed; it must be said, in fairness, that no study of the text, not even Syme 1983, 12–29 (his most concise statement of his final conclusions), has persuasively addressed the compositional order of the lives.

36 The use of Dio is possible but cannot be proven: the arguments of Kolb 1972 are comprehensively disproved in Barnes 1978, 78–89, while the use of Dio alleged in Zinsli 2014, 36–46, is nowhere definitive.

up Philip, Decius, Trebonianus Gallus, and Aemilian is genuine or another imposture has been much, if inconclusively, debated; given that the archetype of the two extant manuscript families was badly disordered, however, it seems unnecessary to postulate an imposture on this point.[37] The author of these middle lives is almost certainly—but not absolutely definitively—the same as the author of the final post-lacuna lives, which are attributed to Trebellius Pollio and Flavius Vopiscus and take up the largest part of the corpus: the Valeriani, the Gallieni, the Thirty (mostly invented) Tyrants, Claudius, Aurelian, Tacitus, Probus, the *Quadrigae tyrannorum*, and the joint *vita* of Carus, Carinus, and Numerianus. Here there are no underlying base texts, merely gleanings from the epitome tradition and some hints of Dexippus.[38] As a result, these lives are almost entirely fiction.

That summary would be conceded by all contemporary scholars, whether they favor single or multiple authorship, whatever their precise opinion about the date of the whole text, and however they regard the sequence of composition and later revision.[39] What is more, recent computer studies, much more robust in their methodologies than the pioneering attempts of the 1970s had been, seem to confirm the foregoing picture: the main imperial lives from Hadrian to Caracalla have a very distinct vocabulary and syntax from the lives that follow the supposed lacuna, while the secondary and intermediate lives show varied and inconsistent similarities with both the early and the late lives.[40] Welcome as that degree of consensus certainly is, it conceals the full extent of disagreement about the date of the *Historia Augusta*, a subject that has rarely been approached without preconceptions and *parti pris*. Too often, consideration of date is driven by *idées fixes* about the work's purpose or *Tendenzen* rather than by the standards of textual criticism we apply with less controversial works. Thus, from the earliest numismatic works of Andreas Alföldi, the pagan revival and the supposed "circle of Symmachus" were the interpretative peg on which that prolific scholar hung his entire vision of the fourth century and its historical dynamic—and thus his understanding of our

---

37 Syme 1971a, 199–203 had already shown how likely the lacuna is to be genuine.

38 The use of Dexippus is not in doubt; the extent of it is: Paschoud 1991.

39 Or *almost* all contemporary scholars: Lippold 1991, 1999, 2002 remained to the end an outlying believer in multiple authorship and Constantinian date, forcing succeeding commentators on individual *vitae*, e.g., Brandt 1996, 21–45, to argue the obvious case for post-Constantinian date and unitary authorship all over again. (Brandt has the great virtue of brevity, over against the generally hypertrophied commentaries in the Antiquitas Reihe 4, Serie 3.) Den Hengst 2002, persuaded by now superseded computer studies (see following footnote), considered the question of multiple authorship, if not date, open.

40 Stover and Kestemont 2016; cf. Marriot 1979; Sansone 1990; Meissner 1997; Tse et al. 1998. Dessau 1889, 378–392 had already laid out the basic arguments for unitary authorship.

THE HISTORIA AUGUSTA   31

text. Johannes Straub then made the *Historia Augusta* Exhibit A for a hitherto undetected genre of pagan historical apologetics, enthusiastically second-ing Werner Hartke's characterization of it as a *Propagandaschrift*.[41] Straub's patronage of the Bonner Historia Augusta Colloquia over many years ensured the dominance of his approach to the text, and its anti-Christian polemic came to be taken for granted rather than discussed. Finally, since the late 1980s, with François Paschoud and Stéphane Ratti, the lost *Annales* of Nicomachus Flavianus, or indeed Flavianus as himself the author of the Historia Augusta, have driven all discussions of date.

There is, in fact, only one absolutely decisive piece of evidence for the date of the *Historia Augusta* in its present form that everyone will concede. The author had read the *Caesares* of Aurelius Victor and borrowed from it a unique error—conflating Didius Julianus with the jurist Salvius Julianus—not shared by other witnesses to the lost *Kaisergeschichte*.[42] There is also a good deal of evidence for the use of Eutropius in the *Historia*, but it all just about leaves open the possibility of the author's having used the *Kaisergeschichte* itself.[43] That means we should not use Eutropius (370) for a *terminus post quem*, and we cannot use the *Kaisergeschichte*, since its date is unknown. That leaves Aurelius Victor, who wrote in 360/1, as a decisive *terminus post quem*. All attempts to detect later *termini post quem* have proved indecisive in one respect or another. What about a *terminus ante quem*? It is in the nature of things that *termini ante quem* are more difficult to pinpoint than *termini post quem*, if only because they so often rely on what is missing in a place where its presence would be expected. To take just one example, it is almost universally argued that Ammianus wrote his *Res Gestae*, or at least Book 22, before 391, because his praise of the Serapaeum could not have failed to register its destruction in that year. There are sound ways to evade that inference, but it hardly matters since the cumulative evidence that Ammianus wrote at a late Theodosian date, after the death of Petronius Probus in circa 388, is overwhelming.

Cumulatively suggestive evidence is not, however, good enough when we come to the *Historia Augusta*, if only because so much scholarly capital is at stake. The standard of proof for a *terminus ante quem* must be sky high. It can-not be merely suggestive or built-up by quantities of the plausible rather than the probative. That is because one can accumulate two or three suggestive

---

41   Hartke 1940, *passim*, most concisely at 161–168: the author was "ein Mann aus der Umgebung des Symmachus" (163). The circle of the "Symmachi Nicomachi" is revived and leaned heavily upon in Savino 2017.

42   *V. Sev.* 17.5–19.4, and Aur. Vict., *Caes.* 20.1; 20.10–30. There are other correspondences but this one is decisive.

43   Chausson 1997; restated, over-speculatively, by Festy 1999b.

passages for almost any single date between 360 and 420.[44] To those, one can add four or five more seemingly supportive passages that turn out, on close inspection, to apply to a much wider range of dates. They therefore offer reinforcement only once one has settled on the first two or three indicators as definitive *a priori*. In other words, they provide evidence of scholarly confirmation bias, not of date, and the *Historia Augusta* has a malign genius for evoking such bias. Even Syme, who acknowledged error in the face of evidence more readily than do most scholars, was disinclined to accept that his cumulative case for 394–395 was uncharacteristically weak: merely plausible at best.

As Alan Cameron recognized—alone of all *Historia Augusta Forscher*—no cumulation of the possible, the plausible, or even the highly likely can suffice with this text. Only irrefragable proof will do and it must come from the rigorous application of philological and text-critical method.[45] And just as dependence of the *Historia Augusta* on the precisely dated *Caesares* of Aurelius Victor offers the only unassailable *terminus post quem*, only the philologically proven dependence of a dated work on the *Historia Augusta* can provide a *terminus ante quem*. The parameters of what constitutes philologically irrefragable proof need to be strictly defined and policed, with no relaxation or special pleading.[46] Quotation is admissible, commonplace topoi are not. As to allusion or intertext, the alleged relationship must be extensive enough and unique enough to allow no cavils. Any possibility of a common source used independently must also be excluded. And any quotation, allusion, or intertext must show the chronological priority of one author over another.

Of the hundreds upon hundreds of allusions that have been adduced over the years, only one will stand up unimpugnably to that level of scrutiny. Since 1927, we have known that Jerome's preface to the *Life of Hilarion*, his only venture into nonfictional hagiography, and the preface to the fictional *Life of Probus* in the *Historia Augusta*, are closely related.[47] That relationship has inspired the hunt for other connections between the authors. In every alleged case, however,

---

44   E.g., the alleged *terminus ante quem* of 399 provided by the description of the Italian provinces in *Tyr. tr.* 24.5 rests on its omission of the province of Valeria, created in that year. Strong evidence, but not strong enough.

45   For the basics of which consult Maas 1958; West 1973; Den Hengst 1991, though still not skeptical enough.

46   Paschoud (and Bleckmann) are honest enough philologists to evade, by silence or oracular assertion, the places where they know their *Quellenforschung* to be at its weakest (e.g., Paschoud 2002, 45–49); of their epigones, one cannot be so sure. But as Den Hengst 1991, 166 put it so well: "I am often amazed by the scope of the author's supposed literary culture and I cannot quite escape the impression that I am learning more about the erudition of the scholars writing about the HA than about the HA itself." *Plus ça change ...*

47   Schmeidler 1927.

THE HISTORIA AUGUSTA   33

scholars have assumed the priority of Jerome, many of whose works are precisely datable.[48] The assumption serves a useful function, if one believes in the centrality of the *Historia Augusta* to a pagan revival, by pushing it well into the 390s, if not indeed much later.[49] But the textual priority between the two prefaces needs to be demonstrated, not assumed. In a posthumous article, expanding on half a dozen pages of *LPR*, Alan Cameron subjected the two prefaces to a text-critical test.[50]

The key is a passage about Alexander at the tomb of Achilles that both authors have in the form known from Cicero's *Pro Archia* 24.[51] The parallels in where they diverge from Cicero are such that we cannot postulate independent use of the same anecdote from Cicero, nor the use of a common intermediary source.[52] None of the main resemblances are mere commonplaces. In five places where Jerome and the *Vita Probi* disagree, the *Vita Probi* is closer to Cicero.[53] Of these, the contrast of *virtutum* and *meritorum* is particularly salient, since these synonyms are not nearly as synonymous in a Christian context in which *virtus* is a common word for miracle.[54] Cameron adduces many more reasons than this to show that Jerome must have imitated the *Vita Probi* and not vice versa.[55] Several things follow: *inter alia*, we may jettison the large and implausibly detailed knowledge of Jerome's biblical commentaries hitherto ascribed to the author of the *Historia Augusta*.[56] More importantly, we can draw some consequences about the date of that work.

---

48 A good example is Schlumberger 1998, otherwise quite sound, and Rohrbacher 2015, *passim*, not.

49 Savino 2017 is an extended argument for a fifth-century date, based on supposed anti-Stilichonian passages and references to Augustine.

50 Alan Cameron 2011a, 764–772; 2020. He also tested the soundness of other supposed reminiscences of Jerome in the *Historia Augusta*: a few are plausible if not proven, while most stand up to neither logical nor philological scrutiny. Only the evidence of the two prefaces really holds up (Barnes 1991 had concurred in this judgment).

51 Jerome, *VHil.* 1.1–4; *VProb.* 1–2.

52 They both begin with allusion to Sallust, continue to the Cicero reference, share a verbal parallel in *tanti viri et talis historia* (HA) and *tanti et talis viri conversatio vitaque* (Jerome), and then both note the incomplete sources available to them on their subjects.

53 The quotations are tabulated at Alan Cameron 2011a, 765.

54 This is a decisive point missed by Barnes 1991; Barnes 1999: there would have been no reason at all for the *Historia Augusta* to alter Jerome's *meritorum* to *virtutum*, but every reason for Jerome to avoid *virtutum* with reference to Achilles.

55 There is no point in restating the elegant argument at length here. It cannot be dismissed with a "non mi sembra convincente," *pace* Savino 2017, 49.

56 Rohrbacher 2015, *passim*, assumes *a priori* that the *Historia Augusta* postdates Jerome, which necessarily begs the most significant question. Paschoud 2001, 42–49, evades the problem of actual textual criticism by citing his "proof" of a late-fourth-century date for the *Historia Augusta*.

We know that Jerome left Rome in 385.[57] In his *De viris illustribus*, written at Bethlehem in 392, Jerome lists his works to that date in chronological order within each genre.[58] The *Life of Hilarion* comes directly after what is conventionally called the *Life of Malchus* but which Jerome calls *The Captive Monk* (a clue, should one want it, to the novelistic as much as/rather than biographical nature of the text).[59] Because of one known historical figure to which it alludes (Evagrius, Nicene bishop of Antioch), the *Captive Monk*/*Life of Malchus* cannot have been written earlier than mid-389, and possibly no earlier than mid-388.[60] A date on either side of 390 for the *Life of Hilarion*, and at very least before 392, is thus about as certain as such dating can be. It follows that the *Historia Augusta* was available to Jerome by 392 and that he drew from the *Vita Probi* his extended *exemplum* about Alexander's fame.[61] Cameron maintains that Jerome must have read the *Probus* before he left Rome: thinking its preface readily adaptable to hagiography, Jerome jotted it down in a commonplace book for future reference.[62]

If true, this would mean that the *Historia Augusta* was already available in the Rome of the early 380s, well before any of the many works its author is so often claimed to have read. But unlike the evidence for Jerome's dependence on the *Vita Probi*, this argument for date is not quite iron clad. Jerome got a lot of Western books while in Bethlehem. He read Ammianus there—he might have read the *Historia Augusta* there as well. And if the *Life of Hilarion* might be as late as 391 or even 392, then the date of the *Historia Augusta* could shift much closer toward one that Chastagnol, Syme, or Paschoud might embrace. One could welcome back in all the many cumulatively suggestive hints that point to the very late 380s to the mid-390s. One could readmit one of Syme's strongest suppositions, that a reference to *ipse ille patriarcha* in the *Quadrigae*

---

57   Jerome, *Ep.* 45.

58   Jerome, *De viris illustribus* 135, on which see Nautain 1980.

59   See in general Leclerq et al. 2007, 185–211; Gray 2015, *passim*.

60   Evagrius *papa* only became bishop of the Nicenes at Antioch in 388/389 according to Theoderet. Summary at Gray 2015, 5–6.

61   In one class of manuscripts (A), the *Vita Hilarionis* carries a dedication to Asella, the pious Christian noblewoman well known to Jerome: see the apparatus *ad loc.* in Leclerq et al. 2007, 212. The text of the first six lines (*VH* 1–2) is also substantively different in several places, less precise in its quotation of Sallust. There are no differences in the manuscript families at *VH* 3–4, where the connection with the *Vita Probi* is strongest. Harvey 2005 argues that this manuscript tradition represents a first draft of the *vita* which was rapidly replaced with the vulgate version transmitted in most manuscript families. If that is so, it *might* push the *terminus ante quem* back further, strengthening the case for Jerome's having read the *Vita Probi* in Rome rather than Bethlehem.

62   Alan Cameron 2011a, 770–772; 2020.

THE HISTORIA AUGUSTA   35

tyrannorum (8.4) is the Jewish Patriarch Gamaliel.[63] It would also suit the very large number of invented characters in the *Historia Augusta* whose names evoke the late 380s and 390s better than the late 370s or early 380s.

Sadly, it is not quite good enough. *Ipse ille patriarcha* cannot be proved to be Gamaliel. None of the invented names excludes the 370s, though they have since Dessau excluded the 290s and 320s. What is more, Jerome's knowledge of Ammianus is neither here nor there: Ammianus was a man from Oriens, probably an Antiochene. He kept up with friends and acquaintances, perhaps even family, there. That his *Res Gestae* should have had an eastern reception is utterly unsurprising. By contrast, the horizons of the *Historia* are western, at times narrowly Roman—what audience would its Latin puns and local Roman knowledge have found in the East? Which is to say that Jerome *is* indeed less likely to have stumbled on the *Historia* in Bethlehem than in Rome, but the possibility simply cannot be excluded. And once we concede that, then all the objections to cumulatively plausible evidence again obtrude. Cameron's Gratianic or very early Theodosian date is quite possible, but it cannot be proven on the grounds of Jerome and the *Vita Probi*. The absolute *terminus post quem* must remain 360. And the priority of the *Life of Probus* over the *Life of Hilarion* provides an irrefragable *terminus ante quem* of 392.

What follows? Reams of nonsense can be consigned to oblivion.[64] Scores of supposed allusions can be discarded, or looked at afresh: if they cannot possibly postdate 392, then they are either not actually allusions or they allude to something other than events post-392. All that is good, and if taken seriously, should make a really substantive difference to analysis of the text. What is more important, in some ways, are the consequences we must draw for any future attempts at dating the text. No such attempt should be treated as legitimate unless or until it meets the standard of proof demonstrated by the comparison of the *Vita Probi* and Jerome's *Life of Hilarion*: proof must exclude the use of a common source, whether primary or intermediary; and it must show irrefragably that one source depends upon the other and not the reverse, i.e., it must demonstrate the chronological priority of one text over the other. If, these conditions having been met, the source on which the *Historia Augusta* depends, or the source that depends on the *Historia Augusta* can be dated, then—and only then—can we declare the existence of a new *terminus post*

---

63 Syme 1971a, 17–29. The earliest letter of the eight that Libanius wrote to Gamaliel, whose son was his pupil, is from 388.

64 E.g., Nardelli 2016, arguing with a deranged subtlety for minute knowledge of the Septuagint on the part of the *scriptor Historiae Augustae*.

36 KULIKOWSKI

or *ante quem*.[65] Until then, the *Caesares* of Aurelius Victor on the one hand, and Jerome's *Life of Hilarion* on the other, are the only *termini* we can accept as unimpugnably proven.

•••

That conclusion may seem somewhat anticlimactic, given the labor required to arrive at it, but the *Historia Augusta* demands minimalist treatment after a century of elaborate hypotheses, mainly disproved or unprovable. There is, however, some chance of progress in light of two discoveries, one very recent. The first arises from the dissertation of Bruno Bleckmann, a book cited in inverse proportion to its actual readership.[66] Bleckmann subjected the treatment of the third and fourth centuries in the middle Byzantine historiographical tradition to a close examination. While he never provided a conspectus of his key passages with which readers might check his arguments, undertaking the exercise confirms that the core of Bleckmann's thesis is correct: there was a lost fourth-century source that was transmitted via another lost source to the history of John Zonaras, which is now the best witness to its existence.[67] Elements of Bleckmann's argument are highly problematical, not least that he identified his fourth-century source as the lost *Annales* of Nicomachus Flavianus.[68] At best incautious, the identification has stuck: most *Flavianforscher* now accept that a complicated, classicizing *Latin* masterpiece lies behind the whole Byzantine conception of late Roman history.[69] This is

---

65 None of these conditions are met by the imperial laws proposed by Honoré 1998, nor by the alleged correspondence of *Car.* 16.1–5 and *Collatio legum* 5.5.2, first proposed by Chastagnol 1976 and since claimed by Ratti as definitive.

66 Bleckmann 1992.

67 I did this for several of Bleckmann's key passages, at the suggestion of Richard Burgess, and I believe Alan Cameron had also done so independently.

68 By naming his lost intermediary source the *Leoquelle*, after the history of Leo Diaconus, which is in fact merely a defective recension of Symeon the Logothete, Bleckmann created lasting confusion about at how many removes from the fourth-century source we now stand. This confusion is compounded by controversy over where (or whether) Peter the Patrician and John of Antioch stand in the transmission. (Alan Cameron 2011a, 659–686 makes a good case for John rather than Peter.) Bleckmann 1996 detects a tetrarchic Latin source to explain the discrepancies between Victor and Eutropius.

69 Paschoud 1994; variously in Paschoud 2006. The otherwise reliable account of the *Historia Augusta* provided by Birley 2003 is damaged by propagating this implausibility. Birley 1996, by contrast—accepting that, as Schlumberger 1976 had long since proved beyond reasonable doubt, the *Epitome de Caesaribus* reflects some elements of a Greek tradition—correctly notes that, if there was indeed a Latin intermediary between the Greek tradition and the *Epitome* (which Schlumberger, to my mind, did not prove), and if

THE HISTORIA AUGUSTA

patently impossible. We know the kind of Latin source that actually got into the Greek tradition: *breviaria* like that of Eutropius and *consularia* like those represented by the *Consularia Italica* tradition that was used by Marcellinus *comes* and in the *Paschal Chronicle*. That last source is, of course, in Greek, and Eutropius was translated into Greek not once but twice.[70] A Latin work on the scale imputed to Flavianus could have had no impact on a Greek historical tradition that wanted nothing more difficult than Eutropius, and even Eutropius in translation.[71]

That said, if one strips away the otiose Flavianus postulate, one sees that Bleckmann did discover something important: a fourth-century classicizing history in Greek, certainly running to Julian's reign and probably to Jovian's, one that is not Eunapius and did not depend entirely on Dexippus for the third century. We can be certain this source existed. I propose to call him Nicht-Eunap. If someone uncommitted to the Flavianus hypothesis were to subject the *Historia Augusta* and Zonaras to an exhaustive text-critical study, new traces of Nicht-Eunap are quite likely to appear. If they do, they might disclose shards of good information hidden amongst the fiction, and they would certainly reveal bits of fiction which the *Historia Augusta* borrowed rather than invented. It is true that Zonaras and other middle Byzantine histories are difficult to work with because they contain so much of the folkloric accretion one finds as early as Malalas.[72] Moreover, particularly in the absence of good modern critical editions, it is very hard to distinguish the use of a common source from cross-contamination between different texts in the stemmatics. Nonetheless, the imprint of Nicht-Eunap is a genuinely new and potentially even significant avenue into the mysteries of the *Historia Augusta*.

The second novelty is the recently discovered Vienna palimpsest containing new fragments of Dexippus.[73] Though much work remains to be done, the fragments have already cast new light on a work nearly as susceptible to misuse as the *Historia Augusta* itself, namely the *Getica* of Jordanes. Jordanes was a sixth-century author, writing pedestrian Latin in Justinian's Constantinople,

---

that intermediary was Flavianus, then several egregious errors stemming from mistranslated Greek seem incompatible with the work of so sage a *pepaideoumenos*: an unnoticed (seemingly even by Birley) but damning indictment of the whole theory.

70 Alan Cameron 2011a, 665–668; Burgess and Kulikowski 2013, 175–187, 224–232.

71 The idea of Eunapius' having used the *Annales* (Festy 1998; cf. Baldini 1999) is particularly far-fetched.

72 Kulikowski 2017b.

73 Martin and Grusková 2014a, 2014b, 2014c. Martin 2017 argues persuasively that the new Dexippus derives from a complete copy of the *Scythica*, rather than from a collection of excerpts like the Constantinian *excerpta* hitherto known.

but he has far too often become an excuse to divagate on his supposed source: a Gothic history by the great Cassiodorus Senator, quaestor and praetorian prefect to the kings of Ostrogothic Italy with intimate access to an authentic *Origo Gothica*, a *völkisch* memory of the Gothic homeland in Scandza.[74] Because Jordanes has served as proxy for the wildest dreams of the old *germanische Altertumskunde*, sober students of his *Getica* have taken as jaundiced a view of his text as Alan Cameron did of Flavianus. The Dexippus palimpsest, however, reveals that hypercriticism, while often methodologically justified, can occasionally be misplaced: some details in Jordanes that were reasonably regarded as inventions turn out not to be. Most sensationally, the name Ostrogotha is not an eponym invented to give the Italian Goths of the sixth century a third-century aetiology. Rather, there in the Dexippus palimpsest stands an Ostrogotha, amidst the kind of circumstantial narrative and local chorographic knowledge that late imitators might suppress but cannot invent. We have always hoped that Jordanes hewed as closely to his lost sources as we can show he did in his use of Ammianus and Priscus.[75] The palimpsest suggests that rather less of Jordanes' account of the third-century history is fictional than is sometimes thought. No one has yet subjected our expanded Dexippus and Jordanes to rigorous comparison but doing so seems likely to reveal hitherto unnoticed use of Dexippus in the *Historia Augusta*, whether or not that adds substantively to the factual evidence for third-century history.[76]

Regardless, even if Nicht-Eunap and Dexippus/Jordanes do disclose meaningful novelties, any historical use we make of the *Historia Augusta* will still need to be minimalist. We know the text is not what it purports to be and trouble has always attended attempts to give the imposture some authentic historical purpose. If, as the foregoing has shown, the text can only be dated to a thirty-year window between 360 and 392, then most of a historian's questions cease to matter. A work anchored so loosely in an historical context forfeits any explanatory value for historical events and can be used as evidence for no one and no group's ideologies or *mentalités*. Rather than dispiriting, we should find this realization liberating. We are free to read the *Historia Augusta* for what it

---

74 See an accurate, if slightly intemperate, summary at Kulikowski 2007.

75 It is on those grounds that Blockley 1983 prints Latin passages of Jordanes as fragments of Priscus on the Vandals and Huns.

76 Christol 1998, circumspect about the Flavianus theory, is right to see the treatment of Aureolus in the *Historia Augusta* as evidence for direct use of Dexippus. Martin 2017, 110–114, makes a good start of drawing new conclusions on the use of Dexippus in the *Historia Augusta* (Zecchini 2017 less so). In terms of the factual material in the *Nebenviten* and the post-Caracalla lives, the summary in Barnes 1978, 32–78 remains basically comprehensive.

THE HISTORIA AUGUSTA 39

is, a very odd piece of literature, and apply to it all the wonderful literary tools available to those who read Achilles Tatius, or Lucian, or Heliodorus.[77] Read as history, the *Historia Augusta* might be trivial, it might be scandalous, easily dismissed. Read as fiction? Has anyone yet done that, or done it for its own sake, without ulterior motive?[78] To read, still more to reread, the *Historia Augusta* is to be struck by its failure to obey any criterion of historicity, ancient *or* modern.[79] It reminds one of mid-period Rushdie. No one goes to *The Moor's Last Sigh* or *The Ground Beneath Her Feet* for insight into the trauma of Partition, or a polemic against the late-twentieth-century music business. They go looking for Rushdie at his most baroquely inventive, drunk on his own capacity for verbal excess, impervious to the fear of failure, safe in the knowledge that if one exorbitant *jeu d'esprit* falls painfully flat, another will be along so fast it will not matter.[80] That is what the *Historia Augusta* looks like: an author growing into and reveling in his own powers, and to hell with anyone who cavils at one or another demonstration of them. If it is liberated from a procrustean historical reading, from the demand that it have some coherent purpose as invective or propaganda or coded *Zeitgeschichte*, a new era in *Historia-August-Forschung* will beckon.

---

77   See, e.g., Morales 2005. I should here note that in the *Historiae Augustae Colloquia* published since the 1990s, there are many fine contributions (by Baratta, Behrwald, Brandt, Bruggisser, Chausson, Moliner, Neri, Stickler, Velaza, Vera and Zawadzki, *inter alia*, too many for individual citation here) that, while unable, given the stakes and the setting, to treat the work in purely literary terms, do much to advance our understanding of the *Historia Augusta* as a work of literature. Note too the scattered contributions on numismatics and stemmatics/reception which deserve to be noted by those outside the Flavianus-bubble.

78   Van Nuffelen 2017 makes a good start, attempting to portray the *Historia Augusta* as deliberately going against highbrow fourth-century taste, but in such an over-the-top way that its *bien pensant* readers would recognize the joke and have all their prejudices against biography confirmed.

79   Dessau 1892, 572, was conscious of this (see Barnes 1997 for the contemporary use of *Fälschung* and why forgery is perhaps not the ideal translation). Syme 1983, 1–11, remains the best short investigation—lucidly skeptical rather than dogmatic—of ancient forgery and its motive, and see now Bleckmann 1999 on the use of ostensibly variant stories as long-standing technique of *Fälschung*. Peter 1911, 405–455 remains fundamental.

80   Cascón 1996 gives a somewhat humorless typology of the humor in the *Historia Augusta*. Schwartz 1987 is rather neglected but shows how the author's mind skipped from text to intertext and fueled his inventions thereby, or the way his use of "privatus" was designed to confuse as much as enlighten (see Beranger 1985, 25). But note the respectful use of Virgil: Velaza 1996.

Acknowledgements

I continue to regret that I did not know Alan Cameron very well, but his work has been a constant presence in my scholarly life since the start. We students of T. D. Barnes swiftly learned to read everything by any scholar for whom Tim showed even passing approbation, and the esteem in which he held Alan's work was far more than passing. I therefore started with *Porphyrius* and *Circus Factions*, worked back to *Claudian* and the great *JRS* articles of the 1960s, and then from *Barbarians and Politics* have read everything new as it appeared. It goes without saying that my own work on the late Roman aristocracy (especially Kulikowski 2017a) would have been impossible without Alan's work on the consular diptychs, the career of Basilius, and the rules of senatorial polyonymy. I wish to thank Gavin Kelly, Justin Stover, Richard Burgess and the participants of the 2019 Edinburgh Historia Augusta Colloquium for their very helpful comments on various versions of this argument.

CHAPTER 4

Ambrose Thinks with Slavery

Noel Lenski

Ambrose of Milan is one of the slipperiest figures of the late fourth century. Thoroughly political, he operated squarely on the razor's edge between church and state, building out the burgeoning power of the Christian episcopacy at the expense of the emperor, yet always doing so behind a cloak of Christian pietism that kept him just beyond the range of imperial assault.[1] Ambrose's skill at running circles around emperors and fellow bishops was matched only by his ability to spin his accomplishments to maximum narrative advantage. It is therefore surprising that Ambrose did not attract more attention from Alan Cameron, who so often trained his powers of analysis on figures just like Ambrose.[2] Whether because Neil McLynn, whose work garnered fulsome praise from Alan, had already deconstructed this champion self-promoter, or simply because he never got round to focusing on this figure so squarely situated in his scholarly field of vision, Alan left Ambrose for others. In this chapter, I take up the challenge of Ambrose in a brief investigation of his understanding of ancient slavery. Although he confronted slavery directly in only one treatise, the problems it poses permeate much of Ambrose's extant writing. This study will therefore show not just how this important late antique author thought about the pervasive problem of owning humans as property, but also how the very phenomenon of slavery played a role in shaping Ambrose's broader thought world and even influenced some important measures he took to prevent mass enslavements. Ambrose thought and worked with slavery because, in his world, slavery was everywhere. It provided an inescapable but also remarkably adaptable metaphor for the understanding of all human relationships of dependency and hierarchy, and it kept open a perennially available avenue for the abuse of power that sometimes stirred Ambrose to take action on behalf of the oppressed.

---

1 The most important studies of Ambrose include Palanque 1933a; Mazzarino 1989; McLynn 1994; Ramsey 1997; Liebeschuetz 2005, 3–26; Sordi 2008. For Ambrose on slavery, see Klein 1988, 9–51; Garnsey 1996, 191–205; Ramelli 2016, 147–151.
2 But see Alan Cameron 1970, 39, 115–116, 219, 237–241; 2011, 34–37, 75–89, 112–126.

© THE TRUSTEES OF COLUMBIA UNIVERSITY IN THE CITY OF NEW YORK,
2021 | DOI:10.1163/9789004452794_005

42   LENSKI

1   Ambrose as Witness and Party to Late Roman Slaveholding

There is no doubt that Ambrose owned slaves. Although this is not attested directly, he came from an elite Italian family of the sort that took slaveholding for granted. His homonymous father was a senator who was serving as pretorian prefect in Gaul at the time he was born, probably in 339.[3] The family hailed from Rome and held estates not just in Italy but also in Africa and perhaps Sicily as well.[4] Ambrose's brother, Uranius Satyrus, was appointed to a western governorship in the early 370s,[5] and Ambrose himself was made governor of the prestigious consular province of Aemilia et Liguria in 374, immediately before his election as bishop of Milan. Their sister Marcellina was consecrated as a holy virgin by none other than Pope Liberius in Rome, and she then spent the rest of her days there living off the proceeds of the family estates.[6]

Apart from these circumstantial indicators, a number of passages in Ambrose's writings make it clear that he understood Roman slaveholding from the perspective of the masterly elite: he thanks God that his brother was an adept estate manager and judicious disciplinarian of the family's slaves;[7] aware of how the concord of masters can be ruined by discord among their slaves, he advises that the former pay close attention to their slaves' whisperings and that they separate slaves who live under a single roof despite being owned by separate masters;[8] he invokes masterly stereotypes praising slaves who are diligent and reviling those who are argumentative or thieving;[9] he upbraids those of his social peers who puff themselves up over the number of slaves and horses in their train;[10] he chastises them for deploying throngs of slaves to prepare and serve their feasts and for prizing bedizened serving girls and exotic barbarian youths;[11] he tantalizingly intimates the sexual liaisons of a female slave

---

3   Paulinus of Milan, *Vita Ambrosii* 3 (Kaniecka 40–42) with Mazzarino 1989, 9–19. On the date, see Palanque 1933a, 480–482.
4   Ambrose, *Exc. Frat.* 1.17–18, 24–26 (*CSEL* 73.218–19, 222–23).
5   *PLRE* I Uranius Satyrus.
6   *PLRE* I Marcellina 1; *PCBE* II.2 Marcellina 1.
7   *Exc. fratr.* 1.40–41 (*CSEL* 73.231): "*Tu enim actor negotiorum, censor servulorum, arbiter fratrum, non litis, sed pietatis arbiter.*"
8   *Abr.* 1.3.10 (*CSEL* 32.1.509–10). *Virg.* 3.38 (*PL* 16.232) even claims that his martyr ancestor Soteris was undone during the Great Persecution by the accusations of her slaves (*servilibus contumeliis*).
9   Diligent: *Exp. Ps. CXVIII* 18.20 (*CSEL* 62.407). Argumentative: *Expl. Ps. XII* 38.9 (*CSEL* 64.190). Thieving: *Off.* 3.22 (*CCSL* 15.161); cf. Paulinus of Milan, *Vita Ambrosii* 43 (Kaniecka 86–88). See also Klein 1988, 29–30.
10   *Expl. Ps. XII* 1.46 (*CSEL* 64.38); *Hex.* 6.52, 57 (*CSEL* 32.1.244, 248); *Tob.* 5.19 (*CSEL* 32.2.527).
11   *Helia* 8.24–25, 9.45–46, 15.54 (*CSEL* 32.2.425–426, 427–438, 444).

with her playboy master;[12] he rails against the use of a slave girl to perform a gynecological inspection of the noble virgin Indicia, who was wrongly suspected of adultery;[13] he had seen slaves tattooed with the name of their master, and sensed their fear of chains, imprisonment, and whipping;[14] he tosses off with elite self-assurance the maxim that "the master never sells anything but a bad slave, and certainly never sells a good one";[15] indeed, he had witnessed slave auctions himself, at which buyers signaled their bids by raising a finger, and leering men drive up the price for beautiful slave girls on the block;[16] and he had been party to manumission ceremonies, where slaves were publicly slapped by way of welcoming them to free society.[17]

Ambrose's clear familiarity with late Roman slaveholding renders it especially striking that he makes only sparing references to the use of slaves in agriculture. In a discussion from his *Exposition on Luke* on the need for constant labor in the service of God he mentions "the slave who plows for you and pastures your sheep," and in his *Apology for the Prophet David* he describes wealthy masters who would punish their unruly slaves by relegating them to remote farm fields (*agelluli*), a fate considered worse than whipping.[18] Even the latter passage, however, implies that many slaves never expected to work the fields, and Ambrose's remaining references to agricultural labor point to a heavy mix of tenants and wage laborers alongside slaves: he not only discourages landowners from abusing their slaves but also encourages them to "pay your wage laborer his wage and do not defraud him of the pay for his labor";[19] he admonishes farm owners not to expel their field hands (*rustici*) from their

---

12   *Ep.* 56[5].20 (*CSEL* 82.2.96): "*ancilla praesto esset alia, quae stupro eiusdem Renati se diceret coinquinatam.*"

13   *Ep.* 56[5].5–6 (*CSEL* 82.2.87): "*Invenisti tibi vile mancipium, procacem vernulam: cur non abutaris pudibundo ministerio et exponas eius modestiam, cum praesertim nihil sanctius in virgine sit quam verecundia?*"

14   Tattoo: *De obit. Val.* 58 (*CSEL* 73.357). Chains and imprisonment: *Tob.* 8.31 (*CSEL* 32.2.535); *Virg.* 1.59 (*PL* 16.205); cf. *Ep.* 56[5].15 (*CSEL* 82.2.92). Whipping: *Fug. Saec.* 3.15 (*CSEL* 32.3.175). On fear in general, see *Ios.* 4.20 (*CSEL* 32.2.87): "*nihil enim tam speciale servitutis est quam semper timere.*"

15   *Expl. Ps. XII* 43.44 (*CSEL* 64.293).

16   *Ep.* 7[37].12, 17 (*CSEL* 82.1.48, 51).

17   *Ep.* 7[37].18 (*CSEL* 82.1.51). On the slap (*alapa*) administered to freedmen at manumission, see Harper 2011, 468–471.

18   *Exp. Luc.* 8.32 (*CCSL* 14.309); *Apol. Dav.* 14.67 (*CSEL* 32.2.345). *CTh* 11.1.12 confirms the ongoing use of slaves in north Italian agriculture.

19   *Tob.* 92 (*CSEL* 32.2.572): "*redde ergo mercennario mercedem suam nec eum laboris sui mercede defraudes, quia et tu mercennarius Christi es et te conduxit ad uineam suam et tibi merces reposita caelestis est.*"

land indiscriminately;[20] his *Exposition on Luke* implies that tenants (*coloni*) were the norm in viticulture;[21] and a long passage in *On the Duties of Ministers* criticizes the expulsion of free laborers from Rome during a food crisis: "if we are deprived of these people, don't you see, we should have to hire other skilled workers to cultivate the land? How much cheaper is it to feed than to buy a farmer?" an indication that these probably acted as market gardeners in and around the city;[22] in *On Naboth* he reminds the wealthy that their happiness depends on the labors of the poor, who supply them with game, fowl, fish, and fruits and who risk their lives to harvest their vines and tree crops;[23] and several other passages also indicate strong familiarity with free, tenant, and hired laborers.[24] Thus, for all that Ambrose clearly understood slavery at first hand, his sizable corpus provides no evidence that northern Italy in the late fourth-century looked anything like M. I. Finley's "slave society."[25] Slavery was thus an everyday part of Ambrose's world, penetrating all sectors of the economy but playing a particularly large role in the domestic labor market and a much more attenuated one in the countryside.

2   Ambrose's Antecedents

Ambrose was hardly the first ancient thinker to have grappled with the problem of slavery. His most obvious antecedent was, of course, Aristotle, whose

---

20   *Exp. Luc.* 8.4 (*CCSL* 14.299–300).

21   *Exp. Luc.* 8.28–29 (*CCSL* 14.340–341). See also *CTh* 13.10.3 = *CJ* 11.48.2 (a. 357) on the management of bound *coloni* on estates in *Aemilia*.

22   *Off.* 3.47 (*CCSL* 15.170): "*Numquid his deficientibus, non alii nobis redimendi cultores uidentur? Quanto uilius est pascere quam emere cultorem?*" On this food crisis, probably in 384, see Palanque 1933b, 349–53; Cracco Ruggini 1995[1961], 112–146, 161–162; Cracco Ruggini 1976, 253–256; Stathakopoulos 2004, 210–213 no. 31; cf. Davidson 2001, 840.

23   *Nab.* 5.18–26 (*CSEL* 32.2.476–480).

24   *Ep.* 36[2].12 (*CSEL* 82.2.9); 73[73].20 (*CSEL* 82.3.45–50); *Iob et David* 1.6 (*CSEL* 32.2.213–214); *Exp. Luc.* 7.228 (*CCSL* 14.293). Ambrose's contemporary Maximus of Turin certainly conceived of north Italian *possessores* as managing a labor force consisting of *rustici* rather than slaves, *Serm.* 91, 107–108 (*CCSL* 23.369, 420–423); cf. Lizzi 1989, 200–201. More on wage labor in Late Antiquity at Banaji 2007, 179–212; Tedesco 2018.

25   Harper 2011, 144–200, 497–509, has overstated the evidence that the fourth-century empire was still a Finleyan "slave society." Based on a much more careful empirical investigation, Vera 1992–93, 1995, 1999, 2012 had already proven that late antique Italy was no longer primarily dependent on slaves for agricultural labor. For further disproof of the Harper model, see Lenski 2017, 2019. Klein 1988, 34–36 also emphasizes the mix of free, bound, and slave labor attested in Ambrose. See also Lenski 2018; Lewis 2018 on the superannuation of the "slave society" paradigm.

AMBROSE THINKS WITH SLAVERY

theory of "natural slavery" posited that some peoples (in Aristotle's case, Greeks) are naturally fitted by the superiority of their intellect and self-control to be masters, while others (barbarians) are better suited by their mental deficits and physical strength to be slaves.[26] This was a theory long thought to have had little purchase in subsequent intellectual history, but Peter Garnsey has argued recently that it reappears in Ambrose—a connection we shall question below.[27]

Stoics from Zeno onward also discussed the question, theorizing that true slavery is a state of mind rather than body, and that slavery is thus a moral condition that can be overcome even by those trapped in physical servitude.[28] For Stoics, all men are capable of virtue provided they access their rational capacities, but those unwilling or unable to do so must on some level remain enslaved, even if juridically they are free. By the same token, proper training of the soul can allow even slaves to escape from the inferior mental condition of servitude, even while continuing to serve.

Ambrose is not known to have had direct knowledge of any of the earliest Stoics, but he was an avid reader of Philo, who had applied Stoic teachings to his own project of demonstrating the compatibility of Hebrew and Greek wisdom.[29] Using the tools of allegoresis, Philo argues that the best illustration of the "every good man is free" dilemma is the story of the brothers Jacob and Esau, who stood for moral opposites: virtue and vice, reason and foolishness, knowledge and ignorance. Thus, although Esau was the elder of the two, he sold his birthright for a bowl of pottage and was subjected to slavery to his brother by order of their father. Moreover, because the story reflects not just the will of the patriarch Isaac but also that of God, it confirms the existence of a class of persons whose intellectual inferiority renders them suitable for slavery.[30] Thus, regardless of Philo's baseline Stoic argument that all good men are capable of attaining true freedom through their intellect, his providentialist outlook pulls him down a path that conceives of some persons as naturally suited to slavery.

---

26 Aristotle, *Pol.* 1.3, 1253b14–1.5, 1255a3; cf. Schofield 1990; Garnsey 1996, 107–127; DuBois 2003, 189–205; Heath 2008.

27 Garnsey 1996, 195–99.

28 On Stoic slave theory, see Garnsey 1996, 128–152; Ramelli 2016, 45–76.

29 On Philo's slave theory, see especially the treatise *Quod omnis probus liber sit*, originally paired with a now lost work on "every bad man is a slave," as well as his *De specialibus legibus* 2.66–85. See also Garnsey 1996, 157–172; Hezser 2005, 58–60, 155–156, 330–335; Ramelli 2016, 82–100. On Ambrose's extensive use of Philo, see Lucchesi 1977; Klein 1988, 44–49; Runia 1993, 291–311; Garnsey 1996, 192–195.

30 Philo *Quod omnis probus liber sit* 57; *Legum allegoria* 3.88–89; *De virtutibus* 208–210; *De congressu quaerendae eruditionis gratia* 175–176.

Paul's letters also provided numerous inroads into the question, inroads that have been explored in studies too numerous to catalog.[31] For this study, it suffices to point to four strains of Pauline thought:

(1) At Romans 9:1–24 Paul argues that the Jacob and Esau story was not simply a tale of enslavement and freedom but also an allegory of the Jewish and Christian races, with the elder sibling Esau (the Jews) risking enslavement to the younger, but morally superior brother Jacob (the Christians);

(2) at 1 Corinthians 7:20–24 Paul encourages those called to Christianity in a state of slavery to accept their servile status rather than challenge it, an idea confirmed in the letter to Philemon which effects the return of the runaway slave Onesimus to his Christian master;

(3) in several deutero-Pauline passages referred to as the "household codes" (*Haustafeln*), slaves are encouraged to be obedient to their earthly masters, even as masters are admonished to treat their slaves with justice (Col. 3:22–4:1; Eph. 6:5–8; Titus 2:9–13; 1 Tim. 6:1–2);

(4) at Gal. 3:28 (cf. 1 Cor. 12:13; Col. 3:11), Paul asserts that "there is neither Jew nor Greek, slave nor free, male nor female, for you are all one in Christ Jesus"—a radically egalitarian message implying equality of gender, nationality, and status in the community of Christians.

Indeed, the Pauline tradition, as also the broader New Testament canon, teems with the language of slavery, such that notions of slavery and servitude permeate all aspects of Christian thought: from Paul's regular references to himself as the "slave of God";[32] to the exhortation to Christians to abandon enslavement to sin and exchange it for enslavement to righteousness;[33] to the crucial concept that Christ's incarnation represented a kind of divine self-subjection to slavery: "Christ, who though he was in the form of God, did not judge equality with God to be a thing for the seizing, but he emptied himself, taking the form of a slave, being made in the likeness of men."[34] The notion of slavery was, in other words, inextricably woven into Christian scripture such that slavery could be taken by all Christians as simultaneously normal (an integral part of the world order) and normative (a paradigm for all hierarchical relationships).

---

31   See for example Garnsey 1996, 173–190; Glancy 2002; Harrill 2006; Ramelli 2016, 101–120.

32   Rom. 1:1 δοῦλος Χριστοῦ Ἰησοῦ; 1 Cor. 4:1; Titus 1:1; Phil. 1:1; cf. James 1:1; 2 Pet. 1:1; Jude 1:1. Ambrose follows Paul's lead in the salutation of *Ep. extra Coll.* 14.1 (*CSEL* 82.3.235): *Ambrosius, servus Christi* ... On the adoption of this self-appellation among early Christians, see Combes 1998, 96–102.

33   Rom. 6:15–25.

34   Phil. 2:5–12.

AMBROSE THINKS WITH SLAVERY

Each of the elements in this rich tradition of slave thought and rhetoric found resonances in Ambrose. This only stands to reason given that Ambrose had direct access to Paul and Philo and familiarity with Stoic ideas through Philo and Cicero. The question of Aristotle's influence is more doubtful. Indeed, as we shall see below, what appear to be Aristotelian strains in Ambrose are more likely to derive from a Platonizing tradition inherited through Basil of Caesarea. From these antecedents Ambrose absorbed, assimilated, and developed the notion that slavery was in fact a sort of sociological metonym for the broader category of subordination, and he built on this assumption in ways that allowed slavery to become a highly productive metaphor in his broader epistemology. Slavery was, to deploy a useful but hackneyed academic cliché, "good to think with."

3 The Stoic Paradox 1—Christianized and Anti-Judaized

For Ambrose, slavery (*servitium*) stood first and foremost for psychic subordination to intellectual and moral superiors. This notion is at the heart of his most extended treatment of the question, cast in the form of a letter (*Letter* 7) to his priest Simplicianus, who would eventually succeed him as bishop of Milan in 397. At twenty-three pages in the modern standard edition, the letter bills itself as an exegetical treatise on the passage at 1 Cor. 7:23: "You have been bought for a price; do not become slaves of men." From the start, Ambrose resorts to the Stoic paradox: "This passage has been pitched and tossed on a great mass of discussion by philosophers, who say that every wise man is free and every fool is a slave."[35] Ambrose explores the idea, particularly in respect to notions of freedom of will versus compulsion. The wise man is always in control of his wishes, desires, and emotions, while the fool is ever in thrall to passions, impulses, and appetites:

> Not every wish is good, but the wise man wishes only that which is good; he hates evil because he chooses what is good. Therefore, if he chooses what is good, as the arbiter of his choice and the decider of his actions, he is free, for he does what he wishes; therefore the wise man is free.
>
> *Ep.* 7[37].19 [*CSEL* 82.1.52]

---

35   *Ep.* 7[37].4 (*CSEL* 82.1.45). Here and throughout, all translations are my own. More on the question of slavery in *Letter* 7 at Klein 1988, 17–21; Garnsey 1996, 192–201.

In adopting this Stoicizing approach in *Letter* 7, Ambrose follows closely Philo of Alexandria, and particularly his most extensive treatise on slavery, *Every Good Man is Free*.[36] Ambrose also takes from Philo a connection between the Stoic paradox and the Old Testament (OT) typology of Jacob and Esau:

> Ultimately the devoted father, who struggled with paternal affection between the two sons, but was conflicted over the judgment—for love rests on family relationship, but judgments are formed based on merits—when he allotted favor to one and mercy to the other, favor to the wise, mercy to the foolish, because he [Esau] was unable to elevate himself to virtue by his own powers nor to progress of his own free will, he [Isaac] gave him a blessing so that he [Esau] could serve his brother and be his slave, thus showing that foolishness is brought so low through servility that servility becomes its remedy; for the fool cannot manage himself, and unless he has a guide, he is ruined by his own desires. The loving and prudent father thus made him a slave to his brother in order that he [Esau] should be managed by his [Jacob's] wisdom.
>
> *Ep.* 7[37].7 [CSEL 82.1.46]

Ambrose demonstrates his commitment to this same complex of ideas and associations by repeating it in several other places in his corpus: in a letter to the priest Orontianus, where he argues that Isaac withheld his benediction from the brute Esau and enslaved him to the wise Jacob for the benefit of both; in a longer treatise *On Jacob and the Happy Life*, where he explains that the good father Isaac was left with no choice but to place the moderate son over the immoderate; and in the *On Paradise*, where Ambrose contends that servitude was a kind of blessing conferred on Esau to bring his unruly nature under control.[37]

In his important study *Ideas of Slavery from Aristotle to Augustine*, Peter Garnsey carefully explicated the relationship between Ambrose and his Philonian model in the development of this complex of notions: that every wise man is free; every unwise man a slave; Jacob and Esau provide the archetypal exemplars of this phenomenon; and Esau—like other fools—actually benefited from his own enslavement to his wiser brother. Garnsey also noted how striking it is that, with the last assumption (the benefit of slavery for

---

36   Ambrose follow's Philo's argument closely (sometimes nearly verbatim) at *Quod omnis probus liber sit* 5, 7–8, 12–13, 19–20, 27–32, 36–40.

37   *Ep.* 20[77].6 (*CSEL* 82.1.149); *Iac.* 2.11 (*CSEL* 32.2.38); *Par.* 14.72 (*CSEL* 32.1.320).

AMBROSE THINKS WITH SLAVERY 49

the enslaved) Ambrose, like Philo before him, grafts onto the Stoic paradox a branch of thought that appears to be redolent of Aristotle's "natural slave theory." Nevertheless Garnsey struggles to explain how this hybridization might have occurred.[38]

What Garnsey seems not to have noticed, even though it had been pointed out by Richard Klein, whose *Die Sklaverei in der Sicht der Bischöfe Ambrosius und Augustinus* Garnsey cites, is that Ambrose is using not just Philo in the development of his thought here but also the work of his own contemporary, Basil of Caesarea.[39] In his *On the Holy Spirit*, which Ambrose read and used as the basis for his own *De spiritu sancto*, Basil discusses the causes of slavery, which he asserts can arise through capture, poverty:

> Or by some wise and imperceptible dispensation, the worse children are condemned to slavery to the wiser and better by the command of their father. Nor would the just interpreter of events even call this a condemnation, but rather a blessing. For it is of greater benefit that the one who, through lack of intellect (δι' ἔνδειαν τοῦ φρονεῖν), does not have the capacity to govern in his nature should become the property (κτῆμα) of the other, in order that he can be guided by the rational capacity of the one who rules him, and resemble the chariot receiving its charioteer or the boat having a steersman stationed at the rudder. Because of this Jacob was master to Esau through the blessing of his father (ἐκ τῆς εὐλογίας τοῦ πατρός), in order that the foolish one (ὁ ἄφρων), the one lacking in intellect to serve as a guide, could be managed by the prudent one (παρὰ τοῦ φρονίμου), even if he did not wish it.
>
> BASIL *De Spir. Sanct.* 20 [*SCh* 17bis.204–206]

The precise parallels with Ambrose's text cited above make it clear that Basil had a direct influence on Ambrose's argument concerning the Jacob and Esau typology and its demonstration that slavery to a wise man is of benefit to the fool.

It is hard to miss the Platonizing allusions to the chariot and boat in Basil, who regularly recurs to Plato—as does Ambrose, although most of his

---

38 Garnsey 1996, 195–199, esp. 196–197: "The transaction is illegitimate—the Stoic doctrine cannot be poured into an Aristotelian mould and retain its identity—whether Ambrose realizes it or not."

39 For Basil's influence on Ambrose, see Klein 1988, 42–44. Importantly, Madec 1974, 133–137 has shown that Ambrose had no direct access to Aristotle; cf. Pépin 1964, 209–216, 532–533.

understanding of Plato appears to be derived from later authors.[40] Indeed, it is likely that Basil's notion of a world in which some persons were inherently slavish and should therefore be relegated to servitude by virtue of (and for the benefit of) their weaker intellects is Platonic. An important pair of articles by Eckart Schütrumpf helps clarify how this could be.[41] Schütrumpf demonstrates that Aristotle's "natural slave" theory owes much to ideas laid out in Plato's *Phaedo* (79c–80a: that the body operates as a kind of slave of the soul) and *Republic* (9, 590c–d: that it is for the slave's own good that he is governed by a rational master; cf. *Resp.* 1, 342b–347a). And indeed, this embryonic "natural slave" theory of Plato's—which speaks exclusively of mental strength and weakness and emphasizes the equal benefits of servitude to master and slave—aligns more closely with Basil's discussion than the Aristotelian line—which contrasts the master's mental powers with the natural slave's physical strength and holds that the despotic relationship primarily benefits the master. Furthermore, Philo's own exploration of the same notion (in *Every Good Man* and the other passages cited at n.30) is also likely to derive from Plato,[42] and perhaps also the middle Stoa,[43] rather than Aristotle. There is thus a much stronger case that Ambrose's theory that slavery was a necessity and a benefit to the mentally challenged derives not just from Philo but also Basil, and that it ultimately traces its origins to Plato rather than Aristotle.[44]

Ambrose not only elaborates on Philo, he also veers strongly from him by turning his predecessor's argument against the Jews. Where Philo had employed the Jacob and Esau story in the service of his larger project of demonstrating the compatibility of Greek and Jewish wisdom, Ambrose follows a path first explored by Paul when he transforms the story into a cosmologically charged

---

40 Madec 1974, 109–132 shows that Ambrose had only indirect access to Plato (through Cicero, Porphyry, and Origen), but sprinkled his works with Platonic concepts, one of his favorites being the "chariot of the soul" metaphor from the *Phaedo*, cf. Courcelle 1958, 90–93.

41 Schütrumpf 1993, 2003.

42 On Philo's Platonism, see Runia 1990.

43 See, for example, Posidonius F 147 (Theiler), which holds that many nations, being unable to care for themselves on account of their intellectual weakness (διὰ τὸ τῆς διανοίας ἀσθενὲς), surrender themselves to service to more intelligent peoples (εἰς τὴν τῶν συνετωτέρων ὑπηρεσίαν).

44 It is notable that one of the few (pseudo) Platonic works Ambrose seems actually to have read is the *First Alcibiades*, from which he is reported to have derived the notion that the soul owns the body, which it rules over like a master, see [Plato] *Alc. I* 129c–131b. This idea shows up in a lost work of Ambrose *De sacro regenerationis*, quoted at Augustine, *Con. Iul.* 2.24 (PL 44.690): "ergo princeps et domina carnis naturaliter anima est, quae domare carnem debet et regere." On the connection, see Madec 1974, 318–323.

allegory for salvation history. In Ambrose's telling, Jacob was not simply a reflection of the rational soul and Esau its irrational counterpart, the two were personifications of the New and Old Testament order:

> Therefore a reward is given to the wise man, but the wise man acts of his own free will, thus, according to the Apostle, the wise man is free. Whence he proclaims: "You have been called to freedom, just don't turn freedom into the occasion for sensuality" (Gal. 5:13). The law is set aside so the Christian does not seem to be subject to the law, and he calls Christians to the Gospel so that they can preach and enact it of their own free will— the Jew under the law, but the Christian through the Gospel. In the law there is slavery, but freedom in the Gospel, where there is understanding of wisdom. Therefore everyone who accepts Christ is wise, and the wise man is free; thus every Christian is both free and wise.
>
> *Ep.* 7.22 [*CSEL* 82.1.51–53]

Ambrose has thus coopted the Stoic binary into a Christian cosmology that assumes the ascendancy of the Gospel as the only access to true wisdom and the only source of true liberation. The Mosaic Law, by contrast, represents foolishness, imperfect wisdom capable of controlling its followers only through fear and constraint, and thus conducing to servitude.

Nor does Ambrose stop with the example of Jacob and Esau as symbols of freedom and slavery, for he refits the same binary to another archetypal story of OT enslavement from earlier in Genesis, Abraham's rejection of his son Ishmael by the slavewoman Hagar in favor of Isaac, his late-born son by his legitimate wife Sara. For Ambrose, Abraham's two sons can be slotted into the same roles as Jacob and Esau, with the slave-son Ishmael representing the Jews (bound to serve the law) and the free-son Isaac standing for the Christians (freed through the remission of sins by the sacrifice of Christ).[45]

Ambrose's discourse is thus troubling both in its apologetic for slavery as a thing of benefit to persons of weaker mental and moral capacity and in its disturbingly racialized view of Judaism as an inherently servile faith. Building on the Stoic paradox "all wise men are free," which he inherited through Philo, he grafts onto it Platonizing concepts of beneficial slavery received from Basil, and then follows Paul in interpreting the Jewish myths of the OT to explain

---

45   *Abr.* 1.4.28 (*CSEL* 32.1.522–523). See also *Ep.* 20.8–9 (*CSEL* 82.1.150) and *Ep.* 65.5 (*CSEL* 82.2.158) for the related metaphor.

the Jews' own intellectual and spiritual enslavement in the postincarnation world order.[46]

4 The Stoic Paradox 2: Joseph and Jesus, Wise Men in Slavery

Explicit in Ambrose's adaptation of the Stoic paradox is, of course, the notion that truly wise men can and do escape the fetters of servility through the exercise of self-control and virtue. This combination was possessed not just by Esau but also by the illustrative OT figure of Joseph. Joseph had, of course, been unjustly subjected to slavery when his brothers sold him to Ishmaelite traders, and he had been forced to serve in the household of the Pharaoh's palace guard Potiphar. There he had been targeted for sexual abuse by Potiphar's wife and unjustly accused of adultery. Nevertheless, far from succumbing to his enslavement and the blandishments of his seductress, Joseph always demonstrated mastery of himself and the situation. Overcoming his imprisonment, he was able to win his way back into the Pharaoh's estimation and to save Egypt and his own people from famine.

Ambrose proposes Joseph as a sort of mascot for the slaves of his fourth-century world, an example of sage-like behavior and noble endurance in the face of physical enslavement, even to unjust masters. This idea is stated most clearly in the treatise *On Joseph*:

> Joseph was a slave, Pharaoh was a ruler; the slavery of the one was more blessed than the rulership of the other. Ultimately all Egypt would have collapsed from famine if Pharaoh had not subjected his kingdom to the plan of this lowly slave (cf. Gen. 41:55–56). Therefore slaves by birth have a reason to be proud; for even Joseph was a slave. Those who have fallen from freedom into slavery because of some necessity have a reason to take consolation. They have a thing to imitate, in order that they might learn that their condition can change, but not their morals, and that there is freedom even among house-born slaves and uprightness in slavery.[47]

---

46 Ambrose is, of course, not the only late antique author to follow Paul in portraying the Jews as a people enslaved to the law, see for example Augustine, *Serm.* 5.5 (*CCSL* 41.55–56); John Chrysostom, *Joh. Hom.* 54.1–2 (*PG* 59.297–298); Philoxenus of Mabbug, *Ascetic Discourses* 7 (Budge 1.198 = 2.191).

47 *Ios.* 4.20–21 (*CSEL* 32.2.87). Interestingly, although Philo composed a treatise *On Joseph*, it does not touch on the "every good man is free" topos, nor does Philo have high regard for Joseph, whom he generally allegorizes as a duplicitous politician.

AMBROSE THINKS WITH SLAVERY   53

The same typological interpretation of the Joseph story is also found in *Letter* 7, cited above, as well as *Letter* 36, and the *Exposition on the Psalms*: despite his noble birth and family wealth, Joseph was sold into vilest slavery and served as a steward and cook, but always proved himself above servitude through his wisdom, self-control, and unshakable morality.[48]

Joseph was paralleled in his equanimity and endurance only by Jesus, who, like Joseph, was also exchanged for a price, although his was no less than the price of human salvation. Ambrose draws the parallel between the two figures directly, signaling Joseph as a precursor to Jesus's incarnation "in the form of a slave" and redemption of his people from slavery to the law. The connection is evident in a passage from *On Faith* which references the crucial passage at Philippians 2:7:

> For according to divine generation the son is equal to God the Father, and according to the assumption of a body he is a slave to God the Father, for he says: "he took on the form of a slave." Nevertheless the son is one and the same being.... Not only did he take on servitude in the person of a man even though he was from the line of David, but he did so in name as well, as you read: "I found my slave David" (Ps. 88:21), and elsewhere: "Lo I shall send my slave to you, and his name is East" (Zech. 3:8 + 6:12). And the Son himself says: "Thus says the Lord, who made me in the womb as a slave for himself, and he said to me: It is great for you to be called my son. Lo I placed you in the testament of my line in the light of the nations, in order that you should abide in safety until the end of the earth" (Is. 49:5–6). Who else is spoken of but Christ "who although he was in the form of God, emptied himself and took on the form of a slave?" (Phil. 2:6–7)[49]

Willing self-subjugation was thus a characteristic of Christ, just as it was of Joseph—the heroes of Old and New Testaments. The archetypal Jewish and Christian sages were, in other words, willing slaves.

Like Paul, Ambrose argues that this paradox creates a necessity for all humans to follow this example by willingly subjecting themselves to slavery to God. Indeed, Ambrose's entire conception of salvation history is punctuated by willing servants. We have already seen that Esau accepted servitude

---

48   *Ep.* 7.11–12 (*CSEL* 82.1.48–49); *Ep.* 36.19–23 (*CSEL* 82.2.13–16); *Exp. Ps. cxviii* 3.27; 12.31 (*CSEL* 62.56–57, 269–270); cf. *Expl. Ps. XII* 43.44 (*CSEL* 64.293); *Spir. Sanct.* 123 (*CSEL* 79.202–203); *Off.* 1.112; 2.20 (*CCSL* 15.41, 104).

49   *Fid.* 5.8.107–108 (*CSEL* 78.255–256). See also *Fid.* 2.64 (*CSEL* 78.78–79); *Ep.* 7.24 (*CSEL* 82.1.55); *Spir. Sanct.* 3.123 (*CSEL* 79.202–203).

to Jacob as something good, that Joseph willingly served Pharaoh, and Christ mankind, but further examples of voluntary servitude abound in Ambrose's corpus: Eve chose to serve her husband (*Par.* 14.72 [*CSEL* 32.1.320]); Abraham served the three angels, two of whom served the third—messianic—one (*Abr.* 1.5.36 [*CSEL* 32.1.530]); Noah served God's orders (*Noe* 47 [*CSEL* 32.1.444–445]); and at the Last Judgment we will all choose to serve God (*Exp. Ps. CXVIII* 12.27 [*CSEL* 62.266–267]). Here Ambrose has stepped well beyond the Stoic paradox into a distinctly Pauline space which not only minimizes the moral implications of servitude but also valorizes it as a positive good.[50] As Paul says at Romans 6:23: "The slave who is called in the Lord is a freedman in the Lord; similarly, whoever is called free is a slave in Christ."[51] Paul's—and thus Ambrose's—Christianity was, in other words, predicated on the concept of servitude, with all Christians subjecting themselves to divine slavery of necessity, but (in theory) of their own free will.

5 The Stoic Paradox 3: Equating Folly with Sin

Not only did Ambrose bend the Stoic paradox by turning servitude into a positive good, and also graft onto it the Old and New Testament heroes Joseph and Jesus as archetypal examples of enslaved sages, he further manipulated Stoic slave theory by equating the Stoic notion of folly with the Christian conception of sin. The fact is that the Stoic paradox occupied many non-Christian thinkers other than Ambrose, including not just Philo in the first century, as we have seen, but also Dio Chrysostom in the second, and even Libanius in Ambrose's own day.[52] These had always hewed close to the notion that mental or moral weakness (ἀφροσύνη) were the root of enslavement without, of course, introducing the distinctly Christian notion of "sin." In *Letters* 7 and 20, discussed above, Ambrose also accesses the idea of folly in his discussion of Esau, who was consigned to serve the morally superior Jacob through his *stultitia*.[53] But in

---

50 See also *Ep.* 20.3 (*CSEL* 82.1.147–48): "*Verum est et servitus libera, quae est voluntaria, de qua apostolus ait*: Qui liber vocatus est, servus est Christi (*I Cor.* 7.22). *Haec est servitus ex animo, non ex necessitate. Itaque nos servi quidem sumus creatoris nostri, sed 'libertatem habemus, quam per gratiam Christi accipimus,' generati ex repromissione secundum fidem.*"

51 See *Fid.* 1.104 (*CSEL* 78.45).

52 Dio Chrysostom, *Or.* 14–15; Libanius, *Or.* 25.

53 *Ep.* 7.6–7 (*CSEL* 82.1.45–46): "*cum divideret ... sapienti gratiam, insipienti misericordiam*"; *Ep.* 20.5–7 (*CSEL* 82.1.149): "*ne sua stultitia praecipitetur et labatur temeritate.*" See also Ambrosiaster, *Comm. Col.* 4.1–3 (*CSEL* 81.3.202–203).

AMBROSE THINKS WITH SLAVERY 55

his more extended treatment of Esau in *On Jacob and the Happy Life* he elaborates the paradox of slavery and freedom in more firmly Christian terms:

> Everyone who does not have the authority of a pure conscience is a slave; everyone who is crushed by fear or ensnared in pleasure or seduced by greed or outraged with indignation or dejected with grief is a slave. Indeed, every passion (*passio*) is servile, "for he who commits sin (*peccatum*) is a slave of sin" (John 8.34), and, what is worse, the one subject to vices is the slave of many sins. He binds himself to many masters so that he is scarcely permitted to exit from slavery.
>
> *Iac.* 2.12 [*CSEL* 32.2.38–39]

Here we watch as Ambrose effects a slide between the Stoic notion of folly or agitation (*passio*) and Christian sinfulness (*peccatum*). Pivoting around a scriptural citation, he naturalizes the equivalency between folly and sin so that the reader barely notices that the two separate but related ideas have become one.

Furthermore, Ambrose casts the sinfulness that is the root of servitude in distinctly ascetic terms that further close the ground between passion and sin: it is Esau's temptation by food and gluttony that lead him into voluntary servitude (*Helia* 11.38 [*CSEL* 32.2.435]); Joseph, by contrast, demonstrates his freedom by fleeing the lustful clutches of Potiphar's wife and thus avoids subjection to true servitude (*Ios.* 5.25 [*CSEL* 32.2.90]). This does not mean, however, that Joseph is fully free, for in Ambrose's Pauline world, there is no escape from some form of slavery. We have just seen that this was true even of Ambrose's star exemplar of freedom, Jesus, who voluntarily subjected himself to slavery as a necessary consequence of his role in salvation history. In the *On Jacob* Ambrose argues that ultimately this necessity applies to everyone:

> The Apostle proclaims: "Do you not know that, because you offer yourselves to someone to be obedient slaves, you are slaves of the one you obey, whether slaves of sin in death or slaves of obedience to justice?" (Rom. 6.16) Therefore, if we are to serve either sin or justice, let us consider on what side the slavery is more tolerable and the fruit richer. But what fruit can there be in death? "For the wages of sin is death" (Rom. 6.23), and thus there is no fruit in it but the loss of modesty, when we are ashamed at what we have done. But it is freedom to serve justice: "indeed whoever is called as a slave in the Lord is a freedman of the Lord. Likewise, whoever is called as a free person is a slave of Christ" (1 Cor. 7:22).
>
> *Iac.* 1.11 [CSEL 32.2.11]

We arrive back at the Pauline passage that sparked Ambrose's lengthy examination of slavery in *Letter* 7, a paradox that animates further commentary elsewhere in Ambrose's corpus.[54] Paul was, as we have seen, obsessed with the metaphor of slavery and its potential for explaining the relationship between man and God. He had thus welded slavery permanently into his cosmological framework. Ever the careful student of the Apostle, Ambrose found himself trapped in Paul's cage, and thus took as a baseline assumption that the human / divine relationship was predicated on the discourse of slavery: there was no escaping slavery, but whereas slavery to sin was ruinous and therefore to be avoided, slavery to God was necessary and natural and thus to be desired.

6 An Alternative Anthropology: Primitive Communism and the Intrusion of Slavery

The only glimmer of light from outside the Pauline cage that Ambrose lets in comes from an alternative to the Judeo-Christian anthropology which he cribs, once again, from the Stoics: primitive utopian communism. This idea is described at several points in his corpus, and particularly in *On the Duties of Ministers* and in the *Hexaemeron* (*On the Seven Days of Creation*).[55] *On Duties*, the earlier of the two, describes a primitive natural order in which God supplied all resources in equal abundance to all of creation's earliest humans: "His plan was that the earth would be, as it were, the common possession of all. Nature thus produced common rights, but greed (*usurpatio*) created private rights."[56] Ambrose professes to have borrowed this idea from the Stoics; it is certainly present in Cicero's *On Duties*, the model for Ambrose's own work, and can be traced in the Stoic tradition back as far as Zeno.[57]

When Ambrose recurs to the idea in the *Hexaemeron*, however, he does so with a clear eye to Basil, whose homonymous treatise Ambrose cribs throughout his own. In the fifth book of Ambrose's *Hexaemeron*, he argues that the earliest humans had formed communities in imitation of the birds, who shared

---

54 *Expl. Ps. XII* 36.16 (*CSEL* 64.82).

55 In addition to the citations below, see *Exp. Ps. CXVIII* 8.22 (*CSEL* 62.163); *Nab.* 1.2, 3.11–12, 12.53 (*CSEL* 32.2.469–70, 474, 498). See also Vasey 1982, 103–114.

56 *Off.* 1.132 (*CCSL* 15.47), part of a broader argument at *Off.* 1.120–133 (*CCSL* 15.47). On this passage, including the translation of *usurpatio* as "greed," see Davidson 2001, 2.571–576.

57 Cicero, *Off.* 1.21–22; *ND* 2.37, 154–162; *Fin.* 3.67. Ambrose also read Seneca, who transmitted the same idea at, e.g., *Ep.* 73.7; 90 *passim*. For attestations in the earlier Stoic tradition, see Davidson 2001, 2.573–576.

AMBROSE THINKS WITH SLAVERY

all benefits—property, labors, rewards, and honors—in a radically egalitarian society:

> No one dared to repress another with slavery (*seruitio*), when the woes he endured would have to be shared by those who succeeded them in rank; no one's labor was severe, for the honor that followed would offer him relief. But afterward the desire of domination (*dominandi libido*) began to make property claims to powers once they had been gained and was unwilling to relinquish them when they were assumed, and later there began to be no common law of service, but slavery instead.[58]

This explanation for slavery's absence from the primitivist utopia is entirely in keeping with a common theme in Ambrose's broader corpus: that nature intended abundance for all, but avarice for money, and the problem of debt that results, introduced the root of all evils.[59] The passage quoted also fits well with an understanding outlined above: no human oppressed another with the excesses of servitude in the primitive utopia because all knew they must exchange service to one another; they were thus locked in a transactional matrix that assumed equal reciprocity by all and for all.

Interestingly, although Basil had supplied Ambrose with his story of bird communism, his version makes no mention of slavery.[60] We need not, however, assume that Ambrose's connection between communistic living and the absence of slavery are original to him. Indeed, there is obvious precedent for the same link in, once again, Philo's *Every Good Man*. In describing the Essenes as a model community of free sages, Philo asserts:

> Not a single slave is to be found among them, but all are free, exchanging services with each other, and they denounce the owners of slaves, not merely for their injustice in outraging the law of equality, but also for their impiety in annulling the law of Nature, who mother-like has born and reared all men alike, and created them as genuine brothers, not in mere name, but in very reality, though this kinship has been put into confusion by the triumph of malignant covetousness (ἡ ἐπίβουλος πλεονεξία).
>
> PHILO, *Quod omnis probus liber sit* 79

---

58 *Hex.* 5.52 (*CSEL* 32.1.178–180); cf. *Hex.* 5.2; 5.66–68 (*CSEL* 32.1.141, 183–184).
59 Calafato 1958; Cracco-Ruggini 1976, 248; Swift 1979; Wacht 1982; Davidson 2001, 2.574–575; Brown 2012, 120–147.
60 Basil, *Hex.* 8.4–5 (*PG* 29.172–177).

Here we find the whole bundle of Ambrose's utopian threads tied in a neat little ball: the absence of slavery, community property, shared services, Nature's apportionment of equality among men, and the disturbance of this equality through the intrusion of greed. This makes it all the more striking that the Essenes make no appearance here, or anywhere in Ambrose's corpus.[61] One cannot help but sense that the same anti-Jewish prejudices that induced him to consider all Jews slaves prevented Ambrose from admitting that Jewish Essenes had so earnestly striven to recreate his longed-for paradisal utopia here on Earth. Thus has Ambrose transformed Philo's Essenes into Basil's birds.

But how *did* slavery enter this utopia? Unsurprisingly, for Ambrose, the answer is sin. The same negative principle that occasioned physical enslavement for individuals and psycho-spiritual enslavement for the mentally and morally weak also unleashed the institution of chattel slavery into human history. Following other Christian (and Jewish) writers, Ambrose holds that humanity was compelled to servility through the sin of Cham, the son of Noah, who had laughed at his father's drunken nakedness and thereby provoked Noah to condemn Cham's son Canaan to perpetual slavery: "Cursed be Canaan, a servant of servants shall he be unto his brethren" (Gen. 9:28).[62]

As noted, Ambrose was not the first to trace the origins of slavery to this OT curse, but he was one of the earliest to treat the question in any detail.[63] He also shows more concern than most with the most troubling aspect of the story—the fact that Noah condemns not Cham, the transgressor, but his son, Canaan, with perpetual servitude.[64] Without claiming to offer a solution, Ambrose ultimately contents himself with the aprioristic assumption that Noah's curse must have been just, in keeping with Noah's righteousness, and could therefore be used to explain how humanity had devolved from the utopian state Ambrose describes in the *Hexaemeron* to a world in which personal enslavement was commonplace.

Lest we be too hard on Ambrose, however, his communistic utopianism is given some real-world potency by the fact that, in his own lifetime, he relinquished his own chattel and real property to the poor and his church, save

---

61 Eusebius, who also draws on Philo, does treat the Essenes at *Praep. evang.* 8.12, including their renunciation of slaves at 8.12.7.

62 *Ep.* 7.6 (*CSEL* 82.1.45–46); *Noe* 120–121 (*CSEL* 32.1.493–494); cf. *Helia* 5.11 (*CSEL* 32.2.419).

63 Ambrosiaster, *Comm. Filip.* 2.7–8 (*CSEL* 81.3.139–140); Augustine, *Qu.* 1.153 (*CCSL* 33.59); Basil, *Spir. Sanct.* 20 (*SCh* 17bis.204–206); John Chrysostom, *Inani gloria* 70–73 (*SCh* 188.170–176); *Genes. Serm.* 4.1 (*SCh* 433.222–239).

64 *Noe* 120–121 (*CSEL* 32.1.493–494); cf. Philo *De sobrietate* 44–47; *Quaestiones in Genesim* 2.65, 77.

AMBROSE THINKS WITH SLAVERY 59

for a portion he kept in usufruct to provide for his sister.[65] To be sure, this donation continued to accrue to his benefit as he deployed the money to construct churches and fund charitable projects in Milan that helped bolster his social prestige and political power.[66] Nonetheless, the monumental scale and radical personal disruption represented by this redistribution represented a marked departure from the long traditions of euergetism so deeply rooted in the Mediterranean aristocratic culture of earlier centuries—and represented a departure taken not just by Ambrose but also by many of his contemporaries in the revolutionary world of the late fourth and early fifth centuries.[67] As we shall see in the final two sections of this study, the same spirit of charitable giving had a direct impact on the lives of at least some slaves, even if it was never deployed to effectuate the abolition of slavery itself.

7 Debt, Enslavement, Redemption

To understand the way in which Ambrose's uncomfortable relationship with property affected his approach to slavery we must return to the fundamentally economic or transactional metaphor underlying the Christian conception of "redemption"—"you have been bought for a price (*pretio empti estis*)," says Paul at 1 Cor. 7:23, the passage that had set Ambrose to thinking about slavery in the lengthy *Letter* 7 with which this study began.[68] Debt was, in Paul's framing and thus in Ambrose's as well, at the very root of salvation, a paradox equally as puzzling as the Pauline enigma, discussed above, that true freedom could be had only through slavery to God. Ambrose is thus convinced that all of mankind is in a relationship of perpetual indebtedness to Christ.[69] Because Christ redeemed humanity—literally bought it back—with his blood, we owe him a debt not in money but in blood.

Debts in silver and gold, by contrast, must be strictly avoided as conduits to enslavement to sin. This is a notion Ambrose explores especially in *On Tobit* where he rails:

---

65   Paulinus of Milan, *Vita Ambrosii* 38 (Kaniecka 80–82); cf. Ambrose, *Ep.* 76.8 (*CSEL* 82.3.112). The skepticism of Mazzarino 1989, 28 n45 should be noted.

66   As was the case with Paulinus of Nola, see Trout 1999; Brown 2012, 208–240.

67   On this new trend of renunciation, see esp. Brown 2012 passim.

68   On the economic basis for the notion of "redemption," see Brown 2015.

69   *Expl. Ps. XII* 36.16 (*CSEL* 64.82); *Exp. Ps. CXVIII* 3.6 (*CSEL* 62.43); *Virg.* 19.126–127 (*PL* 16.299–300).

60   LENSKI

> At the same time note that moneylending has been judged to be the basis
> for sin, for whoever could bind himself to the moneylender would eas-
> ily flee the Lord; moneylending is the root of lying and the cause of bad
> faith. "I did not sell you," he says, "but you have been sold for your sins
> (*peccatis vestris*)" (Is. 50.1). Thus whoever binds himself to a moneylender
> sells himself, and what is worse, he sells himself not for bronze but for
> sin (*culpa*).[70]

Indeed, for Ambrose debt was not simply a path to enslavement to sin but also
to the literal enslavement of the body. This we learn from the same treatise at
a point where Ambrose brings his diatribe to life with examples of debtors he
had recently seen forced to sell their own children in the wake of a devastating
food shortage:

> I have seen a miserable spectacle, children brought to auction for their
> parents' debt and held as heirs of his misfortune who could not be shar-
> ers in his inheritance, and the creditor shows no shame at such a horren-
> dous abomination. He presses, he urges, he proclaims, "They were fed by
> my money, so they should acknowledge slavery in recompense for their
> sustenance (*mea ... nutriti pecunia pro alimonia seruitium recognoscant*);
> they should be subject to bidding for this expense; the spear should be
> shaken for the price of each one." Is it not improper to shake the spear
> when a human life is at stake? Is it not improper to come to auction when
> a person's fate is on the line? This is the inhumanity of the lender, this the
> stupidity (*stultitia*) of the borrower.[71]

Ambrose makes the same claim to having witnessed the sale of children in
his *On Naboth*, where he portrays in vivid coloring the anguished internal
monologue of a father faced with the impossible task of selecting which of his
children to sell in order to sustain the rest of his brood.[72] Both works are part
of a larger part of the Ambrosian corpus that criticize the hording of wealth

---

70   *Tob.* 8.31 (*CSEL* 32.2.535–536); cf. *Tob.* 21.81–82 (*CSEL* 32.2.567); *Nab.* 6.28 (*CSEL* 32.2.482–3).

71   *Tob.* 8.30 (*CSEL* 32.2.534–535). The sale of children into long-term indenture first became legal under Constantine (*CTh* 5.10.1 [a. 319]; 4.8.6 [a. 323]; cf. *Frag. Vat.* 34 [a. 313], with Vuolanto 2003), who opened this avenue to the destitute at the same time he began the process of criminalizing the exposure of infants.

72   *Nab.* 5.18–26 (*CSEL* 32.2.476–480). In this treatise, Ambrose cribs heavily from Basil *Homilia in illud Lucae destruam horrea mea* 4 (*PG* 31.268–269), but the assertion that he had personally witnessed such incidents recently remains valid.

AMBROSE THINKS WITH SLAVERY

and the inhumanity of the rich; both also explore the same notion discussed above, that God intended the earth to be shared by all in common, even if the hoarding of wealth now disrupts this plan.[73] They were thus part of a consistent effort in Ambrose's pastoral campaign to combat social inequality with pen and pulpit.

But in this specific instance, Ambrose may have gone farther; he may actually have helped to convince the emperor to rescind the very sales he laments. The *On Tobit* can be dated within a broad window between 376 and 390, but the *On Naboth* offers clues that point to a much more precise dating in 389.[74] It seems highly likely that both are nearly contemporary, and both describe the aftereffects of the food shortage in northern Italy just mentioned. The same shortage is also discussed by Ambrose in his *On Joseph* and in a letter of Symmachus, both datable to 388, when a famine seems to have arisen in northern and central Italy in the wake of the suppression of the usurper Magnus Maximus.[75]

All these passages can also be connected to a law of Theodosius I, issued from Milan on March 11, 391:

> All those bound into servitude by the pitiable fortune of their parents while seeking sustenance (*dum victum requirit*) should be restored to their original freeborn status. Nor should anyone demand repayment of the purchase price, given that they have already received satisfaction from the servitude of a freeborn person over a considerable period of time (*Nec sane remunerationem pretii debet exposcere, cui non minimi temporis spatio servitium satisfecit ingenui*).
>
> *CTh* 3.3.1

There can be no proving it, but it seems plausible that Ambrose's lobbying played a role in the issuance of this constitution. It is well known that Ambrose exercised an outsized influence over emperors throughout the course of his bishopric: from his close collaboration with Gratian on matters of faith, to his blockage of Valentinian II's negotiations with the Roman Senate over the Altar of Victory, to his refusal to cede a church in Milan to Valentinian's homoian troops, to his manipulation of Theodosius I over the destruction of

---

73   *Nab.* 3.11–12 (*CSEL* 32.2.474); *Tob.* 8.31 (*CSEL* 32.2.536); cf. Vasey 1982, 143–181.

74   *On Tobit*: Ramsey 1997, 58. *On Naboth*: Vasey 1982, 22–25.

75   *Ios.* 7.38 (*CSEL* 32.2.99–100); Symmachus, *Ep.* 2.52. For the food shortage, see Palanque 1933b, 353–355; Cracco Ruggini 1995[1961], 163; 1976, 241 n25; Stathakopoulos 2004, 214–215 no. 33.

the Callinicum synagogue, to his public shaming of Theodosius for the massacre of random citizens in Thessalonica following public riots, Ambrose regularly confronted and bested the emperors resident in and around Milan in the ecclesial-political chess games he so loved to orchestrate.[76] We know that Theodosius issued a law in 390 imposing a thirty-day cooling off period before the imposition of imperial execution orders in the wake of Ambrose's cajoling after the emperor's misconceived ruthlessness against the crowds of Thessalonica.[77] Nor is Ambrose the only late antique bishop known to have played a role in the formulation of imperial legislation.[78] Given the clear and public concern with the fate of children sold in the aftermath of the 388 famine that Ambrose expressed ca. 390 in *On Tobit* and *On Naboth*, it is more than plausible that in 391 the seasoned bishop convinced a world-weary Theodosius to rescind those sales and bar demands for repayment on the original loans, now three years old (*non minimi temporis spatio*), just as the emperor was preparing to depart Milan for Constantinople that same spring.[79]

8 Redemption in Action

Ambrose was able to perform his concern for the redemption of those who had been unjustly enslaved in even more public fashion in the instance of prisoners taken captive by foreign foes. The mass ransom of captives had been an occasional undertaking of the Roman government since Republican times, but this delicate business had not involved cult foundations until the Christian church began ransoming those captured by foreign peoples in the third century CE. Taking its cue from Christ's claim to have come "to proclaim freedom for prisoners" (Luke 4:18; cf. Isa. 61:1–2), the church is first attested playing this role of redeemer under Cyprian of Carthage (Cyprian, *Ep*. 62.4 [*CCSL* 3C.384–388]), but Ambrose truly moved the process into the mainstream.

---

76 McLynn 1994 offers the most nuanced treatment. See also Lizzi Testa 2019 on Ambrose's attention to protocol in his communications with the emperor.

77 *CTh* 9.40.13 with Ambrose, *Ep. extra Coll.* 11[51] (*CSEL* 82.3.212–218); Rufinus, *HE* 12.18. See more at McLynn 1994, 315–330; Liebeschuetz 2005, 262–269.

78 See Lenski 2016 on the role of Augustine and Aurelius of Carthage in prompting the issuance of legislation against the Donatists.

79 Theodosius departed Milan within two months of issuing *CTh* 3.3.1, see Seeck 1919, 278. Note that Theodosius was still in Milan when he issued the first of a series of strictly anti-pagan measures (*CTh* 16.10.10, Feb. 24) that would open the door to widespread temple destruction in the course of that same year. Here too, Ambrose's influence might be suspected. Similar conclusions about Ambrose's influence on imperial legislation in 391 are reached at Palanque 1933a, 250–254; Vuolanto 2003, 174–175 n16.

AMBROSE THINKS WITH SLAVERY 63

In the early 380s he undertook a massive ransoming campaign to secure the release of those taken prisoner by barbarians during the Gothic wars of 376–381. He discusses the incident at two points in his *On the Duties of Ministers,* where he is at pains not just to recommend his behavior to future clerical leaders, but also to defend himself from detractors against his ransoming scheme. These, he contends, were mostly "Arians," who chided him for having broken up church vessels to pay for the redemptions; Ambrose responds that it was far better to preserve the freedom and—in the instance of females—purity of the captives than it would have been to preserve the vessels:

> Therefore, the highest mark of generosity is to redeem captives—and especially when it is from a barbarian enemy that concedes not the slightest shred of humanity to mercy except what their greed might recover from the redemption money. And to submit to another's debt if the debtor is insolvent and is straitened for a payment legally owed but unavailable because of poverty, and to feed small children, and look after orphans.[80]

Ambrose thus recommends that future generations of clerics follow his lead in freeing captives to foreign enemies. He also extends the imperative to spend church resources freehandedly in order to cover the liberation of those caught in the bonds of debt or poverty—again a reflection of his striving against the insuperable tides of inequality.[81]

As the empire's borders crumbled in the course of the century and a half to come, the church took on an increasingly important role as the primary redeemer of Romans taken captive by non-Roman peoples. Ambrose is quick to point out in his reply to Symmachus' *Relatio* to Valentinian II on the Altar of Victory, this (inter alia) set Christian churches apart from the temples.[82] To be sure, Ambrose's decision to purchase the freedom of the Gothic prisoners of the 380s was motivated by more than a purely altruistic desire to enact a scriptural mandate. The scheme by all means permitted Ambrose to build support for his leadership by stoking fear and furor against barbarians and by amassing political capital among those whose freedom he had purchased. Even so, it is hard to deny the positive impact these efforts must have had on the lives of those who were liberated, let alone its importance as a model for the

---

80   *Off.* 2.70–71 (*CCSL* 15.122); cf. *Off.* 136–143 (*CCSL* 15.146–147); Paulinus of Milan, *Vita Ambrosii* 38 (Kaniecka 80–82). See also Davidson 2001, 744–748, 789–795; Klein 1988, 26.
81   See also *Exp. Ps. cxviii* 8.41 (*CSEL* 62.175).
82   *Ep.* 73[18].16 (*CSEL* 82.3.43).

64 LENSKI

ecclesiastical management of redemptions in the decades and even centuries to come.[83]

Moreover, although Ambrose never saw his way to launching a critique of the institution of slavery as such, he certainly did help to shape emergent trends among the Christian clergy that directed sharp social critique against slaveholder abuses.[84] He openly accused masters who sexually exploited their slaves of violating the commandment against adultery.[85] He encouraged masters to abide by the Pauline household codes, ordering not just slaves to be obedient to their masters but also masters to treat their slaves with respect.[86] And he encouraged masters to remember their shared nature with their slaves, all of whom were equals before their common master—God.[87] In other words, for all that Ambrose was a convinced believer in the inevitability and even desirability of slavery, he was also a staunch critic against the abuse of slaves.

9   Conclusion

It is difficult to trace a consistent line of thought in Ambrose's approach to slavery. Apart from *Letter* 7, he offers no extended treatment of the question, which he generally confronts casuistically and mostly explores only as a metaphor with which to explicate other matters. Ambrose came from a slave-owning family and appears to speak from experience on matters of slave management, yet much of his thought on the matter traces to the influence of literary and theological forebears, in particular Cicero, Philo of Alexandria, and Basil of Caesarea, and especially to Jewish and Christian scripture, above all Paul. Like many imperial writers, Ambrose was convinced of the validity of the Stoicizing paradox that "every good man is free, and all fools are slaves." Having received this idea from Philo, Ambrose added a new strain to it by arguing that the morally and mentally weak both deserve slavery and benefit from it. This he appears to have derived not from Aristotle's "natural slave" theory, but from Platonizing notions inherited through Basil. He also borrows Philo's connection

---

83   More on the politics of redemption from captivity by Christian leaders at Klingshirn 1985; Lenski 2011, 2014; López 2013, 57–63. For the impact in Byzantine society, see Rotman 2009, 27–57. Cf. Fynn Paul 2009 for the development of sectarian anti-slaving zones inside the territories of the north-western Europe.

84   On this pattern, see Ramelli 2016.

85   *Abr.* 1.3.19, 1.4.22–26 (*CSEL* 32.1.515, 517–520); *Par.* 13.65 (*CSEL* 32.1.324).

86   *Ep.* 36.31 (*CSEL* 82.2.20); *Ep. extra Coll.* 14.112 (*CSEL* 82.3.295); cf. Klein 1988, 34–35.

87   *Exhort. Virg.* 3 (*PL* 16.337); *Exp. Luc.* 5.84, 8.28–29 (*CCSL* 14.162–163, 340–341); *Exp. Ps. CXVIII* 20.17 (*CSEL* 62.453–454).

of the Stoic paradox to the Genesis story of Jacob and Esau, although he adds a Pauline twist to that by making the two typological figures stand in not just for the free sage and the enslaved fool but also for the broader Christian and Jewish communities. Unabashed in his simultaneous appropriation and abnegation of Jewish traditions, he also equates Joseph and Jesus as exemplars of true freedom's ability to express itself even in a condition of slavery. He then further develops the paradox by equating Stoic folly with Christian notions of sin.

A separate strain of thought posits a primitive communistic utopia without private property and slavery. This had been overturned with the introduction of wealth, making slavery nothing less than a corruption of mankind's original freedom, ruined by the accumulation of riches. Here too one can find Stoic precedent, absorbed by Ambrose through Cicero and Basil. Strikingly, however, the discomfort with wealth born of these convictions led Ambrose not only to relinquish his personal fortune but also to labor on behalf of those unjustly enslaved due to debt or capture. In this vein, he labored to free children sold into slavery by their parents during a famine in 388, perhaps even extracting a law from Theodosius effecting their release in 391. He also orchestrated the liberation of captives seized by the Goths in their wars against the Romans in the 370s and 380s.

Ambrose was thus at once an apologist for the institution of slavery and a social activist against some of its more egregious injustices. Although he understood human slavery to be an evil contrary to the paradisal equality intended by God and nature, he accepted it as an inevitability and even a social necessity in the postlapsarian world. Indeed, he even elevated slavery to the status of a totalizing paradigm for relations of subordination, following Paul's paradox that all humans must serve either sin or Christ. His was thus a muted critique not aimed at overturning slavery so much as blunting its edges with consolatory rhetoric and occasional sprinklings of political influence and dollops of cash.

Acknowledgements

Mine are the fondest memories of Alan Cameron, whose acquaintance I first made at his Riverside Drive apartment in 1992 as he helped me discover my dissertation topic in an area already well charted by his work, with whom I then remained in contact for the 25 years following, and whose final article on diptychs he published under my editorship at the *Journal of Late Antiquity*. There are few who could outdo his wit and none who will surpass his intellect. We can only be grateful that so much of both survive in his scholarship.

CHAPTER 5

Rutilius Namatianus, Melania the Younger, and the Monks of Capraria

Gavin Kelly

The elegiac poem of Rutilius Namatianus *De Reditu Suo*, 'On his Return', which describes his sea-voyage from Rome to his native Gaul in the autumn of 417, left little impact in Antiquity.[1] But ever since its rediscovery in 1493, it has charmed readers, a late antique poem admired even by those who do not generally love late antique poetry. Rutilius' meter and language are classicizing, his debt to Vergil and Ovid is plain, and he is the last Latin poet we know to have been a pagan; these facets, combined with his poignant praises of the Roman world-empire in his hymn to Rome, gave him a nostalgic place at the end of many histories of Latin literature. In part because of the poem's sense of place and landscape on the voyage up the Italian coast, it has been particularly popular in Italy, where it has even inspired a film.[2]

The last pagan Latin poet, perhaps the last pagan prefect of Rome, seems a most appropriate topic with which to honor Alan Cameron.[3] Alan's most important scholarly contribution on our poet came in an early article of 1967: 'Rutilius Namatianus, St. Augustine, and the Date of the *De Reditu Suo*'.[4] Rutilius was writing—or at least his poem is set—in the 1169th year of Rome (1.135–6): 'although with a thousand years and sixteen decades completed, your ninth year besides is passing'.[5] But given uncertainties in the calendar which it is not necessary to elaborate here, there has been debate as to how to interpret this information. It was long thought that Rutilius' voyage belonged to the autumn

---

1 Sidonius is Rutilius' only certain reader from antiquity (e.g., Brocca 2003–2004, 285–290), though suggestions have been made about possible echoes in the *Epigrammata Bobiensia*; Russo 2019 has now identified the influence of Rutilius on the verse of Paul the Deacon in the late eighth century.
2 Claudio Bondì (dir.), *De reditu—il ritorno* (2004).
3 Whether you consider Rutilius the last known pagan prefect of Rome (he held the office briefly in mid-414) will depend on whether you accept Alan Cameron's argument for the Christianity of his friend Volusianus, appointed prefect during Rutilius' journey (1.415–428, and see n.11 below).
4 Alan Cameron 1967b; see also Alan Cameron 1970, 250–251.
5 *Quamuis sedecies denis et mille peractis*
   annus praeterea iam tibi nonus eat.

© THE TRUSTEES OF COLUMBIA UNIVERSITY IN THE CITY OF NEW YORK,
2021 | DOI:10.1163/9789004452794_006

of 416. Jérôme Carcopino had argued that the actual date was 417, while in his book on Rutilius of 1961 Italo Lana argued for 415.[6] Alan followed Carcopino, but refined the latter's argument from astrological references and added an allusion to St Augustine as part of the proof. The overwhelming weight of the evidence is on his side, and his argument is made much more efficiently than Carcopino's or Lana's. Classical scholars, reconstructing texts and events on the basis of limited evidence, cannot have more than faint hope that a new source will be discovered and prove their theories correct. But that is exactly what happened to Alan in this case. Six years after his article came out, Mirella Ferrari published a scrap of parchment, dateable to ca. 700, which was reused to patch up the lower margin of a page of a Turin codex (F IV 25, folio 22r). It contained two fragmentary passages from the lost parts of Rutilius' second book.[7] In the second the poet sings the praises of the Master of the Soldiers and future emperor Constantius III, and refers to his second consulship—precisely in 417. So Alan was proved right.[8]

But Rutilius Namatianus is also found, as one would expect, in the long cast-list of *The Last Pagans of Rome*, where a part of a chapter is dedicated to analysis of the author's attitude to Christianity. Although Alan Cameron concurs (with near certainty, at any rate) with the general view that Rutilius was a pagan, he adduces the praises of Constantius as evidence against interpreting the poem as pagan polemic, and argues that the passages that have been seen as attacks on Christianity would not have seemed so to contemporaries.[9] The central focus of this article is one of these passages. The poet's voyage home to Gaul takes him past the island of Capraria (modern Capraia). The sight of Capraria, an established monastery when Rutilius sailed in autumn 417, provokes the poet into a tirade against monks (1.439–52). After discussing individual points of the passage (second section), I suggest that this passage makes coded reference to one of the great celebrities of fifth-century monasticism, Melania the Younger (third section), and to explore the implications of this link for our understanding of both Rutilius and Melania. Before that, however,

---

6 Carcopino 1928 (reprinted and amplified 1963); Lana 1961, ch. 1.

7 Ferrari 1973, 12–13, 15–30.

8 Some Italian literary scholars have clung loyally but most unconvincingly to Lana's date of 415: see, e.g., Brocca 2004, 170–184. Note also a curiosity, Stéphane Ratti's republication of Carcopino 1963 in the French electronic journal *Anabases* with a short prefatory article entitled 'Rutilius Namatianus: Jérôme Carcopino avait raison!' (Ratti 2012). He explains how Carcopino's arguments had been definitively confirmed by the discovery of the Turin fragments. But though he has a full scholarly apparatus, Ratti never mentions the name of Alan Cameron, seemingly unwilling to acknowledge that he too was right.

9 Cameron 2011a, 207–218, esp. 208.

68 KELLY

I would like to show why we might expect Rutilius' poem to contain such a coded reference (first section).

1 *De reditu suo* as a *poème à clé*

Rutilius' readers have long had the feeling that this is poetry strongly directed at a particular social or literary circle. Throughout the poet's journey, places skirted prompt reflection on the recent past, and people encountered prompt passages of praise or blame. In particular, the first book alone has nine passages in praise of aristocratic friends, almost all of them praised specifically as holders of high office; the Turin fragments from the second book, discovered in 1973, add a tenth.[10] Some scholars tended to identify the friends of Rutilius as being universally pagans, members of the circle of Symmachus, and an incidental achievement of Alan Cameron's in *LPR* is to show both how weak the evidence for that is in several cases, and how misguided it is to link those named to Symmachus, fifteen years dead at the time of Rutilius' voyage.[11] There is also a series of invectives, including that provoked by the monks of Capraria. A second and equally vigorous antimonastic passage is found at the island of Gorgo; the attack is on a specific hermit rather than cenobites, an unnamed aristocrat who gave up his marriage and his wealth for a filthy and degraded life there (1.515–26). Previously, an encounter with a disagreeable Jewish landlord prompted a forceful—indeed notorious—antisemitic rant (1.381–99), and at the beginning of the second book, there is an attack on the late generalissimo Stilicho (2.41–60).

A related quality which can also be seen in *De reditu suo* is that it appears to be, to some extent, a *poème à clé*, a work in which some items are reported without names being given, in a way that would nevertheless have been understood by well-informed early readers. In a simple form, this comes with the poet's references to his friend Rufius Antonius Agrypnius Volusianus. The name by which he was generally known (the diacritic), Vŏlŭsĭānus, would not fit into elegiac verse. When first mentioned (1.170–2), he is *Rufius ...| qui Volusi antiquo deriuat stemmate nomen / et reges Rutulos teste Marone refert*

---

10   1.165–178 Volusianus and his father Albinus; 1.207–216 Palladius and his father Exuperantius; 1.267–276 Messala; 1.415–428 Volusianus again; 1.465–474 Albinus; 1.491–510 Victorinus; 1.541–558 Protadius; 1.575–596 Lachanius, the poet's father; 1.599–614 Decius and his father Lucillus. In Book 2, fr. A11–16 (and beyond?), Marcellinus. Of these, only the youthful Palladius is not referred to as an office holder.

11   On the view that all Rutilius' friends were pagans, see e.g., Corsaro 1981, 86; Alan Cameron 2011, 362, and 188–189 on Protadius, and 196–197 on Volusianus.

(Rufius, who derives his name from the ancient line of Volusus, and recalls the Rutulian kings, as witnessed by Vergil). Alessandro Fo has suggested that the poet reveals somewhat more of Volusianus' full name by the juxtaposition of the words **Volusi antiquo**.[12] And at Volusianus' second appearance, the metrical problem is specifically indicated (1.419–422): 'I should like to embrace your true name in my poem, but a harsh rule shuns some feet; your *cognomen* will come in my verse, dearest Rufius; by it my page sings you before now.'[13] This sort of self-conscious circumlocution is not so rare in ancient poetry (one might exemplify from one of Rutilius' major models, Ovid's *Ex Ponto* 4.12.1–16) and the code is hardly difficult to break.

A rather more complex example of coded language arises when the poet's party halts at Portus Herculis (modern Porto Ercole, on the south of Monte Argentario). The rebel consul Lepidus had camped there in 78 BC, and this leads into an enumeration of four wicked Lepidi of Roman history, including the triumvir (1.295–306). The passage ends (1.307–312):

> nunc quoque—sed melius de nostris fama queretur:
> iudex posteritas semina dira notet.
> nominibus certos credam decurrere mores?
> moribus an potius nomina certa dari?
> quidquid id est, mirus Latiis annalibus ordo,
> quod Lepidum totiens reccidit ense malum.

> Now too ... but rumour will do better at complaining about our times. Let posterity be the judge that marks this ominous race. Should I believe that fixed characters run in names, or rather that fixed names are given to characters? Whatever the answer, there's an astonishing pattern in Latin histories, in that Lepidan infection so often recurs with the sword.

The poet seems about to indicate a modern recurrence of the name Lepidus in the person of a contemporary villain, but interrupts himself. There is clearly a fifth Lepidus, or more than one further Lepidus,[14] not identified in the text (though quite what we are to infer about him or them will depend on the interpretation of the obscure line 1.312). As it happens, a plausible conjecture has

---

12   Fo 2004, 180–191, esp. 189.

13   *optarem uerum complecti carmine nomen,/ sed quosdam refugit regula dura pedes./ cognomen uersu †uenerist, carissime Rufi;/ illo te dudum pagina nostra canit.* I translate *ueniet* (Vessereau) for the unmetrical *ueneris*.

14   So Castorina ad loc.

been made, by A. Zumpt in 1837: one of the very few attested Lepidi of Late Antiquity is Claudius Lepidus, a former provincial governor, *magister memoriae*, and *comes rerum privatarum*, who, probably in the first decade of the fifth century, helped his brother and brother's wife in the establishment of a walled Christian community called Theopolis ('the city of God'!) at Sisteron in Provence.[15] The fifth Lepidus is usually thought to be not this man but his more famous brother, Claudius Postumus Dardanus, who as praetorian prefect of Gaul in ca. 411–413 had played a significant and violent role in putting down the usurpation of Jovinus, and who was still execrated by members of the Gallic aristocracy half a century later (see Sidonius *Ep.* 5.9.1).[16] Fo has argued for the existence of a cryptographical hint at the name Postumus Dardanus in the words *posteritas* (1.308) and *dari* (1.310).[17] Whatever our conclusions, this passage shows that Rutilius is prone to coded language when speaking negatively about his contemporaries. Similarly, the ascetic on Gorgo is left unnamed, and in one of the fragments discovered in 1973 there is a reference to a *praedo sagatus* (fr. A16), a brigand in a military cloak, seemingly otherwise unnamed (a usurper, perhaps?).[18] All this suggests that we should be ready to see potential coded reference in other passages too, such as that concerning Capraria.

A second preliminary assumption to be made about the Capraria passage is that it should be read alongside other passages of invective in the work. This applies particularly, perhaps, to the antisemitic passage and the attack on the hermit, but we should also bear in mind the passage just discussed on the fifth Lepidus (which, if it refers to Dardanus or his brother, could be related to their status as founders of a Christian community), and the attack on the late generalissimo Stilicho in the second book. In most of these passages, a generalized attack arises from the example of one particular individual. In fact, practice and methods of invective have much in common across these passages.[19]

---

15 *CIL* 12.1524 = *ILS* 1279. On the date see *PLRE* 2 s.v. Dardanus.

16 See Zumpt 1837, 81–83; Lana 1961, 61–73; among recent literature supported by Fischer 1986 and Fo 2004; for a contrary view see Frye 1993.

17 Fo 2004, 179.

18 Sivan 1986, 526, argued for a reference to Alaric. It could of course be that in this case the name of the individual was on the lost left-hand part of the page (though there is little room for it) or was revealed after the end of the fragment.

19 For the importance of reading these passages together see also Verbaal 2006, 168–180.

2   The Monks of Capraria and Rutilius' Invective

Processu pelagi iam se Capraria tollit:
    squalet lucifugis insula plena uiris.   440
ipsi se monachos Graio cognomine dicunt,
    quod soli nullo uiuere teste uolunt.
munera Fortunae metuunt, dum damna uerentur:
    quisquam sponte miser, ne miser esse queat?
quaenam peruersi rabies tam stulta cerebri,   445
    dum mala formides, nec bona posse pati?
siue suas repetunt factorum[20] ergastula poenas,
    tristia seu nigro uiscera felle tument,
sic nimiae bilis morbum adsignauit Homerus
    Bellerophonteis sollicitudinibus: 450
nam iuueni offenso saeui post tela doloris
    dicitur humanum displicuisse genus.

On the advance over the main Capraria now raises itself: the island is dingy, full of men who shun the light. They call themselves by a Greek surname, *monachoi*, because they wish to live alone without any witness. They fear the gifts of Fortune, while they dread her losses: would anyone to escape misery live of his own choice in misery? What stupid madness of a distorted brain is it not to be able to endure good things because you fear bad ones? whether they seek the slave-houses as their punishment for their deeds, or whether their sad innards swell with black bile. It was even so that Homer assigned the disease of excessive gall to Bellerophon's troubles: for it was after the arrows of a savage grief that the stricken youth is said to have conceived his loathing for the human race.

The island of Capraria lies around 50 kilometers west of from the Tuscan coast, roughly on the same latitude as Populonia (from where Rutilius was setting out) and as the northern tip of Corsica, a further thirty kilometers to the west. The island can be seen from the Tuscan coast in the right weather, and there

---

20   The reading of the archetype was *fatorum* (**VR**); Sannazaro suggested *factorum* in the margin of **V**, and Pio's editio princeps (**B**) printed *ex fato* (also a conjecture). For confusion in the ms tradition between *facta* and *fata* cf. 1.92 (where the second *facta* should be emended to *fata*).

72   KELLY

is no reason to doubt that Rutilius and his crew saw it, but they are unlikely to have sailed very close and its inclusion was far from inevitable (the poem is not, after all, a faithful diary[21]). There had been monks on Capraria for at least twenty years at the time when Rutilius was writing, following a general trend toward monastic establishments in the islands both of the Tyrrhenian Sea and the Adriatic.[22] We learn from Orosius (*Hist.* 7.36.4) that there was an established monastery there early in the year 398 when Mascazel landed at the island on his way to Africa to fight against his brother Gildo. In the same year, Augustine sent a letter to an abbot named Eudoxius (*Ep.* 48).

A number of remarks on this text may be made. First, the overall charge against the monks of cutting themselves off from the world through hatred of the human race associates this passage with the attack on the hermit of Gorgo (*homines terrasque reliquit*, 1.521), but there is also a similarity with the attack on the Jewish innkeeper as *humanis animal dissociale cibis*, 'an animal cut off from human foods' (1.384).[23] The association of the object of invective with animals is also present in the second antimonastic passage: the hermit of Gorgo is described as transformed in his mind by his *secta*, just as the bodies of Odysseus' sailors were by Circe's magic (1.525–526). His assimilation to a spiritual pig reinforces the suggestion of the previous line that in his delusion the wretch believes that heavenly things can feed on filth (*infelix putat illuuie caelestia pasci*, 1.523).[24] A similar association could also be identified within this passage, as Latin readers would probably associate the word *lucifugi* with Vergil's *Georgics* 4.243, where it denotes the beetles, *blatti*, that threaten to eat the bees' honey.

Line 442 glosses the word *monachi* in the previous line, as an unpoetic loanword from Greek, in which it was also a neologism.[25] Although glossing Christian words was not necessarily a sign of hostility, it seems to be so in this

---

21   See Paschoud 1978, esp. 325.

22   The standard work is Jenal 1995; see esp. 1.121–125 and 429–431.

23   Note how the Kosher practice of avoiding certain foods, especially animals, is turned round to call the Jew himself an animal and how the hapax *dissociale* creates an allusion by opposition to the Aristotelian idea of man as *animal sociale*, represented in Latin by Seneca (*Ben.* 7.1.7, *Clem.* 1.3.2) and Lactantius (*Div. Inst.* 6.10.10, 17.20; *Epit.* 29.2).

24   *Illuuies* also of course summons up the stereotype of monks as unwashed, as does *squalet* in our passage (1.440).

25   That said, this was not the word's first appearance in poetry: cf. Damasus *Carm.* 78.7, Paul. Nol. *Carm.* 17.219 (AD 400), 24.331 (?AD 400); it seems likely that Rutilius was aware at least of the poetry of Paulinus (see Guttilla 1994–95 and n.35 below). It was a recent word in Greek too: Eunapius in similar fashion refers to τοὺς καλομένους μονάχους (*VS* 468), and a famous epigram of Palladas (*AP* 11.389) played on the neologism, asking εἰ μοναχοί, τί τοσοίδε; τοσοίδε δέ, πῶς πάλι μοῦνοι;/ ὦ πληθὺς μοναχῶν ψευσαμένη μονάδα ('If *monachoi*,

RUTILIUS NAMATIANUS, MELANIA THE YOUNGER 73

case.[26] A detail of the gloss is also worth questioning: the words *nullo teste*, with no witness, which are strictly speaking redundant alongside *soli* rendering *monachi*, might perhaps evoke the other meaning of *testis*, suggesting that these men (metaphorically or even literally) have made themselves eunuchs for the kingdom of heaven's sake (Matthew 19.12). This double entendre is not unfamiliar in Latin literature, as for example in an extended passage near the end of Plautus' *Miles Gloriosus* (1420 and 1426).[27]

The interpretation of line 447 is unusually ambiguous by the standards of the author. The issues, all interrelated, are: (1) does *ergastula* mean prison-workhouses for slaves (the primary meaning), or is it here (also well-attested) a metonym referring to the slaves from such a workhouse?[28] (2) And is it therefore nominative (as in the latter case) or accusative plural in apposition to *suas ... poenas*? (3) Should we read *fatorum* or *factorum* and is the genitive plural dependent on *ergastula* or on *poenas*? In my view, the association of islands with imprisonment as a punishment makes it preferable to see *ergastula* as slave workhouses, in apposition to *suas poenas factorum*, but other interpretations are possible.[29]

The critique of monasticism as misanthropic culminates in the marked and extended use of the example of Bellerophon, which is carefully marked as an allusion to Homer. In this, it shares features with both the other antimonastic passage, in which the *secta* that inspires ascetic withdrawal is compared to Circe's magic (1.525–526), and the anti-Jewish invective, where the Jewish landlord at Falesia is called *hospite conductor durior Antiphate* (1.382)—a landlord harsher in his hospitality than Antiphates, the cannibal king of the Laestrygonians in *Odyssey* 10 (esp. 105–132). The citation of the Greek hero Bellerophon ostensibly looks to Homer *Iliad* 6.200–205:

---

why so many? Being so many, why again "alone?" O multitude of *monachoi* laying false claim to solitariness!')

26   This phenomenon in Greek and Latin historiography is the subject of one of Alan Cameron's earliest articles, co-authored with Averil Cameron (1964).

27   For this play on words seen Adams 1982, 67, who additionally cites Plautus *Curc.* 31, Phaedr. 3.11.5, Mart. 7.62.6, *Priap.* 15.7. I would also draw attention to an inspired conjecture by Michael Hendry on Juvenal 6.311, which has been accepted into Braund's Loeb text. The drunken Roman matrons urinate in the streets on the way home and then indulge in spontaneous outdoor lesbian sex. The paradosis is *in uices equitant et luna teste mouentur* (they take it in turns to ride and thrash about, witnessed by the moon). Hendry 1996–1997, 256–257) emends to *nullo teste* ('with none to witness/ without male genitalia').

28   *TLL* s.v. *ergastulum*, B1 (5.2.758.3–23).

29   See in particular Bertotti 1969, n.40 (on pp. 106–107). If *ergastula* is the subject, a translation might run 'if the workhouse slaves demand their own punishments for their crimes'.

ἀλλ' ὅτε δὴ καὶ κεῖνος ἀπήχθετο πᾶσι θεοῖσιν,
ἤτοι ὃ κὰπ πεδίον τὸ Ἀλήϊον οἶος ἀλᾶτο
ὃν θυμὸν κατέδων, πάτον ἀνθρώπων ἀλεείνων·
Ἴσανδρον δέ οἱ υἱὸν Ἄρης ἆτος πολέμοιο
μαρνάμενον Σολύμοισι κατέκτανε κυδαλίμοισι·
τὴν δὲ χολωσαμένη χρυσήνιος Ἄρτεμις ἔκτα.

But when Bellerophon came to be hated of all the gods, then he wandered alone over the Aleian plain, devouring his own soul, and shunning the paths of men; and Isander his son was slain by Ares insatiate of battle, as he fought against the glorious Solymi, and his daughter was slain in wrath by Artemis of the golden reins.

In dealing with western writers of the fourth and fifth centuries it is common for scholars to wonder whether vaunted knowledge of Homer is direct, indeed whether the author in question has a functional knowledge of Greek. This has been the case with Rutilius here and elsewhere: in one other ostensibly Homeric reference in the work (just before the departure from Rome), Homer is at the very least mediated through Ovid.[30] In this case too, there are Latin models that deserve to be taken seriously, above all the most important poetical engagement with asceticism that had yet been written in Latin, the verse-letter exchange between Ausonius and his former pupil Meropius Pontius Paulinus, the future bishop of Nola, written in the first half of the 390s. Together with his wife Therasia, and shortly after the deaths of their infant son and of his brother, Paulinus started selling their property and made a commitment to celibacy and asceticism.[31] In Ausonius' *Ep.* 29 (= 21 Green), he complains about the unknown person who has dissuaded Paulinus from replying to his letter, hoping that they live wretchedly in the wilderness (70–72):

> ... ceu dicitur olim
> mentis inops coetus hominum et uestigia uitans
> auia perlustrasse uagus loca Bellerophontes.

Just as once, lost in mind and avoiding the intercourse and footprints of men they say wandering Bellerophon marked out the pathless places.

---

30   1.195–6; cf. *Od.* 1.57–9. See Tissol (2002) 441–2.

31   The bibliography on this correspondence is very considerable but see for example: Trout 1999, 67–77; Rücker 2012; Brown 2012, 208–216; Fielding 2017, 22–51 (all of whom mention Rutilius' allusion).

Ausonius' summary of the example of Bellerophon shows clear engagement with a passage of the *Tusculan disputations* (3.63), in which Cicero discusses excessive reactions to the deaths of one's loved ones and quotes the relevant passage of Homer in his own verse translation—Ausonius reproduces a half-line almost unchanged.[32] Paulinus replied to this jibe, as well as to Ausonius' previous comparison of Therasia to Tanaquil (*Ep.* 28 (=22 Green) 31), taking the attack on an unnamed person stopping him from writing as being a reference to himself—perhaps rightly.[33] The engagement with Ausonius' ideas goes across his two verse-letters,[34] but is particularly found in the following lines (Paulinus *Carm.* 10.189–192):

> Ne me igitur, uenerande parens, his ut male uersum
> increpites studiis neque me uel coniuge carpas
> uel mentis uitio: non anxia Bellerophontis
> mens est nec Tanaquil mihi sed Lucretia coniunx

> So do not chide me, revered father, as though I had turned to these pursuits perversely and do not twit me with my wife or with defect of mind. Mine is not the perturbed mind of Bellerophon, nor do I have as wife a Tanaquil but a Lucretia.

That Rutilius alludes to Ausonius and Paulinus seems certain, since the evidence for his knowledge of the former is unquestionable and that for his knowledge of the latter strong, since the use of a minor mythological *exemplum* from Homer to apply to monasticism is so distinct, and since the parallels go beyond simply the quoted passage.[35] For some readers, the interaction with the Latin texts has seemed primary, and scholars have expressed doubts about whether Rutilius actually had direct knowledge of Homer, partly because there

---

32 *ex hoc evenit, ut in animi doloribus alii solitudines captent, ut ait Homerus de Bellerophonte:*
    Qui miser in campis maerens errabat Aleis
    Ipse suum cor edens, hominum uestigia uitans.
    (So it happens that some seek out deserted places when pained in spirit, as Homer says of Bellerophon: 'who in wretched grief would wander on the Alean plains, eating his own heart, avoiding human tracks.')

33 See, e.g., Fielding 2017, 30–31.

34 E.g., there is further engagement with the figure of Bellerophon at 10.157–159.

35 Rutilius could be seen as echoing some of the language of Paulinus' *Carm.* 10 (e.g. 133, 134, 150 *perversus*; 135 *stulta Dei sapiens*; 197 *humanis ... locis*). The reference to a madness in the brain (*rabies ... cerebri*), however, goes beyond Ausonius and Paulinus's equivalents (*mens vaga, mentis inops, mentis uitio* etc.).

are several differences from Homer.[36] Others will be discussed below, but most significantly, Homer does *not* attribute Bellerophon's troubles to an excess of black bile, i.e. melancholy (nor do Ausonius/ Paulinus).

This difference is in fact not such a strong argument for Rutilius being ignorant of Homer, since the idea that Bellerophon's 'eating up his heart' and isolating himself from humanity were to be associated with an excess of black bile has a long tradition.[37] The older *Scholia* (*Scholia vetera* **bT** ad *Il.* 6.202a) gloss the words ὃν θυμὸν κατέδων (eating out his heart) with the explanation that 'he did not, as the newer writers say, isolate himself suffering from black bile, but grieving at the loss of his sons'.[38] The much later commentary of Eustathius (which however embraces much earlier material) at the same line points to one representative of the 'newer writers' who hold this view, glossing the whole line: 'i.e. fleeing from association with people, because spinning into melancholy, as Aristotle too reports in his own *Problems*'.[39] And indeed in *Problems* 30, 953a, Aristotle talks about melancholy, with examples including Ajax and Bellerophon, quoting these lines for his discussion of the latter. This does not prove beyond all doubt that Rutilius' knowledge of Homer was direct, but the fact that he is clearly aware of aspects of the Greek exegetical tradition is very suggestive. The interpretation is not otherwise attested in Latin, and my inference would be that Rutilius almost certainly did read Homer in the original, and in a text with marginal scholia.

Rutilius' passage is violently hostile to monasticism, but its view of renunciation of the world as the result of mental illness was not culturally isolated. Christians like Ausonius could call excessive devotion to asceticism into question, particularly if it involved members of the upper classes. Ausonius in particular was writing in the aftermath of the execution of the extreme ascetic Priscillian of Avila and some of his aristocratic followers.[40] The idea of a link

---

36   For doubt as to knowledge of Homer at this point, see Duval 1968, 185; Doblhofer 1970, 6–12; 1972, 31–33, 49–51; see also Doblhofer 1983, 74–77. I incline rather to the view of Tissol 2002, 439–441 that Rutilius follows a practice well known in earlier Latin writers of alluding to Homer through an intermediate text: what I would call—adapting Thomas 1986—a 'window allusion' (see Kelly 2008, 209–211, and for further references Tissol 2002, 441n13). See also Fo 1992 on this passage and on 1.195–196.

37   A point first made in print, as far as I know, by Fielding 2017, 32–33.

38   οὐχ ὡς οἱ νεώτεροί φασι, μελαγχολάνας, ἀλλ' ὀδυνώμενος ἐπὶ τῇ τῶν παίδων ἀπωλείᾳ ἐμόναζεν.

39   ἤγουν ἐκφεύγων τὴν μετ' ἀνθρώπων συνδιατριβήν, οἷα εἰς μελαγχολίαν ἐκκυλισθείς, καθά καὶ Ἀριστοτέλης ἐν τοῖς οἰκείοις ἱστορεῖ Προβλήμασι.

40   Trout 1999, 67–77.

between withdrawal and melancholy was part of a wider discourse, and can be paralleled even in as unapologetic an ascetic as Jerome.[41]

3   Melania the Younger?

I now wish to make a conjecture. I have argued that Rutilius' poem sometimes expresses itself in a coded way, and I would like to suggest that, along with other aspects of the passage, the specific reference to the monks' disease as *melancholia* is meant to hint at the name of Melania the Younger, who, with her husband Pinianus, was perhaps the most famous sponsor of monasticism in this period.[42] Melania was lauded by contemporaries, including Paulinus of Nola and Palladius in the *Lausiac History*, but the most detailed account comes in the life attributed to Gerontius, written not too long after her death in 439 and soon translated into Latin. A scion of an immensely rich and noble Roman family and granddaughter of another famous aristocratic ascetic, she was married to Pinianus, from a similarly exalted background, when she was in her fourteenth and he in his seventeenth year. According to Gerontius, she longed for a life of chastity from the start (*Vita Melaniae* 1). At any rate, after she had had two children and both had died, at the age of 20, she and Pinianus decided to renounce the world and began to liquidate their vast holdings of land and slaves and to give away the proceeds. This involved fighting the opposition of many senators (there were threats of confiscating the property they cared so little for to pay off Alaric's Goths) and, according to Gerontius, of members of their family—though her father relented on her deathbed and her mother Albina later joined her in asceticism.[43] Their departure from Italy shortly before the Gothic sack of Rome in 410 was not an easy one. Melania, Pinianus, and Albina spent the rest of their lives founding monasteries around the Mediterranean on the proceeds of their sales, eventually settling in Palestine in 417. Melania was always controversial, and could be seen as either a woman of

---

41   Jerome Ep. 125.16: *sunt qui humore cellarum immoderatisque ieiuniis taedio solitudinis ac nimia lectione ... uertuntur in μελαγχολίαν et Hippocratis magis fomentis quam nostris monitis indigent.*

42   *PLRE* 1, s.v. Melania 2, Valerius Pinianus 2. The bibliography is extensive: see above all Clark 1984; Chin and Schroeder 2017 (on both Melaniae); and Brown 2012, 291–300, 322–325, 365–366. The standard edition of the life is Gorce 1962, and of the Latin version Laurence 2002; on the historicity of the life, see also Barnes 2010, 249–252.

43   See esp. Giardina 1988 and Brown 2012, 294–299, for how and why their senatorial peers were understandably alarmed.

male virtues and a figure of extraordinary generosity, or an unstable, anorexic, celebrity-hunting poor-little-rich-girl.

What should Capraria, where we hear only of male monks, have to do with Melania, a female monastic—and one who at the dramatic date of *De reditu suo* had just begun her residence in Palestine? At an early stage of her ascetic life, when she was still in Italy, her biographer lists Melania's and Pinianus' already worldwide benefactions (*Vita Graeca* 19):

Νήσους δὲ οὐκ ὀλίγας ὠνησάμενοι ἁγίοις ἀνδράσιν ἐδωρήσαντο· ὁμοίως δὲ καὶ ἀσκητήρια μοναχῶν τε καὶ ἀειπαρθένων ὠνησάμενοι τοῖς οἰκοῦσιν αὐτὰ ἐχαρί- σαντο, χρυσίον ἑκάστῳ τόπῳ τὸ ἱκανὸν παρέχοντες

Having bought not a few islands they gave them to holy men; likewise having bought monasteries of monks and eternal virgins they gifted them to those that lived there, providing each place with a sufficiency of gold.[44]

So Melania and Pinianus could well have bought and endowed a pre-existent monastery on Capraria. In that case, contemporary readers would have been prepared for a reference.

In arguing for a reference to Melania, one may start with the simple fact of her celebrity. Rutilius' reference to those who dread the gifts of fortune because they fear her losses (1.443) may imply a particular concern with those renouncing great wealth rather than humbler monastics; the losses of fortune then could refer to the death of her children, which, in Palladius' account, played a major role in Melania and Pinianus' withdrawal. But this possible relationship is made very much more forceful by the *exemplum* of Bellerophon, marked specifically as being from Homer. As noted above, there is good reason to think that Rutilius knew Homer directly, but the allusion has details that are either not in the *Iliad* or actually in conflict with it. The first is that, in Homer,

---

44   The equivalent passage of the Latin life is as follows (*Vita Latina* 19.3, 5): *quantas uero insulas ementes, monachis praestiterunt loca et regiones ... 5. coeperuntque et monasteriis praebere, et ipsa monasteria ementes donant monachis et uirginibus, et aliquibus certum pondus auri tribuentes*. The scholarly consensus is that the life was originally written in Greek, though as the current Greek version has undergone some redaction, the Latin version can offer valuable material. See Clark 1984, 4–13; Laurence 2002, 109–141; Laurence 2002, 301–315, has a useful table setting out parallels and divergences between the lives. *Vita Latina* 19.4 contains material which *Vita Graeca* places after 19.5 (note that no edition of the Greek life has yet been published with sentence divisions).

Bellerophon came to be hated by the gods and avoided men; subsequently his children were killed by the gods. In Rutilius (here, to be fair, he follows Homeric exegetical tradition), the process is reversed: it was *after* the arrows of a savage grief (*saeui post tela doloris*) that Bellerophon came to hate the human race. This fits well with the narrative of Melania and Pinianus' life in Palladius' *Lausiac History* (more on this below), where depression from the loss of their children drives Pinianus, at least, to retreat from the world. Secondly (a lesser point), Bellerophon is described as a youth, a *iuuenis*: without going into the exact parameters of being a *iuuenis*, it clearly seems a better fit for Pinianus and Melania, who gave up the world at the ages of 23 and 20, than for Bellerophon, the father of adult children.[45] Thirdly, and crucially, Homer has Bellerophon 'devouring his own heart', but Rutilius claims falsely that Homer refers to the disease of excessive black bile (though this interpretation of 'eating his own heart' might of course be found in the exegetical tradition). The specific reference to Homer invites the reader to translate *nigro felle* and *nimiae bilis* into Greek, and I suggest that the answer is Melan(chol)ia.

In support of the idea of a play on names, I have already shown that this is not the only such play in Rutilius' poem. Nor is it the only such play in fifth-century texts on the name of Melania. It is well known that her grandmother, St Melania the Elder, was also referred to punningly by St Jerome as a woman 'whose name of blackness (*nomen nigredinis*) bears witness to the shades of perfidy'.[46] An interesting parallel comes in a work of fifth-century martyr-fiction, the *Passio Eugeniae*.[47] Eugenia is the daughter of a governor of Alexandria who has left her family to become a Christian, disguised as a young man. As Eugenius, she cures the quartan fever of a matron of Alexandria called Melanthia, and unwittingly becomes the object of her lust and lavish gifts, both of which are rejected. When Melanthia starts making physical advances, Eugenia reproves her, with the words (11) *recte Melanthiae nomen habere cognosceris: nigredinis enim repleta perfidia nigra diceris* (rightly you

---

45 Note also that *iuuenis* is also used for the aristocratic hermit of Gorgo (1.519).

46 Jerome Ep. 133.3: *Evagrius scribit ad eam cuius nomen nigredinis testatur perfidiae tenebras.*

47 See now Lapidge 2017, 228–249, for an accessible translation, and for a summary Matthieu Pignot, Cult of Saints, E02490: http://csla.history.ox.ac.uk/record.php?recid=E02490. Citations adopt Lapidge's chapter numbering; he translates the version *BHL* 2667, thought to be the earlier recension, as edited by Mombritius 1910, 2.391–397 (a reprint of a late fifteenth-century edition), correcting the text as he goes (as I have done above). For the other version (*BHL* 2666), see *PL* 73.605–624. I am grateful to Kate Cooper for pointing me to this passage.

are known to have the name Melanthia: full of the treachery of blackness, you are called black). In another recension of the same passion, the similarity to Jerome is even greater: *recte nomen tuum nigredinis testatur perfidiam* (*PL* 75.612).[48] Melanthia is an *illustris femina* (13), she has infinite wealth (11), and the echo of Jerome's words makes it even more obvious that she is meant as a lightly disguised version of one of the Melaniae.[49] There are thus parallels for plays on Melania's name.

I have left until last one final piece of the argument. In the passage immediately preceding this digression, we have news that almost sends Rutilius back to Rome, that an admirable young man of noble family, already praised earlier in the poem (1.167–178), has just been appointed prefect of Rome (1.415–428). Rufius Volusianus is lauded in the two passages for his ancestry, his political participation, and for his impressive career. But he was also the brother of Melania's mother Albina. Although he had corresponded with Augustine on his objections to Christianity, he was baptized twenty years later on his death-bed following pressure from Melania (*Vita Melaniae* 54–55). The juxtaposition would be particularly apt between the devoted public servant Volusianus and his troublesome relatives.

If my proposal that Rutilius hints at the name of Melania is accepted, it has interesting corollaries regarding contemporary attitudes to—and perhaps also the basic facts of—her ascetic renunciation. Rutilius would be implying that Melania and Pinianus' renunciation of the world was the result of mental imbalance after the death of their children. This explains the chronological reversal of Homer's Bellerophon, and coheres with Palladius' account of her in the *Lausiac History*. It clashes, however, with the testimony of Gerontius' *Life*, as the comparison below shows:

---

48   Cf. also *PL* 73.615: *O Melanthia, nigredinis nomen, et tenebrosa Melanthia* (O Melanthia, name of blackness, shady Melanthia). The story continues with the rejected Melanthia accusing 'Eugenius' of rape; the trial goes before the governor, and Eugenia simultaneously proves that she could not have committed the crime and reveals herself as his runaway daughter.

49   This would argue for a slightly earlier date than 475–500, suggested by Lapidge 2017, 232: the dating is dependent on comparison to other *Passions*, themselves imprecisely dated.

RUTILIUS NAMATIANUS, MELANIA THE YOUNGER

Palladius *Lausiac History* 61.2–3	Gerontius, *Vita Melaniae Graeca* 1 (tr. Clark)
[After their two male children both die, she addresses Pinianus:]	[After marrying, but desiring to abandon worldly life, she pleads with Pinianus:]

'If you should choose to practice asceticism with me according to the rule of continence, I acknowledge you both as master and lord of my life. But if this seems oppressive to you because you are young, take all my possessions, and give freedom only to my body so that I may fulfil my desire for God, sharing in the virtue for God of my grandmother, whose name I bear. For if God wanted us to remain in this world and have enjoyment from it, he would not have taken my children in untimely manner.'[50]

'If, my lord, you consent to practice chastity along with me and live with me according to the law of continence, I contract with you as the lord and master of my life. If, however, this seems burdensome to you and if you do not have the strength to bear the burning passion of youth, just look: I place before you all my possessions; hereafter you are master of them and may use them as you wish, if only you will leave my body free so that I may present it spotless, with my soul, to Christ on that fearsome day. For it is in this way that I shall fulfil my desire for God.'

At first, however, he neither accepted her proposal nor did he, on the other hand, completely rule out her plan. Rather he replied to her in these words: 'If and when by the ordinance of God we have two children to inherit our possessions, then both of us together shall renounce the world.'[51]

| [In the end Pinianus is persuaded.] | [A daughter is born and consecrated as a virgin; later (5) her prematurely born son dies.] |

---

50 εἰ μὲν αἱρῆσαι συνασκηθῆναι κἀμοὶ κατὰ τὸν τῆς σωφροσύνης λόγον, καὶ δεσπότην σε οἶδα καὶ κύριον τῆς ἐμῆς ζωῆς· εἰ δὲ βαρύ σοι τοῦτο καταφαίνεται ὡς νεωτέρῳ, πάντα μου λάβων τὰ πράγματα μόνον ἐλευθέρωσόν μου τὸ σῶμά, ἵνα πληρώσω μου κατὰ Θεὸν ἐπιθυμίαν, κληρονόμος γενομένη τῆς μάμμης τοῦ ζήλου, ἧς καὶ τὸ ὄνομα ἔχω. 3. Εἰ γὰρ ἐβούλετο παιδοποιεῖν ἡμᾶς ὁ Θεός, οὐκ ἄν μου ἐλάμβανεν ἄωρα τὰ τεχθέντα.

51 εἰ μὲν βούλει, φησίν, κύριέ μου, ἀγνεύειν συν ἐμοὶ καὶ κατὰ τὸν τῆς σωφροσύνης συνοικισθῆναί μοι νόμον, καὶ κύριόν σε καὶ δεσπότην τῆς οἰκείας ζωῆς ἐπιγράφομαι· εἰ δὲ τοῦτό σοι ἐπαχθὲς καταφαίνεται, καὶ οὐκ ἰσχύεις ἐνέγκαι τὴν πύρωσιν τῆς νεότητος, ἰδοὺ πρόκεινταί σοι ἅπαντά μου τὰ ὑπάρχοντα ὧν ἐντεῦθεν ἤδη δεσπότης γενόμενος χρῆσαι καθὼς βούλει, μόνον τὸ σῶμά μου ἐλευθέρωσον, ἵνα τοῦτο σὺν τῇ ψυχῇ μου ἄσπιλον παραστήσω τῷ Χριστῷ κατὰ τὴν ἡμέραν

82   KELLY

Palladius was writing around 420, when Melania was still alive, whereas the biography was written not long after her death in 439. It has long been clear that at this point Gerontius has based his narrative on Palladius (indeed this is one of the clinching arguments for the life's original composition in Greek),[52] but has adapted it. The fact that has attracted most interest is that Palladius' Melania explicitly draws attention to the fact that her ascetic aspirations are modeled on those of her grandmother, Melania the Elder, whereas this is simply suppressed in the *Vita*: Gerontius nowhere names or explicitly refers to the elder Melania, probably because she was theologically *persona non grata*.[53] But there are other divergences. Palladius describes two male children, the *Vita* a girl and a stillborn boy. For Palladius, Melania's request to her husband comes after the death of her two children; for the *Vita* she was set on virginity from the start. Indeed, Melania's statement in Palladius that "if God had wanted us to remain in this world ... he would not have taken in untimely manner the children born to us" is twisted by Gerontius by being put into the mouth of Pinianus, who promises that once they 'have two children to inherit their property, they will retreat from their worldly existence. The overall effect of Gerontius' changes is to date Melania's wish to renounce the world to the very beginning of her marriage. This of course fits with the abundant circumstantial detail of Gerontius' hagiography, with stories including that of her being forced to visit the public baths by her parents and only pretending to bathe (2), and with its overall tenor, implying a heroic and victorious battle with her relatives. So although the *Vita*'s version of Melania and Pinianus' renunciation has probably gained more attention (understandably: after all Gerontius was a confidant of Melania in her later life and makes her the focus of his much longer narrative), the evidence of Rutilius, if accepted, supports Palladius' earlier account of how Melania and Pinianus came to renouce the world. Finally, the close comparison to the Greek sources suggests that we should probably see Rutilius as concerned above all with Pinianus' failure to behave as a Roman aristocrat should and his capitulation to the wishes of his wife: Bellerophon will therefore be a figure for Pinianus, and *melancholia* for the negative external influence of Melania.

ἐκείνην τὴν φοβεράν· οὕτω γὰρ πληροφορήσω τὴν κατὰ Θεόν μου ἐπιθυμίαν. Ὁ δὲ οὔτε ἐπένευ-σεν ἐξ ἀρχῆς τῇ προθέσει αὐτῆς, οὔτε πάλιν παντελῶς ἀπέστρεψεν αὐτὴν τὰ ῥήματα ἀπεκρίνατο· "Ὅταν, τοῦ Κυρίου κελεύσαντος, τοὺς διαδόχους τῶν ὑπαρχόντων ἡμῖν δύο παῖδας κτησόμεθα, τότε κοινῶς ἀμφότεροι τῷ κόσμῳ ἀποτασσόμεθα.

52   For details see Clark 1984, 9–10

53   On this *damnatio memoriae* see Clark 1984, 148–151.

4   Conclusions

The diary-style format of *De reditu suo*, with first-person narration predominantly in the present tense, combines with the strongly expressed emotions and swings of mood to give a sense of a highly personal poem; this character is reinforced by the associations of the elegiac metre. And yet the personal is inextricably connected to the political. The friends that the poet encounters are virtually all members of the aristocracy of service and men of high rank, and are commended precisely for their service, rank, and inherited qualities.[54] The places he encounters remind him of political events, and across the poem he gradually creates a picture, composed of fragments of memory and opinion, of contemporary political circumstances: the poem becomes a meditation on the Gothic sack of Rome, its causes and consequences, and the other connected problems of contemporary politics.[55]

I have argued for a hitherto unnoticed covert reference in Rutilius' poem: in attacking the monks of Capraria he alludes to the most notorious example of withdrawal from the world of the last decade or so, by Melania and Pinianus. If this is accepted, Rutilius' reaction becomes less an outburst against a social phenomenon that he dislikes in general terms and more in tune with the rest of the poem: the passage calls to mind aristocrats who do not live up to their obligations to the state and the expectation of begetting heirs. Given the disputes that raged over the disposal of Melania and Pinianus' property when Alaric was threatening the city in 408–410 and funds were badly needed by the Senate, the passage becomes more closely tied to the series of reflections on the Gothic crisis.

This evocation of Melania and Pinianus also strongly supports Alan Cameron's view that this and Rutilius' other invective against monasticism 'would not have struck most lay Christian contemporaries as offensive'.[56] After all, we know what problems their Christian family and peers in the Senate had

---

54   An interesting reverse confirmation: when Rutilius is supplied with a magistrate's *carpentum* and horses to enter Pisa by a tribune who had reported to him as Master of the Offices, the man's name is left out, presumably as not senior enough (1.561–562).

55   Among the images that build this picture: the need to rebuild Gaul (1.19–30); the problems of land travel in Italy caused by the Goths (1.37–42); of the slow healing of Rome's scars after her misfortunes, with evocations of Pyrrhus and Hannibal (1.115–140); oblique reference to the defeat of the Goths in 416 (1.141–142); how the island of Giglio harbored refugees from Rome during the Gothic siege (1.331–336); Victorinus' status as a refugee from the capture of Toulouse (1.493–510); the crimes of Stilicho (2.41–60), where the sack of Rome is at last directly addressed. Finally, fragment B lauds the current holder of Stilicho's old office, Constantius, for restoring Roman pride.

56   Alan Cameron 2011, 218.

with the couple's renunciation. He acknowledges, however, that Rutilius perhaps felt greater indignation at monasticism than his Christian contemporaries (and indeed the language of Rutilius is far more rebarbative than, say, that of Ausonius a generation earlier). Cameron rightly bases his argument on a reading of all four invective passages (adding those against Jews and against Stilicho). One could object, of course, that pagan contemporaries might have read these passages rather differently. Some individual phrases might seem to attack Christianity more broadly, but in a way that would always be deniable.[57] *The Last Pagans of Rome* has shown how difficult it is to identify pagan aristocrats after the prohibition of the traditional cults in 391/2: they fade out of view as their religion was driven from the public sphere. Obvious clues like priesthoods on career inscriptions are no longer available. Rutilius Namatianus is one of the last to be visible, and is only so because we happen to have a personal poem, and even in that, it is striking how much a distinctive pagan aristocratic viewpoint shares with Christian aristocratic viewpoints.

Acknowledgements

It is an honor to offer this essay in affectionate memory of Alan Cameron. The names of all those who have heard versions of this piece and have made useful comments elude me, but I would like to acknowledge help of various sorts from Cornelia van der Poll, Kate Cooper, Fabio Guidetti, Michael Hendry, Calum Maciver, and Adriano Russo, as well as from this volume's editors.

---

57   Above all, 1.525 *num, rogo, deterior Circaeis secta uenenis* and perhaps also 1.389 *radix stultitiae.*

CHAPTER 6

Late Antique Homeric Exegesis in the *Greek Anthology*

Arianna Gullo

One of the essential and, at the same time, conspicuous aspects of Greek literary culture in Late Antiquity is certainly Hellenism, that linguistic and cultural background (*paideia*)[1] inherited from the ancient models[2]—first of all Homer,[3] boundless source for late antique and, later, Byzantine rhetoric. Christianity, then, crucially contributed to merging Greek and Latin culture. Therefore, the classical Greek world, which we usually consider a homogeneous entity, does not exclude Late Antiquity: in fact, the former embraces the latter, as its last, notable artistic expression. The same phenomenon can be observed in the Roman world. In this way, there is no break or interruption, but evolution and continuity within the classical literatures *par excellence*.

Research starting from these methodological assumptions is particularly productive for Greek poetry in Late Antiquity. It is not hard to identify in it the signs of a learned and intellectual diction derived from the previous tradition. Earlier erudite Greek poetry was certainly aware of specific exegetical and stylistic procedures employed for studying and interpreting Homer: these techniques can be already recognized in the Hellenistic age, and in fact turned out to be the *raison d'être* of Alexandrian poetry. However, since the focus of modern scholarship on the topic has been on the Hellenistic age alone,[4] in this chapter I aim to investigate Homeric exegesis in Late Antiquity, in a literary genre showing centuries-long development—epigram. My study will be limited to literary epigram,[5] a subgenre showing development over several centuries, and I will present examples from Gregory of Nazianzus, Christodorus of Coptos, and Agathias Scholasticus, thus spanning a chronological range from the fourth to the sixth century CE. All the cases here presented come from

---

1 See, e.g., Brown 1992, 35–70.
2 Agosti 2006–2007, 2008, 2009, 2010a, 2010b, 2011a, 2013, 2015a, 2016a, 2016b; see also Waltz 1931, particularly 10–12 and 14–15; Averil Cameron 2006, 14–15; Alan Cameron 2007b.
3 See most recently Agosti 2004, 2011b.
4 See, e.g., Rengakos 1992, 1993, 1994, 2007. See also Hunter 2005; Trajber 2017.
5 For the presence of Homer in late antique epigraphic epigram, see most recently Agosti 2017.

© THE TRUSTEES OF COLUMBIA UNIVERSITY IN THE CITY OF NEW YORK,
2021 | DOI:10.1163/9789004452794_007

the so-called *Greek Anthology*, a huge collection of poems which is our main source for Greek epigram.

The contribution of the preceding Greek epigrammatic tradition to the genre in Late Antiquity is remarkable, and a particular aspect of this contribution is crucial: the complex and extremely varied relationship between Homer and epigram.[6] In general, one may observe this relationship in the fictitious funerary epigrams dedicated to Homer himself,[7] as well as in those poems in which, as if in a "miniature" *epos*, Homeric heroes star. The diversity of Greek epigrams on Homer ranges, through the ages, from poems on the tombs of the Homeric heroes and ekphrastic epigrams on the artistic representations of Achilles, Patroclus, Ajax, Hector, Menelaus, and so on, to poems narrating single epic episodes in the turn of a few elegiac distichs, to epigrams on the speeches uttered by the protagonists of the *Iliad* and the *Odyssey* and reworked in concise and witty lines, to poems containing more or less literal Homeric quotations.[8] Beyond this readily evident and macro-level imitation of Homer, one may observe a formal and linguistic imitation standing on the line between the art of poetry and the broad area of ancient exegesis. Specifically, late antique Greek poetry continued the debate on Homeric language, which had been vital since the archaic age. This debate basically consisted in recovering Homeric words that were (and are) particularly interesting from a lexical point of view, as well as rare terms (the so-called *hapax* and *dis legomena*) and/ or difficult ones, better known as *glossai*, interpreted in the light of the scholiographic tradition. In some cases, nonetheless, this reflection was not limited to the banal and passive reuse of these Homerisms, which were often exhumed merely to show off erudition.

Attempts to explain the controversial or uncertain meaning of a Homeric *glossa* or *hapax* might also be embedded in the lines themselves; in such cases, these poets employed the *glossa* or *hapax* (especially an adjective) together with another word, whose meaning was clearer. By putting the two terms next to each other, in a synonymic pair, they reproduced, poem by poem, the individual interpretations debated by the Alexandrian philologists. Alternatively, they might take their own personal stand without directly using the Homeric rarity. In these cases, instead of the Homeric word, they used *one* of the lexical alternatives offered by the scholiographic tradition to explain the ambiguous meaning of that word itself. Moreover, if a poet wished to imitate or quote a

---

6 The study by Skiadas 1965 is fundamental. See also Gutzwiller 2017; Harder 2007, 2017; Sistakou 2011; Tsagalis 2008, 262–268; 2017; and, in general, Durbec and Trajber 2017.

7 See, e.g., Bolmarcich 2002.

8 See, in general, Pralon 2017.

Homeric passage that may display textual differences, the Homeric *interpretatio* could result in a conscious choice between two or more versions (readings or variants) of the Homeric text. The Homeric reading or variant preferred by the late antique poet was then embedded in the texture of the verse.

Actually, Hellenistic epigram, differently than epigram in earlier and later epochs, tended to develop and exploit subtler allusions to Homer, especially from a linguistic point of view: it dynamically took part in the philological activity of its time. There is thus a key element to appreciate that distinguishes the exegetical practice on Homer in Hellenistic poetry and epigram from that of late antique poetry and epigram. The former, firmly rooted in the Alexandrian culture, made the study of Homeric epic a field of philological knowledge set apart, a subject on its own, that dealt with problems of text editing, language, and style. In contrast, late antique erudition aimed to suggest a continuous comparison with its former models. For this reason, the most common method of Homeric *interpretatio* in Late Antiquity was allegory, even though this aspect does not characterize epigram.

Another aspect to take into account is the massive influence of Nonnus of Panopolis on late antique poetry, including epigram. By imitating and outdoing Homer, Nonnus became the predominant model for late antique poetry of the fifth to sixth centuries CE from a linguistic, stylistic, and metrical point of view.[9] Nonnus' poetry is learned in every aspect: rare myths and the most uncommon geographical terms are preferred, as well as neologisms—especially adjectives. Behind a (seemingly) neutral lexical choice, he admirably hides his own stance about *vexatae questiones* of Homeric exegesis. Therefore, for each epigrammatic case selected, I was first compelled to check whether the Homeric rarity was used by Nonnus too. If not, the case was evidently not problematic; if so, instead, I had to verify, on a case-by-case basis, whether the exegetical solution proposed by the epigrammatist derived from a direct reading of the Homeric text in the light of the scholiographic tradition, or was rather filtered through the Nonnian use of the word examined. I excluded those cases that can be explained by Nonnian influence. In the following sections I will show examples, grouped by exegetical typology, of uses of various Homerisms in late antique literary epigrams.[10]

---

9 On the definition of the so-called *stile moderno* (modern style), that is, the metrical and language style codified in late antique literary poetry, which finds its supreme manifestation in Nonnus of Panopolis (hence it is called "Nonnian," though it was not properly elaborated and developed by him), see, e.g., Whitby 1994; Agosti and Gonnelli 1995. The label of "Nonnian" poets applied in particular to the *Cycle* epigrammatists, including Agathias, should now be put into perspective: see Gullo, forthcoming a.

10 The texts of the Greek epigrams are those of Beckby 1967–1968. All translations are mine.

88   GULLO

1   **Homeric *Hapax Legomena* and Late Antique Epigrammatic
       Cleverness**

This section discusses two epigrams in which a Homerism is used in its most
uncommon meaning. In these cases the poet deviates from his contemporaries
and former fellow epigrammatists by recovering the Homeric word as a rarity.
The first example comes from an epigram ascribed to Agathias Scholasticus
(*AP* 9.204 = 33 Viansino) on the stone thrown by Ajax at Hector (H 206–272);
according to the tradition, the rock was preserved as a tool to show one's
own strength:

> Μή με τὸν Αἰάντειον ἀνοχμάσσειας, ὁδῖτα,
>   πέτρον ἀκοντιστὴν στήθεος Ἑκτορέου.
> εἰμὶ μέλας τρηχύς τε· σὺ δ' εἴρεο θεῖον Ὅμηρον,
>   πῶς τὸν Πριαμίδην ἐξεκύλισα πέδῳ.
> νῦν δὲ μόλις βαιόν με παροχλίζουσιν ἀρούρης   5
>   ἄνθρωποι, γενεῆς αἴσχεα λευγαλέης.
> ἀλλά μέ τις κρύψειεν ὑπὸ χθονός· αἰδέομαι γὰρ
>   παίγνιον οὐτιδανοῖς ἀνδράσι γινόμενος.[11]

In composing his poem, Agathias takes inspiration from H 268: Ajax is here
depicted as a champion with extraordinary strength.[12] Through the solemn
speech uttered by the rock, which first talks about itself and then about its era,
concluding with a negative evaluation of contemporary mankind, Agathias
proposes his own model of heroism, now lost, because men are not strong any-
more, but weak and feeble.

Let us consider the adjective λευγαλέης (l. 5), which occurs fourteen times
in Homer; according to the scholiographic tradition, it is employed in turn in
the following meanings:[13]

---

11   "Wayfarer, do not hoist me, the stone / of Ajax, darter of Hector's breast. / I am black and
        rough; yet ask divine Homer / how I made the son of Priam rolling on the ground. / Now
        men, shame of a weak generation, / hardly manage to move me a little from the ground. /
        But let someone hide me in the dust; I am ashamed to / have become the toy of worth-
        less men."

12   The poem contains references to other Homeric passages as well: l. 3 μέλας τρηχύς τε ~
        H 265 = Φ 404 μέλανα τρηχύν τε (the rock thrown by Hector at Ajax before the latter hits
        him by an even bigger stone); l. 4 με παροχλίζουσιν ἀρούρης ~ M 448 ἀπ' οὔδεος ὀχλίσσειαν
        (*sc.* λᾶαν); ll. 5–6 ~ M 447–449 τὸν δ' οὔ κε δύ' ἀνέρε δήμου ἀρίστω / ῥηϊδίως ἐπ' ἄμαξαν ἀπ'
        οὔδεος ὀχλίσσειαν, / οἷοι νῦν βροτοί εἰσ'· ὁ δέ μιν ῥέα πάλλε καὶ οἶος.

13   See *ThGl* s.v.: (a) "perniciosus," "difficilis," "gravis" (I 119; N 97; Ξ 387; Υ 109; Φ 281; ε 312;
        ο 359); (b) "miser," "aerumnosus," "calamitosus" (ο 399; π 273; ρ 202; ρ 337; υ 203; ω 157); (c)

LATE ANTIQUE HOMERIC EXEGESIS IN THE GREEK ANTHOLOGY   89

(1)   ὀλέθριος, χαλεπός ("baneful," "mournful"): I 119; N 97; Ξ 387; Υ 109; ο 399;
      υ 203;
(2)   ἄδοξος ("inglorious," "ignoble"): Φ 281 = ε 312; ο 359; π 273 = ρ 202 = ω 157 ~
      ρ 337;
(3)   ἀσθενής ("weak"): β 61.

Agathias avoids the predominant meanings of λευγαλέος attested in the *scholia*
(ὀλέθριος, χαλεπός, and ἄδοξος),[14] and prefers the marginal sense of "physically
weak" (ἀσθενής),[15] recorded only in Aristonicus' Σ on β 61a1,[16] and in the Σ ex.
on β 61a1 and V on β 61c:

> Homer β 60–61
> ἡμεῖς δ' οὔ νύ τι τοῖοι ἀμυνέμεν· ἢ καὶ ἔπειτα
> λευγαλέοι τ' ἐσόμεσθα καὶ οὐ δεδαηκότες ἀλκήν.[17]

> Σ β 61 Pontani

> Ariston.
> a1. λευγαλέοι τ' ἐσόμεσθα· ἀντὶ τοῦ λοιγαλέοι, παρὰ τόν λοιγὸν ἀντὶ τοῦ ἀσθε-
> νεῖς. HMᵃTx ex.
> a1. λευγαλέοι τ' ἐσόμεσθα· [...] ἀσθενεῖς φανησόμεθα [...] HMᵃT V
> c. λευγαλέοι· ἀσθενεῖς BE²GHMᵃPVY ἀδύνατοι. HMᵃVY
>   See Σ bt Υ 109 Erbse; Σ ε 312 Pontani

The adjective λευγαλέος occurs more than once in Homer, but it is only attested
in β 61 with the meaning ἀσθενής ("weak"): in this respect, it is a *hapax*. Agathias

---

"invalidus" (β 61). *LfgrE* s.v. does not record the meaning "weak" for β 61, but "miserable"
(kümmerlich). The other meanings supplied for the remainder of the occurrences are
"fatal" (I 119); "leidbringend" (N 97; Ξ 387; ο 399; υ 203); "aggressiv" (Υ109); "schlimm" (Φ 281;
ε 312); "erbarmungswürdig" (ο 359); "schäbig" (π 273 = ρ 202 = ρ 337 = ω 157). It is interesting
to observe that λευγαλέος and λυγρός are connected, because they share the same I.-E.
root *lougos (lat. *lugeo*): in N 237 συμφερτὴ δ' ἀρετὴ πέλει ἀνδρῶν καὶ μάλα λυγρῶν ("courage comes from fellowship even of very weak men"), λυγρός means "weak," like in σ 107.

14   These are also the meanings recorded s.v. in *Suid.* λ 312 and *EM* 561,30.
15   Modern translators of Agathias' epigram understand λευγαλής as "miserable," "pitiful."
16   Actually, the Σ bT on Υ 109 (λευγαλέοις ἐπέεσσιν ἀποτρεπέτω καὶ ἀρειῇ) explains the adjec-
     tive λευγαλέοις with εὐτελέσι καὶ ἀχρείοις; however, the most appropriate meaning here is
     χαλεποῖς.
17   "We are not capable to keep it off at present; for sure we shall / then be found weakling
     and knowing nothing of strength." None of the modern translators interprets λευγαλέοι
     with "weak," but always with "unhappy," "wretched."

90 GULLO

himself seems to be willing to explain his own text and provide us with the interpretive solution by using at l. 8 the adjective οὐτιδανός, which is often glossed with ἀσθενής in ancient *scholia* and *lexica*.[18] In addition, let us consider a passage from Juvenal's *Satires*:[19] Here the degeneration of mankind, which began with the age of Homer, is stated:

> nam genus hoc vivo iam decrescebat Homero;
> terra malos homines nunc educat atque pusillos.[20]

Juvenal's passage is recorded in the *TLL*[21] among those in which the adjective *pusillus* is used for living beings *qui sunt infirmi*, that is, "weak" indeed.

In Agathias' time, Homer's works were not merely texts read in school. They had truly become, in every aspect, the reference texts of classical *paideia*. Agathias shows a particular inclination to use a rare gloss. Let us consider another case of recovering a Homeric rarity in the work of this epigrammatist: in Homer Z 133–135 Diomedes asks Glaucus to reveal his identity, because he does not want to fight against the gods. For Lycurgus was punished by the gods for having chased Dionysus and his nurses:

> [...] αἳ δ' ἅμα πᾶσαι
> θύσθλα χαμαὶ κατέχευαν, ὑπ' ἀνδροφόνοιο Λυκούργου
> θεινόμεναι βουπλῆγι.[22]

The meaning of the problematic Homeric *hapax* βουπλήξ (l. 135) is still debated. The ancient scholiasts gave different interpretations of the word:[23] it

---

18 Σ D A 231/Z^S van Thiel οὐτιδανοῖσιν· οὐδενὸς λόγου ἀξίων (~I^S), ἀσθενῶν. ZYQA^ti; Σ on Nicander *Th.* 385d οὐτιδανήν· μικρὰν K² ἐλάττονα bm ἀσθενή. f; Σ on Oppian *C.* 1.438 οὐτιδανοί· ἀσθενεῖς; Σ on Oppian *H.* 1.767 οὐτιδανής· ἀσθενοῦς, μικρᾶς; Σ on Oppian *H.* 2.144 οὐτιδανός· ἀσθενής, μικρός, εὐτελής, ὀλίγος; Hesychius o 97 Latte οὐτιδανός· οὐδαμινὸς v ἀσθενής p ἄψυχος, οὐδενὸς ἄξιος gn οὐδὲ λόγου; *EGud.* o p. 442,52 Sturz οὐτιδανοῖσιν, ἀσθενέσιν, οὐδενὸς λόγου ἀξίοις (see schol.-epim. A 231, b Dyck); Zonaras o p. 1479,30 Tittmann οὐτιδανός. ὁ ἀσθενὴς ἢ ὁ οὐδενὸς λόγου ἄξιος.

19 15.69–70.

20 "For the human race was already in decline when Homer lived; / now the earth produces men who are sinful but worthless."

21 See *TLL* x,2 (fasc. xvii) 2738,9–11; 25–27.

22 "[...] All of them together / threw down their wands on the ground, stricken / with an ox-goad by murderous Lycurgus." The lines are quoted in Heraclitus, *Quaest. Hom.* 35.2.

23 Σ T Z 135b D (~) Erbse βουπλῆγι· μάστιγι ἢ πελέκει. T (πελέκει: see Porphyry on Z 129 Schrader; Σ on Oppian *H.* 3.557; 4.481; 5.152; EM 371,41); Σ D Z 135/Z^S van Thiel βουπλῆγι· μάστιγι ἐκ βοείου δέρματος γινομένη πρὸς τὸ πλήσσειν, ἢ πέλεκι ᾧ τὰς βοῦς κτείνουσι. Z ~ T; ↑ Σ D Z 135/Y^S van Thiel βουπλῆγι· τῷ πελέκει, ὅτι ἐν αὐτῷ τυπτόμενοι οἱ βόες ἀναιροῦνται. οἱ

LATE ANTIQUE HOMERIC EXEGESIS IN THE GREEK ANTHOLOGY

may indicate an ox-goad (basically a spur), an ax, or a sort of whip. The *LfgrE* s.v. explains the term as "ax" or "goad," but tends to assign to it the latter meaning, which is probably correct in the Homeric context.[24] What about the late antique poets? Neil Hopkinson correctly believes that Nonnus might understand the noun βουπλήξ as a synonym of πέλεκυς ("ax").[25] Quintus of Smyrna and Paul the Silentiary interpret βουπλήξ as "ax" as well,[26] and this was the most common meaning even in earlier authors.[27] I did not find certain attestations of βουπλήξ = βούκεντρον ("ox- goad") or μάστιξ ("whip"): beyond those cited so far, the remainder of the strictly literary passages in which βουπλήξ occurs, do not allow us to state whether it should be understood as a synonym of βούκεντρον, μάστιξ, or πέλεκυς.[28] 31 If, in an epigram by Agathias (*AP* 6.41 = 65 Viansino) the Homerism is recovered in one of its two most unusual meanings, and particularly in that used in its first attestation by Homer himself ("goad"), that would be truly remarkable. In that case, Agathias would deviate from his contemporaries and his models (notably Nonnus), who interpret βουπλήξ as "ax." However, Agathias does not directly use the word itself. The epigram records the farmer Callimenes' dedication of agricultural tools to Demeter. The first three lines of the poem contain a list of the offerings:

δὲ μάστιγι ἐπεὶ ἐκ βύρσης γίνεται. YQI(T)G* (πέλεκυς - μάστιγι: see Apollonius the Sophist p. 52,7 Bekker; Hesychius β 953 Latte); Eustathius *in Il.* p. 629,51 βουπλήξ δὲ βούκεντρον ἢ πέλεκυς βοὸς ἀναιρετικὸς ἢ μάστιξ γιγνομένη ἀπὸ τμήματος βύρσης (for βουπλήξ δέ - βύρσης: see *synag.* β 80 Cunningham; Photius β 238 Theodoridis; for βουπλήξ - βούκεντρον: see Pausanias the Grammarian β 15 Erbse; *Lex. art. gramm.* p. 430,12 Bachmann; *Suid.* β 455 Adler; Zonaras β p. 398,11 Tittmann).

24 Most of Homer's modern commentators and translators understand the word as "goad."

25 Hopkinson 1994, 14–15. The word occurs twenty-three times in Nonnus: see Peek 1968–1975, 3: s.v.

26 For Quintus of Smyrna: seven occurrences in the *Posthomerica*. For Paul the Silentiary: *S. Soph.* 522.

27 So Timo *SH* 778.1; Leonidas of Alexandria *AP* 9.352.3 = *FGE* XXIX 1972; Pseudo-Lucian *Philopatr.* 4; Oppian *H.* (four occurrences: see Eutecnius the Sophist *Par. in Opp. H.* 5.5; 5.8 Papathomopoulos); *EM* 37,41.

28 See Teucer *FGrHist* 274 F 1a; Oppian *C.* 1.154 (likely "ax": see Eutecnius the Sophist *Par. in Opp. H.* p. 11,17 Tüselmann); Anonymous *Hymn. GDRK* 56.11; Theodore Prodromus *Rhod. et Dos.* 7.261; John Cinnamus *Ethop.* 48; Eustathius Macrembolites *Hysm. et Hysm.* 4.13.12 (likely "ax"); Nicephorus Basilaces *Progymn.* 47; Nicetas Choniates *Hist.* p. 383,22 van Dieten (likely "whip"); *Or.* p. 72,30 van Dieten. The word is attested several times in grammar handbooks (7x in Herodian; 1x in Arcadius; 17x in Theodosius; 21x in Choeroboscus; 2x in Gennadius Scholarius): in these sources βουπλήξ occurs in long lists of words without any further specification; same in Eustathius *in Il.* p. 629,56 and *in D.P.* p. 558,12; Σ *in Aesch.* (2x); Σ *in Lyc.* (1x); *EGud.* (2x).

Χαλκὸν ἀροτρητὴν κλασιβώλακα νειοτομῆα
  καὶ τὴν ταυροδέτιν βύρσαν ἐπαυχενίην
καὶ βούπληκτρον ἄκαιναν ἐχετλήεντά τε γόμφον
  Δηοῖ Καλλιμένης ἄνθετο γειοπόνος,
τμήξας εὐαρότου ῥάχιν ὀργάδος· εἰ δ' ἐπινεύσεις   5
  τὸν στάχυν ἀμῆσαι, καὶ δρεπάνην κομίσω.[29]

The phrasing βούπληκτρος ἄκαινα (l. 3) is not attested elsewhere. The two-ending adjective βούπληκτρος, -ον only occurs in this epigram by Agathias, so the word is a true *hapax*. In fact, it may be a formation by Agathias himself on the basis of βουπλήξ. The noun ἄκαινα, instead, is first attested in the third century BCE, in Callimachus and Apollonius Rhodius. With regard to this, the *scholion* on Apollonius' *Arg.* 3.1323b Wendel, which also contains a quotation from Callimachus, is truly interesting:

> ἀκαίνη· ἀντὶ τοῦ κέντρῳ. ἄκαινα δέ ἐστι μέτρον δεκάπουν, Θεσσαλῶν εὕρημα, ἢ ῥάβδος ποιμενικὴ παρὰ Πελασγοῖς ηὑρεμένη· περὶ ἧς Καλλίμαχός φησιν [*Aet.* 1 fr. 24.7 Pf. = 26 Massimilla = 24 Harder]· "ἀμφότερον, κέντρον τε βοῶν καὶ μέτρον ἀρούρης." L^g P[30]

The *scholion* explains that Apollonius uses the word ἄκαινα in a sense to mean "goad" (κέντρον). It also states that, beyond the ox-goad, ἄκαινα may also designate a land measurement. This semantic dualism is confirmed by Callimachus.

As already pointed out, Agathias does not employ directly βουπλήξ, but uses the word ἄκαινα, which should gloss and explain the former in a sense to mean "goad." However, as we have already seen, ἄκαινα can mean both "ox-goad" and "ten-foot measurement." Therefore, in order to make his choice even more precise, Agathias ingeniously combines ἄκαινα with βούπληκτρος ("which pushes the oxen"), an adjective formed after βουπλήξ, which allows the poet to dispel any doubts about his stance. This is a truly Hellenistic learned pun embedded in an epigram: there is a gloss explaining another gloss. Agathias not only

---

29 "The bronze of the plough breaking clods and breaking / up a fallow, the hide binding the bull under the neck, / the ox-goading spike, and the bolt of the plough-handle / the farmer Callimenes dedicated to Demeter, / after cutting the back of his well-ploughed field. If you / grant me to reap the corn, I will bring you a sickle too."

30 "With an *akaina*: instead of 'with a goad. *Akaina* is a measure of ten feet, a Thessalian invention, or the crook of the shepherds discovered by the Pelasgians; in regard to this Callimachus says: 'both of them, ox-goad and land measurement.'" See Hesychius α 2231 Latte; *EGen.* α 286 Livadaras ἀκαίνη δέ ἐστι Θεσσαλικὴ ῥάβδος τὸ καλούμενον βούκεντρον; *ESym.* α 49/53 Lasserre; Photius α 702 Theodoridis; *EM* 43,48; *synag.* α 216 Cunningham.

LATE ANTIQUE HOMERIC EXEGESIS IN THE GREEK ANTHOLOGY 93

indirectly recovers a Homeric rarity (βουπλήξ), voluntarily deviating from the common use of the word found in his contemporaries, he also uses a *terminus technicus* (ἄκαινα), which can have various meanings, in a particular sense in order to explain the Homeric *hapax*.

2   'Glossing Homer'

This section discusses two cases in which the late antique epigrammatists challenge themselves to explain a Homeric rarity.[31] In so doing, they take their own view and at the same time, take part in the ancient scholarly debate by either adopting one of the interpretations already recorded in the scholiographic tradition or proposing a new, original one. The first example concerns the meaning of the adjective ὁμοίϊος in an epigram by Gregory of Nazianzus, while the second one comes from Christodorus' ekphrastic poem on the baths of Zeuxippus in Constantinople and deals with an use of the word αὐλός as an equivalent for "neck."

Let us start with the case taken from Gregory's epigram. Consider first Homer Δ 315–316, where Agamemnon addresses Nestor:

> ἀλλά σε γῆρας τείρει ὁμοίϊον· ὡς ὄφελέν τις
> ἀνδρῶν ἄλλος ἔχειν, σύ δὲ κουροτέροισι μετεῖναι.[32]

The *iunctura* γῆρας ὁμοίϊον is also attested in *h.Ven.* 244, where Aphrodite addresses Anchises:

> νῦν δέ σε μὲν κατὰ γῆρας ὁμοίϊον ἀμφικαλύψει
> νηλειές.[33]

Let us examine the adjective ὁμοίϊος, which I translated differently on purpose in the two passages under examination, respectively from the *Iliad* and the *Homeric Hymn* to Aphrodite. It is important to recall the ancient meanings applied to the word according to the scholiographic tradition. Homer's ancient commentators debated the precise meaning to assign to ὁμοίϊος. From Aristonicus' *scholion* on Δ 315a we know that glossographers understood ὁμοίϊος

---

31   I owe the title of this section to Sistakou 2007.

32   "Yet wretched old age weakens you; if only some other / man had your age, and you were one of the young men!"

33   "Now wretched, pitiless old age shall throw its mantle over / you."

94 GULLO

as κακός ("bad," "cruel").[34] The same interpretation is supplied by the exegetical *scholion* on γ 236.[35] On the other hand, according to Σ T on Δ 315b,[36] as well as V on γ 236c1[37] and c2,[38] ὁμοίϊος means "common" (= ὁμοῖος). The same idea is found in Apollonius the Sophist:[39]

ὁμοίίου πτολέμοιο· οἱ μὲν γλωσσογράφοι τοῦ κακοῦ· ἀπίθανον δὲ τοῦτο. Ὅμηρος γὰρ πᾶσι τὸ ὁμοίως συμβαῖνον ὁμοίιον λέγει· ὡς καὶ τὸ γῆρας καὶ τὸν θάνατον, οὕτως οὖν καὶ τὸν πόλεμον, ὅτε μὲν γὰρ τὸ γῆρας, "ἀλλά σε γῆρας τείρει ὁμοίϊον·" ἐπὶ δὲ τοῦ θανάτου, ἐπεὶ κατὰ πλεῖον περὶ πάντας ἐστίν.[40]

Apollonius' criticism mirrors the tradition of Aristarchus. Going against the glossographers' interpretation, based upon one context only,[41] Aristarchus seemingly understood ὁμοίϊος as "what happens in the same way to everyone," that is, "common." In Σ D on Δ 315[42] we read an attempt at an etymology for

---

34   Σ A Δ 315a Ariston. Erbse ⟨ὁμοίϊον·⟩ ὅτι οἱ γλωσσογράφοι ὁμοίϊον τὸ κακόν. A^im

35   Σ ex. γ 236d Pontani ὁμοίϊον] [...] ὃ δέ ἐστι πᾶσιν ἐξ ἴσου κακόν, ἐκεῖνο καὶ 'ὁμοίϊον' ῥηθήσεται, ἤτοι κοινὸν κακόν. B (see glossogr. fr. 24 Dyck; Eustathius *in Il.* 476,46 Ἀπίων γοῦν καὶ Ἡρόδωρός φασιν ὅτι οἱ γλωσσογράφοι 'ὁμοίϊον' κατὰ διαίρεσίν φασι τὸ κακόν).

36   Σ T Δ 315b ex. | D | sch. (?) Erbse γῆρας ⟨-⟩ ὁμοίϊον· τὸ ὁμοίως πᾶσι χαλεπὸν | καὶ κοινῇ ἐπερχόμενον. T

37   Σ V γ 236c1 Pontani ὁμοίϊον· τὸν ὁμοίως ἐπὶ πάντας κατὰ φύσιν ἐρχόμενον. HM^aTVy

38   Σ V γ 236c2 Pontani θάνατον μὲν ὁμοίϊον] κοινόν, EGHPs φυσικόν, Es τὸν ὁμοίως πᾶσι ἐπερχόμενον. BEs (see Σ D O 670 van Thiel).

39   P. 120,29 Bekker.

40   "War *homoiios*: glossographers understand 'evil' which is unlikely. For Homer calls *homoiios* what happens equally to everyone; like old age and death, so then war (is *homoiios*) too. When talking about old age, he says indeed 'yet old age, common to all, weakens you'; as for death, (it is *homoiios*) since it concerns all in general."

41   According to Dyck 1987, 153 the glossographers depend on a comparison of various passages for this interpretation.

42   ὁμοίϊον· τὸ ὁμοίως πᾶσι χαλεπόν. ZYQXIT | ἰστέον δὲ ὅτι ὁ ποιητὴς πανταχοῦ τὸ ὁμοίϊον ἐπὶ τοῦ φαύλου λαμβάνει, οἷον ὡς ἐνταῦθα "ἀλλά σε γῆρας τείρει ὁμοίϊον" καὶ "ἀλλ' ἤτοι θάνατον μὲν ὁμοίϊον οὐδὲ θεοί περ καὶ φίλῳ ἀνδρὶ δύνανται ἀλαλκέμεν ὁππότ' ἂν (γ 236~7) τέλος ἔλθῃ ὁμοίϊου πολέμοιο" (~ Γ 291 + ω 543). ZYQXA UIG ("*Homoiion*: what happens equally to all. It needs to be known that the poet absolutely derives *homoiios* from *faulos* ['mean,' 'bad'] as in that passage 'yet old age, evil for all, weakens you' and 'yet surely not even the gods can keep off death, which is cruel to all, from men, however much loved by them, when the equally wretched war comes to an end.'"). For τό - χαλεπόν see Σ D Δ 444; I 440; O 670 van Thiel; *Suid.* o 309 Adler; Eustathius *in Il.* p. 477,1 (see app. van der Valk); *in Il.* p. 662,34–36; *in Il.* p. 790,63–64; *in Od.* p. 1465,24; see also Hesychius o 758 Latte; *EGud.* γ p. 303,13 de Stefani; *EM* 624,24.

ὁμοίϊος,[43] which is probably due to Aristarchus' influence; according to van der Valk, this would then exclude Erbse's hypothesis by which Σ D depends on the glossographers.[44] Finally, the *scholion minor* Lundon on Δ 315, attested in *P.Dura* 3,11, records ομοιιον· κακον *vel* κοινον. To sum up, given the uncertainty in the context, as for example in Δ 315—old age is common to everyone, but it is also bad because it deprives Nestor of the energy to fight—ancient commentators understood ὁμοίϊος as equivalent either with ὁμοῖος ("equal," "even") or with κακός ("bad," "cruel").[45]

One may wonder whether ὁμοίϊος carried any trace of this semantic ambiguity[46] still in Late Antiquity. In most cases the late antique usage of ὁμοίϊος is equivalent with ὁμοῖος. However, it seems that at least in one case Gregory of Nazianzus closely refers to this problem of Homeric exegesis in a funerary epigram dedicated to his mother Nonna.[47] In the poem, where the adjective ὁμοίϊος is again associated with γῆρας,[48] Gregory does not make a choice between the two possible meanings of the word according to the exegetical tradition ("even" and "bad"), but leaves the *aporia* unsolved, by concealing through the context the mention of the two different interpretations that the memory of a learned reader should recall:

Οὐ νόσος οὐδέ σε γῆρας ὁμοίιον, οὔ σέ γ' ἀνίη,
  καίπερ γηραλέην, μῆτερ ἐμή, δάμασεν·
ἀλλ' ἄτρωτος, ἄκαμπτος ἁγνοῖς ὑπὸ ποσσὶ τραπέζης
  εὐχομένη Χριστῷ, Νόνν', ἀπέδωκας ὄπα.[49]

---

43 Modern scholars have different views about the origin of the word: see, e.g., Athanassakis 1976; Rengakos 1994, 119–120.

44 van der Valk 1963–1964, 1:258. See Erbse 1953, 170.

45 Stephanus' *ThGl* s.v. ὁμοίϊος refers to ὅμοιος. *LfgrE* s.v. records the following meanings under ὁμοίϊος: (a) "gemeinschaftlich," "solidarish," "keinen vershonend"; (b) "der alle Menschen trifft," "involvierend." Δ 315 and *h.Ven.* 244 are grouped under (b).

46 According to Livrea 1972, 241–242 such ambiguity is reflected in Apollonius Rhodius *Arg.* 4.62 νῦν δὲ καὶ αὐτὴ δῆθεν ὁμοίης ἔμμορες ἄτης, where ὁμοίης, which here replaces ὁμοίϊης because the latter is metrically impossible, would indicate that Medea's love is evil but, at the same time, common to all creatures.

47 *AP* 8.50. There might be ambiguity in Nonnus *D.* 5.344 αἴθε μοι ἄλγος ὄπασσεν ὁμοίϊον (Actaeon, torn to pieces by his dogs, wished for himself the same fate as Tiresias, which is also evil). It is hard to say. More likely, since the word ἄλγος already embraces the idea of evil, here ὁμοίϊον means just "even," in order to avoid redundancy.

48 *AP* 8.50.1.

49 "Neither sickness, nor wretched(?) age, nor grief subdued / you, mother, even if you were old; / yet unwounded, unbent, at the holy feet of the altar, you, / Nonna, in the act of praying, returned your voice to Christ."

96   GULLO

The last case in which the *iunctura* γῆρας ὁμοίϊον occurs, beyond the three shown so far, is a passage from Quintus' *Posthomerica*;[50] here Priam addresses Diomedes, who then replies back:

"[...] καὶ γάρ ῥα μακρὸν πέλει ἀνέρι κῦδος
ἄνδρα νέον κτείναντι καὶ ὄβριμον· ἢν δὲ γέροντα
κτείνῃς, οὔ νύ τοι αἶνος ἐφέψεται εἵνεκεν ἀλκῆς.   195
τοὔνεκ' ἐμεῦ ἀπὸ νόσφιν ἐς αἰζηοὺς τρέπε χεῖρας
ἐλπόμενός ποτε γῆρας ὁμοίϊον εἰσαφικέσθαι [...]."
Ὣς φάμενον προσέειπε κραταιοῦ Τυδέος υἱός·
"Ὦ γέρον, ἔλπομ' ἔγωγ' ἐσθλὸν ποτὶ γῆρας ἱκέσθαι·
[...]."[51]

One might hypothesize that Gregory depends here on Quintus, whose work he certainly knew. However, in Quintus' passage there is no ambiguity at all: here ὁμοίϊον clearly means "even," "equal," as the poet himself seems to point out through the phrasing ἐσθλόν [...] γῆρας at l. 199, which could hardly lead to understanding the previous ὁμοίϊον as "evil" or "bad." Therefore, Gregory must be imitating Homer here, and alluding to the debate on the interpretation of the gloss. It does not matter if the glossographic interpretation is suspected to have arisen from the frequent association of ὁμοίϊος, in Homer, with nouns bearing a negative concept.[52] It makes no difference if the semantic differentiation between ὁμοίϊος and ὁμοῖος is secondary to the phonological one: to Gregory the *aporia* becomes the basis for a refined, learned pun.

Let us now pass to the second case of this section, taken from Christodorus' ekphrasis, which likely dates from 503 CE or shortly after. Once the poem's context as a work originally composed for the court was forgotten and got lost, the ekphrasis entered the *Greek Anthology*, in which it survives in its entirety as its Book 2. As Alan Cameron argued,[53] the structure of the ekphrasis itself, as well as the use of the hexameter verse, which was common in the contemporary literary and epigraphic epigrammatic tradition, contributed to the fact

---

50   13.197.

51   "[...] 'To slay a young and strong man is an enormous / glory; but if you smite an old man, / no praise will then follow for your courage. / Therefore turn from me your hands against young / men, if you ever hope to reach old age such as mine.' / So he spoke; the son of strong Tydeus replied: 'Old man, I do hope to reach honoured age [...].'"

52   See, e.g., πόλεμος (*passim*); θάνατος (γ 236); νεῖκος (Δ 444); see also Theocritus 22.172 νεῖκος [...] ὁμοίϊον.

53   Alan Cameron 1973, 106.

LATE ANTIQUE HOMERIC EXEGESIS IN THE GREEK ANTHOLOGY

that Christodorus' poem was understood as a series of sixty-five ekphrastic epigrams on the statues adorning the baths of Zeuxippus in Constantinople. Lines 228–240 describe the statue of an athlete (a wrestler or, less likely, a boxer) whose identification remains uncertain.[54] In particular, lines 239–240, in spite of expressing a banal idea, are characterized by a sequence of rare words and unusual, baroque metaphors, which almost prevent their understanding:

καὶ παχὺς ἀλκήεντι τένων ἐπανίστατο νώτῳ
αὐχένος εὐγνάμπτοιο περὶ πλατὺν αὐλὸν ἀνέρπων.[55]

In particular, the metaphor αὐχένος [...] περὶ πλατύν αὐλόν is unprecedented and unparalleled:[56] seemingly, it describes the neck of the wrestler, by emphasizing its stretched form.[57] For this pattern Christodorus might be influenced by the exegesis of Homer P 297–298, although the use of this *locus difficilis* looks a bit forced. The Homeric passage refers to the battle around the body of Patroclus becoming more and more violent. Hippothous, a Trojan warrior, fastened a belt around the ankle of the dead, and dragged the corpse into the melee. Then Ajax, darting, stuck a javelin into Hippothous' head; immediately his brain, covered in blood, splattered out through the wound:

ἐγκέφαλος δὲ παρ' αὐλὸν ἀνέδραμεν ἐξ ὠτειλῆς
αἱματόεις.[58]

The word αὐλός is used three times in the *Iliad*, twice in the *Odyssey* and twice in the *Homeric Hymns*: it means "pipe" (musical instrument) in K 13, Σ 495, and in the two occurrences from the *Homeric Hymns*.[59] In τ 227 αὐλός designates the clip to fix Odysseus' cloak, whereas in χ 18 the word means "spurt" of blood. The last occurrence (P 297), that is, our passage, is the most problematic: much debate developed in ancient scholarship on the expression

---

54 See Tissoni 2000 on Christodorus 228–230, 180–182.
55 "His nape stood out thick atop his powerful back, creeping / upwards around the broad tube of his flexible neck."
56 In Anonymous *AP* 14.58.1–3 the object of the riddle, an artichoke, speaks in the first person: here, however, it is αὐχήν (neck) that is metaphorically used to indicate the stalk of the artichoke, whereas αὐλός, even though employed in a simile to indicate, once more, the stem, preserves its original meaning of "reed," "tube."
57 See Tissoni 2000 *ad loc.*, 185.
58 "The blood-soaked brain spurted up from the wound / along the pole."
59 *h.Merc.* 452; *h.* 14.3.

παρ' αὐλόν of P 297, as shown by the related *scholia* bt[60] and D,[61] as well as Eustathius' commentary.[62] According to them, in P 297 αὐλός may designate:

(a)   the pole or the length of the spear (Σ bT; Σ D);
(b)   the point of the spear (Eustathius);
(c)   a dimension (height) of the helmet, understood as a narrow and lengthened object (Σ D);
(d)   the hole in the helmet from which Hippothous' brain spurted (Σ D; Eustathius);
(e)   gush of blood (Σ bT; Σ D; Eustathius).[63]

Stephanus' *ThGl* s.v. αὐλός records the Homeric passage among those in which the word designates the spurt of blood. According to *LfgrE* s.v., instead, in this case αὐλός would rather indicate the tang of the spearpoint which is fixed into the spear shaft: this interpretation is accepted by several modern commentators and translators.[64]

---

60   Σ bT P 297 ex. Erbse παρ' αὐλόν· τινὲς τὸ ξύλον τοῦ δόρατος, ἐπεὶ καὶ τὰς αἰγανέας 'δολιχαύ-λους' (ι 156) φησίν. οἱ δὲ τὸν ἄκρον ἐξακοντισμὸν τοῦ αἵματος, ὡς ἐκεῖ ἄνω πηδήσαντος τοῦ ἐγκεφάλου [...] b (BCE³E⁴T ("Along the *aulos*: for some it is the wood of the spear, because (*sc.* Homer) calls even the javelins *dolichaulous* ['with long tubes']. For others the highest spurt of blood, because in that passage it is as though the brain would jump up").

61   Σ D P 297/Z^S van Thiel ἐγκέφαλος δὲ παρ' αὐλόν ἀνέδραμεν· ὁ δὲ ἐγκέφαλος παρὰ τὴν ἀνά-τασιν τοῦ κράνους σφόδρα καὶ ἐκτεταμένως τῇ τοῦ αἵματος ῥεύσει συνεξέρρευσεν. αὐλὸς γὰρ λέγεται πᾶν τὸ στενὸν καὶ ἐπίμηκες, κατὰ μεταφορὰν τοῦ ὀργάνου. [...] νῦν οὖν αὐλόν φησιν τὸν τοῦ αἵματος ἀκοντισμόν. ἔστι δὲ ὅτε καὶ τὸ ἐπίμηκες τοῦ δόρατος(?). ZYQUI^mG. T^r ἢ τὴν ὀπήν. ("The brain spurted up along the *aulos*: the brain ran out very much and continuously together with the flow of blood along the height of the helmet. As a matter of fact, *aulos* is anything narrow and oblong, for analogy with the musical instrument. [...] Therefore, now [*sc.* Homer] calls *aulos* the spurt of blood. From time to time the length of the spear too. Or the hole"). For αὐλός - ὀργάνου see Σ V χ 19 Dindorf αὐλὸς αἵματος· πᾶν γὰρ τὸ στενὸν αὐλὸν ἔλεγον· Σ on Pindar *P.* 4.404 Drachmann ὀρθὰς δ' αὐλακας· διὸ καὶ αὔλακες εἴρηνται παρὰ τὸν αὐλόν. πᾶν δὲ ἐπίμηκες οὕτω φασίν.

62   Eustathius *in Il.* p. 1107,61 αὐλὸν δὲ λέγει ἢ τὸ ὀξὺ τοῦ δόρατος, ἐπεὶ καὶ αἰγανέας δολιχαύλους που λέγει τὰς μακροξύλους, ἢ τὸ τρῆμα τῆς κυνέης τὸ διὰ τοῦ ἔγχεος. καὶ ἄλλως δὲ αὐλὸν τὸν ἐξακοντισμόν φησι καὶ τὴν ἐπίμηκη φορὰν τοῦ αἵματος. αὐλὸς γάρ, ὡς καὶ προεδηλώθη, πᾶν τὸ ἐπίμηκες καὶ οὐδὲ πλατύ. ("[*sc.* Homer] calls *aulos* the point of the spear, because he calls even the javelins made of a long wood *dolichaulous* ['with long tubes'] somewhere, or the perforation in the helmet caused by the spear. Otherwise, he calls *aulos* the spurt and extensive rush of blood. As shown previously, *aulos* is indeed anything oblong and not broad").

63   Following Homer, Nonnus employs αὐλός in the meaning "spurt" three times (*D.* 4.454; 30.143; 44.105). In the remainder of the occurrences he keeps the meaning "pipe." It is certainly significant that a Nonnian poet like Christodorus employs αὐλός only once, exploiting a metaphorical sense which is not attested in Nonnus.

64   For example, van Leeuwen, Leaf, Bayfield, Mazon, Murray, Edwards. Others, accepting what the scholiographic tradition asserts, understand αὐλός either as a part of the helmet,

LATE ANTIQUE HOMERIC EXEGESIS IN THE GREEK ANTHOLOGY

I firmly believe that Christodorus was determined to make his own contribution here to the scholarly debate over the meaning of αὐλός in Homer P 297, because he disagreed with all the interpretations provided by the scholiographic tradition. The point here is not the interpretation of αὐλός in the Homeric passage: we need to understand how Christodorus interpreted it and how he reused the metaphor for his own work. Christodorus, visualizing the image of Hippothous' brain pouring down slowly along his neck, understood αὐλός as "neck." One may add another hypothesis to justify Christodorus' understanding of αὐλός as "neck." The Σ on P 297 states that Hippothous' brain spurted out "along the height of the helmet": a free reading of it could have led Christodorus to explain αὐλός as that part of the human body identifiable with the neck.[65] The idea that anything narrow and stretched in shape is called αὐλός (hence, the helmet and the human neck as well), for analogy with the musical instrument, might contribute to Christodorus' interpretation. It is important to recall here that a wrestler has no armor, and that the Mycenaean helmet, as well as the one used in the Geometric period, whose features fit the descriptions of the helmet attested in Homer, was very extended in height.[66] Therefore, the word αὐλός, which might indicate in Homer a lengthened part of the helmet (or the helmet itself, stretched in shape), is used by Christodorus in the sense of an oblong part of the wrestler's naked body "armor," the "neck." The tight relationship with the Homeric text is further supported by the fact that Christodorus employs ἀνέρπων, an incisive verb which clearly recalls the ἀνέδραμεν of Homer P 297.

3   Homeric Variants and *poetae docti*

As noted in the introduction, it is possible to spot cases in which the late antique poet seems to make an actual choice between two variants in the Homeric text. We shall go back again to Christodorus of Coptos and to the description of the unknown athlete's statue (ll. 233–237); his beard and thick hair, as well as his harsh expression and mighty build, are highly praised:

---

particularly the frontal part, or as the javelin itself. The former interpretation may be also influenced by the debated epithet αὐλῶπις, applied to the helmet in E 182; Λ 353; N 530; Π 795.

65   The only other case in poetry in which αὐλός designates a part of the body is seemingly Oppian *C.* 1.189 ὀρθοτενεῖς δολιχοί τε ποδῶν περιηγέες αὐλοί, where it refers to the part of the legs of a horse between knee and fetlock ("shanks"). In Hippocrates *Mul.* p. 126,8 Littrè αὐλός is the uterus. In Pollux (2.72) human nostrils are called αὐλοί.

66   See Snodgrass 1967, figs. 7–8, 17, 23–24, 43–44.

100   GULLO

> ἔπνεεν ἠνορέης· λάσιος δέ οἱ εἵλκετο πώγων
> καὶ φόβον ἠκόντιζον ἀεθλητῆρα παρειαὶ
> καὶ κεφαλῆς ἔφρισσον ἐθειράδες· ἀμφὶ δὲ πυκνοῖς   235
> μυῶνες μελέεσσιν ἀνοιδαίνοντο ταθέντες
> τρηχαλέοι· [...][67]

Attention should be paid to the word ἐθειράδες ("hair") at l. 235, which is apparently not attested elsewhere. However, a *scholion* on a passage from Theocritus claims it to be a Homeric variant:[68]

> ἐθειράζοντες· κομῶντες τὰς τρίχας, οὐ γενειῶντες, ὥς τινες. ἔθειρα γὰρ ἡ θρὶξ τῆς κεφαλῆς. ὅθεν Ἀρίσταρχος ἐν Ὁμήρῳ (π 176) ἔγραψε· "κυάνεαι δ' ἐγένοντο γενειάδες ἀμφὶ γένειον", οὐκ "ἐθειράδες." KGEAT[69]

The scholiast on the Theocritean passage states that Aristarchus would introduce the Homeric reading γενειάδες ("beard") into π 176, because ἔθειρα means "hair of the head," and is not suitable for the hair around the chin.[70] The same alternation of readings is attested in *EM* 225,54:[71]

> γενειάδες, αἱ κατὰ τῶν γενείων γενόμεναι τρίχες· τινῶν γραφόντων ἐθειράδες· παρὰ τὸν τόπον ἐν ᾧ πεφύκασι.[72]

---

67   "He had an air of valor: he had a shaggy trailing beard, / his cheeks shot competitive fear and / the hair on his head bristled; around his thick / limbs his stretched muscles swelled / in bulges; [...]."

68   Σ on Theocritus 1.34b Wendel.

69   "*Etheirazontes*: with long hair, not beard, like some reckon. As a matter of fact, *etheira* is the hair on the head. Therefore, Aristarchus with regard to Homer wrote: 'the beard about his chin turned black,' not 'the hair.'"

70   Ἀρίσταρχος was conjectured by Lehrs and accepted by Wendel: the manuscripts bear the reading Ἀριστοτέλης. Van der Valk 1963–1964, 2:588–590 (see also van der Valk 1949, 50–51), asserted that the scholion on Theocritus was a forgery. Rejecting Lehrs' conjecture (Ἀρίσταρχος) and keeping the transmitted reading, he believed that Aristotle, interested in biological phenomena, may have explained ἐθειράδες in a passage now lost and understood it to mean "hair." He also thought that Aristotle may have added that Homer's text showed γενειάδες. Van der Valk concluded that the source of the Theocritean scholion erroneously retained the γενειάδες that was a conjecture by Aristotle. This entire hypothesis looks very convoluted and somewhat implausible. In particular, the confusion between Ἀρίσταρχος and Ἀριστοτέλης is banal and obvious, as pointed out by Wendel in his apparatus. Van der Valk's hypothesis has not gained wide acceptance.

71   Eustathius in *Od.* p. 1798,63 mentions both the variants too. See also Eustathius *in Il.* p. 696,64; p. 1059,7; *in Od.* p. 1799,21.

72   "*Geneiades*, hair growing about the cheeks; some write *etheirades*; it depends on the area where it grows up."

LATE ANTIQUE HOMERIC EXEGESIS IN THE GREEK ANTHOLOGY   101

In π 175–176 Homer describes the effects of the transformation of Odysseus, helped by Athena in order not to be recognized by his son Telemachus:

ἂψ δὲ μελαγχροιὴς γένετο, γναθμοὶ δ' ἐτάνυσθεν,
κυάνεαι δ' ἐγένοντο γενειάδες ἀμφὶ γένειον.[73]

At l. 176 most manuscripts bear the reading γενειάδες, accepted by almost all the modern editors of the *Odyssey*. Only G (= Laur. 32.24, tenth century), the oldest manuscript of the *Odyssey* handed down to us, and U (= Mon. 519 B, fourteenth century) transmit the variant ἐθειράδες,[74] printed in the *editio princeps* of the *Odyssey* by Demetrius Chalkokondyles (1488), in Stephanus' edition (1566), in another edition dated 1541, and in von der Mühll's edition (1946). Usher, the Teubner editor of the Homeric centos composed by Eudocia, prints ἐθειράδες as well (*Homer*. 1280), as well as Schembra, the Brepols editor of the same text for the *Corpus Christianorum, Series Graeca* (*Homer*. 1, 1287).

Since in the Homeric scholion on π 175[75] there is some criticism about the fact that in ν 399 (and 431) Odysseus' τρίχες are said to be ξανθαί ("blonde") and not κυάνεαι, it is plausible to think that Aristarchus, wishing to avoid the inconsistency, may have corrected κυάνεαι δ' ἐγένοντο ἐθειράδες ("the hair turned black") to κυάνεαι δ' ἐγένοντο γενειάδες ("the beard turned black"). If this hypothesis is accepted, evidently the Theocritean scholion was not considered a forgery at the time, and ἐθειράδες was believed to be a supposed variant!

In two passages respectively by Dio Chrysostom and Synesius, the two writers stress how Homer enjoys describing his characters' hair.[76] Particularly with regard to the black hair of Odysseus, they both quote a Homeric passage which seems to be partially equivalent with π 176:

κυάνεαι δ' ἐγένοντο ἔθειραι.[77]

---

73   "His dark color came back to him again, his jaws firmed, / and the hair that grew around his chin turned black."

74   However, the second hand in U amends ἐθειράδες into γενειάδες, and adds the abbreviation γρ': this may mean that the variant was taken from a model that was an edition equipped with variants.

75   Σ ν 399 Dindorf [...] καὶ πῶς ἐν τῇ μεταμορφώσει φησὶ "ξανθὰς δ' ἐκ κεφαλῆς ὀλέσω τρίχας" (ν 399); φαμὲν οὖν πρὸς τὸ πιθανὸν τῆς φαλακρώσεως. αἱ γὰρ ξανθαὶ τρίχες ἀραιαί εἰσι καὶ εὐχερῶς φαλακροῦνται [...] H. Q. ("[...] And how can (*sc.* Homer) say that during the transformation 'blonde hair disappeared from his head'? Therefore, we state that [he puts it this way] in order to make baldness plausible. As a matter of fact, blonde hair is thin and falls easily out [...]").

76   Dio Chrysostom: *Or.* 39 von Arnim (*Enc. com.*). Synesius: *Or.* 3.43 Terzaghi (*Calv. enc.*).

77   "The hair turned black."

The word ἔθειραι, at any rate, takes us back to ἐθειράδες. It is hard to say whether Dio and Synesius report just a variant or the *vulgata* between first and fourth century CE, or even the text from a common *florilegium*. The most convincing hypothesis is certainly that Dio quotes by heart (this would explain ἔθειραι, which is more usual than ἐθειράδες), and that Synesius depends on Dio. In the Imperial age, then, ἐθειράδες was likely perceived as a variant in every aspect.

For the purposes of the theme examined in this chapter, it does not matter whether ἐθειράδες is a correction by Aristotle (or Aristarchus) or not, and if the Theocritean *scholion* states the truth. As a real *poeta doctus*, Christodorus recovers—being the only one to do it so faithfully—what he perceives as a Homeric rare variant, ἐθειράδες, in its right meaning and in the same metrical position as Homer.[78] Moreover, at l. 235 of Christodorus' poem, κεφαλῆς allows the cultivated reader to appreciate the philological juxtaposition with the *Odyssey*. And further, the *clausula* ἀμφί in both Homer (π 176) and Christodorus (l. 235) is an even stronger testament to the tight relationship between the two texts.

•••

The diligent dedication of Gregory of Nazianzus, Christodorus of Coptos, and Agathias Scholasticus both on poetical and philological grounds results in the usage they make of controversial Homerisms for literary aims. Not only Homer, but Homeric philology as well becomes a significant intertext for late antique epigram and adds a substantial factor for its understanding and interpretation.

The cases examined in this chapter show that the late antique epigrammatists perfectly assimilated the preceding exegetical techniques into their works. Therefore, these poets can be considered "Hellenistic" in every aspect, not just from the point of view of content and style. Given the fact that these literary epigrams addressed a very cultivated audience, the readers were probably challenged by the poets to "spot" the Homeric rarities embedded within the lines. The situation changes if we shift to the epigraphic epigrams showing Homerisms: since exposed/exhibited inscriptions might be read by anyone, therefore, there were different kinds of audience; those who were learned enough could catch the allusion, but a large part of the "passers-by" was not able to identify the scholarly reference.

---

78   See Tissoni 2000 *ad loc.*, 183.

I hope to have shown that this research field, of which here I presented only an essay, is clearly rich and productive: given the long life of epigram and its unique tendency to continuous and unpredictable experimentation, it would be advisable to extend the same kind of investigation to late antique literary and inscriptional epigram more broadly, as well as to Byzantine epigram. In doing so, new responses to Homeric reception will be revealed by observing how Hellenistic exegesis is treated in epigram throughout the centuries.

Acknowledgements

I first met Alan Cameron in April 2014 at the American Academy in Rome, where he was a visiting scholar in residence: I was then a PhD student in Classics at the Scuola Normale Superiore in Pisa, and working on the *Greek Anthology*. In time he became my primary advisor, at least in an unofficial sense, and in 2015 he came to Pisa to serve as the external examiner on my PhD committee. My personal as well as intellectual debt to him is enormous: he believed in me, even and especially when I did not. He went out of his way to help me, and I only regret that we had so little time together. I consider it a great honor to be able to acknowledge his extraordinary learning, astuteness, and insight, and to thank him for his inspiration.

CHAPTER 7

Returning to the Wandering Poets

New Poems by Dioscoros of Aphrodite

Jean-Luc Fournet

A tribute to Alan Cameron could not fail to evoke what is one of his most magisterial and innovative articles, 'Wandering Poets: A Literary Movement in Byzantine Egypt'. Moreover, it is no accident that at the end of his life and more than fifty years after he wrote it, he decided to publish a selection of his articles in a volume with a title that very symbolically picked up the title of that pioneering paper.[1] This was certainly the study that most impressed and stimulated me when I began, exactly thirty years ago, to work on a doctoral thesis about one of those 'wandering poets', Dioscoros of Aphrodite (or Aphrodito). Thus I hoped that he would agree to be a member of my thesis 'jury', without much expectation that he would accept. However he said yes, and was kind enough to cross the Atlantic to take part in the academic ritual of a thesis defence.

Remembering that first meeting, I should like to pay tribute to the memory of that great scholar by offering him a new papyrus text of the 'wandering poet' to whom I dedicated my thesis. It is true that one can ask whether some new poems by Dioscoros are really a worthy present for Alan. We know how much the compositions of this minor Egyptian poet of the sixth century—who came from a family that had Coptic as its mother tongue and is known by a dossier of papyri (one of considerable size: it contains poems in his own hand, books from his library, and also business papers)—have been the subject of scholarly mockery. Two scholars have written that Dioscoros' poems are 'the morass of absurdity into which the great river of Greek poetry emptied itself'.[2] Alan, however, in his 2016 revision of his 'Wandering Poets' wrote: 'I regret in 1965 joining in the long-standing custom of mocking Dioscoros's metrical incompetence'.[3] He had now fully realized that behind the clumsiness of form (accentuated by the preparatory nature of the rough drafts that have come

---

1 Alan Cameron 2016b.
2 Bell and Crum 1925, 177. On the ferocious critiques to which Dioscoros has been subjected, see Baldwin 1984a, 327–331; and more recently Fournet 1999, 1:1–3.
3 Alan Cameron 2016b, 15.

© THE TRUSTEES OF COLUMBIA UNIVERSITY IN THE CITY OF NEW YORK,
2021 | DOI:10.1163/9789004452794_008

down to us) there is much that illuminates the cultural profile of the village élites of the late Roman Empire and helps to understand their literary trends, which are too often overshadowed by the great figures that tradition has preserved. So I have no scruples about dedicating to his memory the publication of these new poetical productions of Dioscoros, whose interest he would have been the first to appreciate.

In fact I should say '*almost* new', since they have been known since the publication of the Dioscoros papyri in the Cairo museum by Jean Maspero in 1916.[4] But because of humidity the roll that contains them has deteriorated and crumbled to such an extent that it is now reduced to a series of fragments placed, not always in order, under six plates of glass (one of which disappeared several decades ago). Its reconstitution is thus quite difficult, and its very darkened colour often makes the text illegible to the naked eye. The verses of Dioscoros are concentrated in the most damaged part of the roll, so much so that Maspero, observing that they 'are now almost entirely illegible, the ink being scarcely darker than the papyrus itself', could only distinguish two titles, and that in only a partial fashion.[5] Leslie S. B. MacCoull does not even include them in her edition of the poems of Dioscoros.[6] In my edition, I have tried to go further than Maspero in proposing readings of some lines that I managed to make out, but my advances were very limited and the main word in the title, which lets us understand the subject of these texts, still escaped me.[7] It was only in 2014 that I was able to take some infrared photos of the papyrus that literally unveiled these texts, enabling me now to offer a more complete edition and above all to identify the subject.

1   The Texts

The sequence of the fragments that I am able to propose is based on the Coptic text on the other side of the roll (which was written first). It consists of an arbitration dated to 28 October 569 – one of the first Coptic texts that is not a letter and hence of great importance for the sociolinguistic history of that language. Since this text is known from a duplicate also found in the archive of

---

4   Maspero 1916.
5   Maspero 1916, 175 (= *P.Cair.Masp.* III 67353 B and C).
6   MacCoull alludes to one of the two poems (*P.Cair.Masp.* III 67353 C), but she limits herself to translating the title (MacCoull 1988, 130).
7   Fournet 1999, 1:449–450 (= *P.Aphrod.Lit.* IV 44 and 45).

Dioscoros,[8] we are able to put the fragments back in their right order—except that for certain parts where we lack parallels in the duplicate. According to the reconstitution based on the Coptic text, the following is the content of the verso of our papyrus:

(1) the endorsement of the Coptic arbitration of 28 October 569 at the top of the roll;

(2) after three lines which I will return to, Poem 1 (l. 1–18) (Figure 7.1):[9]

FIGURE 7.1 Poem 1. Infrared image: Jean-Luc Fournet; image processing: Fabrice Bessière, Collège de France

---

8 *P.Cair. Masp.* II 67176[r] + II 67275[r] + III 67351[r] + P.Alex. inv. 689[r] + *BKU* III 503 + Corpus Christi College (Cambridge), Ms. 541[r]. See Fournet 2010, 125–130. I am preparing an edition of this text in collaboration with Anne Boud'hors, who has helped me greatly in the reconstitution of the fragments of *P.Cair.Masp.* III 67353.

9 One notes that the lines of the poems are almost all broken near the middle by a *vacat* that cannot be explained by reference to colometry. A *vacat* in the same place, but narrower, can also be seen in the middle of the lines of the document (3). I propose to explain this by a defect in the surface of the papyrus (absence of vertical fibres, easily visible in the first three fragments, ll. 5–14), which would have led Dioscoros to jump the defective part. But this defect then seems to disappear, while Dioscoros continues to place a *vacat* within each line. See Jones 2016, 375, for the same phenomenon in a poem of Dioscoros, *P.Aphrod.Lit.* IV 46. See also *P.Aphrod.Lit.* IV 28 and 43, where Dioscoros again introduces metrically unjustified spaces in the middle of lines without there being, as far as I can see, any material defect that would explain the anomaly.

RETURNING TO THE WANDERING POETS   107

Fr. 5i + f + g + e + h

↓   ⟦......⟧

⳨ Δεῖξον ἐμοὶ . . [   ]   ⟦   ⟧
   [Δ]εῖξον ἐμο[ὶ   ] *traces ?*
   Δεῖξον ἐμοὶ σέθε[ν] . . .

5 ⳨ Τίνας ἂν εἴπη λόγ(ους) Ὅμηρος *vac.* παρακαλῶν τὴν Θέτιν ἔνοπλον δεῖξαι
       αὐτῷ τὸν Ἀχιλλέα;
   Πότνια Θέτις, κόσμησον'. . ρ[1/2 ?]   *vac.* . . ϊον υἱέα . ε . ς·
   ὡς πά[ρ]ος ἐν πτολέμοισι σὺν   *vac.* ἔντεσι πάντα δα[μ]άζων,
   ὡς πά[ρο]ς ἐν πτολέμοισιν ἀριστεύων *vac.* ἐνὶ χάρμη
10 τε . (.)[.] . . . κ[.] . ι ξίφος ⟦. .⟧ ἀργυρόε *vac.* ντά τε τόξα τιταίνων
   χαλκοχίτων φορέων 1? αμι .   *vac.* . . . . .ς
                              Ἀχιλ   *vac.* λῆα φῶτα χαράττω
   ὥς κεν ἐνὶ γραφίδεσσιν ὁ⟦. ⟧   *vac.* μοίϊον ἄνδρα χαράττω
   βίβλοις ἀπαγγέλλουσιν ἐμοῖς πολ   *vac.* εμήϊα ἔργα
                         . . ερα
   . . . . ε . . . εγωντεγλισημεν   *vac.* ἀληθέα θαύματ' ἰδέσθαι
15 . α καὶ ἐν π . . . . *vac.* 1? ε . ιο . ςκα . . ιςςως
   . εαλλοφ . . ε . . . κατεν   *vac.* ἤρατο ⟦α⟧νηλέϊ χαλκῷ.
   . α . ν . . . ος Αἰακιδάω[ν] ἄφθι   *vac.* τον ὑμνοπολεύω
   . . . (.)
   [   ] . . ον . . . . ι *vac.* ⟦ ± 7 ⟧ κατὰ δῆριν ἀητ{τ}αν.

5i : 5 Ȧ ‖ l. εἴποι ‖ 7 ϊον υϊέα ‖ 11 χαλκοχιτων : κοχιτων in rasura ‖ 12 μοιϊον ‖ χαρατ'τω
‖ 13 απαγγελλουσιν : απαγγελλ supra εμοις scriptum ; cf. comm. ‖ εμηϊα ‖ 14 init-
ium in rasura (fort. . . ερα vestigia textus prioris) ‖ θαυματ' ϊδεϲθαι ‖ 15 ω̅ϲ vel ο̅ϲ
(ω vel ο in rasura) ‖ 16 νηλει : fort. diaeresis in lacuna ‖ 17 ὑμνοπολευω ‖ 18 αητ'ταν.

'Show me [...]
Show me [...]
Show me your [...]

1

|⁵ What words would Homer use when asking Thetis
to show him Achilles in arms?
Lady Thetis, prepare⁷ [...] your son [...]. As before, in wars, conquering all
with his arms, as before, in wars, excelling in the close fighting, [...] |¹⁰ bran-
dishing his spear and his silver bow, with his tunic of bronze, bearing [...] so
that I can put in writing mortal Achilles¹⁰ in my books that describe the works

---

10   Text before correction: 'so that I can describe this man just as he is'.

108   FOURNET

of war [...] real marvels to see |[15] [...] slew with pitiless bronze. I sing of the
immortal [offspring] of the Aeacids [...] in the insatiable combat'.

1–3   Cf. below, p. 123.
5   Compare the title of this ethopoia to that of, e.g., *AP* IX 465 (Τίνας ἂν εἴποι
      λόγους Ἀλθέα (l. -αία) παρακαλοῦσα τὸν Μελέαγρον;) or *AP* IX 463 (Τί ἂν
      εἴποι Ἕκτωρ ὁρῶν τὸν Ἀχιλλέα ἐν τοῖς ὅπλοις;).
7   Πότγια Θέτις: false quantity. Dioscoros should have used the form πότνα
      (e.g. πότνα θεά, *Od.* V 215). But he was probably influenced by the use of
      πότνια at the beginning of a line, e.g. at *h.Cer.* 54 and 492 and *h.Terra* 6, as
      well as nine times in the *Hymns* of Callimachus.
      κόςμηςον? : doubtful reading, though it seems unavoidable. Rather than
      'prepare (for battle)' (cf. Peek 1973, *s.v.* 1), the word has the sense of 'dress',
      or 'equip oneself', as in Nonnos, *D.* XLVI 92 in a similar context (ἔντεσι
      κοσμηθέντα 'you who are equipped with your arms').
8–9   ὡς πά[ρ]ος: this phrase, unknown to Homer (who uses ὡς τὸ πάρος περ),
      appears in the same *sedes* in AR III 635 and especially in Nonnos (nine
      occurrences). The repetiton of this expression indicates that the speaker
      wants Achilles to become again the warrior he was in the past, equipped
      with his new arms.
      ἐν πτολέμοισι(ν): cf. ἐν πολέμοισι in Nonnos, *D.* XXVI 316 (same position)
      and ἐνὶ πτόλεμοις in Nonnos, *D.* XX 219 (same position), itself repeated
      from AR I 467 (same position) and Quintus Smyrnaeus, III 254, 394
      (same position).
8   σὺν ἔντεσι: Homeric phrase, always in this position (*Il.* V 220; VI 418;
      XIII 331, 719), taken up by AR and Quintus but not attested in Nonnos.
      πάντα δα[μ]άζων: cf. Nonnos, *D.* XXXIII 139 (ξύμπαντα δαμάζω |).
9   ἀριστεύων ἐνὶ χάρμῃ: cf. the ethopoia *AP* IX 468, 2 (ἀριστεύειν ἐνὶ χάρμῃ |).
      The phrase ἐνὶ χάρμῃ goes back to Quintus Smyrnaeus (nine times) and
      Nonnos (six times), always in the same position.
10   χ[.].ι ξίφος: perhaps χ[αί] οἱ ξίφος ?
      ξίφος [[..]] ἀργυρόεντά τε τόξα τιταίνων: the combination ξίφος/τόξα goes
      back to Homer, *Il.* III 17–18. The clausula τόξα τιταίνων goes back to *Il.*
      VIII 266, and is appreciated by the late Egyptian poets (Claudian, *AP* V
      86, 1; Nonnos, *D.* XXVII 258, XXIX 127; Musaeus, *Hero and Leander* 17; *BKT*
      V/1, pp. 114–117 (Mertens-Pack³ 349; TM 64988; Heitsch 1964, Suppl. 10),
      l. 40 (and 42 with another mode).
      ἀργυρόεντα: rare adjective (ἀργυροειδής is preferred), attested, before
      Dioscoros, only in Nicander, *Alexiph.* 54; Eudocia, *S. Cypr.* II 181, and (at
      an unknown date) in *AP App.* II 601, 1.

RETURNING TO THE WANDERING POETS

11 χαλκοχίτων: Homeric adjective, always in the plural in Homer. The nominative singular is common in Nonnos (five occurrences, three of them in the same position: *D.* XX 345; XXVIII 297; XXIX 329).

12 ἐνὶ γραφίδεσσιν ... χαράττω: cf. l. 25, ἐνὶ γραφίδεσσι χαράττω. On this favourite phrase of Dioscoros, cf. *P.Aphrod.Lit.* IV 1, 4 n. (add as a poetical example, almost contemporary with Dioscoros, Agathias, *AP* IV 3, 118 [= 4, 72]: ὅσσαπερ ἢ γραφίδεσσι χαράξαμεν). On χαράττω 'write', which is to be found in the documentary prose of this period as well as in the poets, see *P.Aphrod.Lit.* IV 2, 7 n. The verb is to be found in an identical Homeric context in the ethopoia *AP* IX 455 (ἐχάρασσε δὲ θεῖος ῞Ομηρος) and in *APl.* 293, 1 (Τίς ποθ' ὁ τὸν Τροίης πόλεμον σελίδεσσι χαράξας).

ὁμοῖϊον ἄνδρα: 'I describe such a man', or, much better, 'this man as he is'. The theme of resemblance is a frequent *topos* in epigrams that refer to statues (see, for example, *SEG* XIII 277, 20 [late imperial]: εἰκόνι λαϊνέῃ πανομοίιον ἐστήσαντο). But the formulation was not a very happy one, and one understands why Dioscoros made the interlinear correction Ἀχιλλῆα φῶτα.

13 Dioscoros began by writing βίβλοις ἐμοῖς, then he crossed out ἐμοῖς and wrote above ἀπαγγέλλουσιν, coming back gradually after that to the previous level of the line.

βίβλοις ἀπαγγέλλουσιν ἐμοῖς: on this phrase, cf. l. 27 n. Dioscoros here commits a heteroclisis (one expects βίβλοις ἀπαγγελλούσαις ἐμαῖς—despite the metrical mistake in βίβλοῖς!). He corrects himself at ll. 27–28 (see p. 111), where he uses the feminine form of the participle (see also ll. 34–35 and 36). It is also possible that he was thinking of the neuter βίβλον, attested in John Geometres, *Hymns* LXXIII 29 (ed. Sajdak 1931)—but that is a rare and late form.

πολεμήϊα ἔργα: Homeric phrase (*Il.* II 338; V 428; VII 296; XI 719; XIII 730, always in the same position).

14 θαύματ᾽ ἰδέσθαι = *Batrachomyomachia* 58, adaptation of the Homeric clausula θαῦμα ἰδέσθαι | (*Il.* V 525; X 439; XVIII 83, 377; etc.).

16 κατενήρατο [[α]]νηλέϊ χαλκῷ: borrowed from Hesiod, *Th.* 316 (ἐνήρατο νηλέϊ χαλκῷ |), who combines two Homerisms, νηλέϊ χαλκῷ (eighteen occurrences in the same position) and κατενήρατο χαλκῷ (*Od.* XI 519, in the same position).

17 Αἰακιδάῳ[ν] ἄφθιτον: the form Αἰακιδάων (the ending is hard to read but is imposed by the metre) is employed only by Collouthos, 275, and Christodoros, *AP* II 296 (but always at the end of the line). The preceding word could be γένος.

ὑμνοπολεύω: cf. *P.Aphrod.Lit.* IV 5, 13 n.

18 κατὰ δῆριν: expression that appears in Dionysius Periegetes, 1051 (in another position), and is picked up by Quintus Smyrnaeus (seven occurrences, in the same position as in Dionysius) and Nonnos (three occurrences, one of them in the same position as in our poem: *D.* XXX 120).
    ἄητ{τ}αν: I see this as an erroneous form of ἄητος, -ον (which only appears in the expression θάρσος ἄητον (*Il.* XXI 395; Quintus I 217), by analogy with ἀήττητος.

(3) a Greek document (list of persons or a rough draft of a contract) written upside down by Dioscoros;
(4) Poem 2 with the same title as the first one, on two fragments that do not join (ll. 19–31) (Figure 7.2):

FIGURE 7.2 Poem 2. Infrared image: Jean-Luc Fournet; image processing: Fabrice Bessière, Collège de France

Fr. 5b

→ ⳨ Τίνας ἂν εἴπῃ λόγους Ὅμηρος   *vac.*   παρακαλῶν τὴν Θέτιν δε[ῖ]ξ[αι αὐτῷ]
20   ἔνοπλον τὸν Ἀχιλλέα;
            οὕτ(ως)·

+   Δεῖξον ἐμοὶ σέθεν υἷα κεκασ   *vac.*   μένον, δῖα θεάων,
    ἔρνος ἀκοντίζειν ὑπερήνορος   *vac.*   Αἰακίδαο·
    ἔμφυτον ἠνορέῃφι δυσάμμορον   *vac.*   ἐκγεγαῶτα,

RETURNING TO THE WANDERING POETS   111

25   πάντοθεν ἀμφιβόητον ἐνὶ γρα   *vac.*   φίδεσσι χαράττω
      [.]...[...].[.]...[...]... ε...ε.   *vac.*   γος ἄφθιτον εἶναι

Fr. 6c

→   βίβ[λον] ἀ[παγγέλ]λουσαν᾿ ἄπερ   *vac.*   τελέεσκεν....(..),
      [βίβλον] ἀπαγγέλλουσαν ἀληθ   *vac.*   ἑα πᾶσιν ὀπά[σσ]ῳ,
      [πα]ντοίων᾿ μεθέπουσαν ἀ   *vac.*   μετρήτων ἀρετάων
30   ζόντος Ἀχιλλῆος παναέθ   *vac.*   λια κυδιανείρης
      ἀργαλέης ἔριδος κακομηχ   *vac.*   άνου Τυνδαρεώνης.

5b : 19 l. εἴποι ‖ **21** ουτ— ‖ **22** υἷα ‖ δῖα θεᾱων ‖ **23** ὑπερηνορος ‖ αιακιδᾱο ‖ **25** αμφι-βοητον : alt. ο ex η corr. ‖ χαρατ᾿τω ‖

6c : 29 αρετᾱων ‖ **30** l. ζῶντος ‖ l. κυδιανείρας ‖ **31** τυνδαρεωνης : τυνδα in rasura.

2

'What words would Homer use when asking Thetis
to show him|²⁰ Achilles in arms?

Show me your son, divine among the goddesses, he who excels at hurling the javelin², the offspring of the arrogant Aeacides. It is a being of innate bravery, born for a wretched destiny, |²⁵ acclaimed everywhere, that I am writing about [...] to be immortal [...] book that relates what he accomplished [...], I bring to all a book that recounts the truth, which contains the terrible ordeals inflicted |³⁰—while Achilles, with his innumerable virtues of every sort², was living—by the tricky Tyndarides, so famous among humans, source of bitter quarrels.'

21   οὗτ(ως): the use of this adverb, typical of papyrus accounts, in which it constitutes the connection between the title and the document itself (the equivalent therefore of a colon), shows how much Dioscoros' documentary practice influences the drafting of his poems (see *P.Aphrod.Lit.*, I, p. 258).

22   κεκασμένον: 'excellent' (Homeric) or 'well equipped', whence 'well armed'. See ll. 22–23 n. The last syllable is treated as short despite the fact that it is followed by a consonant, perhaps under the influence of Homer who uses this adjective always with a short last syllable (κεκασμένε, -νὄν). Charles de Lamberterie has pointed out to me that this phenomenon occurs in

two other Homeric words (ll. 31 κακομηχάνου and 50 κεχαρισμένην) whose last syllable is always short in Homer (κακομηχάνοῦ, -ε and κεχαρισμένε, -α, -ὅς). This systematic mistake is a further proof of Homer's impact on Dioscoros.

δῖα θεάων: clausula dear to Homer (*Il.* V 381, VI 305, XIV 184, XVIII 205, 388, XIX 6, XXIV 93). In the last two passages it is applied to Thetis.

22–23 The construction and the sense of the infinitive ἀκοντίζειν pose a problem. The simplest solution would be to take it with κεκασμένον, with this word meaning 'to excel at'. The sense is then rather flat, and the position of ἀκοντίζειν, postponed to the next line and inserted after ἔρνος, would be strange. One is tempted to consider other solutions, but none is convincing: (1) it would make a more interesting sense to see in ἀκοντίζειν an 'infinitive of destination', the subject of which would be Homer: 'show me your son (…), so that I can aim at the offspring of the arrogant Aeacid'. Dioscoros would be playing on the sense of the verb by comparing the writer's instrument, the pen, to a javelin: the target that is aimed at becomes the subject that is being treated. The image might continue with the use in l. 25 of χαράττω, which as well as meaning 'write' can also mean 'scratch', hence 'wound'. In the figurative use of ἀκοντίζειν, Dioscoros was perhaps also influenced by Nonnos' use of this verb with μῦθον ('let fly a speech', *D.* XXXIV 299) as an equivalent of 'say', or by Pindar's metaphorical use of it (*N.* IX 55 or *I.* II 35, where the javelin is a metaphor for the poet's art). (2) Keeping the same construction, one might also suppose that Dioscoros has given ἀκοντίζειν the same sense as ἀνακοντίζειν 'make [something] gush forth' (a common verb in Nonnos): 'show me your excellent son (…), so that (by means of my poem) I can make him gush forth (= so that I can make him appear, give him life)'. This solution, which I owe to Gianfranco Agosti, would be tempting if it did not rest on a lexical confusion, a minor one it is true. (3) ἀκοντίζειν also has the sense of 'cast its rays, shine' (see Euripides, *Ion* 1155), which could give us here 'show me your son (…), so that (by means of my poem) he can shine …'. (4) Achilles could equally well be the subject of ἀκοντίζειν taken in its banal sense: 'show me your son (…), so that the offspring of the arrogant Aeacides should hurl his javelin (sc. now that he is newly armed)'. But I do not understand the idea that this infinitive would add: Homer does not ask Thetis to show him Achilles in arms so that the latter can rush off to fight, but so that he can become the subject of the poem. I have hesitatingly kept the simplest construction even though it gives a very uninteresting sense.

RETURNING TO THE WANDERING POETS

23 ἔρνος: the term that Thetis herself uses about her son in *Il.* XVIII 56 and 437 (ὃ δ' ἀνέδραμεν ἔρνεϊ ἶσος : 'he has grown like a young shoot').
ὑπερήνορος Αἰακίδαο: Peleus, son of Aeacus. Dioscoros has certainly misunderstood the adjective in giving it a positive sense ('very brave') which *a priori* the root could justify. However it suits Achilles well.

24 ἔμφυτον ἠνορέῃφι: it is tempting to give the adjective a passive sense, but that is not attested: 'who is naturally endowed with courage'. Should we try to connect this passive sense with the use of ἔμφυτος in the papyri to apply to a vine (*P.Hamb.* I 23, 16, from the archive of Dioscoros)?
δυσάμμορον: this adjective used in this position recalls *Il.* XIX 315, XXII 428, 485, which were followed in particular by Apollonius Rhodius (seven occurrences) and Quintus Smyrnaeus (nine occurrences).
ἐκγεγαῶτα: clausula which appears in *h.Cer.* 237. On the influence of the Homeric hymns on the poetry of Late Antiquity, see Agosti 2016c.

25 ἀμφιβόητον: for this adjective, a Dioscoros favourite, cf. *P.Aphrod.Lit.* IV 4, 35 n.
ἐνὶ γραφίδεσσι χαράττω: cf. l. 12 n.

26 ἄφθιτον εἶναι: same clausula in another ethopoia by Dioscoros, *P.Aphrod. Lit.* IV 43, 8 (on the subject of Achilles). Naïm Vanthieghem proposes to read immediately before this γένος 'immortal race'.

27 βίβ[λον] ἀ[παγγέλ]λουσαν³: there is perhaps a trace of ink before βίβ[λον]. See Paul the Silentiary, *Hagia Sophia* 779: | βίβλον ἀπαγγέλουσαν ὅσα κτλ., where the book in question is the Bible (see l. 36 n.). We find this expression in the plural at l. 13. The verb has here the sense of 'relate, describe' (cf. Lampe, *s.v.* 2). The beginning of this line (repeated at the following one) may suggest that Dioscoros knew Paul the Silentiary's poem. There would be no chronological objection: Paul's *ekphrasis* had been read in public for the inauguration of Hagia Sophia in 562 or 563. And there are other echoes of Paul in the poems of Dioscoros: besides, in our papyrus, the beginning of l. 36 (see comm. *ad loc.*), see *P.Aphrod.Lit.* IV 3, A^r, col. I, 1 (= *Hagia Sophia* 197). But we cannot exclude a lost common model (as is the case with *P.Aphrod.Lit.* IV 5, 19 = *Hagia Sophia* 213, since this poem is at least ten years earlier than Paul's; both must have been inspired by Nonnos, *D.* XXV 437, although the metrical position is different). In fact, the number of echoes of Paul in the work of Dioscoros inclines me to prefer the hypothesis of a direct influence. Paul's poem, an encomium of the emperor and his achievement, must have circulated quite quickly across the empire, probably helped by the authorities, who could justifiably see it as useful propaganda. Dioscoros, at that time in the capital of one of the provinces, could easily have had access to it.

114   FOURNET

βίβ[λον: singular with a collective sense (cf. ll. 34 and 36). See Garulli 2017, 142 (with other poetic examples concerning Homer) and above all Agosti 2010c, 13–14 and 22–23, for the cultural background of the use of this term to refer to the works of Homer.

28   [βίβλον] ἀπαγγέλλουσαν : see l. 27.

πᾶσιν ὀπά[σσ]ῳ = Nonnos, *Par.* X 99 (same position). See also, at the end of the line, Ps.-Apollinaris, *Par.Ps.* XXXVI 47 (πᾶσιν ὀπάζει) and Sophronios, *Anacr.* IV 38 (πᾶσιν ὀπάζων). The Homeric poems are seen as giving access to the truth about humans and the world (cf. l. 40). Their encyclopaedic and moral content is privileged at the expense of their diegetic content.

29   Cf. Dioscoros, *P.Aphrod.Lit.* IV 35, 4: παντοίης μεθέπεις, ὅτ᾽ ἀμετρήτων ἀρετάων. The genitive [πα]ντοίων² ... ἀμετρήτων ἀρετάων depends on Ἀχιλλῆος in the following line or on a substantive in the preceding line.

30   ζόντος: for the mistake, cf. *P.Aphrod.Lit.,* I, p. 343, § 1. The contracted form ζῶντ- is exceptional in Homer (*Il.* I 88, in a different *sedes*) who prefers the Ionian form ζώοντ-. It is not found in epic poets such as Apollonius, Quintus, or Nonnos.

παναέθλια: 'terrible (παν-) ordeals/exploits', *hapax* derived from ἀέθλιον (epic form for ἆθλον or ἆθλος), which has here not the sense of 'prize' (ἆθλον) of a contest or 'contest' (ἆθλος), but of 'ordeals, exploits', which can be the meaning of ἄεθλον/ἆθλον, as it is in Nonnos (*D.* IX 181: ἄεθλα νεηγενέος Διονύσου; XXV 242: ἆθλα μὲν Ἡρακλῆος). The idea of ordeals emerges from the adjective *πανάεθλος (for πανάεθλιος), 'who has endured all the ordeals' (a synonym of ἀεθλοφόρος, which is used about Christian martyrs), which Dioscoros employs in documents (see below, p. 131). There had apparently been some variation (-ιον/-ον) in the ending of this word as in the word used in our poem.

30–31 The meaning can be also: 'the terrible ordeals caused in Achilles' life (...), by the bitter dispute over the tricky Tyndarides'. See the following notes.

30   κυδιανείρης: to be taken here in a passive sense ('glorified by men') as in its other two attestations in Dioscoros (*P.Aphrod.Lit.* IV 17, 25 and 51, 1). I make this adjective depend on Τυνδαρεώνης, but one could also make it depend on ἔριδος ('discord so (unhappily) celebrated among mankind'). On this word, see *P.Aphrod.Lit.* IV 17, 25 n. The only attested genitive is κυδιανείρας (*Scholia vetera ad Iliadem* IX 441); this hyperionism is also committed by Dioscoros with the accusative (*P.Aphrod.Lit.* IV 17, 25: κυδιανείρην).

31 ἀργαλέης ἔριδος κακομηχάνου Τυνδαρεώνης: it is not clear how to understand this sequence of genitives. According to the Homeric parallels, κακομηχάνου could go equally well with Τυνδαρεώνης (Helen uses the word to describe herself at *Il.* VI 344) or with ἔριδος (cf. *Il.* IX 257: ἔριδος κακομηχάνου in the same position). We note a hyper-Homerization of language in which several Homeric references telescope themselves and overlap.

On the metrical error in κακομηχάνου, see l. 22 n.

ἀργαλέης ἔριδος: citation of Solon, *Fr.* 4, 38 West 1972 = *Fr.* 3, 38 Gentili and Prato 1988.

Τυνδαρεώνης: this appellation for Helen is typical of the poetry of late antique Egypt (Tryphiodoros 473; Collouthos 378; Christodoros *AP* II 167; Dioscoros, *P.Aphrod.Lit.* IV 34, 5).

(5) an act of disinheritance (ἀποκήρυξις) in Greek dated 12 November 569, written by someone other than Dioscoros;
(6) after a long *vacat*, Poem 3 is written the other way up, on three fragments which do not join (Figure 7.3):

FIGURE 7.3 Poem 3. Infrared image: Jean-Luc Fournet; image processing: Fabrice Bessière, Collège de France

116 FOURNET

Fr. 6h

→ Εἰς τὰ Ὁμήρια
ϡ Ζώοις αἰέν, Ὅμηρε, τεὸς χρόνος οὔ[ποτ' ὀλεῖται]·
   βίβλον ἔχεις πολύμολπον ος.[
35 παντοίως μεθέπουσαν …[

- -

Fr. 6d[11]

→ [β]ίβλον ἀειζώο<υ>σαν ̣(.) πυκίνης σοφί[ης ≃]
   [.]̣ερπει   ῥήτρης[ ]

- -

Fr. 6a+b+g+k

- -

→ πᾶσιν ̣[± 6]   ± 7   [
   …… πρ…..coς…[   ]…[
40 εἴσ[ω]ʾ τ' ἀμφιέπουσαν ἀληθέ[α μ]υθολογεύειν,
   πάντοθεν ἀ[γ]γέλλουσαν …. vac. τη…. εγος.̣.
   [..].…………ει.…[.].[…].̣.ρου
   .c.………..[.(.)]ν vac. πολύμυθον ἀρίστων
   …[.….] ἀμφεκόμισσα κ[αὶ ὣ vac.]μοσα καρτερὸν ὅρκον·
45 οὐρανὸς λλ…ην [πολ vac. υʾ]φεγγέα κύκλα σελήνης·
   εἰσὶν ἅπασιν ….τ. [.. vac.]. ἀστέρες ἥρωες ἄνδρε[ς]
   κου…ερ. ιεταα.ινα vac. γηρα………..[
   ἔμπεδον ἀστυφέλικτον ὅ vac. σης γενεῆς βίον ἔσχον
   ὑμνητῆρες ἀφαυροὶ νοήμ vac. ονες εὐεπιάων
50 τοσσατίην ἀρετὴν κεχαρισμ vac. ένην..χρ…[.]..ρες. vac. αυ[.]ον
   ἱμερόεις ἀμίμητος Ὅμηρο[ς vac…]τοεισς.ε….η

---

11 The position of this fragment is doubtful. The verso is blank, like Fr. 6h. Both of them are to be placed after the Coptic contract, the end of which is preserved in Fr. 6 a+b+g+k. But the relationship between 6h and 6d is elusive. Should Fr. 6d be placed laterally with respect to 6h?

RETURNING TO THE WANDERING POETS

in the right-hand margin between ll. 42 and 46:

52   ᵃ οὐκ ἐα.̣ [---] ᵇ ἀεὶ ζώοντ[---] ᶜ ἔπειτ.̣ [---]ᵈουσι πτ[---] ᵉ σὴν ἀρετὴν [---]
      ᶠτες ὅσο[

6h : 32 l. Ὁμήρεια.
6d : 36 ζωοσαν : ω ex ο corr.
6a+b+g+k : 49 ευεπιᾱων ‖ **51** ἵμεροεις ‖ **52** ante ουκ' signum 🖿 ‖ ουκ' ‖ ζωοντ[:
ω ex ο corr.

3
'Encomium of the Homeric poems

May you live forever, Homer: your time will never perish. You are the author
of a book so melodious [...],|³⁵ which contains so completely [...] a book of
profound wisdom that lives on and on¹² [...]|⁴⁰ and contains truths for repeat-
ing, which pronounces everywhere [...] eloquent among the best [...] I have
brought [...] and I have taken a powerful oath. |⁴⁵ Heaven [...] the shining disk
of the moon. For all the [...] stars are heroes [...] from which lineage I/they
hold an existence that is firm and untroubled. The singers of hymns, poor
connoisseurs of poetry [...]|⁵⁰ so much of virtue [...] desired and inimitable
Homer [...].'

32   τὰ Ὁμήρια: on how to understand this expression, see below, pp. 122–123.
33   Ζώοις αἰέν = Dioscoros, *P.Aphrod.Lit.* IV 11, 51 (same position). Cf. also 6, 21;
      7, 19; 10, 39; 14, 42; 18, 53; 20, 12; 30, 3 (ἀεὶ ζώοις); 22, 6 (‖ Ζώοις ἀλύπως).
      τεὸς χρόνος οὔ[ποτ' ὀλεῖται] = Dioscoros, *P.Aphrod.Lit.* IV 10, 36 (preceded
      by an imperative and by a vocative). Cf. also 6, 4; 9, 1 and 17, 26 (where
      the subject is τεὸν or τὸ σὸν κλέος, which would have been more suitable
      here). The clausula οὔ[ποτ' ὀλεῖται] is borrowed from Homer, *Il.* 11 325 and
      VII 91 and *Od.* XXIV 196, which was picked up by Hesiod, *Fr.* 70, 7.
34   βίβλον: see l. 27 n.
      πολύμολπον: very rare word (synonym of the no less rare πολυμελπής,
      Pollux, *On.* IV 67), which is first attested here (otherwise it occurs in
      John Geometres, *Poèmes en hexamètres et en distiques élégiaques*, ed. van
      Opstall 2008, poem 300, 51, on the subject of the swallow). Here the sense
      may be passive: 'very celebrated'.
35   παντοίως μεθέπουσαν: cf. l. 29 ([πα]ντοίων? μεθέπουσαν) and Dioscoros,
      P.Aphrod.Lit. IV 35, 4 (‖ παντοίης μεθέπεις).

---

12   It is not certain that this line belongs here.

36 [β]ίβλον ἀειζώο<υ>σαν: this is an echo of Paul the Silentiary, *Hagia Sophia*, 777–779 μῦθον ἀειζώοντα πιφαύσκων, | λαιῆι βίβλον ἔχων ζαθέων ἐπιίστορα μύθων, | βίβλον ἀπαγγέλλουσαν, ὅσα κτλ. (the beginning of 779 is identical to that of ll. 27–28—see also l. 13). On the substantive, see l. 27 n.

πυκινῆς σοφί[ης: cf. *Or. Sib.* 1, 91 (| καὶ πυκινὴ σοφίη). See also Dioscoros, *P.Aphrod.Lit.* IV 10, 35 (τὰ μήδεα πυκνὰ σοφίης |).

37 I do not understand why these two words are separated.

ῥήτρης: cf. Dioscoros, *P.Aphrod.Lit.* IV 4, 19 (Ῥήτρης εὐρυνόο[ι]ο δια- μπερὲς ἔμπλεος ἦσθα).

40 ἀμφιέπουσαν ἀληθέ[α μ]υθολογεύειν: Dioscoros has perhaps decided to use ἀμφιέπω with an infinitive in the sense of 'try to' ('a book trying to tell truths'). Note that elsewhere in his poems (*P.Aphrod.Lit.* IV 24, 26; 30, 4; 34, 9; 50, B 4), he uses it in the same position as here (except in 30, 4) but with an accusative, with the sense 'to have, benefit from' (see 30, 4 n.). That is the sense that I have kept in the translation. For the idea, see l. 28.

ἀμφιέπουσαν: the placing of the verb in this form is influenced by Nonnos, *D.* XLII 466 (| μούνην ἀμφιέπουσα μίαν Χάριν).

μ]υθολογεύειν: clausula going back to Homer, *Od.* XII 453.

43 πολύμυθον: same as in *Od.* II 200 and in Quintus Smyrnaeus XII 557.

44 This line is near to Dioscoros, *P.Aphrod.Lit.* IV 35, 3 (Σὸν μέλος ἀμφε- βόησε καὶ ὤμοσε καρτερὸν ὅρκον): ἀμφεβόησε has been replaced by ἀμ- φεκόμισσα while the second hemistich is almost identical. But I do not understand its sense in the context of the present poem.

ἀμφεκόμισσα: cf. Dioscoros, *P.Aphrod.Lit.* IV 32 A 10 (same position). Dioscoros provides the earliest occurrences of this verb (which is not a *hapax*, contrary to what I claimed at 32 A 10 n.: see *LGB, s.v.*), to which he seems to give a weakened sense.

ὤ]μοσα καρτερὸν ὅρκον: on this Homeric expression, see Dioscoros, *P.Aphrod.Lit.* IV 35, 3 n.

45–46 Is Homer here compared to a star? See, for example, Leonidas of Tarentum, *AP* IX 23; Alcaeus of Messina, *AP* VII 1; Antipater of Sidon, *AP* VII 6. For l. 45, see perhaps Philip, *AP* IX 575 (Οὐρανὸς ἄστρα τάχιον ἀποσβέσει ...| ... | ἢ ποτε Μαιονίδαο βαθυκλεὲς οὔνομ' Ὁμήρου | λήθη γηραλέων ἁρπάσεται σελίδων, 'Heaven will quench its stars ... before the glorious name of Homer of Maeonia falls prey to the oblivion of his ancient writings') or Antipater of Thessalonica, *APl.* 296, 7 (πάτρα σοι τελέθει μέγας οὐρανός, 'Your homeland, that is the great heaven'). These lines could also refer to a Homeric 'catasterism' (see, for example,

RETURNING TO THE WANDERING POETS 119

Renaud 2003). N. Zito (oral communication) asks whether l. 46 might be an allusion to the myth of the Dioscuroi (who are near-homonyms of Dioscoros!), about whom Homer says (*Od.* XI 304) that after their death they alternated stays in the underworld with stays in heaven (the catasterism is thus implicitly evoked) and whom certain later texts present as stars that come to the aid of mariners. So perhaps we should read κοῦροι at the beginning of l. 47. Finally, this passage could be praising the astronomical knowledge that Homer demonstrates.

45 οὐρανός: the usual position of this word in Nonnos (eight times out of nine).

[πολυ?]φεγγέα: one could also restore [εὐ]φεγγέα (cf. Nonnos, *D.* x 191: εὐφεγγεῖ κύκλῳ).

κύκλα σελήνης = Moschos, *Europa* 88; Leonidas of Tarentum, *AP* IX 24, 1; *Or. Sib.* IV 57; Dionysius Periegetes 720; Nonnos, *D.* XVI 163, XXII 353, XXIV 198, XXXVI 477, XXXVIII 34, XLI 410; *AP App.* III 120, 1 (always in the same position).

48 ἔμπεδον ἀστυφέλικτον ... βίον: cf. Gregory Nazianzenus, *Carmina de se ipso* II, 1, 567–568 ed. Tuilier and Bady (= *PG* XXXVII 1012, 8), βίον δ' ἐπὶ ἄλλον ἐπείγειν | ἔμπεδον, ἀστυφέλικτον. The sequence ἔμπεδον ἀστυφέλικτον at the beginning of the line is typical of Gregory: *Carmina de se ipso* II, 1, 18, 13; 2, 4, 125 and 2, 6, 11 (= *PG* XXXVII 1263, 1; 1515, 1; and 1543, 5). As for ἀστυφέλικτος, an adjective that Dioscoros was fond of (four other occurrences in his poems), cf. *P.Aphrod.Lit.* IV 10, 19 n.

βίον ἔσχον: cf. Theocritus, *Epigr.* VI 340, 3 (β. ἔσχε |).

49 ὑμνητῆρες: a rare word that appears in Alcman (*Fr.* 159, 1, ed. Page 1967), and then in Oppian, *Hal.* III 7 and Greg. Naz., *Carmina dogmatica* et *moralia* (*PG* XXXVII 452, 4; 515, 5; 529, 3 and 541, 14)—authors who never use the word at the beginning of a line.

νοήμονες εὐεπιάων: I understand νοήμων here as going with the genitive in the sense of 'connoisseur', which is a very rare construction (Lampe, *s.v.* 2, cites only Chrysippus of Jerusalem, *Encomium in Joannem Baptistam*, p. 37, 10–11, ed. Sigalas 1937: ὦ ἔρημος ἡ νοήμονας τῶν θείων καὶ ἐπουρανίων μυστηρίων τοὺς ἀνθρώπους ἐκδιδάσκουσα). Elsewhere Dioscoros uses the term in its classical sense (*P.Aphrod.Lit.* IV 11, 30).

εὐεπιάων: same form in the same position in Dioscoros, *P.Aphrod. Lit.* IV 11, 27. This genitive plural is typical of late poetry (Heitsch 1963, XXXIV (*Encomium Heraclii ducis*) 33; Christodoros, *AP* II 407; John of Gaza, *Ekphrasis* 39 (ἐγκύμονες εὐεπιάων) and 100; Claudian (on this post-Nonnian Claudian, cf. Alan Cameron 1970, 11–12), *AP* I 28, 1—at the end of the line in every case). On 'poetry', more specifically epic, as the

120   FOURNET

meaning of εὐεπίη, cf. John of Gaza, *Ekphrasis* 39 n., ed. Lauritzen 2015, 74, and Magnelli 2004, 272n15.

50   τοσσατίην ἀρετήν = Dioscoros, *P.Aphrod.Lit.* IV 5, 14; 14, 40; 18, 36 (and in another case, 36, 16). On τοσσάτιος, cf. *P.Aphrod.Lit.* IV 5, 14 n.

κεχαρισμένην: the metrical position of this participle goes back to Homer, *Od.* XVI 184 and XIX 397 (the poet usually uses it in a different position), and see also Nonnos, *Par.* XIX 51. For the last syllable treated as short, see l. 22 n.

51   ἱμερόεις = Dioscoros, *P.Aphrod.Lit.* IV 13, 11 (also in 35, 10 in a different case, and in 35, 12–13 in a different position). This Homeric term (*Od.* X 398) is a particular favourite of Nonnos, who uses it eight times in the same position, and is followed notably by Musaeus, 20.

ἀμίμητος: this term first appears in poetry with Nonnos (*Par.* IX 114; X 149; *D.* VIII 265; XXIX 200; XXXVI 412; XLIII 402). Dioscoros only uses it elsewhere in his trimeters (*P.Aphrod.Lit.* IV 11, 19 ; 25 B 3).

2   Date

The writing of Poems 1 and 2, framed by two dated documents, is thus situated between 28 October and 12 November 569. Poem 3 should belong to the same time or be later than 12 November. If it is later, it cannot be by much, given the commonality of content and form it shares with 1 and 2.[13] These poems date in any case from the period when Dioscoros had left Aphrodite and was staying in the provincial capital of the Thebaid, Antinoopolis, where he practised the profession of notary (from the end of 565 or the beginning of 566 until 15 November 570 or 573).[14] It is unusual that we can date the composition of a literary work and put it in its original milieu so precisely. We shall see later how much a contextual analysis can bring to the understanding of this text.

3   Genre and Subjects

But precisely what kind of text are we dealing with here? We have two types of poem, all written in dactylic hexameters: the first two (1 and 2) belong to the genre of ethopoia, a speech put in the mouth of an individual that was considered to be appropriate to his character (*ēthos*), personality, and

---

13   See further, pp. 124–125.
14   Cf. Fournet 1999, 1:321.

RETURNING TO THE WANDERING POETS 121

situation.[15] Both have the same title, beginning with a formula typical of ethopoiai:[16] Τίνας ἂν εἴπῃ (l. εἴποι) λόγους Ὅμηρος παρακαλῶν τὴν Θέτιν ἔνοπλον δεῖξαι αὐτῷ τὸν Ἀχιλλέα; ('What words would Homer use when asking Thetis to show him Achilles in arms?'). We have to do here with a completely unique poetic subject: an ethopoia that not only bases itself on a Homeric subject, like so many others (I shall return to this point), but whose speaker is the poet himself. In the vast repertory of ethopoiai known in Greek and Latin down to the thirteenth and fourteeth centuries (more than 270), there are no others that make Homer the speaker.[17] To date we only have an ethopoia of Hesiod contained in a papyrus of the end of the third or the beginning of the fourth century,[18] but the fact that Hesiod introduces himself at the beginning of the *Theogony* might justify making him speak in an ethopoia. Otherwise I only know one other ethopoia in which an author is made to speak, namely Aeschines in the work of another Egyptian writer, Theodore of Cynopolis (5th–6th c.);[19] there too we have to do with an author who is in the habit of speaking in the first person and whose historical role made him a potential subject for an ethopoia. But the mysteriousness of the figure of Homer, an author who does not reveal himself in his work, did not make him a natural subject for an ethopoia. In fact, if numerous ethopoiai are put in the mouths of characters in the *Iliad*, and to a lesser extent of those in the *Odyssey*, and if, more rarely, Homer could be the subject of one,[20] our two ethopoiai are the only ones to have attempted to make Homer speak.[21] More astonishing still, Homer finds himself projected into his work and speaks to his own characters, specifically Thetis[22] (after she had provided Achilles with new arms forged by Hephaistos when the hero decided to return to the fight after the death of

---

15   On this genre, see Amato and Schamp 2005.

16   On this formulaic title, see Fournet 1992, 255.

17   See the exhaustive list of ethopoiai provided by Amato and Ventrella 2005.

18   *P.Oxy.* L 3537 (Mertens-Pack³ 1857.320; TM64335). On this piece, see Agosti 1997 and Jarcho 1999.

19   Ed. Schissel 1929–1930. Cf. Amato and Ventrella 2005, 217n14.

20   Thus *AP* IX 455 (Τίνας ἂν εἴποι λόγους Ἀπόλλων περὶ Ὁμήρου;).

21   Was Dioscoros innovating? It is difficult to say. Certainly his poetical work is not characterized by its originality and it is possible that he was using a framework that others had exploited without leaving us any trace. But Dioscoros' 'Homeromania', which I shall come back to later, seems to me to account for these pieces and their atypical character.

22   That was no accident: Thetis was considered, in spite of her secondary role, as an emblematic character in the *Iliad*, if at least we believe Alcaeus of Messenia, *AP* VII 1, 5–6, who presents the *Iliad* as the 'glorification of Thetis, her son and the combats of other heroes' (Θέτιν κύδηνε καὶ υἱέα καὶ μόθον ἄλλων | ἡρώων).

Patroclus),[23] with Dioscoros abolishing all distance between the author's present and the past of the story. To crown everything, Homer 'does a Homer', since his words are a rhapsody of Homeric syntagmas.[24]

Poem 3 belongs to another genre. Its title, Εἰς τὰ Ὁμήρια, is susceptible to several interpretations. I originally asked myself whether τὰ Ὁμήρια might refer to a festival in honour of Homer.[25] For a long time the poet was the subject of festivals, sometimes in the framework of a cult and sometimes not,[26] in which, notably at Oxyrhynchos in the second and third centuries, spectacles were organized based on episodes in the Homeric poems, acted by Homerists (ὁμηρισταί).[27] If a cult of Homer was obviously impossible at the time of Dioscoros, festivals in honour of the Poet at which there were Homeric recitations or poetry competitions are readily imaginable. It so happens that we have proof of the existence of such a festival, known precisely as Ὁμήρια, thanks to a papyrus of unknown provenance dating from the beginning of the fourth century.[28] But we are two-and-a-half centuries later, and nothing proves the existence of such events in the second half of the sixth century.[29] In the absence of proof of the survival of this festival, I think that it is more reasonable to take τὰ Ὁμήρια to mean 'Homeric poems', understanding the word ἔπη (literally 'Homeric lines') or, at a pinch, ποιήματα.[30] The εἰς at the beginning, in

---

23 Il. XVIII.

24 See the notes to ll. 8, 10, 11, 13, 14, 24, 33, 40, 43, 44, 50, 51. Homerisms certainly form part of the 'epic code' conventional in hexameter epigrams, but here they are doubly motivated and invested with a strong significance because it is Homer who speaks and because his words come from a Homeric cento. Dioscoros makes use of intertextuality: thus l. 22, δῖα θεάων was used by Homer on the subjet of Thetis; l. 23, ἔρνος is used by Thetis on the subject of Achilles. Dioscoros reaches the point of saturating his verse with Homerism by putting together various Homeric expressions: see l. 31 n. on the subject of ἔριδος κακομηχάνου Τυνδαρεώνης. On the different levels of 'Homericity', see Agosti 2017, 237–241. Even Dioscoros' metrical mistakes can be explained by a Homeric influence (see l. 22 n.).

25 The expression Εἰς τὰ Ὁμήρια makes one think, mutatis mutandis, of the title of P.Aphrod. Lit. IV 21–22: Ἐγκώμια δι᾽ ἰάμβων ἤτοι ἰαμβεῖα εἰς τὰ γενέσια Κωσταντίνου διοικητοῦ (Enkōmia or iambeia for the birthday of Kōstantinos the diœcētēs).

26 At Alexandria, cf. Visser 1938, 41 (on the subject of Aelian, Varia Historia, XIII 22); and Petrovic 2017.

27 Husson 1993; Hillgruber 2000, 2001.

28 SPP XX 85 (provenance unknown, date certainly 320/321 [BL VIII 466]): τῷ [α]ὐτῷ ἐν ἑορτῇ Ὁμηρίων κν(ίδια) κ.

29 Rita Lizzi suggests to me that we may have to do here, more modestly, with school contests. The hypothesis is interesting, but for the moment it is not supported by any document from Byzantine Egypt. I found no trace of the use of this adjective to refer to these certamina in Egypt.

30 For Ὁμήρεια ἔπη, cf. Herodotus V 67, as well as Eudocia, Homerocentones, apol. 17, or APl. 125, 3. For Ὁμήρεια ποιήματα, cf. Phrynichos, Praeparatio sophistica, ed. J. de Borries,

RETURNING TO THE WANDERING POETS

the sense of 'in honour of', is typical of eulogies.[31] So we have here an *enkōmion* of Homer's work.

4 The Poet at Work

Thus this papyrus offers us three compositions celebrating Homer and his work. If they are interesting for the reception and perception of Homer in early Byzantine times (I return later to this), they also provide the most eloquent testimony of ancient poetical autographs that has come down to us. Our roll allows us in fact to follow the poet's process of composition as if we were looking over his shoulder while he was writing. I shall not elaborate on the 'corrections' that Dioscoros makes between the lines[32] or on the additions in the margins:[33] this sort of thing one encounters in Dioscoros' other poems.[34] I merely point out that the first line of Poem 2 (l. 22: Δεῖξον ἐμοὶ σέθεν υἷα κτλ.) seems to have given Dioscoros some difficulty: it is repeated three times above poem 1 (ll. 2–4)—unfortunately the state of the papyrus does not allow us to follow the work of reformulation.[35]

More interesting is the relationship between the three compositions, and what we can learn from this about Dioscoros' creative processes. I mentioned that the two ethopoiai have the same title: one may ask whether Dioscoros tried to compose two ethopoiai on the same subject, or whether, dissatisfied with the first version, he decided on a second. We only have a single example of a poem he wrote in two versions:[36] a eulogy of a *dux* that has come down to us in two versions, on two different papyri, each corresponding to a stage of composition, but where, leaving aside the order of the lines, the poetic material is fairly similar in the two versions. The same cannot be said of our two ethopoiai; we are dealing with two very different poems, apart from some similarities:

    Fr. 33* (ἁμαρτάνουσιν οὖν οἱ λέγοντες Ὁμηρικὸν ποίημα. Ὁμήρειον γὰρ δεῖ λέγειν). On the term Ὁμήρειος, see Garulli 2017, 141–149, 152–154.

31   Cf., in Dioscoros, the titles of *P.Aphrod.Lit.* IV 4, 7, 8, 9, 14, 15, 21 and 32.

32   Lines 12, 14, 50.

33   Line 52.

34   See Fournet 1999, 1:291–297.

35   One can ask why this line, which should have introduced Poem 2, was worked on in another location. I think that Dioscoros took advantage of the *vacat* at the top of the roll to work up the line before writing the definitive version in the correct place (l. 22).

36   *P.Aphrod.Lit.* IV 18 and *P.Bagnall* 26. On literary 'autographs' in general see the bibliography given in *P.Bagnall*, p. 100 n. 14.

·1, l. 12 : ὡς κεν ἐνὶ γραφίδεσσιν Ἀχιλλῆα φῶτα (ex ὁμοίϊον ἄνδρα corr.) χαράττω ≈ 2, l. 25 : πάντοθεν ἀμφιβόητον ἐνὶ γραφίδεσσι χαράττω

·1, l. 13 : βίβλοις ἀπαγγέλλουσιν ἐμοῖς πολεμήϊα ἔργα ≈ 2, l. 27 : β[ί]β[λον] ἀ[παγγέλ]-λουσαν? ἅπερ τελέεσκεν . . . .(..)

But no line is repeated exactly. It is thus probable that Dioscoros tried to write two texts on the same subject in the manner of companion pieces or *Konkurrenzgedichte*, according to a tradition that goes back to archaic times and in virtue of which the same author composed several epigrams on the same subject, to show his skill at *variatio* and his poetic virtuosity.[37] The phenomenon intensified in Late Antiquity as we can see in the epigraphic epigrams.[38] An earlier papyrological example can be seen in the two epitaphs commissioned by Zeno from a local poet to commemorate the death of his dog Taurōn:[39] one is in hexameters, the second, introduced by ἄλλο, 'another poem', is in elegiac distichs. But by contrast with these two epitaphs, it is not the difference of metres that justifies Dioscoros' having 'doubled' his poem: how could he have honoured Homer except in hexameters? He probably tried to handle his subject in different ways for reasons I shall come back to when I examine the purpose of these pieces.

As for Poem 3, the eulogy of the Homeric poems, we notice some cross-references when we get to the second ethopoia:

2, ll. 27–30 :
  β[ί]β[λον] ἀ[παγγέλ]λουσαν? ἅπερ τελέεσκεν....(..)
  [βίβλον] ἀπαγγέλλουσαν ἀληθέα πᾶσιν ὀπά[σσ]ω
  [πα]ντοίων? μεθέπουσαν ἀμετρήτων ἀρετάων

can be compared with

3, ll. 34–36 :
  βίβλον ἔχεις πολύμολπον ος.[
  παντοίως μεθέπουσαν ...[
  [β]ίβλον ἀειζωο<υ>σαν .(.) πυκίνης σοφί[ης ⌣]

---

37 Cf. Fantuzzi 2010.
38 Cf. Robert 1948, 81–82, and Agosti 2015b, 60–61, who takes a particular interest in the way in which these duplicates were arranged on the stone.
39 *P.Cair.Zen.* IV 59532 (Mertens-Pack³ 1761; TM 65682) = *SB* III 6754; *SP* III 109; *Supplementum hellenisticum* 9977. Cf., most recently, Pepper 2010.

RETURNING TO THE WANDERING POETS

and with 3, ll. 40–41:

εἴσ[ω]ʼ τʼ ἀμφιέπουσαν ἀληθέ[α μ]υθολογεύειν,
πάντοθεν ἀ[γ]γέλλουσαν....τη....εγος..

From one poem to the next we find the same formulations. I incline to think that the second ethopoia, notably the evocation of the Homeric poems by Homer himself, gave Dioscoros the idea of composing a third piece of a different kind, entirely dedicated to these poems. And it is not impossible that Dioscoros had sketched this poem before the writing of the Greek document that preceeds it (5), turning the roll upside down and starting writing from the other end, perhaps to compose at a same time as the second ethopoia a poem on a similar subject.

5   Why These Texts?

The fundamental question which now has to be asked is the purpose of these texts, which contrast sharply with Dioscoros' other poetical production. That consists mainly of poems 'de circonstance' addressed to notable persons who could help him. Homer could do nothing for him! Why then make the effort to write these epigrams on such an untimely subject?

The genres to which our three poems belong offer us the beginning of an answer: the ethopoia and the eulogy are two of those roughly twelve προγυμνάσματα or 'preparatory rhetorical exercises',[40] the list of which partly stabilizes with Theon (first century) and which were to constitute for centuries the framework for the teaching of rhetoric.[41] Thus they have an eminently educational value that the treatises on rhetoric emphasized and which emphatically conditioned the literary production of imperial and late antique times. Ethopoia, regarded by some as one of the 'most perfect *progymnasmata*',[42] is without any doubt the one that has left the greatest quantity of evidence in the papyri—an indication of the central place it occupied in the pedagogical system of those times.[43] The two ethopoiai of Homer are not the only ones we have from Dioscoros; we have four others:

---

40   Fable, story, saying, maxim, protest/confirmation, commonplace, eulogy/reprimand, parallel, ethopoia, description, thesis, law proposal.

41   These two exercises are combined elsewhere in the papyri: cf. *P.Oxy.* L 3537 (cited in n. 18) and the Codex of Visions in *P.Bodmer* XXX–XXXVIII (see Fournet 1991, 264).

42   Τῶν τελεωτέρων προγυμνασμάτων ἐστὶ καὶ ἡ ἠθοποιΐα (*Schol. ad Aphthonium*, ed. Walz, *Rhet. Graec.* I, p. 52, 2–3).

43   Cf. Amato and Schamp 2005.

P.Aphrod.Lit. IV 41: ethopoia of Apollo: '<What words would be used> by Apollo after Hyacinth and Daphne had been changed into plants?' [hexameters]

P.Aphrod.Lit. IV 42: ethopoia of Achilles: 'What words would Achilles use when dying because of Polyxena ?' [hexameters]

P.Aphrod.Lit. IV 43: ethopoia on the death of Achilles (title partly lost) [hexameters]

P.Aphrod.Lit. IV 46: ethopoia of Polyxena (no title) [hexameters]

Certainly, in so far as the poets of late antiquity used the 'progymnastic' genres as the framework for a new poetic independently of their primary educational function, the ethopoiai of Dioscoros can also be considered as poems independent of their educational function, governed by the principle of *art pour l'art*. In the list of ethopoiai down to the fourteenth century, Eugenio Amato and Gianluca Ventrella classified those of Dioscoros as 'literary ethopoiai', while the others that have survived on papyrus are considered to be 'éthopées scolaires', 'school ethopoiai'.[44] This distinction, which seems artificial to me in that the distinction between a school exercise and a literary composition is difficult to put into practice,[45] has a good chance, in the case of Dioscoros, of being mistaken. I am now persuaded that the ethopoiai of Dioscoros constitute one indication among many that Dioscoros took on the functions of a teacher with a number of students. I do not have the time here to develop my argumentation or to give an account of the crucial evidence; I do this in a recent article.[46] Let it be sufficient to say that the ethopoiai of Dioscoros take on another sense besides other texts from his library such as the actual school texts written by students (conjugation tables, metrological tables), pedagogical models in Dioscoros' hand (a glossary, metrological tables, a *Life of Isocrates*, a didactic poem from the *Palatine Anthology* on the ancient Greek games), as well as non-school works that had an educational role (copies of the *Iliad* and of scholia on that work, stuffed with glosses). It is difficult not to see these ethopoiai as poems composed by Dioscoros for his pupils, to teach them rhetoric—or more exactly poetical rhetoric—at the same time as the language of Homer, as well as some mythology and mythical history. They could even

---

44 Cf. Amato and Ventrella 2005, 217–218 for Dioscoros and 223–225 for the other ethopoiai on papyrus. They agree with the position that I developed in my study of the ethopoia (Fournet 1992, 263). But there (263n61) I raised the possibility that these texts belong in a school setting, a hypothesis that I repeated in Fournet 1999, 2: 688–690, and developed recently in Fournet 2019, 210–213.

45 See Agosti 2005, 39–45.

46 Fournet 2019.

RETURNING TO THE WANDERING POETS

be corrections to exercises that Dioscoros had set for his pupils. In the present case, the fact that the same subject is treated twice is explicable by the educational nature of these texts.

The pupils in question could have been his children. The poems were written at Antinoopolis at a time when his son Peter was receiving training there from the accountant (*psēphistēs*) of the public school of Antinoopolis, as is attested by an unpublished document in Berlin (P.Berol. inv. 25715) and another badly published one in London (*P.Lond.* v 1706).[47] We do not know whether his other children (Victor, Theodosia, etc.)[48] were then at the right age to benefit from his teaching. Dioscoros may also have had paying pupils, but we have no evidence of that.

6   Over-Homerizing Ethopoiai

It will have been noticed that, with one exception (*P.Aphrod.Lit.* IV 41), Dioscoros' ethopoiai all centre on the main figure in the *Iliad*, Achilles, even though the situations are not always borrowed directly from the *Iliad*.[49] Thus they perfectly reflect not only the place of the figure of Homer in the Greek epigram,[50] but above all his almost exclusive place in Greek teaching.[51] They constitute an ideal complement to the study of the Homeric poem itself as carried on by Dioscoros with his pupils, which is attested by the corrections and glosses in the copies of the *Iliad* and the scholia on the *Iliad* that Dioscoros owned. They form part of a real school poetic that developed in late antiquity, of which the poet-*grammatikos* (or -*grammatistēs*) is the emblematic figure.[52]

The two new ethopoiai, with their 'over-Homerizing' tone, which adds something to the other Dioscoros ethopoiai (Homeric subject, with in addition Homer as a speaker who cites himself), are a new testimony to the hegemonic

---

47   See Fournet 2009, 118–119.

48   They were of an age to rent a piece of land in 580 (*SB* XXII 15522, to which we should join P.Cair. inv. SR 3733 (23a and b)).

49   On the Alexandrian legend of the love affair of Achilles and Polyxena, which was very popular in early Byzantium, Fournet 1999, 2:652.

50   See the classic study of Skiadas 1965; and more recently Pralon 2017 and Hunter 2018, 4–24.

51   With regard to the immense bibliography on the place of Homer in schools, beyond the classic study of Verdenius 1970, completed for the imperial period by Ibrahim 1976–1977 and, more specifically for Egypt by Davison 1956, I simply refer to a few recent studies: Cribiore 1994, 2001, p. 194–197, 204–205, 226; Hock 2001; Díaz Lavado 2007; Sandnes 2009.

52   See the numerous examples given by Alan Cameron 1965 (reprinted in Alan Cameron 1985, 1; and recently revised in Alan Cameron 2016b, ch. 1).

128 FOURNET

place that Homer occupied in the inspiration of the writers of ethopoiai.[53] This is well exemplified by the ethopoiai preserved in papyri,[54] the ones in *Palatine Anthology* IX 449–480,[55] and those in prose in Libanius.[56] The reasons are mostly these:

(1) Homer was himself considered a reservoir of ethopoiai since about half of his poems are in direct speech. And because of his art of characterization, which is brought out by Aristotle (*Poetics* 1460 a 9–11), Homer was considered the ideal model for authors of ethopoiai, as the rhetoricians point out, endlessly indicating the ethopoiai in his work that correspond to their typologies.[57]

(2) Homer was the poet par excellence. The ethopoia was a *progymnasma* considered by the ancients to be one of the most useful for learning to write poems,[58] and in consequence it became a genre that was practised in verse. Homer provided his metre, his lexicon, his characters and his situations.[59]

(3) Homer was also regarded as a model orator.[60] Hermogenes for example considers him not only the best of poets but also the best orator and the best *logographos*.[61] The ethopoia is a preparatory exercise for rhetoric and was considered one of the most formative ones because, according to the fifth-century orator Nicolaos, it contributes to all branches of eloquence (encomiastic, judicial, and deliberative), not to mention the art of letter writing.[62] So Homer was essential for the practice of oratory.

---

53 See Ureña Bracero 1999.

54 See Fournet 1992, 261.

55 A fairly coherent series, later than the mid-fifth century (Wifstrand 1933, 170), 'many if not all' of which 'come from the same hand, or at any rate from the same school' (Alan Cameron 1967c, 60).

56 Webb 2010. For the *progymnasmata* of Libanius, see Gibson 2008. For the attribution to Libanius, besides Gibson, p. XXIII–XXV, see Ureña Bracero 2007.

57 Ureña Bracero 1999, 319–320; Robert 2015, 79–80.

58 E.g. Quintilian, *Inst.* III 8, 49: 'utilissimum vero haec the exercitatio vel quod duplicis est operis, vel quod poetis quoque (…) plurimum confert' (this exercise is very useful, whether because it demands a double effort, or because it is also very advantageous to the poets too).

59 On the relationship between ethopoia and poetry, see Viljamaa 1968, 17–18, 116–124; and especially Agosti 2005.

60 See Knudsen 2014. For the Byzantine period, see especially Browning 1992, 135–136.

61 Hermogenes, Περὶ ἰδεῶν λόγου, ed. Rabe (1913), 389, 21–27: τοῦτ' ἂν ῞Ομηρος εἴη κατὰ τὴν ποίησιν, ἣν δὴ πανηγυρικὸν λόγον ἐν μέτρῳ λέγων εἶναί τις οὐκ οἶμαι εἰ διαμαρτήσεται, ἐπεὶ κἀνταῦθα ὁμοίως ἀναστρέφει τὸ πρᾶγμα, καθάπερ ἀνέστρεφεν ἐπ' ἀμφοῖν κἀκεῖ· ἀρίστη τε γὰρ ποιήσεων ἡ Ὁμήρου, καὶ ῞Ομηρος ποιητῶν ἄριστος, φαίην δ' ἂν ὅτι καὶ ῥητόρων καὶ λογογράφων, λέγω δ' ἴσως ταὐτόν.

62 Thus Nicolaos, *Progymnasmata*, ed. Felten (1913), 66, 16–67, 9: ῎Εστι δὲ καὶ τοῦτο τὸ προγύμνασμα πρὸς τὰ τρία εἴδη τῆς ῥητορικῆς χρήσιμον· καὶ γὰρ καὶ ἐγκωμιάζοντες καὶ κατηγοροῦντες

RETURNING TO THE WANDERING POETS

In short, everything combined to link the Homeric poems and the ethopoia closely together, to the point that, in spite of Christianity and its impact on written culture in general and on poetry in particular, there was a deliberate choice not to cut the ethopoia off from its Homeric cultural reference in order to Christianize it.[63] It can in fact seem strange that, with the exception of two ethopoiai with Old Testament subjects in the Codex of Visions in the Bodmer collection (5th c.)[64] and nine ethopoiai with Old and New Testament subjects in the Book of Chreia (Girk' Pitoyic') preserved in Armenian but very probably going back to a Greek model of the fifth century,[65] we have to wait till the twelfth century before the ethopoia addresses Christian subjects. But all this is due to the fact that teachers very soon gave up on the synthesis that certain poets had attempted in the fourth and fifth centuries by putting biblical subjects into Homeric dress.[66] As the historian Socrates explains very well with regard to the efforts of the Apollinares, which he considers to be useless, the art of reasoning is not taught by Scripture but exclusively by Greek *paideia*.[67] So it is better to separate the two and educate oneself in both in parallel rather than attempting an empty synthesis that could only result in a reciprocal emasculation. Christianizing the *progymnasmata* made no more sense than putting the Gospels into Homeric verse. So education continued to be based on Homer, as a model of poetry and rhetoric, at the risk of a kind of cultural sclerosis that bridled imagination and paralysed originality.[68] Dioscoros, like the rest, submitted to the dictate of 'all-Homer'; but he went much further.

καὶ συμβουλεύοντες ἠθοποιιῶν πολλάκις δεόμεθα· ἐμοὶ δὲ δοκεῖ καὶ πρὸς τὸν ἐπιστολικὸν ἡμᾶς γυμνάζειν χαρακτῆρα, εἴ γε καὶ ἐν ἐκείνῳ δεῖ τοῦ ἤθους τῶν τε ἐπιστελλόντων καὶ πρὸς οὓς ἐπιστέλλουσι ποιεῖσθαι πρόνοιαν. αὐτὸ δὲ τὸ ἐπιστολικὸν εἴτε ὑφ' ἓν τούτων τῶν τριῶν ἀνάγεται εἴτε ὑφ' ἕτερον, οὐ τοῦ νῦν ἐστι καιροῦ σκοπεῖν, ἄλλως τε ἐπειδὴ καὶ περὶ αὐτῶν ἐν τοῖς περὶ ἐγκωμίων ἀρκούντως ὡς πρὸς εἰσαγωγὴν ἐλέχθη.

63 Fournet 2020.

64 *P.Bodm.* XXXIII, fol. 21ʳ, 17–39: τί ἂν εἴποι ὁ Καιν ἀποκτείνας τὸ[ν Ἀβηλ;] ('What words would Cain have spoken after killing Abel?'); and XXXV, fol. 21ᵛ, 32-fol. 23ʳ, 2: τ[ί ἂν εἴπ]οι ὁ Αβελ ἀναιρηθεὶς ὑπὸ τοῦ Καιν ('What words would Abel have spoken after being killed by Cain?').

65 Fournet 2020, 80–82.

66 Besides the paraphrases of the Old and New Testaments that Apollinaris, father and son, are supposed to have written in Homeric, tragic, comic, and Pindaric verse (Socrates, *HE* III 16, 3–5, and Sozomen, *HE* V 18, 3–4; see Agosti 2001) and the ethopoiai in *P.Bodm.* just referred to, one can cite the *Paraphrase of the Gospel of John* of Nonnos (ca. 440–450), the *Paraphrase of the Psalms* of Pseudo-Apollinaris (ca. 460), the *Homeric Centones* of Eudocia (ca. 440–460), not to mention hagiographies in hexameters such as the *De Sancto Cypriano* by Eudocia, the lost *patria* by Theodorus of Alexandria (Fournet 2003) or the *Life and Martyrdom of Saint Thecla* by Basil of Seleuceia, known only from Photius (see Fournet 2003, 532n49).

67 Socrates, *HE* III 16, 7; 17–18.

68 See Robert 2015, 80: 'Quoique la personne d'Homère fût ainsi vénérée et encensée, son texte n'en était pas pour autant figé dans un respect sclérosant, annihilant toute velléité

7 Dioscoros Homer-mad?

His dossier testifies in fact to the invasive presence of Homer in every area of written culture, not only the educational and the literary, but the quotidian as well. Dioscoros adapted Homerism to every form of writing. I will not enlarge on the subject because I have dealt with it elsewhere.[69] It will be enough to summarize the facts:

- Homer was present in his library in the form of a codex containing the *Iliad* and another containing *scholia ad Iliadem*, with which he must have educated himself and which he used in turn in his teaching.[70]
- Homer is the author who most influenced his poems.[71] Dioscoros even cites him by name as a model of eloquence in general.[72]
- Homer was one of the criteria of selection according to which Dioscoros constructed a little anthology of documents (one petition and three letters) which could be useful to him in his own writing: the two letters that have been preserved (the third is damaged and unpublished) have in common that they contain a Homeric citation.[73] Homer is an ornament that the letter-writer cannot do without.
- Not only the letter writer, but also the writer of petitions, another genre very much practised by Dioscoros: Homer appears a number of times in Dioscoros' petitions, in citations, syntagmas, and echoes.[74]

---

de création ou tout effort d'imagination. De fait, les poèmes homériques étaient perçus comme un entrelacement d'épisodes, de thèmes, que rhéteurs et étudiants pouvaient à loisir reprendre : ils avaient toute licence de jouer avec le texte homérique, de s'en inspirer, de le considérer comme un matériau de travail. Comme référent culturel fondamental, les poèmes homériques étaient parfaitement connus des étudiants, c'est pourquoi il était intéressant de s'appuyer sur eux pour les sujets d'exercice : la signification des situations ou des personnages prélevés devait leur apparaître immédiatement. Les rhéteurs envisageaient donc les textes homériques comme un vivier de formules, d'histoires, de passages remarquables, permettant de s'entraîner à développer une virtuosité oratoire, mais n'en fournissant pas un modèle à proprement parler.' This Homerism was so omnipresent that it became insipid and quasi-mechanical, to the point that Palladas mocked it in his epigrams (see, for example, Alan Cameron 1967c and the note to *Anthologia Graeca* IX 395 (VIII, p. 193 in the Budé edition)).

69 Fournet 1995, 2012, 146–150.
70 *P.Aphrod.Lit.* I and II. See Fournet 1995, 302–306; 2019, 203–206.
71 See Fournet 1995, 306–310; 1999, 1:298–303; 1999, 2:673–676.
72 *P.Aphrod.Lit.* IV 4, 22. See also 6, 11 and 9, 4 (on these passages see Livrea 2001), where, according to the procedure of the lop-sided *synkrisis*, Homer seems to serve as a supporting character for the recipient of the poem.
73 *P.Cair.Masp.* III 67295, III, 2–3 and 28. See Fournet 2012, 142–144, 147.
74 Fournet 2012, 144–148.

RETURNING TO THE WANDERING POETS

Certainly all this corresponds quite well with the cultural tendencies at work in late antique prose, which was marked both by a recovery of Atticism and by an infatuation with a sophistic, archaic, and poetic lexicon.[75] Dioscoros' archive contains documents written by people other than Dioscoros that attest to the impact of Homer on the lexicon.[76] But Dioscoros seems to me to testify to an influence of Homer that, because of its outrageous and untimely nature, goes beyond the aesthetic canons of the period. I will simply give three examples:

(1) The first is the division of an inheritance that is not in Dioscoros' hand but which I think he helped to draw up (*P.Cair.Masp.* III 67313):[77] here we encounter the Homeric word αὐτοκασίγνητος to designate the banal term 'brother'.[78] The word is of course unknown in the papyri and is not attested, to my knowledge, in the prose literature (except when there is a reference to Homeric usage). It is hard to understand the use of this term, which adds nothing whatsoever, in a genre of document that, unlike a petition, has no use for *pathos* or rhetoric.

(2) In the same document, we meet the very curious adjective, similar to the one in Poem 3, line 30, πανάεθλος, 'who has endured everything', denoting the eponymous martyr of a church.[79] This term derives from the Homeric word ἄεθλος 'ordeal' (Attic ἆθλος), used here in place of ἄεθλιος ('struggling, enduring hardships'). This is not a *lapsus calami* because the expression is attested two other times, both in the archive of Dioscoros, one of them in his own hand.[80] That is what according to me confirms that the text of this division of an inheritance was indeed devised by Dioscoros even though it was not written by him.

---

75 For the development of a poetic lexicon in the documentary papyri, Zilliacus 1967, 71–83.

76 I gave an example in Fournet 2012, 149–150, namely λήϊα, a Homeric term that one meets in an affidavit written by someone other than Dioscoros and in various authors such as John Chrysostom.

77 This is a notarized document very probably drawn up in the *statio* where Dioscoros worked at Antinoopolis. Parallels such as *P.Cair.Masp.* II 67151–67152 show that Dioscoros drafted a first version that was then copied out neatly by another person. See also *P.Cair. Masp.* III 67315 (in the hand of Dioscoros) next to II 67156–67157 (both in another hand, but with additions by Dioscoros). Work on these *duplicata* in Dioscoros' archive remains to be done.

78 L. 64–65: καὶ προσεπὶ τούτοις λελογχέναι | ὁ[μοίως πρόσωπ]α δύο αὐτοκασίγνητα.

79 L. 55: ἐκκλησίας τοῦ παναέθλου μάρτυρος Ἄπα Θεοδώρου.

80 *P.Cair.Masp.* II 67162, 8 (Antinoopolis, 568), loan contract in the hand of Dioscoros: πανσέπτου Θεοῦ οἴκου τοῦ [πα]ναέθλου μάρτυρος ἄπα Βίκτορο\ς/; *SB* XVIII 13298ᵛ, 1–2 (Antinoopolis, 556–570), loan contract:] τοῦ παναέθλου | [μάρτυρος.

(3) In another division of an inheritance, this time in his own hand, Dioscoros uses in a banal expression the Ionian form of the word ὄνομα (used by Homer), which is entirely inappropriate.[81] Here too nothing motivates the recourse to this form in such an anodyne document and in such a hackneyed expression.

We are dealing here with unmotivated, forced, parasitic Homerisms which, in my view, are part of a phenomenon that has not so far been looked at closely enough and is totally separate from the Homerizing practices of the educated milieux of Late Antiquity. You almost have the impression that these Homerisms are stylistic slips of the pen due to a sort of uncontrolled 'Homeromania' and that they are the result of a failure to appreciate and distinguish different linguistic registers or to gauge the stylistic differences that normal practice required. Dioscoros knew Homer well, and that it was *de bon ton* to Homerize, but he did not always understand when to do it and when he was over-stepping the conventionally imposed limits. In fact, his Homerizing excesses paradoxically could be evidence of imperfect linguistic knowledge. In that respect it is good evidence of the limits of a Copt's Hellenism, notwithstanding his high level of education.

His 'Homeromania' is sometimes involuntary or untimely, but its excesses remain nonetheless a sign of the strong desire on the part of these Coptophone élites to participate fully in Byzantine Hellenism, to be part of the culture of the Empire. Their Egyptian origins and their distance from the centre of power only accentuated their determination to be in line with this common culture—a determination which could sometimes translate into excesses or clumsiness.

This is what seems to me to be the cultural background of Dioscoros' poems, which are like poetic UFOs as far as their subjects are concerned but are symptomatic of a culture still obsessed by the great poet and by poetry.[82] Apart from the fact that they are the only 'archaeological' evidence for a certain poetic-rhetorical form of instruction, they are the last witnesses of cultural values that the age of Justinian wished to display, and which were soon to enter a decline that the Arab conquest irremediably confirmed.

---

81   *P.Cair.Masp.* III 67314, Fr. 3, 7–8: ἀνθομολογοῦμεν καὶ ἡμεῖς οἱ προγ[εγρα]μμέν[οι] | κατ' οὔνομα ὁμογνήσιοι ἀδελφ[οί] καὶ υ[ἱοί] σου π[έντε τὸν ἀριθμόν] 'we too recognize each other in turn, we five brothers, your legitimate sons whose names have severally been given above ...'.

82   The eulogy of the Homeric poems is to be related to the epigram on Homer in the *Certamen Homeri et Hesiodi* 309–314 (ed. Allen) that was still being copied in the 6th/7th century, as we know from P.Duk. inv. 665 (Mertens-Pack³ 77.02; TM 64713), ed. Menci 2012.

Acknowledgements

I wish to thank for their suggestions Gianfranco Agosti, who has read this chapter, the members of my seminar at the Collège de France and the École Pratique des Hautes Études, as well as the members of the Oxford Byzantine seminar (especially Marc Lauxtermann), to whom I was able to present these poems in the context of a conference at the Oxford Centre of Byzantine Research (6 June 2019). I am grateful to William V. Harris for translating this chapter into English.

CHAPTER 8

The Lost *Farnesianus* Manuscript

Uncial Capitals for the Bishops of Rome

Carmela Vircillo Franklin

1   Introduction

Alan Cameron was keenly interested in the reception of texts, in their travels and diffusion through diverse cultural and linguistic contexts, and in the transformations brought about by textual transmission in the preprint era.[1] As a detective, on the trail of often faint and barely visible signs, Alan illuminated the past through his reconstruction of the history of texts. He did this most splendidly, to my mind, in his mapping of the peregrinations of the *Greek Anthology*, a story that begins with a collection of poems put together by Meleager of Gadara in the first century BCE, and is transformed through additions, deletions, and revisions both in manuscript and print during the Middle Ages and the Renaissance, when even Erasmus and Thomas More came across its path.[2]

I share Alan's scholarly interest in the transmission of texts and books, frequently the subject of our conversation. My chapter in this collection dedicated to his memory pays homage to his vast contribution to the field of textual reception by reconstructing an imposing manuscript written in uncial capitals that has been lost, the Farnesianus codex of the *Liber pontificalis*.[3] Its textual and physical characteristics as recreated from evidence surviving from the seventeenth and eighteenth century, I will argue, locate the execution of this grand codex within the book culture of mid-ninth-century Rome.

---

1   Principal Manuscripts discussed in this article:
    Biblioteca Apostolica Vaticana, Reginensis latinus 2081; Biblioteca Apostolica Vaticana, Vaticanus latinus 3321; Biblioteca Apostolica Vaticana, Vaticanus latinus 3835 (*Agimundus Homiliary*, vol. 1); Biblioteca Apostolica Vaticana, Vaticanus latinus 3836 (*Agimundus Homiliary*, vol. 2); Biblioteca Apostolica Vaticana, Vaticanus latinus 3764; Biblioteca Apostolica Vaticana, Vaticanus latinus 3762; Paris, Bibliothèque nationale de France, MS 10318 (Codex Salmasianus); Rome, Biblioteca Vallicelliana, B.25 II (Codex Juvenianus).

2   Alan Cameron 1993a.

3   This *Farnesianus* manuscript should not be confused with other "Farnesiani," including the Farnesianus Codex of Festus in Naples, all linked to the library of the Farnese family.

© THE TRUSTEES OF COLUMBIA UNIVERSITY IN THE CITY OF NEW YORK,
2021 | DOI:10.1163/9789004452794_009

2   The *Liber pontificalis*

The *Liber pontificalis* is our most important literary source for the history of Rome and its popes from Late Antiquity to the Carolingian era, the contemporary counterpart to the city's vast archaeological and building remains. Composed at the Lateran Palace's chancery, the administrative center of the church of Rome, from the late sixth century to the late ninth century, the chronicle was constituted as a continually evolving series of papal *gesta*, a new "Vita" added at every new pontificate, a work of reference and institutional memory.[4] It begins with the "Life of Peter" and ends, incomplete, early in the papacy of Stephen V (885–891). Its contents were endowed with fundamental authority for asserting the primacy of the Roman church, its customs and institutions throughout the Middle Ages, and well beyond.

The *Liber pontificalis* was widely copied in the Middle Ages, a fluid text that has survived in more than one hundred manuscripts. Numerous others have perished. Why mourn the loss of the *Farnesianus*, and attempt to recover its witness? There is first the philological imperative. Textual scholars of Greek and Latin have been trained to reconstitute texts that have come to us imperfect, incomplete, contaminated during the long durée of manuscript transmission. Since the Renaissance and even more after the adoption of the Lachmann method in the nineteenth century, the reconstruction of a text as close to the original as possible has been central to philologists. For the *Liber pontificalis*, as for similar texts updated continuously over the centuries, the importance of antiquity is multifaceted, as antiquity of manuscript frequently is coupled with incompleteness of contents. The complexity of the textual diffusion of the *Liber pontificalis* is reflected in the groupings of the manuscript witnesses by the two modern critical editors of the text, Louis Duchesne and Theodor Mommsen.[5] The manuscripts of the papal chronicle have been divided into five recensions, A–E, with A and B constituting the oldest recensions (and shortest chronological textual span), and E representing the latest recension, including the last lives composed in the ninth century. Yet, even within the more intricate manuscripts' panorama of such a shifting text, the *Farnesianus* stands out. If it had survived, the *Farnesianus* would be textually and graphically significant. It would be one of the oldest witnesses of the papal chronicle,

---

4 The bibliography on the *Liber pontificalis* is enormous. A basic bibliography is found at https://tinyurl.com/y6emgkag. For recent historiography see Gantner 2014, 16–26.

5 Duchesne I, 1886; II, 1892; III, 1957 (incorporating corrections and updates by Cyrille Vogel). Mommsen 1898. Mommsen's edition ends in 715; the second part was planned, but never published.

yet reaching up at least to the Life of Pope Sergius II (d. 847), just a few years before the text comes to an end.[6] Most significantly, it would be the oldest of the manuscripts of the E recension, which contains the last portion of the *Liber pontificalis*. And, if my argument that the codex was produced in Rome is correct, the *Farnesianus* would be the oldest known manuscript of the *Liber pontificalis* to survive from the city where the papal chronicle was composed over the centuries.[7]

Graphically, the *Farnesianus* is also significant. The manuscript, which must have been copied at the earliest after 847 (when Pope Sergius II dies), was written in large uncials, the script tied to the city of Rome and its texts for centuries. No manuscript of the *Liber pontificalis* written in this majuscule script survives, except for the additions in an imitation uncial script in the *Lucensis* (Lucca, Biblioteca capitolare feliniana 490). This composite codex contains the oldest complete copy of the papal chronicle up to 715, and was written in Lucca in a minuscule script dated to the late eighth century. Two later portions of the *Liber pontificalis* were added in uncial letters in the early ninth century, by scribes whose lack of training in this script is betrayed by the use of many minuscule elements, and who were most likely attempting to replicate a Roman exemplar.[8] All the other surviving manuscripts of the *Liber pontificalis* are in minuscule. Yet we know from the surviving evidence that in Rome itself uncial script continued to be used until the beginning of the ninth century. The question behind this chapter—was the *Farnesianus* copied in Rome?—is an obvious one, suggested by the city's scribal history and its attachment to uncial script. But it has never been posed because the manuscript no longer exists. Yet, its exploration could record the use of uncials well beyond the beginning of the ninth century, and enrich the scribal landscape of the city in the second half of the ninth century, documented at present only by eight manuscripts, all written in minuscule.[9]

---

6 The oldest surviving manuscripts are the *Neapolitanus* palimpsest fragment (7th c.; Class B); the *Taurinensis*, another palimpsest fragment (8th c.; Class B); the *Lucensis* (8th–9th c.; Class A), all older than the *Farnesianus*. Of the numerous ninth-century manuscripts, only two are certainly older than the *Farnesianus*, Leyden Vossianus 60 (Class C) and Cologne 164 (Class B), which reach to Pope Stephen II (d. 757) and Stephen III (d. 772), respectively. Duchesne I, clxiii–ccvi.

7 The oldest surviving manuscript from Rome is the Vatican Library's Vaticanus latinus 3764 from the late eleventh century, discussed below.

8 Duchesne I, CLXIV-CLXVI; Gantner 2013, 73–77.

9 Ammirati 2020; Supino Martini 2012, 3–10.

THE LOST FARNESIANUS MANUSCRIPT

3 The Discovery of the Manuscript

The *Farnesianus* was first discovered by the leading humanist in Baroque Rome, the German Lucas Holste,[10] who had trained in Latin and Greek at Leiden, and then in Paris. After his conversion to Catholicism he moved to Rome in 1627, where he would head the city's three greatest libraries of the seventeenth century until his death in 1661: the Barberini Library (from 1636),[11] the Vatican Library (from 1653), and the Library of Queen Christina of Sweden after her abdication (from 1655).

Perhaps around 1650, when surveying the rich ducal library at the Farnese Palace, Holste found the manuscript he would call "Farnesianus."[12] He had been collecting materials since at least 1636 to correct mistakes he had found in the inadequate *editio princeps* of the *Liber pontificalis* printed in Mainz in 1602.[13] His brief description of the manuscript as written in "majuscule letters, a codex of unsurpassed antiquity, older than which nothing I believe exists of this kind," reflects the value humanists placed on the age of a manuscript witness.[14] Holste recorded in his own hand this brief description of the manuscript he called the *Farnesianus*, on a sheet at the front of his own copy of Mainz's printed edition. In the margins of the Latin text in the same book—his copy of the printed Mainz edition—Holste added the variants of the *Farnesianus* manuscript, collating it entirely against the printed version. In the same margins he recorded carefully also textual lacunae, crucial evidence for the reconstruction of the text of the *Farnesianus*. For the codex as seen by Holste already lacked portions at the beginning and at the end, and also pages in the middle section. It began in the Life of Pope Silverius (536–537), and ended in the middle of the Life of Sergius II.[15] Holste's collation in effect preserved the text of the *Farnesianus* as it existed in the middle of the seventeenth century. But he is completely silent about the manuscript's physical

---

10 Known also as Lucas Holstenius (b. Hamburg, 1596; d. Rome, 1661). On Holste, and particularly on his work as a librarian, see Vian 2001.

11 Holste retained this charge until his death in 1661, even after he was named librarian of the Vatican Library in September 1653.

12 Holste 1817, no. XCV, 402–406 (letter to Jacobus Sirmondus [Jacques Sirmond, 1559–1651] of May 1650).

13 Anastasius Bibliothecarius 1602. The authorship of the entire *Liber pontificalis* had been wrongly attributed to Anastasius Bibliothecarius (810–878) by humanists in the circle of Bartolomeo Platina and the Vatican Library in the late fifteenth century. See further, Franklin 2017, 608–610.

14 "*M. S. Farnesiani scripti litteris maiusculis, quo nihil antiquius extare puto in hoc genere.*" Biblioteca Apostolica Vaticana, Reginenensis latinus 2081, added page at the beginning.

15 For a full list of the contents, see Levison 1911.

138 FRANKLIN

characteristics, the size or appearance of the codex, except that it was written in ancient majuscule letters.

After Holste's death in 1661, his annotated copy of the Mainz edition came to the Vatican Library, where it was used by its prefect Emmanuel Schelstrate for his history of the ancient church published in 1692.[16] Schelstrate brought the news of Holste's discovery to the attention of scholars, and quoted his predecessor's brief description of the *Farnesianus*, which, to his regret, could no longer be found in Rome. Schelstrate's statement, however, that the *Farnesianus* ended with the Life of Hadrian I, who died in 795, was an error,[17] and led to confusion, even among modern editors of the papal chronicle.[18] Holste's annotated copy of the Mainz edition is today at the Vatican Library, Reginensis latinus 2081.[19]

There is no further news of the *Farnesianus* until Francesco Bianchini (1662–1729) searched for it while preparing an annotated and illustrated edition of the *Liber pontificalis* in five volumes, under the patronage of Pope Clement XI. Francesco Bianchini is known for his scientific and mathematical works, and for historical works in Italian.[20] His unappreciated edition (in Latin) of the *Liber pontificalis* remains a monument to the Age of Enlightenment's emphasis on observation and material evidence.[21] Deeply involved in archaeological projects, Bianchini was a material philologist *avant la lettre*. He thus was particularly keen to find the 'ancient *Farnesianus*' which could serve as a contemporaneous material witness of the Carolingian rulers' recognition of papal dominion over central Italy, now being questioned by Protestants, and, more practically, challenged by the territorial ambitions of the Dukes of Parma and Piacenza. For Bianchini, whose knowledge of the *Farnesianus* came from Schelstrate's *Antiquitas Ecclesiae*, thought that the *Farnesianus* ended with the papacy of Hadrian I (d. 785) and was thus a document contemporaneous with the establishment of the papal state by King Pepin, and its confirmation by

---

16   Schelstrate 1692.
17   Schelstrate made this mistake most likely because he did not leaf through Holste's entire copy of the Mainz edition. I will provide a full description of this book in a future study of Holste's philological work.
18   Including Duchesne's first discussion of the *Farnesianus* (I, cc), corrected in the second volume (II, i–ii).
19   Although a printed book, it is cataloged as a manuscript because of Holste's collation notes.
20   For some of what follows, see also Franklin 2017.
21   Bianchini 1718–1735. The fourth volume was edited posthumously by Francesco's nephew, Giuseppe Bianchini. A planned fifth volume was never published.

THE LOST FARNESIANUS MANUSCRIPT 139

Charlemagne, in 756 and 775 respectively.[22] Making use of the vast network of papal and princely Rome, Bianchini found the *Farnesianus* through a retainer of the Farnese family in early 1719, at the Farnese Palace in Parma, where a portion of the ducal library had been moved sometime after 1653.[23]

Bianchini collated the *Farnesianus*, but quickly and incompletely, when compared to Holste's thoroughness. His great contribution to our knowledge of the *Farnesianus* is the documentation of his detailed observations of the codex as a material object. A friend and follower of Jean Mabillon (1632–1707), the "father" of modern paleography, Bianchini was the first scholar to apply to medieval manuscripts the rules developed by Mabillon for the dating and authentication of medieval charters. Bianchini thus compared the *Farnesianus'* uncial script to Mabillon's published plates to confirm the antiquity of the codex. The physical witness of this manuscript was thus more important than later manuscripts containing the same text. He took advantage of the developing technology of engraving in print to reproduce the physical manuscript as closely as possible. He produced engravings from five different pages of the *Farnesianus*, from facsimiles drawn by hand, and included them in the second volume of his edition of the *Liber pontificalis* published in 1723.[24] The first facsimile (Figure 8.1) was made in Parma in September 1719, and then engraved in Rome. This page was chosen because it contained an entire papal biography, the short Life of Pope Eugenius I (d. 657). On one page, therefore, the format of an entire biography could be replicated, from the capital initial to the formulaic ending, which illustrates the use of dates and numbers, inconsistent graphic signs. The other four engravings were made a year later in October 1720 (Figures 8.2–8.4). Three engravings, spread over three pages, reproduce the long passage relating to the Donation of Pepin and its confirmation by Charlemagne (in the Life of Pope Stephen II), just as it appeared copied over three pages in the *Farnesiasnus*. The three-page engravings constitute a "photographic" reproduction of the manuscript. Bianchini included a fifth engraving on the last page of this trio (Figure 8.4), the opening of the Life of Pope Paul I from the *Farnesianus*, which includes the pope's portrait. This was no doubt a decision driven by Bianchini's interest in papal iconography and particularly the ancient series of papal portraits on the walls of St. Paul's

---

22 Or at least to people who remembered these events. It is not clear whether Bianchini saw the *Farnesianus* in the same condition as Holste had seen it. It seems at least possible that the last piece at the end of the *Farnesianus*, containing the fragment of Sergius II's Life, had fallen out and been lost during the transportation to Parma.

23 For the removal of the Farnese library to Parma in 1653 and to Naples in 1734, see Scipioni 2013, 1698n50.

24 Bianchini II, xxiii, lvii–lix.

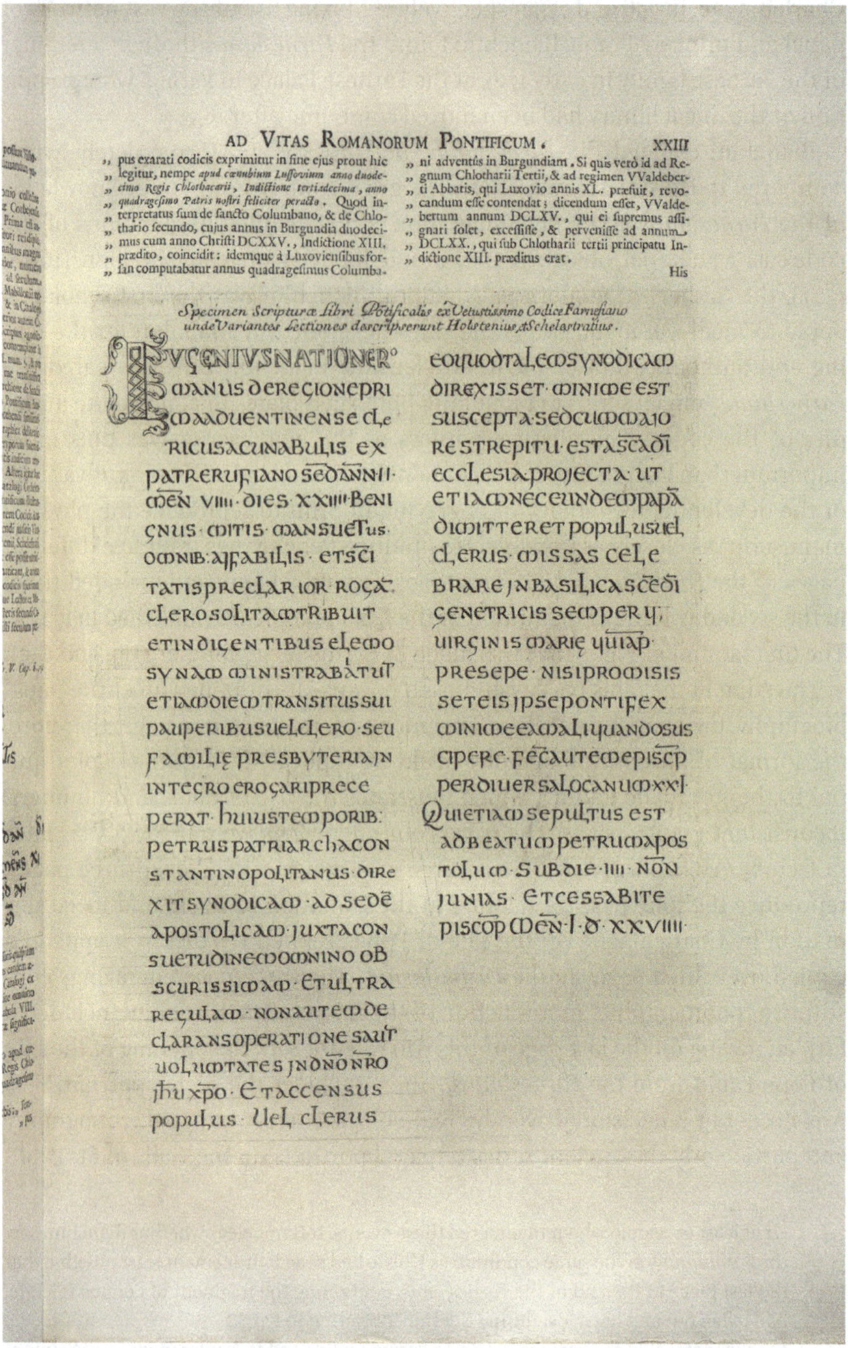

AD VITAS ROMANORUM PONTIFICUM. XXIII

„ pus exarati codicis exprimitur in fine ejus prout hic „ legitur, nempe *apud cœnubium Luſſovium anno duodecimo Regis Chlothacarii, Indictione tertiadecima, anno quadrageſimo Patris noſtri feliciter peracto*. Quod interpretatus ſum de ſancto Columbano, & de Chlothario ſecundo, cujus annus in Burgundia duodecimus cum anno Chriſti DCXXV., Indictione XIII. prædito, coincidit: idemque à Luxovienſibus forſan computabatur annus quadrageſimus Columbani adventûs in Burgundiam. Si quis verò id ad Regnum Chlotharii Tertii, & ad regimen VValdeberti Abbatis, qui Luxovio annis XL. præfuit, revocandum eſſe contendat; dicendum eſſet, VValdebertum annum DCLXV., qui ei ſupremus aſſignari ſolet, exceſſiſſe, & perveniſſe ad annum DCLXX., qui ſub Chlotharii tertii principatu Indictione XIII. præditus erat.

His

Specimen Scripturæ Libri Pōtificalis ex Vetustissimo Codice Farnesiano unde Variantes Lectiones descripserunt Holstenius, et Schelestratius.

HUGENIUS NATIONE RO
MANUS DE REGIONE PRI
MA ADUENTINENSE CLE
RICUS A CUNABULIS EX
PATRE RUFIANO SED ANN II
MEN VIIII DIES XXIIII BENI
GNUS MITIS MANSUETUS
OMNIB ADFABILIS ET SCI
TATIS PRECLARIOR ROGA
CLERO SOLITAM TRIBUIT
ET INDIGENTIBUS ELEMO
SYNAM MINISTRABAT UT
ET IAM DIEM TRANSITUS SUI
PAUPERIBUS UEL CLERO SEU
FAMILIE PRESBYTERIA IN
INTEGRO EROGARI PRECE
PERAT HUIUS TEMPORIB
PETRUS PATRIARCHA CON
STANTINOPOLITANUS DIRE
XIT SYNODICAM AD SEDE
APOSTOLICAM IUXTA CON
SUETUDINEM OMNINO OB
SCURISSIMAM ET ULTRA
REGULAM NON AUTEM DE
CLARANS OPERATIONE SAUT
UOLUNTATES IN DNO NRO
IHU XPO ET ACCENSUS
POPULUS UEL CLERUS
EO QUOD TALEM SYNODICAM
DIREXISSET MINIME EST
SUSCEPTA SED CUM MAIO
RE STREPITU EST A SCA DI
ECCLESIA PROJECTA UT
ET IAM NEC EUNDEM PAPA
DIMITTERET POPULUS UEL
CLERUS MISSAS CELE
BRARE IN BASILICA SCE DI
GENETRICIS SEMPER U
UIRGINIS MARIE QUIA AP
PRESEPE NISI PROMISIS
SET EIS IPSE PONTIFEX
MINIME EAM ALIQUANDO SUS
CIPERE FEC AUTEM EPISCP
PER DIUERSA LOCA NUM XXI
QUIETIAM SEPULTUS EST
AD BEATUM PETRUM APOS
TOLUM SUB DIE IIII NON
IUNIAS ET CESSABIT E
PISCOP MEN I D XXVIIII

FIGURE 8.1 Bianchini 2:xxiii. C 4237. 18 F. Widener Library Special Collections, Harvard University

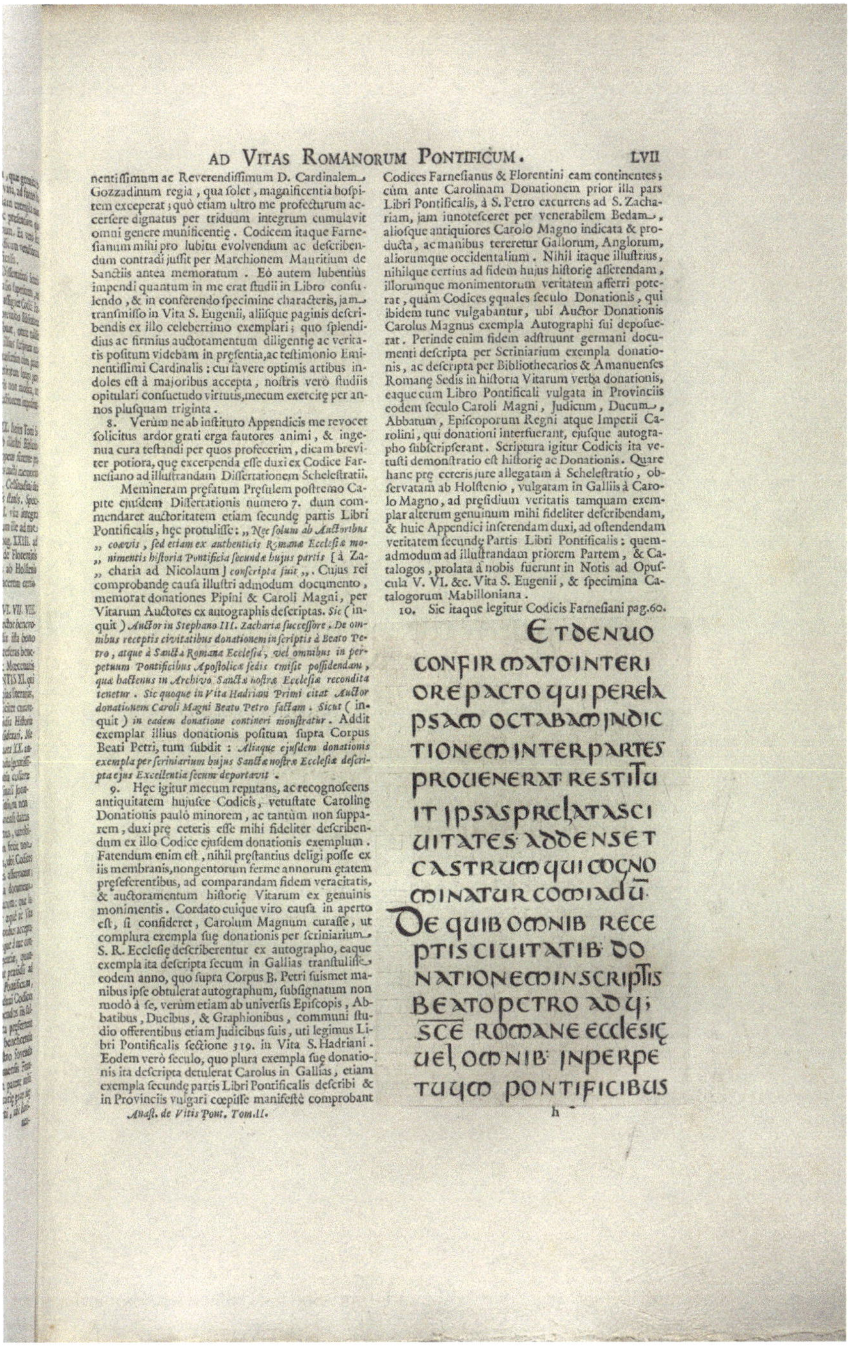

AD VITAS ROMANORUM PONTIFICUM. LVII

nentissimum ac Reverendissimum D. Cardinalem Gozzadinum regia, qua solet, magnificentia hospitem exceperat; quò etiam ultro me profecturum accersere dignatus per triduum integrum cumulavit omni genere munificentię. Codicem itaque Farnesianum mihi pro lubitu evolvendum ac describendum contradi jussit per Marchionem Mauritium de Sanctiis antea memoratum. Eò autem lubentiùs impendi quantum in me erat studii in Libro consulendo, & in conferendo specimine characteris, jam transmisso in Vita S. Eugenii, aliisque paginis describendis ex illo celeberrimo exemplari; quo splendidius ac firmius auctoramentum diligentię ac veritatis positum videbam in pręsentia, ac testimonio Eminentissimi Cardinalis: cui favere optimis artibus indoles est à majoribus accepta, nostris verò studiis opitulari consuetudo virtutis, mecum exercitę per annos plusquam triginta.

8. Verùm ne ab instituto Appendicis me revocet solicitus ardor grati erga fautores animi, & ingenua cura testandi per quos profecerim, dicam breviter potiora, quę excerpenda esse duxi ex Codice Farnesiano ad illustrandam Dissertationem Schelestratii.

Memineram pręfatum Pręsulem postremo Capite ejusdem Dissertationis numero 7. dum commendaret auctoritatem etiam secundę partis Libri Pontificalis, hęc protulisse: „*Nec solum ab Auctoribus* „ *coævis, sed etiam ex authenticis Romanæ Ecclesiæ mo-* „ *nimentis historia Pontificia secundæ hujus partis* [à Za- „ charia ad Nicolaum] *conscripta fuit* „. Cujus rei comprobandę causa illustri admodum documento, memorat donationes Pipini & Caroli Magni, per Vitarum Auctores ex autographis descriptas. *Sic* (inquit) *Auctor in Stephano III. Zachariæ successore. De omnibus receptis civitatibus donationem in scriptis à Beato Petro, atque à Sancta Romana Ecclesia, vel omnibus in perpetuum Pontificibus Apostolicæ sedis emisit possidendam, quæ hactenus in Archivo Sanctæ nostræ Ecclesiæ recondita tenetur. Sic quoque in Vita Hadriani Primi citat Auctor donationem Caroli Magni Beato Petro factam. Sicut* (inquit) *in eadem donatione contineri monstratur*. Addit exemplar illius donationis positum supra Corpus Beati Petri, tum subdit: *Aliaque ejusdem donationis exempla per scriniarium hujus Sanctæ nostræ Ecclesiæ descripta ejus Excellentia secum deportavit*.

9. Hęc igitur mecum reputans, ac recognoscens antiquitatem hujusce Codicis, vetustate Carolinę Donationis pauló minorem, ac tantùm non supparem, duxi prę ceteris esse mihi fideliter describendum ex illo Codice ejusdem donationis exemplum. Fatendum enim est, nihil pręstantius deligi posse ex iis membranis, nongentorum ferme annorum ętatem pręseferentibus, ad comparandam fidem veracitatis, & auctoramentum historię Vitarum ex genuinis monimentis. Cordato cuique viro causa in aperto est, si consideret, Carolum Magnum curasse, ut complura exempla suę donationis per scriniarium S. R. Ecclesię describerentur ex autographo, eaque exempla ita descripta secum in Gallias transtulisse eodem anno, quo supra Corpus B. Petri suismet manibus ipse obtulerat autographum, subsignatum non modò à se, verùm etiam ab universis Episcopis, Abbatibus, Ducibus, & Graphionibus, communi studio offerentibus etiam Judicibus suis, uti legimus Libri Pontificalis sectione 319. in Vita S. Hadriani. Eodem verò seculo, quo plura exempla suę donationis ita descripta detulerat Carolus in Gallias, etiam exempla secundę partis Libri Pontificalis describi & in Provinciis vulgari cœpisse manifestè comprobant Codices Farnesianus & Florentini eam continentes; cùm ante Carolinam Donationem prior illa pars Libri Pontificalis, à S. Petro excurrens ad S. Zachariam, jam innotesceret per venerabilem Bedam, aliosque antiquiores Carolo Magno indicata & producta, ac manibus tereretur Gallorum, Anglorum, aliorumque occidentalium. Nihil itaque illustrius, nihilque certius ad fidem hujus historię asserendam, illorumque monimentorum veritatem afferri poterat, quàm Codices ęquales seculo Donationis, qui ibidem tunc vulgabantur, ubi Auctor Donationis Carolus Magnus exempla Autographi sui deposuerat. Perinde enim fidem adstruunt germani documenti descripta per Scriniarium exempla donationis, ac descripta per Bibliothecarios & Amanuenses Romanę Sedis in historia Vitarum verba donationis, eaque cùm Libro Pontificali vulgata in Provinciis eodem seculo Caroli Magni, Judicum, Ducum, Abbatum, Episcoporum Regni atque Imperii Carolini, qui donationi interfuerant, ejusque autographo subscripserant. Scriptura igitur Codicis ita vetusti demonstratio est historię ac Donationis. Quare hanc prę ceteris jure allegatam à Schelestratio, observatam ab Holstenio, vulgatam in Galliis à Carolo Magno, ad pręsidium veritatis tamquam exemplar alterum genuinum mihi fideliter describendam, & huic Appendici inserendam duxi, ad ostendendam veritatem secundę Partis Libri Pontificalis: quemadmodum ad illustrandam priorem Partem, & Catalogos, prolata à nobis fuerunt in Notis ad Opuscula V. VI. &c. Vita S. Eugenii, & specimina Catalogorum Mabilloniana.

10. Sic itaque legitur Codicis Farnesiani pag. 60.

ET DENUO
CONFIRMATO INTERI
ORE PACTO QUI PERELA
PSAM OCTABAM INDIC
TIONEM INTERPARTES
PROUENERAT RESTITU
IT IPSAS PRELATAS CI
UITATES ADDENS ET
CASTRUM QUI COGNO
MINATUR COMIACU
DE QUIB OMNIB RECE
PTIS CIUITATIB DO
NATIONEM INSCRIPTIS
BEATO PETRO ADQ;
SCE ROMANE ECCLESIE
UEL OMNIB INPERPE
TUUM PONTIFICIBUS

Anast. de Vitis Pont. Tom. II. h

FIGURE 8.2 Bianchini 2:lvii. C 4237. 18 F. Widener Library Special Collections, Harvard University

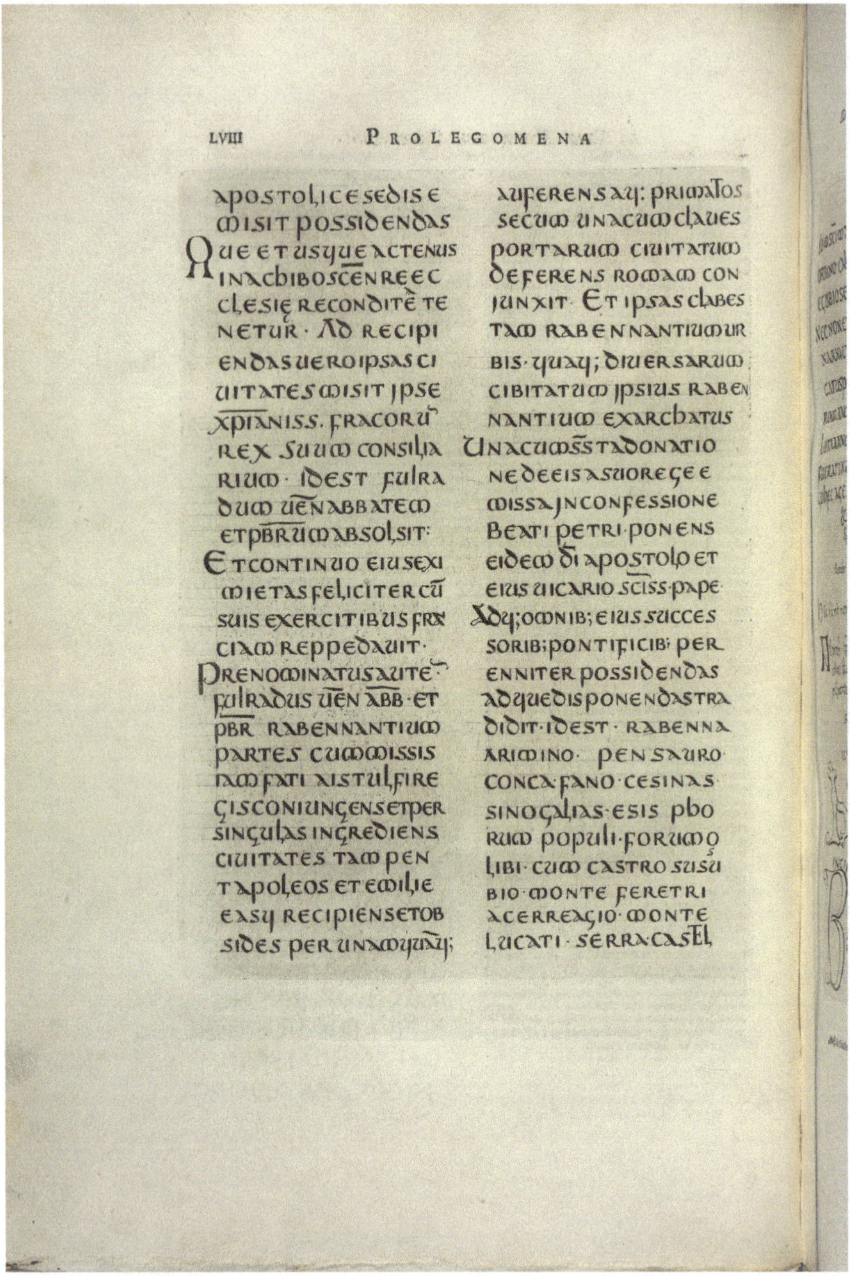
LVIII PROLEGOMENA

apostolice sedis e
misit possidendas
Que et usque actenus
in archiboscenie ec
clesie reconditē te
netur. Ad recipi
endas uero ipsas ci
uitates misit ipse
xpianiss. francorū
rex suum consilia
rium. idest fulra
dum uen abbatem
et pbrum absolsit:
Et continuo eius exi
mietas feliciter cū
suis exercitibus fra
ciam reppedauit.
Prenominatus autē
fulradus uen abb. et
pbr rabennantium
partes cum missis
iam fati aistulfi re
gis coniungens et per
singulas ingrediens
ciuitates tam pen
tapoleos et emilie
easq recipiens et ob
sides per unamquamq;

auferens aq: primatos
secum una cum claues
portarum ciuitatum
deferens romam con
iunxit. Et ipsas claues
tam rabennantium ur
bis quaq; diuersarum
cibitatum ipsius raben
nantium exarchatus
Una cum sstadonatio
ne de eis a suo rege e
missa in confessione
beati petri ponens
eidem di apostolo et
eius uicario scīss pape
adq; omnib; eius succes
sorib; pontificib; per
enniter possidendas
adque disponendas tra
didit. idest rabenna
arimino. pensauro
conca fano cesinas
sinogalias esis pbo
rium populi forum o
libi cum castro susu
bio monte feretri
acerreagio monte
lucati serracastel

FIGURE 8.3 Bianchini 2:lviii. C 4237. 18 F. Widener Library Special Collections, Harvard University

THE LOST FARNESIANUS MANUSCRIPT

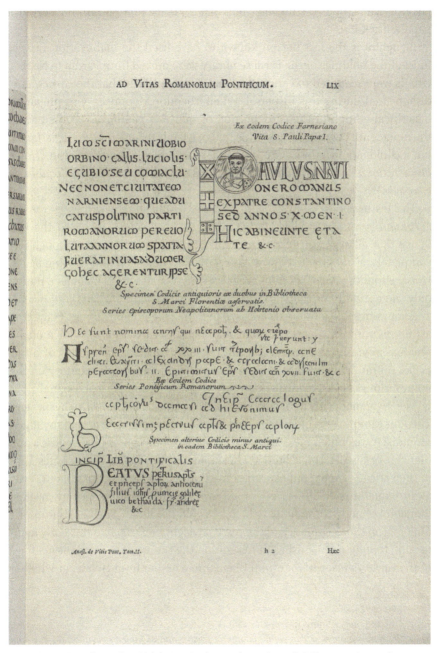

FIGURE 8.4   Bianchini 2:lix. C 4237. 18 F. Widener Library Special Collections, Harvard University

Basilica, which he had studied as material evidence for determining accurate papal succession.

Bianchini is the last person known to have used the manuscript. In 1734 most of the holdings of the Farnese library were moved from Parma to Naples. Others were scattered to various libraries. It seems likely that the *Farnesianus* disappeared during this dispersal. When Theodor Mommsen was preparing his critical edition of the early portion of the *Liber pontificalis* at the end of the nineteenth century, he asked his Italian friends to look for the *Farnesianus*, but it could not be found, as he wrote in his introduction to the edition: "*Hodie desideratur, neque quamquam adiutus diligenter ab amicis Italis quicquam de eo rescivi.*"[25]

The testimony of only two but complementary direct witnesses for the *Farnesianus* remains today. Lucas Holste, the philologist, recorded the evidence that allows us to reconstruct the text of the *Farnesianus*, though not completely, as the manuscript was already then damaged and missing pages. Holste supplies almost no evidence for its physical nature as an object, noting only the antiquity of the codex as denoted by its script, "*litteris maiusculis,*" and not minuscule letters as were used in more recent manuscripts. Bianchini, astronomer and material historian, supplied us with visual evidence of the physical manuscript through a set of carefully executed facsimiles of a few pages, reproducing both script and images. His detailed commentary on the manuscript as an object further assists us in envisioning the lost original.

The two modern editors of the *Liber pontificalis*, Louis Duchesne and Theodor Mommsen, considered the evidence of both Holste and Bianchini.[26] Mommsen was much more thorough in his exploitation of both Holste's and Bianchini's textual collation. He consulted Holste's handwritten notes kept in the Vatican Library, but expresses frustration that he was not able to verify all of Bianchini's collation, as printed in Bianchini's edition, directly against Bianchini's handwritten notes, which he could not find.[27] Such is Mommsen's philological thoroughness and the textual weight he assigns to this early manuscript, that he distinguishes in his edition the source of the variant readings of the *Farnesianus*, whether from Bianchini, whether from Holste, or whether

---

25   Mommsen, xciv.

26   I discuss their editions in Franklin 2018.

27   "*Variam lectionem a Bianchinio enotatam frustra quaesivi inter schediasmata eius tam Romae in bibliotheca Vallicelliana quam Veronae in capitulari, sed fieri potest, ut fugerint nos inter adversaria illa amplissima.*" (I searched in vain for Bianchini's record of variants among his papers both in Rome at the Biblioteca Vallicelliana and in Verona at the Capitular Library, but perhaps it is possible that they escaped us among those most ample notebooks), Mommsen, xcv.

THE LOST FARNESIANUS MANUSCRIPT 145

supported by both. Mommsen's regret for the loss of the *Farnesianus* stems from the antiquity of the manuscript and its excellent readings, which join it to even older manuscripts.[28] This important textual observation will be further explored below. Yet, despite such close attention to the text, Mommsen pays hardly any attention to the images Bianchini had provided. When he discusses the age of the lost manuscript, he does so only from the evidence of its contents, the inclusion of the biography of Sergius II (844–847), without reference to the testimony provided by the script, for which he had used the older, generic term "*quadratis litteris*" rather than the more precise "*uncialibus*."[29]

Duchesne did not make full use of Holste's collation. In numerous places, his edition's apparatus criticus does not reflect the *Farnesianus*' reading as transmitted by Holste. Duchesne grouped the *Farnesianus* with the most recent recension of the *Liber pontificalis*, the E recension, but he did not emphasize, as Mommsen would, that the *Farnesianus* also preserved in places older (and correct) readings. However, he paid greater attention to the physical characteristics of the *Farnesianus* as represented in Bianchini's edition. He noted the manuscript's physical rarity, using precise nomenclature in referring to its script: "a Latin manuscript written entirely in uncials in the middle of the 9th century ... is a great paleographical rarity, especially when one is not dealing with a Bible or a liturgical manuscript." Its luxurious manufacture led Duchesne to speculate that "such a book could not have been executed except by a high ranking person." And he compared it to the Vatican Library's Vaticanus latinus 5007, a manuscript in uncials containing the *gesta* of the bishops of Naples, written ca. 800. He was thus linking text and script, drawing a parallel between the use of lavish uncial script and the genre of the two texts—the episcopal *gesta*.[30] He did not, however, pursue any discussion of the context in which the *Farnesianus* could have been copied. Nor has the *Farnesianus* been included in any of the standard catalogs and surveys of Latin manuscripts, except for one. Paul Lehmann, in his appendix to Ludwig Traube's *Zur Paläographie und Handschriften*, includes the *Farnesianus*, "*nunc deperditus*," among his list of Latin uncial manuscripts, but leaves a blank for the category "*Schriftheimat*."[31]

Considered together, the textual evidence recorded by Holste's hand and the material evidence transmitted through print by Bianchini place the *Farnesianus* within Rome's written culture in the second half of the ninth

---

28   Mommsen, xcvi.

29   Mommsen, xciv. Mommsen's use of the term "*quadratis litteris*" for the *Farnesianus* is puzzling. The differentiation among majuscule scripts and their nomenclature had been established by Scipione Maffei in the middle of the eighteenth century.

30   Duchesne II, i–ii.

31   Lehmann [1909] 1965, 183.

century. This might seem the obvious answer to fill in Lehmann's blank, given that the *Liber pontificalis* was continuously composed in Rome over centuries. The text of every manuscript ultimately goes back to a Roman exemplar, but only a very small number of the surviving manuscripts were written in Rome. While we know from literary sources, and especially from the *Liber pontificalis*, that there was a considerable production of books in Rome during the eighth and ninth centuries, we have meager material evidence that escaped the ruin of the tenth and eleventh centuries, when Rome was sacked repeatedly, and the great library that had been gathered at the Lateran Palace from well before the sixth century was dispersed.[32] There is no surviving manuscript of the *Liber pontificalis* made in Rome before the late eleventh century.

In what follows, I will first, using Holste's collation, investigate the text of the *Farnesianus* as an early witness of the E recension of the *Liber pontificalis*, the Roman "vulgate" that surfaces in the manuscripts only in the eleventh century, and link it particularly to two manuscripts, one written in Rome (Vaticanus latinus 3764), and one copied from a Roman exemplar (Vaticanus latinus 3762). I will also argue that a singular version of the Life of Pope Sergius II, transmitted only by the *Farnesianus* and transcribed by Holste, represents a uniquely Roman version of the papal Life. Turning then to Bianchini's evidence, I will consider the *Farnesianus*' script and its decorated initials to show how closely these visual characteristics echo those found in Roman books that are closest chronologically to the lost codex.

4   The Text

The *Farnesianus* was cataloged by Duchesne as belonging to the E group of manuscripts, the most recent recension of the *Liber pontificalis* containing the lives of the ninth-century popes. This recension was made up by revising, and adding to, the earlier recensions.[33] Its manuscripts are highly contaminated.[34] Within the textual web of the E manuscripts, the *Farnesianus* is the oldest, and is closest to the next oldest, Vat. lat. 3764, copied, as we now know, in Rome in 1085–1086, by a scribe using the typified Roman version of Caroline minuscule,

---

32   Bilotta 2011. The fundamental work on the Lateran Library remains De Rossi 1886.

33   See Duchesne I, ccxiii–ccxvii, for a discussion of the E recension, whose manuscripts are included in Mommsen's Class III (discussed at xciii–cv), retaining, however, Duchesne's manuscript sigla.

34   Duchesne included six principal manuscripts in the E group (I, cxcv–cciii). Two more need to be added, both from the first half of the twelfth century (Vat. lat. 3762; and Tortosa, Biblioteca capitular, MS 246).

THE LOST FARNESIANUS MANUSCRIPT 147

"romanesca."[35] The manuscript, which includes several texts relating to the popes in addition to the *Liber pontificalis*, was a product of "significant value, as shown by the excellent quality of its parchment, the calligraphic nature of its script, and the elegance of its initials."[36] The identification of the Roman scriptorium that produced Vat. lat. 3764 remains unexplored. It may well have been written at the Lateran.[37] Vat. lat. 3764 manifests the revival of interest in the papal chronicle and related historical texts in Roman scriptoria beginning in the eleventh century.[38]

The close textual relationship between the *Farnesianus* and the E recension, and particularly Vat. lat. 3764, is amply documented in Duchesne's and Mommsen's apparatus.[39] Duchesne furthermore concluded that Vat. lat. 3764 and the *Farnesianus* formed a subgroup of the E recension. The relationship of the *Farnesianus* to another witness of the E version of the *Liber pontificalis* circulating in Rome at this time has not been noticed. It also helps to strengthen the argument for the "romanitas" of the text of the *Farnesianus*. This is the version of the papal chronicle put together by Cardinal Pandulphus Romanus, a follower of Pope Anacletus II during the schism of 1130. Pandulphus revised the original text (which, as we saw, ended in the ninth century) and brought it up to his own days, ending with the papacy of Honorius II (d. 1130). Pandulph's continuation of the *Liber pontificalis* is not pertinent here. His version of the original portion of the *Liber pontificalis*, on the other hand, is another witness to the Roman E recension, closely related to Vat. lat. 3764. It is also linked to the *Farnesianus*.[40] The *Liber pontificalis* of Cardinal Pandulphus derives from the same textual tradition as Vat. lat. 3764, the version of the papal chronicle

---

35 Best described in Supino Martini 1987, *passim* but especially 132–135, which corrects both Duchesne and Ignazio Giorgi (1897), who had assigned this manuscript to Farfa Abbey's scriptorium, in northern Lazio. Technically, the *Mutinensis* (Modena, Biblioteca capitolare, VII C, ordine I, n. 12) from the eighth century is older. But this is a canonical collection, in which only extracts from the *Liber pontificalis* from Peter to Leo I are included (Duchesne I, cxcvi). No stemma has been created for these contaminated manuscripts.

36 Supino Martini 1987, 132–133.

37 For the book production of the Lateran Basilica at this time, see Supino Martini 1987, 46–56.

38 Franklin 2013.

39 Hence, it is not surprising that Holste's collation of the *Farnesanus* did not yield an excessive number of variants, for the Mainz edition was based by and large on a copy of Vat. lat. 3764.

40 Pandulph's version of the *Liber pontificalis* survives in two manuscripts: Vat. lat. 3762, copied in 1142 directly from the Roman exemplar, almost certainly from Pandulph's own autograph; the other, Tortosa, Biblioteca capitular, MS 246, from the mid-twelfth century, which was only partially copied from Pandulph's exemplar, and is excluded from this discussion. See further, Franklin 2013, 8–12.

circulating in Rome in the eleventh century, what might be called the Roman vulgate of the papal chronicle. It is therefore particularly significant that Pandulph's version and the *Farnesianus* share variants that Mommsen (who did not consider the manuscripts of Pandulph's text fully) had identified as unique mistakes in the *Farnesianus*, "readings unique to it [the *Farnesianus*], but mendacious or suspect."[41] I cite here only one example of such unique mistakes identified by Mommsen in the *Farnesianus*, which is also found in Pandulph's version. In the Life of Pope John III (d. 574), the Romans tell Emperor Justinian and his wife Sophia that such are the abuses of Narses that they would rather serve (*deservimus*) the barbarians: "*Aut libera nos de manu eius, aut certe et civitate Romana et nos gentibus deservimus.*"[42] Instead of *deservimus*, the *Farnesianus* reads *deserimus* (we abandon) while Pandulph has *deseremus* (we would abandon), most likely Pandulph's grammatical correction of his exemplar's reading.[43] The problematic language of this passage was cause for numerous corrections as shown by its rich apparatus criticus in both modern editions. However, only the *Farnesianus* and Pandulph share this error. This example and similar variants found in Mommsen's and Duchesne's apparatus reveal the lost codex as an earlier exemplar of the same textual stream from which the E recension derives, and as particularly close to its earliest surviving Roman manuscripts.

Mommsen also remarked that the *Farnesianus* on several occasions preserved the correct reading of the older recensions, unlike the other E manuscripts.[44] But he did not explore the significance of the hybrid nature of the manuscript's text. There are many readings that show that the *Farnesianus* retains the reading of the older recensions, whether correct, as was important to Mommsen, or in error,[45] while the E redaction has a different word, frequently reflecting the more "standard" Latinity of the eleventh and twelfth centuries. In the account of the repairs, undertaken by Pope Gregorius II

---

41 "*Subieci lectiones ex hoc libro enotatas ei proprias aut mendosas aut suspectas,*" Mommsen, xcv. Mommsen lists fourteen such suspect readings; I have found three of them in Vat. lat. 3762; but one must keep in mind that Pandulph revised the original text of the papal chronicle significantly.

42 Duchesne I, 305, l. 11; Mommsen, 157–158. Davis 1989, 62 translates the passage as "Either deliver us from his hand or we and the Roman citizenry will serve the barbarians." The emperor in question was actually Justinian's nephew Justin II, whose wife was Sophia.

43 Vat. lat. 3762 f. 42v (Pandulph); Reg. lat. 2081, p. 60 (note in Holste's hand, left margin).

44 Mommsen, xcvi. Mommsen singles out the reading *hieraticos*, the correct reading preserved only by the *Farnesianus* and a manuscript of the B class. (Mommsen, 182, l. 15; Duchesne I, 337, l. 10).

45 This evidence is, therefore, additional to what was singled out by Mommsen as representing the *Farnesianus'* "correct" text.

THE LOST FARNESIANUS MANUSCRIPT   149

(715–731), of the Church of Santa Croce in Gerusalemme that had been long left "uncovered," the earlier recensions of the text and the *Farnesianus* read *distecta*; all the surviving manuscripts of the E recension read *detecta*.[46] The *Farnesianus* in this case preserves the original reading of the older recensions, not the more standard *detecta* of the E recension. The late antique and rare word *distectus* is attested in the works of Avitus;[47] the replacement of this unusual late antique word with a more standard Latin term illustrates the increasing standardization of Latin lexical usage in the E recension. Similarly, both the earlier recensions and the *Farnesianus* use *serrari* in the meaning of "to bolt" rather than the standard *serari*[48] when Pope Sergius II orders that "all the doors" of the Basilica of St. Peter "be shut and bolted" until the intentions of the Frankish king of Italy, Louis II, could be ascertained.[49] Many additional examples can be cited.

Even this brief, but more nuanced, examination of the *Farnesianus* text underscores two points. One is that its text is closer to the text of the older recensions than are the other manuscripts of the E recension, that it represents an earlier point in the evolution of the E recension away from the original text. The second conclusion is that, despite this, the *Farnesianus*'s textual links (both in errors and in correct readings) to the Roman manuscripts of the E recension—Vat. lat. 3764, observed by earlier editors, and Vat. lat. 3762 (Pandulph's redaction)—make a strong argument for the "romanitas" of its text.

The version of the Life of Pope Sergius II (844–847) uniquely contained in the *Farnesianus* is also evidence of the origins of the *Farnesianus* codex in Rome. This Life of Pope Sergius is different from the version transmitted in all

---

46 "*Hierusalem ecclesiam sanctam quae multo fuerat distecta tempore*" (Duchesne I, 401, l. 4 and *app. crit*). Duchesne, however, does not exclude the reading of the *Farnesianus* (*distecta*) from his note "detecta E" embracing all E manuscripts, including the *Farnesianus* (= E[5] in both Duchesne's and Mommsen's editions). See Reg. lat. 2081, f. 97, outside margin: "dist." in Holste's hand. Mommsen's editions stops in 715.

47 Lewis and Short [1879] 1969, 597. The *Oxford Latin Dictionary* (*OLD*), which includes only words attested by 200 CE, does not have "*distectus*," nor does Du Cange's *Glossarium* (1710).

48 "*Serro, serrare*" is a late Latin verb meaning "*to saw*," Lewis and Short, 1680–1681; only its cognates (*serra, serratus*) are attested in the *OLD*. "*Sero, serare*" is the correct word for "to bolt." But the word "*serrare*" in the meaning of "to bolt" is attested in Du Cange, s.v. "*serro, serrare*."

49 Duchesne II, 88, l. 21, where, however, the accurate reading of the *Farnesianus* ("*serrari*" in Reg. lat. 2081, p. 250, outside margin note in Holste's hand) is not included in the *apparatus criticus*.

other manuscripts of the *Liber pontificalis* in two ways.[50] First, it is much more detailed, containing abundant and precise topographic information missing from or highly abbreviated in the other version, and fuller lists of papal donations to local religious institutions. Second, it alone contains the account of the Arab raiding party of August 846, when the "Saraceni" managed to land at the mouth of the Tiber, defeated the defending Roman force, and pillaged the churches outside the Aurelian Walls, including the Basilica of St. Peter and that of St. Paul. The narrator, who exhibits direct knowledge of these events, lays the blame for the disaster at the feet of Pope Sergius, who is portrayed as a weakling under the sway of his simoniac brother, and unable to govern and protect the city.[51] This narrative offers a completely unflattering portrait of the pontiff. The Life ends, incomplete, in the middle of a sentence.[52]

The version of the Life of Sergius transmitted in all the other manuscripts of the *Liber pontificalis* is shorter, eliding many of the details of the *Farnesianus'* account. Furthermore, it omits completely the antipapal passage recounting the Arabs' incursions in Rome's neighborhood. But it ends with the traditional formula summarizing the details of the pope's ordinations, and of his death and burial.

The reasons behind the double redaction of the Life of Sergius II have been debated.[53] Here it is important to stress that the singular Life of Sergius II in the *Farnesianus* offers additional textual support for the manuscript's Roman origins. For it is clear that the *Farnesianus* version is the first, original Life of Sergius, reflecting knowledge of local topography and papal documents which could only be available to an inhabitant of the city, with access to the papal archive (*scrinium*) and chancery (*vestiarium*), and that it was replaced in later manuscripts by a blander, less detailed Life of the pontiff.[54] The preservation of the first, longer Life of Sergius in the *Farnesianus* speaks to the local roots of this copy of the *Liber pontificalis*. Similarly, the account of the Arab incursion and its negative portrayal of the pope can only be understood as representing local, Roman politics. This passage, placed in an awkward position in the

---

50   Duchesne II, iii–iv, 91–101, where the two versions are printed in parallel columns.

51   Duchesne II, 97 l. 17–101 l. 4.

52   Holste did not indicate whether the Life is incomplete because pages were missing at the end, or if the text itself was left incomplete.

53   Some see it as reflecting conflicts within Rome and the papal court over the role of the Carolingians and the Byzantine rulers as protectors of the papal see; Osborne 2011, 222–236, esp. 226–227.

54   On the writing of the ninth-century Lives of the *Liber pontificalis*, see Herbers 2009 and Bougard 2009. The abbreviation of papal Lives by eliminating details that have no longer significance (such as gifts to churches) is frequent in the *Liber pontificalis*.

middle of an otherwise traditional Life, may well have originated as a marginal note which was at a second stage incorporated into the text, or, less likely, from a sudden change in author.[55] In any case, such an addition could only have originated in Rome, and its migration into the text best explained as occurring where the papal chronicle was regularly copied and brought up to date, in the papal chancery and related offices.

5 Material Evidence

To the textual evidence provided by Holste we can add the evidence of script and decoration provided by Francesco Bianchini to strengthen the argument in favor of the Roman origins of the lost *Farnesianus*.

5.1 *Uncial Script*

Created in Late Antiquity, uncial was a majuscule script employed in both Latin and Greek alphabets.[56] Now believed to have originated in Italy, the script was used as a formal book hand throughout Western Europe in the early Middle Ages. It was exported to the north from Rome, frequently transmitting biblical and patristic works, most notably to England (from the sixth century) and to Frankish lands, where uncial was then imitated for especially luxurious books. Uncial became closely associated with the church of Rome, and its literary, liturgical, and legal traditions.

By the late eighth century, when Caroline minuscule had become the dominant book hand, uncial was reserved within most of Europe almost entirely for deluxe Gospels. In Italy, the use of uncial continued for all kinds of texts through much of the eighth century, but well-developed minuscules, including Caroline, were increasingly used as common book hands.[57] In Rome, however, uncial remained the standard book hand for longer than anywhere else, and minuscule acquired dominance much later. Several manuscripts, all in uncials, have been localized in Rome from the late eighth and early ninth century, but none have been dated to the middle or second half of the ninth century, as would be our *Farnesianus*. All eight manuscripts surviving from Rome from the second half of the ninth century are written instead in Caroline minuscule.[58]

---

55 Duchesne II, iii–iv. For an example of marginal notes which migrated into the text of the *Liber pontificalis*, see Franklin 2019.

56 A brief history of the script is found in Bischoff 1990, 66–72.

57 Bischoff 1994, 44.

58 See Ammirati 2020, for the list. These minuscule manuscripts are also discussed in Supino Martini 2012.

Some of the latest uncial manuscripts from the end of the eighth century and the beginning of the ninth now assigned to Rome will serve as points of comparison for the *Farnesianus* in the discussion that follows.[59] Two of these provide clear internal evidence of their Roman origins. One is the *Homiliary* of Agimundus, a collection of homilies arranged according to the liturgical year, originally in three volumes, only two of which survive (Vat. lat. 3835 and 3836: *CLA* I, 18a, 18b).[60] The copying of the homiliary can be located precisely at Rome's Church of Ss. Philip and James (today's Basilica dei Santi Apostoli) because of the colophon written by the scribe, who names himself as "the priest Agimundus" in the "*Basilica apostolorum philippi et iacobi.*"[61] Especially important for my argument are the quaternios added at the turn of the ninth century (ff. 55–70 of Vat. lat. 3836), written slightly later than the rest of the homiliary. The second manuscript provided with internal evidence of its Roman origins is the well-studied Juvenianus Codex of the Vallicelliana Library in Rome, dated to the turn or first quarter of the ninth century (Vall. B.25. II: *CLA* 4.430).[62] The manuscript is named after the subdeacon Juvenianus, who may have been its scribe-artist, as he appears with an inscription in a full-page presentation miniature offering the codex to St. Lawrence. The book contains biblical texts—the Acts of the Apostles, and the non-Pauline Epistles, as well as the Apocalypse followed by the first book of Bede's commentary.

In addition, four more uncial manuscripts have convincingly been attributed to Rome for this period mostly on the basis of script: (1) the important glossary Vat. lat. 3321, from the beginning of the ninth century;[63] (2) the *Salmasianus* (Paris, BnF MS 10318), from the late eighth to early ninth century, containing the Latin Anthology;[64] (3) Vat. lat. 1342, from the same period, a canonical

---

59 On these uncial manuscripts, see Petrucci 1971; Ammirati 2020, with earlier bibliography.

60 Osborne 1990, 80–81, and figures 5 and 6. Ammirati 2020. The digitized manuscript is available at the website of the Vatican Library: https://tinyurl.com/y6e7677p and https://tinyurl.com/y42t6nmz.

61 "*Qui legis obsecro ut oris pro scriptore ut per apostolorum principum solvatur vincula agimundi pro peccatori sicut inutili scriptori deo caeli grates Basilica apostolorum philippi et iacobi,*" Vat. lat. 3835, f. 329^r.

62 Osborne 1990, 82 and figure 7; Zonghetti 2005; Ammirati 2020. The digitized manuscript is available at https://tinyurl.com/y4jalhcl.

63 Ammirati 2020; 2007. The digitized manuscript is available at the website of the Vatican Library: https://tinyurl.com/yy4u78mx.

64 Spallone 1982; Reeve 2011, 55–56. The digitized manuscript is available on the Gallica website of the Bibliothèque nationale de France: https://tinyurl.com/yyxb82vj.

THE LOST FARNESIANUS MANUSCRIPT 153

sylloge;[65] (4) BAV, Reg. lat. 9, containing Roman liturgical texts, written by a hand similar to Agimundus'.[66]

The *Farnesianus*, if written in Rome around the middle of the ninth century as indicated by the presence of the Life of Sergius II, would be more recent than all of the surviving manuscripts in uncials, including the ones listed above. It would thus confirm the long life of uncial script in the papal city, and in fact extend it; furthermore, its large and controlled letters would also argue for a more nuanced perspective of ninth-century Roman uncials as representing a period of decline and demise, an evaluation of script as an organism with a life cycle from birth to maturity to decline and death.[67]

The script of the *Farnesianus* and its decorative initials come to us through the filter of the new forms, transferred from the handwritten parchment page, to the handwritten facsimile, to the engraved print, as we saw above, and it must be assessed cautiously. Bianchini discusses at length his efforts to ensure that the engravings be accurate, as faithful to the manuscript as possible.[68] The drawing for the first engraving (Figure 8.1), of the Life of Pope Eugenius I, was executed by "an expert calligrapher" in Parma under the supervision of Marchese Maurizio de Sanctis, a retainer of the Farnese Duke, who has left a detailed account of the process, which entailed the composition of an entire alphabet "to reflect each letter, both in the thickness of the stroke and their size and height so that there is no difference between the facsimile and the original."[69] Bianchini adds also that after he had the handmade facsimiles engraved in Rome, he sent back a proof of the printed engraving to the Marchese for comparison with the original. The Marchese thus could compare

---

65   Most important is the hand that wrote the uncials in ff. 54^r–69^v: Petrucci 1971, 118–119; Ammirati 2020. The digitized manuscript is available at the Vatican Library website: https://tinyurl.com/yyjj3xjb.

66   Ammirati 2020; Petrucci 1971, 119. The digital copy is available on the Vatican Library website: https://tinyurl.com/yxlvfc2n.

        There is great disagreement about the Roman origins of a very few other uncial manuscripts, and they are excluded from consideration here. These include: Paris, BnF, N. A. lat. 2334; Cambrai, B. M. 386; and Vat. lat. 7809. I also exclude the few Greek or bilingual manuscripts in uncial and attributed to Rome. See Ammirati 2020.

67   As viewed, for example, in Petrucci 1971, particularly 98–100, 114–121.

68   See further, Franklin 2017, 621–628.

69   Bianchini 2, xxiv col. 2, where de Sanctis' letter of September 15, 1719, is quoted (in Italian). The process of printing both letterpress and intaglio (i.e. from a copperplate) has been little studied. It involves two separate processes as printing letterpress takes an impression from a raised surface, while engraving picks up ink from the lines engraved in a flat plate. A useful introduction is Gaskell 2004, esp. 229–230, concentrating, however, on England.

154   FRANKLIN

the *"typum"* (facsimile) sent by Bianchini to the *"prototypum"* in Parma, and certify in a letter that indeed there was complete agreement between the original and the copy. The proofs of some of Bianchini's engravings from the *Farnesianus* are found among Bianchini's papers at the Vallicelliana.[70] The other four facsimiles were made in 1720 by Bianchini himself, who had been trained in drawing and used this skill to record his observation of material data.[71] Both sets of engravings (Figures 8.1–8.4) were made in Rome, but their engravers remain anonymous.

Bianchini does not discuss the script's traits in any detail to argue for the antiquity of the *Farnesianus*, as would a modern paleographer, but relies completely on its images, stressing in his discussion that they are a faithful reproduction of the manuscript, implying that the facsimiles and engravings were executed at scale. As we saw above, in his attempt to record precisely his observations, Bianchini reproduced the Donation of Pepin spread over three pages, an effort to duplicate in print the image of the Donation precisely as transmitted in the manuscript. One of these pages is a full-page reproduction of the *Farnesianus* (Figure 8.3), as is also the facsimile of the Life of Pope Eugenius (Figure 8.1). Each page has two columns of 28 lines per column, and occupies the same area in the printed page, 30×19cm of Bianchini's larger writing area.[72] If three or four centimeters are added to account for the folios' margins typical in a manuscript of this size, the lost *Farnesianus* would have measured 34×23cm. The reconstruction of the quires of the codex by Wilhelm Levison resulted in a book of more than thirty-two quaternios, for a total of at least 256 folios, of which only 80 survived when Holste and Bianchini saw the *Farnesianus*.[73] The *Farnesianus* thus would have been a sizable book and taller by several centimeters than our comparanda,[74] more in line with

---

70   *"aeri incidi feci Romae ad exempli ad me transmissi normam singulos characteres vitae S. Eugenii, et impressionis nostrae typum cum prototypo conferendum eidem reddi curavi,"* Bianchini 2, xxiv col. 2. The proofs of the printing of a few of the engravings alone—i.e., before the text was added—are found in Fondo Bianchini, T. 153. Of the ones discussed here, I was able to find only the proof of the first portion of the Donation of Pepin (Figure 8.2).

71   Franklin 2017, 627–628.

72   The actual scale of the script is corroborated by the fact that the area occupied by each of the plates of full-page reproductions from the *Farnesianus* is smaller than that of the simply printed pages of Bianchini's volumes (as can also easily be seen in Figure 8.1).

73   Levison 1911, 433–438. The majority of Roman books were arranged in quaternios (i.e., four double sheets, or eight folios). Spallone 1982, 43.

74   The *Juvenianus'* written surface is of varying height, but never larger than 24×18, and the size of the full page is 31×23. The measurements of the *Agimundus* are: vol. 1 24.5×20 and

THE LOST FARNESIANUS MANUSCRIPT   155

the measurements of a contemporary Gospel book.[75] Its two-column format, extremely rare at this time except for books used in the liturgy, also signifies a luxurious product.[76]

The printed images, despite the inevitable distortion and uniformity introduced by the processes of transferal through three media (original manuscript, hand copy, print), replicate letters clearly exhibiting the characteristics of late Roman uncials, according to the typology of the script established by paleographers and scholars of Rome's written culture.[77] In the images reproduced by Bianchini, we find the unmistakable flattening of the written lines combined with the heaviness of script that is typical of late Roman uncials, as in all the manuscripts listed above.[78] Very characteristic of late Roman uncial script are the flattened d, which curves back, its vertical shaft almost parallel to the bowl of the letter, as we see in Bianchini's prints;[79] and the a with the loop in the shape of a leaf or triangle, rather than round, as can be seen more clearly in Figures 8.2, 8.3, and 8.4. Late Roman uncial is also typified by the addition of short lines to the horizontal shaft of letters, sometimes curled underneath ("forkings"). In the reproduced images these characteristics are most visible in the letter L, as in the last line of the first column in Figure 8.1, but they can be found also in the L's of the images from Pope Stephen's Life (Figures 8.2–8.4). The curves added to the top of the first shaft of the U's in the *Farnesianus* is a parallel practice.[80]

Most striking in Roman uncial manuscripts is the breakdown of the old squareness of the script, illustrated particularly by the taller L and T, rising above the other letters, as is visible throughout these images. Also widespread in Roman books is the squeezing of letters at the end of the line, and we find instances of this practice also in the *Farnesianus*. In Figure 8.1, there is an

---

      30×24.9; vol. 2 22×19 and 29.5×24.7. The measurements of the *Salmasianus* are 23–24.5×19 and 32×24.5. These measurements come from the *CLA* plates, as cited above.

75   Such as a Gospel book from the late eighth century, written in central Italy, which measures 38×17.5cm (*CLA* I, 51).

76   Of the books we have been discussing, only the *Agimundus*, a liturgical manuscript, is written mostly in two columns of 26–28 lines.

77   The most detailed treatment is Petrucci 1971, especially 98–100, 114–121. A most useful summary is provided in Ammirati's discussions (2020) of Vat. lat. 3321, which she locates in Rome; Ammirati 2007.

78   Close similarities can be observed particularly with the *Agimundus* manuscript, the *Salmasianus*, and Vat. lat. 3321 (a good example is the hand that wrote f. 172 in the last).

79   For example, in Figure 8.2 (l.11, small initial "d"), and at the end of the next line, and two lines below.

80   The *Farnesianus*' curvy U is very similar to that used in the *Salmasianus* (see, for example, *Salmasianus*, 229 Figure 8.9).

example at the end of the first line, and "Tus" at the end of the seventh line (first column), where the "us" is written in what could be called minuscule, a sign of script-mixing, not uncommon in late Roman uncials.[81] The *Farnesianus* also shows the mixing of Roman capitals and uncial letters that is found in Roman exemplars. The opening line of the Life of Eugenius (Figure 8.1) is in Roman capitals, but the second and third E (GE; NE) are uncial. The entire appearance of this incipit in the *Farnesianus* closely resembles one found in Vat. lat. 3321, where, in a title in Roman capitals, there are three uncial E's in addition to one Roman capital E.[82] As in the other examples of later Roman uncials, the *Farnesianus* also shows a greater use of ligatures, especially of the T, written in ligature with E (Figure 8.3, second column, last line), and the N, in ligature with A, in the opening line of the Life of Paul I (Figure 8.4).

The orthography of the script, and particularly the confusion of v and b, is striking: *cessabit* (for *cessavit*), *archibo, Rabennantium, clabes, cibitatem*, etc.[83] This usage, known as betacism, is widely attested in contemporary Roman written materials, including inscriptions.[84]

5.2   *Decorated Initials*

Roman manuscripts from the late eighth and early ninth century display a new interest in the use of ornamentation for initial letters, following the decorative programs developed in scriptoria of France and the British Isles. These patterns include the incorporation of zoomorphic and human forms within letters, interlace design and acanthus leaf flourishes, as well as bright paint colors.[85] Their use has been particularly highlighted in the *Agimundus Homiliary* and

---

81   Two lines below it, a horizontal "m" is found (*"rogam"*); I find this final-m abbreviation above a vowel in the *Salmasianus*, 2, l. 14; and in the *Juvenianus*, f. 64[r], l. 6. In the *Farnesianus*, the final-m is not always abbreviated.

82   Vat. lat. 3321, f. 132[r]. It is noteworthy that the capital E occurs in an AE diphthong (in the word "*differentiae*").

83   The first example is from Figure 8.1, second column, next to last line; the rest from Figure 8.3. There is a far higher occurrence of this phenomenon in the second set of prints, the only slight indication that a different scribe may be at work.

84   See, for example, Vat. lat. 3321, f. 68[r] for *berecundia* rather than *verecundia* (first word of third column). The confusion of b and v has also been noted in the *Agimundus Homiliary* (see f. 60[r], where the original *bitam* has been corrected to *vitam*, as in Osborne 1990, 80 and n33). The *Salmasianus* also exhibits these orthographic traits (Spallone 1982, 64) which had caused Traube to suggest a Spanish copyist. The use of *ebangelista* to refer to Mark the Evangelist in the mosaic inscription in the church of San Marco (ca. 830) is a close chronological parallel I owe to John Osborne.

85   My discussion here follows Osborne 1990. See also Spallone 1982, 44–47. Scholars have disagreed on the transmission route of these decorative styles to Rome (Osborne 1990, 76), but that issue is not of concern here.

THE LOST FARNESIANUS MANUSCRIPT   157

in the *Juvenianus*, the only manuscripts that have been localized in Rome with
certainty. The facsimiles published by Bianchini include only two illustrations:
the E at the opening of the Life of Eugenius, Figure 8.1 as we saw above; and
the P at the beginning of the Life of Paul I (Figure 8.4), which was chosen by
Bianchini to illustrate papal iconography, a subject in which he held a keen
interest. We can be certain that the lost codex had one decorated initial at the
beginning of every papal Life, along the model of those for Eugenius and Paul,
adding up to a total of at least 104.[86] There were also smaller rubricated initials
within the text, as can be seen in Bianchini's plates, where, instead of color, a
thicker ink stroke is used.

The difference between the simpler E at the beginning of Eugenius' Life
and the more complex, and larger, P at the beginning of Paul I's Life suggests
that a broad range of decorative levels was used, as is the case with the comparanda. Their loss is incalculable. Still, the two reproduced by Bianchini offer
compelling additional support for the Roman origin of the *Farnesianus*, for
they exhibit similar motifs that have been highlighted in late uncial manuscripts localized in Rome, and especially in the *Agimundus Homiliary* and the
Juvenianus Codex, including interlace design, the enclosure of the human
form in the bowl of a letter, the replacement of the arms of letters with floral
shapes, and the addition of acanthus flourishes.

The decorated capital P in the *Farnesianus* (Figure 8.4) shows in its bowl
the portrait of Pope Paul I, who wears the pallium and has his right arm in a
gesture of blessing, while holding a book with his left hand (not represented).
The P's decoration recalls both the initial P of the *Agimundus* with the portrait
of Mary in its bowl (Figure 8.5),[87] and the portrait of the Apostle Peter in the
bowl of the even more elaborate P of the *Juvenianus* (Figure 8.6).[88] Here, at
the opening of his First Letter, Peter is figured as bishop, with the pallium, his
right hand raised in blessing, while he holds a large key with his left in a frontal
stance that parallels Pope Paul I of the *Farnesianus* (Figure 8.4). The decorated
P at the beginning of the Life of Pope Paul in the *Farnesianus* is also similar
in decoration and design to the mirror-image letter q at the beginning of the
text *De Remediis salutaribus* in the *Salmasianus*, which encloses an animal
rather than a human form (Figure 8.7).[89] The letters in these last comparanda,
however, are much richer in decoration, and are also painted. The one-color
decorated initials of the *Farnesianus* as printed cannot compete with their

---

86   As Sergius II is 104th in succession from St. Peter.
87   Vat. lat. 3836, f. 64^r (Osborne 1990, 81 and figure 5).
88   Biblioteca Vallicelliana MS B.25 II, f. 51^r (Osborne 1990, 83 and figure 9).
89   BnF, MS lat. 10318, 262. Cf. Spallone 1982, table III.

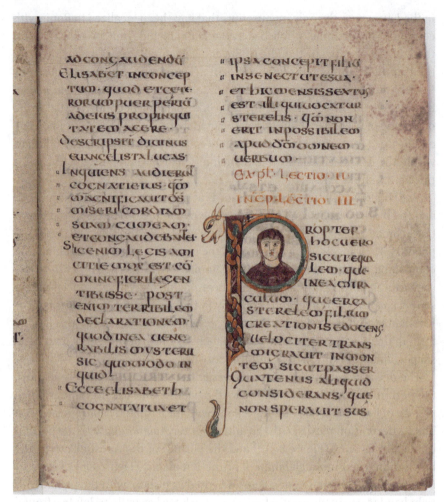

FIGURE 8.5 Biblioteca Apostolica Vaticana, Vaticanus latinus 3836 (*Agimundus Homiliary*, vol. 2), f. 64[r]

showiness.[90] It is very likely, however, that the initials in the *Farnesianus* were painted, but were not so duplicated in the printed engraving.[91]

---

90   Frequently, the scribe was also the decorator, as might have been the case for the surviving *Farnesianus* initials. But the more complex ornamentation of the *Agimundus* and *Juvenianus* manuscripts was more likely the result of collaboration between scribe and artist. The close collaboration between miniaturist and scribe in the planning of the *Juvenianus* has been noted; Zonghetti 2005.
91   Bianchini's work does include one colored plate, replicating the relics of Pope Leo I that were moved to their new tomb in April 1714 (Franklin 2017, 618–619). It is also possible of course that the *Farnesianus* was left unfinished and the initials not painted.

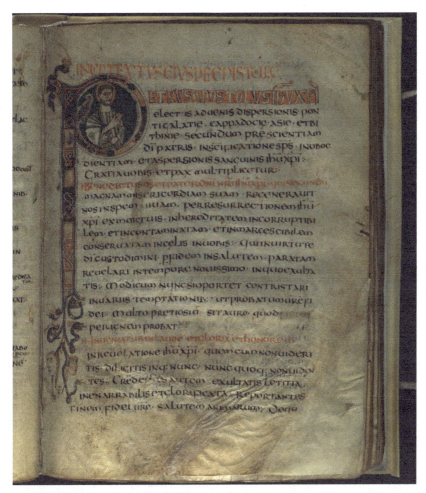

FIGURE 8.6 Rome, Biblioteca Vallicelliana, B.25 II (Codex Juvenianus), f. 51ʳ
PHOTO BY SIRIA SARMIENTO

The vertical stems of both the P and E initials in the *Farnesianus*, decorated with interlace and acanthus leaf, also recall the initials of the earlier books, where acanthus leaves appear in their more lavishly ornamented initials. The initial E of the *Farnesianus* (Figure 8.1) is noteworthy also for the loss of its horizontal strokes, its arms, which here have become floral decorations. In Agimundus' book, the highly decorative E (Figure 8.8)[92] also loses its original arms, replaced by two floral stems, and a blessing hand—a more complicated composition, but typologically similar to the E of Eugenius.

---

92   Vat. lat. 3836, f. 67ᵛ (Osborne 1990, 81 and figure 6).

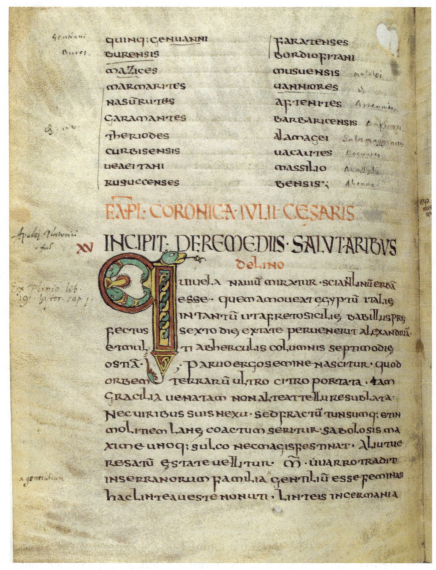

FIGURE 8.7 Paris, Bibliothèque nationale de France, MS 10318 (Codex Salmasianus), 262 (view 272)

The symmetrical acanthus flourishes that extend from the top and bottom of the letter E in the *Farnesianus* (Figure 8.1) to meet at the center of the letter's back, slightly overhanging in the margin, are echoed in the Roman manuscripts, as can be seen in the capital L of the *Salmasianus* (Figure 8.9). More generally, the geometric designs of the *Farnesianus*' E and P, and their acanthus ornamentations, are found in the initials of all the earlier books.

THE LOST FARNESIANUS MANUSCRIPT

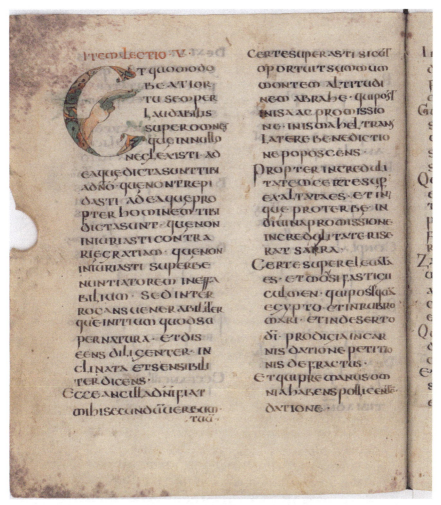

FIGURE 8.8 Biblioteca Apostolica Vaticana, Vaticanus latinus 3836 (*Agimundus Homiliary*, vol. 2), f. 67^v

It is true that the initials from the *Agimundus Homiliary* and especially those of the Juvenianus Codex are more elaborate and larger than those in the *Farnesianus*. This is not surprising since the homiliary, arranged according to the liturgical calendar, was clearly meant to be used for the reading of the homilies during the liturgy. As a book used in public worship it was subject to a higher degree of luxury. The *Juvenianus* is also a religious book, a biblical compendium, part of the liturgical library of the religious institution for which it was produced. Perhaps the more modest painted initials of the *Salmasianus*, not a liturgical book, but a secular collection, are a more plausible reflection of what the initials in the *Farnesianus* looked like. The *Salmasianus* has many

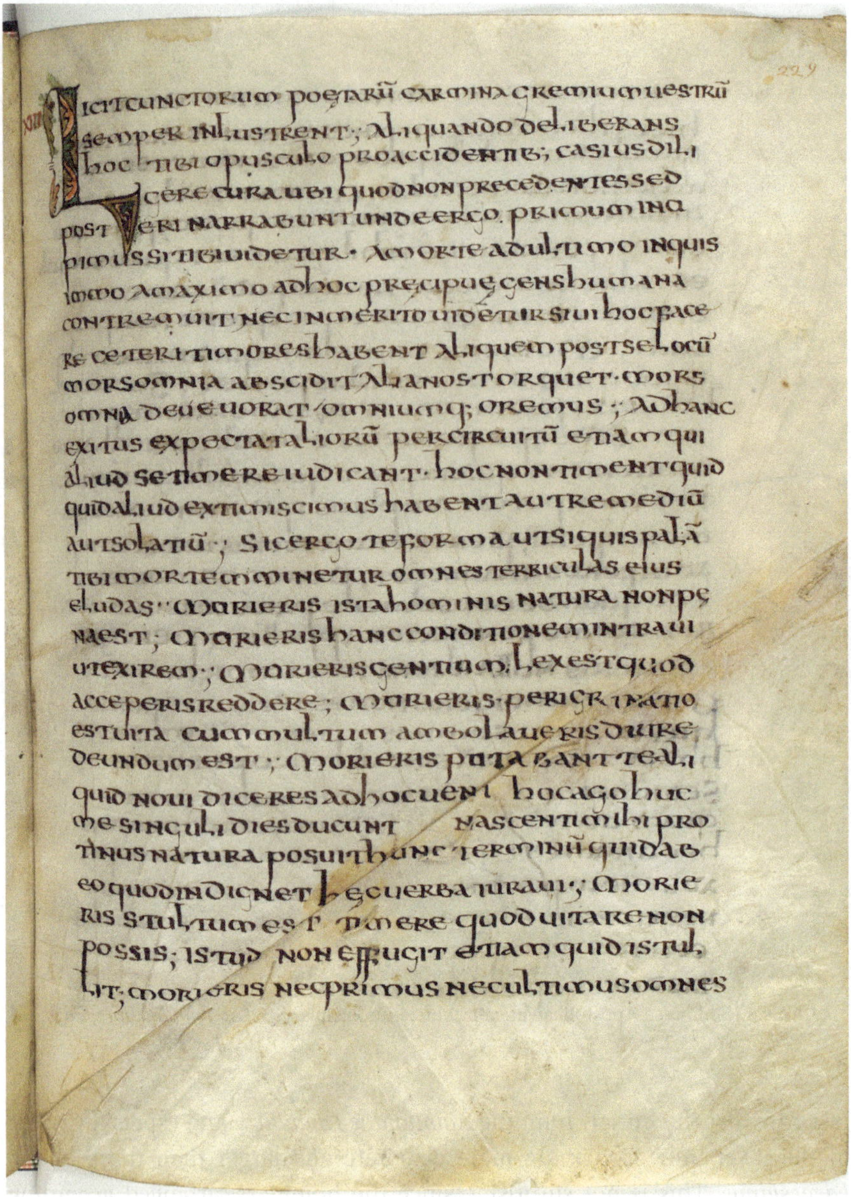

FIGURE 8.9   Paris, Bibliothèque nationale de France, MS 10318 (Codex Salmasianus), 229
(view 239)

decorated initials of different sizes and richness of decorative motifs. Both the
relatively short M whose outside "arms" are in fact acanthus leaves (Figure 8.10),
and the taller L discussed above (Figure 8.9) might be taken as closer to the
decorative register of the *Farnesianus*, recalling the lost manuscript's modest E of Eugenius (Figure 8.1) and the more complex P of Paul (Figure 8.4),

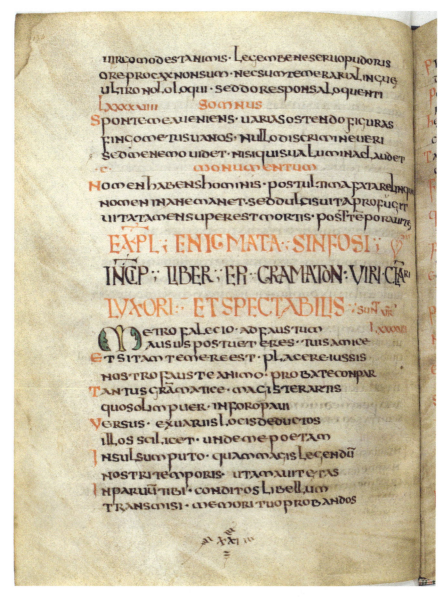

FIGURE 8.10 Paris, Bibliothèque nationale de France, MS 10318 (Codex Salmasianus), 156 (view 166)

keeping in mind that the initials in the *Salmasianus*, an actual manuscript, are painted.[93] The *Salmasianus* also contains several very highly decorated initials, such as the large A on p. 144 (Figure 8.11), whose first slanted line has been substituted by a fantastic fish biting the other line, and thus forming the A, an

---

93   https://tinyurl.com/y4ajnn3m.

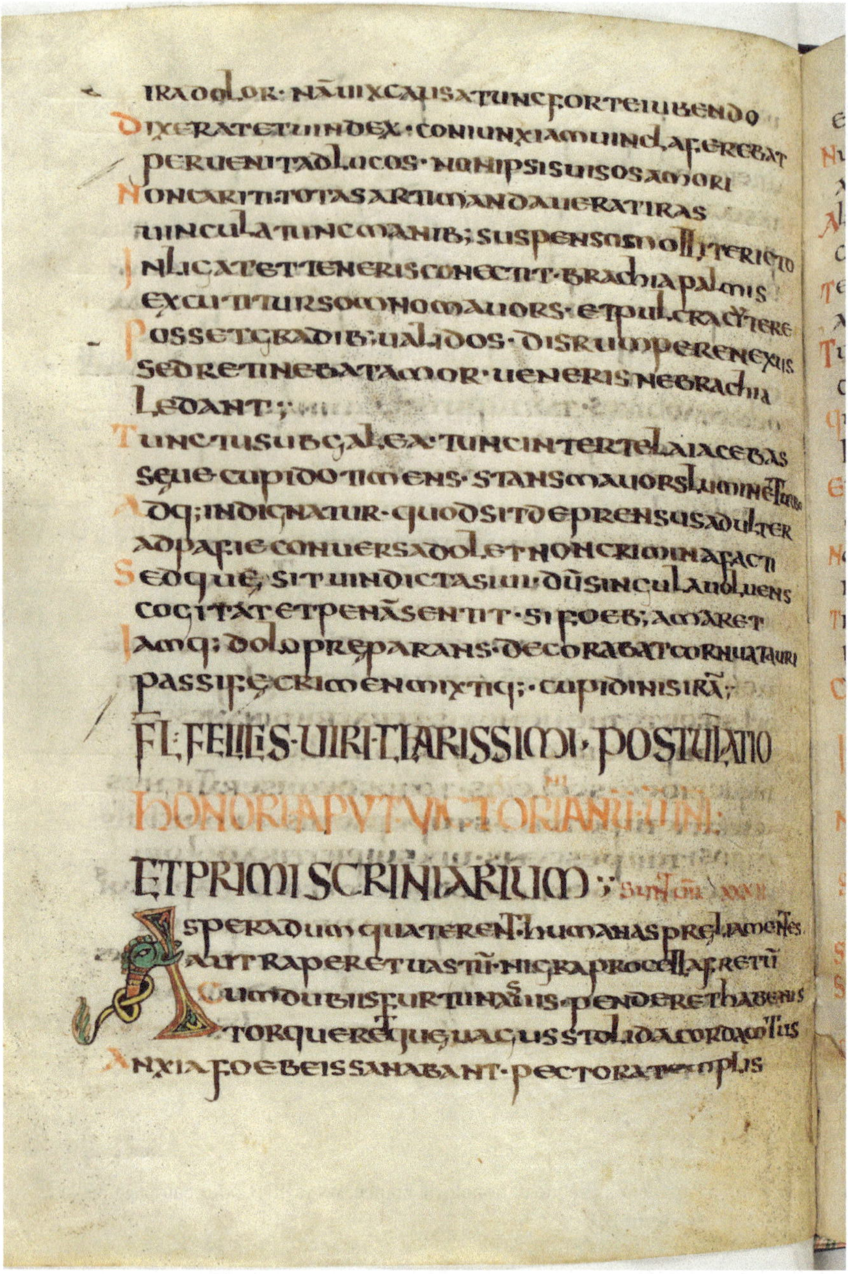

FIGURE 8.11   Paris, Bibliothèque nationale de France, MS 10318 (Codex Salmasianus), 134 (view 144)

THE LOST FARNESIANUS MANUSCRIPT   165

example of the use of zoomorphic motifs in contemporary Roman books.[94] Neither of the two *Farnesianus* initials has a zoomorphic motif such as this. But when we consider that only about two percent of the decorated letters contained in the entire *Farnesianus* are available for comparison, and that they share characteristics with those of surviving books, we must consider it likely that the *Farnesianus* also included similarly ornate and complex decorated initials in addition to the two published by Francesco Bianchini primarily to illustrate historical points.

6   Conclusions

Literary sources from the middle of the eighth century to the late ninth century evoke a thriving book production in Rome, and at the Lateran in particular.[95] Chief among witnesses is the *Liber pontificalis*, which sheds light on the library of the popes and related offices, including the *scrinium*, where particularly important documents and books were kept,[96] and the *vestiarium*, an early chancery. The Life of Pope Gregory II (715–731) relates that the future pope, when a subdeacon, was charged with the care of the "bibliotheca."[97] Beginning with the pontificate of Paschal I (817–824), the office of "bibliothecarius" of the Roman church is regularly mentioned. The *Liber pontificalis* also highlights the gift of books richly ornamented with gold and silver, which the popes gave to churches in Rome and Italy, beginning in the papacy of Leo IV (847–855). More modest books were also given, as must have been the sixteen codices that Pope Stephen V gave to Roman churches, as narrated in his Life, at the very end of the *Liber pontificalis*.[98] The correspondence between Frankish rulers and the curia also offers evidence that numerous gifts of books were made by the papacy to the Carolingians as early as the eighth century, and then in increasing numbers in the ninth. Precious books were also exchanged between the popes and the Byzantines. These details highlight the significance of books as valuable objects especially in this period of Carolingian cultural influence.

---

94   https://tinyurl.com/y303fj44.

95   The most detailed discussion is Supino Martini 2012; Ammirati 2020 provides updates.

96   Such as Charlemagne's diploma of donation to Pope Hadrian I, as stated in the pontiff's Life; Duchesne I, 498, ll. 15–30.

97   Duchesne I, 396, l.6 and 410, n1 ("... *bibliothecae ei cura commissa*").

98   Supino Martini 2012, 38 and notes.

The second half of the ninth century is particularly rich in literary information on the writing activity at the Lateran through several figures associated with its library and scriptorium. The best known is Anastasius Bibliothecarius (810–878), ex-antipope, secretary to Pope Nicholas I (858–867) and prolific author and translator from the Greek, who may even have written some of the ninth-century papal Lives.[99] The working copy of his translation of the Greek Acts of the eighth ecumenical council, executed in 870–871 by several scribes at the Lateran, and with his notes and corrections, survives (Vat. lat. 4965).[100] Both text and notes are written in the Roman version of Caroline minuscule, romanesca.

Yet, in comparison to the literary testimony, there survives meager material evidence for book production during this period. For the ninth century, as we have seen, only a few uncial manuscripts from the very beginning of the century remain, and nothing else until the last quarter of the ninth. By this time, the material evidence is all in minuscule, as we saw above.

The reconstruction of the *Farnesianus*, and its plausible localization in Rome in the middle or later in the ninth century, is therefore particularly precious. It was at this time, during the pontificates of Nicholas I and his successor Hadrian II from the mid-850s to the mid-870s, that the composition of the *Liber pontificalis* was being renewed, written no longer by anonymous minor officials of the Curia, but by literati, such as Anastasius Bibliothecarius himself, and his colleague John the Deacon, best known for his biography of Gregory I, based, as he said, on abundant materials obtained "*de scrinio sanctae sedis apostolicae*."[101] Viewed against the increased literary and scribal revival of ninth-century Rome, the *Farnesianus*, a grand book transmitting the history of the popes, written in large and beautiful uncials, and with painted initials, can be seen as adding another facet to these developments within the papal court. The pioneering paleographer of romanesca script, Paola Supino Martini, wondered how the change from uncial to minuscule took place in Rome, where the uncial majuscule, tied to the traditions of the Roman church, had held such prestige and authority since the sixth century. She opined that the demise of uncial had happened slowly, and not dramatically, and pointed out as an example of uncial's tenacity the continued use of uncial script in the salutation of

---

99   Arnaldi 1961, 25–37. John the Deacon (Johannes Hymmonides) and Gaudericus of Velletri must be added to Anastasius. All three made substantial use of materials in the archives and library of the Lateran; Bougard 2009, 131–134.

100 Supino Martini 2012, 29–30; Bilotta 2011, 64–69. The identification of this manuscript as Anastasius' "working copy" is discussed in Leonardi 1967.

101 Johannes Diaconus, *PL* 75, col. 61.

THE LOST FARNESIANUS MANUSCRIPT 167

papal letters into the tenth century, and in both private and public epigraphic materials. Most importantly, she showed that romanesca's most characteristic traits are vestiges of uncial—the flattening of lines, the a with the bowl in the shape of a leaf, and numerous others.[102] The *Farnesianus*, written as Roman minuscule had gained ascendancy, is a witness of continuity within the city's scribal culture.

My argument that the *Farnesianus* was produced in Rome has been pursued through both the textual and the material evidence transmitted by two scholars who actually saw and studied the now lost manuscript, the humanist Lucas Holste and the scientist and historian Francesco Bianchini. The indirect recovery of the textual evidence of the *Farnesianus*, as has been done here from Holste's glosses in the margin of his printed edition of the *Liber pontificalis*, is familiar philological practice. Philologists often make use of indirect evidence in textual criticism when they use citations by other authors, at times even in a different language. A closer parallel to the case of the *Farnesianus* is the use by editors of classical texts of the collation notes of Renaissance humanists, such as Politian, taken from manuscripts that have since disappeared.[103] As philologists we are forced to reconstruct texts from imperfect evidence, from witnesses that contain mistakes, lacunae, and willful additions and omissions. My comparisons of Bianchini's facsimile of the *Farnesianus*—its appearance, script, and decorations, and even size—with real objects, manuscripts that still survive, however, is less conventional. Yet, it is not unrelated to the common attempts at the reconstruction from drawings and images, both handmade and in print form, of lost objects, including buildings, as is the case of Rome's old Basilica of St. Peter's, whose appearance, obfuscated by its Renaissance renovation, has been reconstructed through prints and written descriptions.[104] My paper has sought to use both the indirect textual evidence transmitted by the glosses of a seventeenth-century scholar, and the material evidence amazingly preserved by an eighteenth-century antiquarian to animate the ninth-century lost *Farnesianus* and its historical context, the written culture of Rome in the second half of the ninth century.

---

102   Supino Martini 2012, 1–27, 58–64.
103   Reynolds 2013, 146.
104   McKitterick et al. 2013.

CHAPTER 9

Late Antiquity Between Sasanian East and Roman West

Third-Century Imperial Women as Pawns in Propaganda Warfare

Anne Hunnell Chen

Due in no small part to the context of our own increasingly globally connected world, there is a growing recognition that the ancient world was far more interconnected than we once realized, and that historiographic factors have shaped disciplinary divides within the Western academic tradition that have in turn obscured fascinating reciprocal cultural exchanges among ancient civilizations. In terms of Late Antiquity, specifically, postcolonial theoretical perspectives have helped us to see past the biased language of Western ancient written sources to reevaluate pejorative narratives that characterize late Roman contact with the Persian Empire as corrupting, and one of the root causes for Rome's decline.[1] In fact, study of the material productions of the late Roman and Sasanian Persian Empires with attention to extraimperial relations reveals that the two powers were highly attuned to one another, and responded to ideological efforts launched from far beyond their own territorial limits. While it has long been recognized that the later Roman Empire's military conflict with their eastern Sasanian neighbors was a defining feature of Late Antiquity,[2] the fact that this rivalry played out on two different, but parallel and complementary, fronts—one militaristic and one propagandistic—has only recently begun to be properly acknowledged and explored.[3] Given the nascency of Romano-Persian cross-cultural studies and the only slightly more mature influence of ancient gender studies, it likely comes as no surprise that imperial women's role with regard to the competitive exchange between the Romans and Sasanians has yet to be foregrounded.

In tribute to Alan Cameron, a generous mentor who encouraged my interest in exploring the myriad internal and external factors that helped to shape

---

1 Rubin 2001, 638; Canepa 2009, 2; Daryaee 2009, xv–xxii; Drijvers 2009, 453–454; Canepa 2010, 9–15.
2 Canepa 2009, 2; Drijvers 2009; Edwell 2013.
3 The seminal study is Canepa 2009. See also Gyselen 2010; Alram and Gyselen 2012, 13–64; Chen 2016.

© THE TRUSTEES OF COLUMBIA UNIVERSITY IN THE CITY OF NEW YORK,
2021 | DOI:10.1163/9789004452794_010

LATE ANTIQUITY BETWEEN SASANIAN EAST AND ROMAN WEST 169

late antique imperial ideological strategy, I offer this brief piece intended to draw attention to this aspect of competitive exchange between the neighboring Sasanian and Roman powers. After a brief historical sketch to set the scene, this chapter aims to show how in the early years of contact and conflict between these empires in the third century, Sasanian and Roman imperial women's acknowledgment in official ideological material—whether through their emphasis or their suppression—was central to the propaganda campaign each empire launched in an effort to speak to issues both at home and abroad.

1 Historical Background: Romano-Sasanian Relations in the Third Century CE

From the second quarter of the third century right through the century's end, the Romans and the incipient Persian Sassanid dynasty were engaged in a near constant state of war.[4] In the first few years of the conflict, the showdown between monarchs was essentially a draw. But in the years between 237 and 260 CE, the tide of the conflict changed significantly, to the detriment of the Romans. At this time, the Romans lost control over important eastern cities, one emperor, Gordian III (r. 238–244), was killed on campaign, and his successor, Philip the Arab (r. 244–249) agreed to what contemporaries saw as unfavorable and humiliating terms for the cessation of hostilities with the Persians.[5] But it was in 260 CE that the Romans would brook what was certainly the biggest misfortune of the period, and possibly the single greatest disaster the imperial Romans had ever suffered at the hands of an enemy. In that year, Sasanian king Šābuhr (r. 240–270) landed a crippling blow, capturing not only a throng of high-ranking Roman officers, but also the Roman emperor himself. The emperor Valerian's (r. 253–260) capture marked the first and only time an emperor had fallen into enemy hands, and the event shook the Roman sense of superiority and invulnerability to its core. To make matters worse,

---

4 Frye 1983, 124–132; Dodgeon and Lieu 1991, 1–3; Dignas and Winter 2007, 18–32; Canepa 2009, 4; Darayee 2009, 2–13; Caldwell 2018.

5 For discussion of the treaty of 244 CE, its terms and reception by the Romans, see Frye 1983, 125; Dodgeon and Lieu 1991, 38–39; Dignas and Winter 2007, 119–122; Canepa 2009, 79. Philip attempted to pass off the treaty as a diplomatic victory by issuing a series of coins praising the *pax fundata cum Persis* (see *RIC* 4.3: 76, no. 69), but the strategy seems to have fallen short of the mark. For discussion of the Western sources' disapproval of Philip and negative attitude toward the peace he negotiated, see York 1972; Dodgeon and Lieu 1991, 38–39. For a chronological survey of early Romano-Sasanian conflict, see Dodgeon and Lieu 1991, 1–3; Dignas and Winter 2007, 18–32, 71–84; Darayee 2009, 2–13.

Šābuhr took advantage of the victory against Valerian to claim thirty-seven cities in the Roman provinces of Syria, Cilicia, and Cappadocia, including the metropolis of Antioch, and deported thousands of Roman soldiers and citizens into Persian territories.[6] Never before had the Romans experienced such a shameful series of defeats with such staying power, but as discussed below, perhaps more importantly, never before had the Romans lost to an enemy that so publicly and pointedly publicized Roman military humiliation.[7]

From the 270s, the Roman state gradually restrengthened, while the later third century saw the Sasanians dealing with a series of successional disputes. After two short intervening reigns, Warahrān II's Sasanian monarchy (r. 274–93) saw internal unrest that may ultimately be to blame for the success of a Roman campaign that captured Ctesiphon under the leadership of Emperor Carus (r. 282–283). Carus' mysterious death would prevent the Romans from advancing further into Sasanian lands or making territorial gains.[8]

However, following the death of Carus, Diocletian (r. 284–305) and his Tetrarchic co-rulers would soon resume the fight with their eastern rivals. After an initial peace treaty with Warahrān II bought both nations time to settle internal matters,[9] including Sasanian dynastic disputes that eventually ended in King Narseh (r. 293–302) taking the Persian throne, war broke out once again.[10] Narseh at first achieved a decisive victory against the Romans in a military confrontation in 297 CE, but it was quickly followed up by an important Roman victory the next year at Satala in Armenia that saw the capture of the Sasanian royal family.[11] More than a half century of intermittent Romano-Persian conflict came to an end with the 298 Treaty of Nisibis. Despite the fact that the agreement clearly favored Roman interests, it ushered in an extraordinarily long period—forty years—of peace between Rome and Persia.[12]

---

6   Šābuhr I's trilingual (Parthian, Middle Persian, and Greek) inscription on the Ka'ba of Zoroaster at Naqsh-e Rustam presents the king's account of his accomplishments in this period. See Huyse 1999; Dignas and Winter 2007, 23, 77–84.

7   Dignas and Winter 2007, 71–84; Canepa 2009, 51–99; Caldwell 2018.

8   Frye 1983, 127–128; Dodgeon and Lieu 1991, 2–3, 97–106; Dignas and Winter 2007, 25–27; Darayee 2009, 10–13. For detailed discussion of the reign of Warahrān II, see Weber 2009.

9   Dodgeon and Lieu 1991, 106; Dignas and Winter 2007, 26–28; Darayee 2009, 12.

10   The bilingual (Parthian and Middle Persian) inscription at Paikui details Narseh's official account of the events that led to his accession; see Frye 1983, 128–130; Skjærvø and Humbach 1983; Darayee 2009, 12–13.

11   Frye 1983, 130–131; Dodgeon and Lieu 1991, 109–114; Dignas and Winter 2007, 86, 122–130; Darayee 2009, 13.

12   Dodgeon and Lieu 1991, 110–114; Dignas and Winter 2007, 28–32, 84–88, 122–130.

LATE ANTIQUITY BETWEEN SASANIAN EAST AND ROMAN WEST

2   Advancing the Propaganda Wars

Šābuhr I's mid-third-century series of stunning victories—including the death of one Roman emperor in battle, the unfavorable forced treaty of a second, and the capture of a third, all within a span of sixteen years—was an opportunity not to be missed. Recently, scholars have begun to recognize Šābuhr's efforts to capitalize on the mid-third-century Sasanian advantage by actively constructing and energetically disseminating an unflattering impression of Roman imperial power, as well as the ways such propaganda provoked response from the Roman court. Since the two great powers shared a number of diplomatic contacts abroad, Persian efforts to shape the Roman international reputation using a variety of media intended for internal and foreign consumption alike were an egregious threat that demanded Roman countermessaging.[13] Following his mid-century successes against the Romans as well as other conquests in Central and South Asia, Šābuhr changed the standard imperial titulature to read, "King of Kings of the Iranians and the Non-Iranians,"[14] clearly advertising what the Sasanians understood as the Romans' newly established status as tributary to the Sasanian court.[15] The insistent differentiation of "Iranian" and "Non-Iranian" lands in this regard seems a deliberate choice that both asserts the status of the Roman emperors as tributaries and servants of the Sasanian monarchs while also signaling to some degree the acceptance

---

13   The seminal study is Canepa 2009, esp. 51–99. See also Dignas and Winter 2007, 71–84; Gyselen 2010; Chen 2016.

14   Interestingly, although Šābuhr I was the first Sasanian monarch to use the extended title on rock inscriptions and on a gold double dinar commemorating the capitulation of Philip the Arab, this revised title was only extended to the regular silver coinage that was used for the bulk of economic activity during the reign of his son, Hormizd I (r. 270–271 CE). It remains unclear why Šābuhr did not carry the revised title over into his silver coinage, but the detail may intimate that Šābuhr was more immediately concerned about disseminating his claim to this revised titulature among external audiences and/or select internal audiences rather than disseminating the claim among the majority of the internal Sasanian audience, considering that gold coinage was reserved for special transactions (either internal donatives or payment/gifts to allies) and that Šābuhr's inscriptions are trilingual (Parthian, Middle Persian, and Greek). Alram 2008, 21; Canepa 2009, 54n8; Alram and Gyselen 2012, 14, 44–45. For the suggestion that Sasanian gold coinage was minted in the fourth century CE not for circulation in Iran but for the payment of foreign populations that were used to payment in gold, see Schindel 2013, 826–827; 2014, 12.

15   What Roman emperors understood as ransom for prisoners or pay-offs for peace, the Sasanian kings interpreted as tribute payments, placing the Roman Empire as subordinate to the Persian Empire. For discussion of the disconnect between Roman and Sasanian understandings of cash payments, see Canepa 2009, 54, 68.

172   CHEN

of the Roman Empire as an ultimately "subordinate but insoluble foe."[16] The modified imperial title was maintained by all of Šābuhr's successors, and verifiably put to use (i.e., explicitly asserted via textual inscription) in the later third century on large-scale stationary monuments, high-value transportable gift objects, and official coinage, and likely also verbally deployed in diplomatic contexts as well. Šābuhr I also communicated an equivalent message in the same contexts—once again on immovable monuments and gifts objects—utilizing unambiguous, internationally legible visual language.[17]

An offhand remark made by the Roman author Lactantius supports the notion that the Persian and Roman rival courts were familiar with the propaganda circulated by their adversaries. It may also signal that Sasanian visual propagation of Roman imperial impotency did not stop with gift objects, rock reliefs, or haughty Persian titulature, and it implies that Sasanian kings continued to capitalize on their third-century successes long after they were won. Lactanius, writing approximately forty years after the capture of Valerian, alleges that the Sasanian king made a point of humiliating the captive emperor by using him as a stepping stool when mounting his horse, and stating when he did so, "This [the humiliated station of the Roman emperor relative to the Sasanian king] is true, and not what the Romans delineate on board or plaster."[18] At the very least, the statement implies the Roman expectation that the Sasanian court was familiar with and motivated to respond to Roman ideological media. In the same passage, Lactantius goes on to say that supposedly, after his death in captivity,

> [Valerian] was flayed, and his skin, stripped from the flesh, was dyed with vermilion, and placed in the temple of the gods of the barbarians, that the remembrance of a triumph so signal might be perpetuated, and that this spectacle might always be exhibited to our ambassadors, as an admonition to the Romans, that, beholding the spoils of their captive emperor in a Persian temple, they should not place too great confidence in their own strength.[19]

Such a showpiece, if it indeed existed, was likely not only on display for Roman ambassadors, but rather a weighty ideological tool wielded for non-Roman

---

16   Edwell 2013, 845.
17   Canepa 2009, 53–74.
18   Lacantius *De mortibus persecutorum*, v, trans. Dodgeon and Lieu 1991, 50.
19   Lacantius *De mortibus persecutorum*, v, trans. Dodgeon and Lieu 1991, 50.

LATE ANTIQUITY BETWEEN SASANIAN EAST AND ROMAN WEST 173

contacts as well.[20] As a Christian Roman reporting on Persian actions and the fate of a Roman emperor considered a persecutor, Lactantius' word must of course be treated with caution. But the passage does at least gesture that the eastern and western rival realms engaged in ephemeral acts of propagandistic combat that made use of diplomatic channels and provocative visual stimuli to communicate with each other and likely also with farther ranging political contacts. The Persian practice of offering enemies' severed heads to the goddess Anāhīd,[21] and the periodic depiction of Roman soldiers presenting severed heads to their emperor on major monuments,[22] adds a hint of credulity to the idea that display of bodily trophies may have been among the tools deployed in the Romano-Persian propaganda war.

Efforts to immortalize Šābuhr's victories over the Romans with methods and media meant to travel beyond the limits of Sasanian territory presented the Roman court with what can be described as an international public-relations crisis.[23] The Tetrarchy's victory for the Romans in 298 CE provided an opportunity to counter Sasanian messaging. An octopylon arch that straddled a main thoroughfare in the imperial city of Thessaloniki was erected to memorialize the achievement. Among the various historical and symbolic scenes encircling the monument's four main piers, is one (Figure 9.1) whose format has been recognized as a Roman appropriation and ideologically significant transformation of a characteristically Persian iconography featuring confronted

---

20 The Romans and Sasanians surely maintained overlapping diplomatic connections with peoples beyond the immediate formal sovereignty of either empire. The bilingual Sasanian Paikuli inscription, for instance, implies that notice of King Narseh's accession, either via courier or envoy, was sent to various rulers in India, the Caucasus, and Central Asia, in addition to Rome; Humbach and Skjærvø 1983. The Roman author Ammianus Marcellinus (XXII.VII.9–10), meanwhile, attests that upon Julian's rise to imperial power in 360 CE, representatives from some of the same nations named in the Persian imperial inscriptions, including India, Armenia, and Persia, hastened to the Roman court to recognize the new western monarch, presumably alerted to the change in Roman authority via diplomatic channels. Additionally, Canepa points to both empires' diplomatic contact in the third century CE with the Kingdom of Aksum in east Africa, and the rulers of the Ḥaḍramawt in the southern Arabian Peninsula. For a general discussion of Roman and Sasanian global contacts and positioning in the third to seventh century CE, see Canepa 2009, 22–31.

21 The tradition is attested by Tabari (The Annals of the Prophets and Kings [Ta'rīkh al-rusul wa-l-mulūk] 2:818–819) and perhaps corroborated by the display of severed heads in Sasanian imperial relief art, such as those prominently featured in Bishapur VI; Boyce et al. 1989; Rubin 2001, 647–648.

22 See, for example, Trajan's column and the Trajanic relief reused and captioned "Liberator Urbis" on the interior of the Arch of Constantine.

23 Canepa 2009, 51–99.

FIGURE 9.1
Galerius and Narseh engaged in equestrian combat. Arch of Galerius, Thessaloniki (B.II.20)
PHOTO BY AUTHOR

FIGURE 9.2
Sardonyx cameo featuring the Sasanian King of Kings capturing Emperor Valerian. Bibliothèque nationale de France, Cabinet des médailles, inv. Babelon 360
PHOTO COURTESY OF MARIE-LAN NGUYEN, VIA WIKIMEDIA COMMONS

equestrian combatants used to the detriment of Roman reputation in the wake of Šābuhr's mid-century victories (Figure 9.2).[24] Elements of Tetrarchic palace layout from the same period that show inspiration from Persian palaces, may be understood in a similar fashion. Like the co-opted iconography, architectural reference to Sasanian models served the dual purpose of "cultural booty" on the one hand, and on the other, functioned to extend the legibility of

---

24   Canepa 2009, 83–99.

LATE ANTIQUITY BETWEEN SASANIAN EAST AND ROMAN WEST   175

the Roman emperor's propaganda to a wider, more international audience.[25] But within this picture of Romano-Sasanian propaganda warfare, the ways in which imperial women functioned to give an impression of the sovereign's power at the rival court and potentially among (mutual) diplomatic contacts has not been fully recognized.

3 Imperial Women as Propaganda Pawns in the Third Century CE

It is not entirely surprising that imperial women's role in this transcultural propaganda war has not been fully recognized. Within the Sasanian Empire, material culture generally, but that containing women's imagery especially, faces certain challenges. In general, the comparatively limited number of modern scientific excavations of Sasanian sites means that much of the transportable Sasanian material culture currently making up a sizable portion of the Sasanian art corpus comes from insufficiently documented contexts, and many of those objects that remain *in situ*, like rock reliefs, lack comprehensive archaeological work in their vicinities.[26] This has meant that the identification of persons depicted on art objects has been highly reliant on iconographically based arguments, and much scholarship over the past decades has been consumed with debating subject matter to the exclusion of other questions.

The iconographic identification of Sasanian imperial women is especially fraught. Whereas Sasanian kings featured together with positively identifying inscriptions on the empire's official coinage, and conveniently bore personalized crowns whose iconography can be utilized for identification purposes in other media where an imperial image is concerned,[27] imperial women only rarely appeared on coinage.[28] In the absence of the numismatic "key" we have for kings' imagery, learned art-historical debate over the past decades has either secured or gathered scholarly consensus regarding the instances wherein Sasanian imperial women are depicted.[29] The iconographic identification of Sasanian queens often relies upon the presence of a number of iconographic details, such as juxtaposition with the image of a Sasanian king, the presence

---

25   Chen 2016.
26   Harper 1983, 1113; Huff 1986; Mousavi and Darayee 2012; Masia-Radford 2013, 920–922; Schindel 2013, 814.
27   Peck 1993; Soudavar 2009, 418; Schindel 2013, 829–833; Alram 2015, 6–9.
28   Choksy, 1989; Brosius 2010; Alram and Gyselen 2012, 15–17, 45–16.
29   For an introduction to issues of gender and sexuality in the Sasanian period, see Darayee 2009, 59–64. For an introductory discussion of written and visual sources pertaining to Sasanian women, see Rose 1998; Daems 2001, 51–60; Brosius 2010.

FIGURE 9.3   Rock relief of Narseh with his queen (right) and a royal child (below). Naqsh-e Rustam III
IMAGE COURTESY OF LIVIUS.ORG

of exclusively royal insignia like the fluttering ribbons of the diadem, or gestures of respect toward imperial figures that allow for differentiation from a female divinity. For instance, the rock relief at Naqsh-e Rustam VIII featuring King Narseh facing a female figure (Figure 9.3) was once thought to represent the king in the presence of the divinity Anāhīd.[30] However, given the presence of all three aforementioned criteria, including the female figure's left hand retracted inside her sleeve as a gesture of respect toward the king, recent scholarly opinion has generally preferred to see her as Narseh's principal wife.[31] This latter detail is one that is paralleled in the depiction of contemporary courtiers attending the king, such as those shown in Šābuhr I's rock relief at Tang-e Chowgan (Bishapur II). It was a gesture meant to protect the King of Kings

---

30   Sarre and Herzfeld 1910, 84–88; Ghirshman 1962, 176; Vanden Berghe 1966, 25; Lukonin 1969, 321; Musavi Haji and Mehrafarin 2009.

31   Shahbazi 1983; Brosius 2010; Overlaet 2013, 314–315. Soudavar 2003, 62–63 and Canepa 2018, 265 prefer the traditional identification of the female figure as a divinity, while Miri 2017, 71 remains noncommittal on the identification.

LATE ANTIQUITY BETWEEN SASANIAN EAST AND ROMAN WEST 177

from bodily pollution. As a mark of subservience, such a gesture is one that a divinity would be unexpected to make toward a mortal king.[32]

Within the Roman realm, material culture related to post-Severan imperial women has inspired less scholarly attention than it ought, due once again to some inherent challenges. First, the half century between the death of Alexander Severus and the ascent of Diocletian and his Tetrarchic co-rulers saw so much tumult in the imperial office that it is difficult to track the changing ideological strategies employed by individual emperors. On a related note, since the imperial office turned over so frequently in this period, emperors had little opportunity to build large-scale monuments. As such, the base of material evidence for the study of Roman empresses of this period is largely limited to coins and free-standing portraits (often with insufficient contextual data) that themselves rely on comparison with numismatic portraits for their identification.[33] And finally, the Tetrarchic Roman emperors of the late third century seem to have intentionally suppressed acknowledgment of imperial women in the ideological realm during the first part of their novel imperial power-sharing arrangement—a point to which we will return presently—and thus the imperial agenda worked just as it was intended, lulling audiences nearly 2000 years later to forget Tetrarchic imperial women's relevance to court politics.[34]

So what evidence is there for imperial women's role in the middle and late third-century propagandistic jockeying that was certainly ongoing between the Persians and Romans at this time? With the advent of the Sasanian empire, the Persian court's use of imperial women in the ideological realm shows both continuity and evolution from the traditions employed by their predecessors. While imperial women were by no means entirely absent from Achaemenid, Seleucid, and Parthian ideological venues, they did not make up an especially prominent and persistent component, especially when compared to the persistence of imperial women's ideological utilization in the Roman Empire.[35] But beginning with the rule of the first Sasanian king, Ardašīr I (r. 224–240), queens featured consistently in official monumental ideological installations, and there is evidence that by the 270s they featured on official transportable objects as well.

Almost every Sasanian ruler that produced a monumental rock installation in support of his reign from the ascendancy of the Sasanian empire through

---

32   Frye 1972, 107; Sundermann 1964, 284; Canepa 2009, 68; Brosius 2010.

33   Wegner et al. 1979; Bergmann 1977; Wood 1986; Kleiner 1992, 360.

34   Chen 2018.

35   Daems 2001; Brosius, 2010. For a brief survey summarizing the various ideological uses to which Roman imperial women were put by succeeding dynasties from the rise of the empire to the early fourth century, see Chen 2018.

FIGURE 9.4 Investiture relief of Ardašīr I. Naqsh-e Rajab III
IMAGE COURTESY OF LIVIUS.ORG

the end of the third century deployed the cultural capital of imperial women in some capacity. Under the founder of the dynasty, Ardašīr I, two imperial women—including the King of King's principal wife—are depicted in the relief at Naqsh-e Rajab III (Figure 9.4).[36] Interesting, and thus far unexplained, is the fact that although these imperial women are undoubtedly depicted for a reason, their backs are turned to the primary action, and they are spatially separated from the primary scene with a baldachin that extends to the picture plane's right where its conclusion remains unmarked. The main scene in this relief shows the supreme Iranian god Ohrmazd's investiture of the king with a beribboned diadem, one of the most potent symbols of kingship at this time, and below, the interaction of the king's grandson Warahrān I and his namesake protector deity—a deity syncretized with Hercules and identified here by means of the large club that he wields in the relief's central space.[37] The choice to include the imperial women's figures in the relief but simultaneously insist upon their visual separation is curious.

---

36   Luschey 1986; Daems 2001, 55; Brosius 2010; Miri 2017, 69–70.
37   Hinz 1969, 123–124 with pl. 59; Shahbazi 1988; Miri 2017, 69–70. For the suggestion that the investing figure is a depiction of high priest rather than the god Ohrmazd, see Overlaet 2013.

FIGURE 9.5 Rock relief of Šābuhr I. Naqsh-e Rajab I
IMAGE COURTESY OF LIVIUS.ORG

An imperial woman may have been included among the figures depicted behind Šābuhr I in his relief at Naqsh-e Rajab I (Figure 9.5), but the limitation of the portrait in question to bust-length leaves some question as to the figure's identification.[38] However, the same king certainly incorporated the women of his imperial house into the trilingual enumeration of his accomplishments at Naqsh-e Rustam. In that inscription Šābuhr uses Parthian, Middle Persian, and Greek to include among his notable accomplishments the commemoration of imperial women with the dedication of sacred fires and prescriptive offerings in their names.[39] The next Sasanian king to rule, Hormizd I, ruled only a year and produced no monumental art that we know of. His successor, Warahrān I, was only in power for a slightly longer reign of three years, and thus only produced a single relief wherein the scene's divine investiture excludes any other attendant figures.[40]

---

38 Lukonin 1969, 189; Harper and Meyers 1981, 34n36; Rose 1998, 41.
39 Shabazi 1998, 58; Huyse 1999; Brosius 2010.
40 On the reigns of Hormizd I and Warahrān I, see Shahbazi 1988; Shayegan 2004; Darayee 2009, 10.

FIGURE 9.6 Coin of Warahrān II with his queen and heir
PHOTO COURTESY OF THE BRITISH MUSEUM; CREATIVE COMMONS
ATTRIBUTION-NONCOMMERCIAL-SHAREALIKE 4.0 INTERNATIONAL
(CC BY-NC-SA 4.0) LICENSE

But a major change is discernible with the ascension of Warahrān II in the mid-270s. This king made concerted ideological use of his family—including his principal wife and crown prince—in what seems to be a consistent and multimedia way that was novel in the Sasanian realm. Conveniently for the purposes of this analysis, Warahrān II featured his wife and heir on his coinage (Figure 9.6), and some of the numismatic issues feature the name of Warahrān's wife inscribed in Middle Persian, removing any ambiguity as to her identity. Warahrān produced types featuring various combinations of his wife and heir(s) throughout his reign.[41]

It has already been recognized since the 1950s that Warahrān's dynastic coins draw inspiration from the centralized mints of the Roman Empire.[42] But the format of conjoined jugate busts of king and supporting female companion on coinage, very often a consort or imperial mother, was a numismatic composition that dated back at least to the Ptolemaic and Seleucid Hellenistic kingdoms, and from there made its way into Roman iconography. From the second century CE, the Romans occasionally began to produce coins that included the facing bust of an heir connected with the principal ruler, but only bronze medallions minted in the reign of Philip the Arab (r. 244–249) combine portraits of the jugate imperial couple with the facing heir in the manner

---

41   Lukonin 1969, 112; Shahbazi 1983; Choksy 1989; Rose 1998, 42–43; Alram and Gyselen 2012.
42   Göbl 1952; 1971, 43; Choksy 1989, 118; Alram and Gyselen 2012, 40–64.

FIGURE 9.7
Medallion obverse featuring jugate busts of Philip I and his wife Otacilla, facing Philip II
IMAGE AFTER GNECCHI 1912, V. 2 PL. 108

later adapted by Warahrān II (Figure 9.7).[43] It is probably not coincidental that the precise formula Warahrān adopted for his novel coinage was one utilized by a Roman emperor known to have paid the Sasanians a hefty ransom and continuing payments aimed at ensuring protection against nomadic incursions.[44] The chronological proximity of the Roman exempla and the geographical and cultural valence of the Seleucid examples may have been involved to a greater or lesser degree in the adoption of related coin iconographies under Warahrān II in the Sasanian era.[45] Warahrān II's numismatic issues have helped in turn to suggest the identification of imperial women incorporated into the rock reliefs composed by him at Naqsh-e Rustam II (Figure 9.8),[46]

---

43 Göbl 1952; Bastien 1994, pl. 63, 9 and 68, 9 (Marcus Aurelius and Commodus), pl. 86, 4 (Macrinus and Diadumcnianus), pl. 94, 6 (Philip the Arab and Philip II). For the medallions of Philip the Arab, see Gnecchi v. 2 pl 108–109.

44 On the peace negotiated between Šābuhr I and Philip the Arab, see Dignas and Winter 2007, 119–122.

45 For general discussion of the ways in which Sasanian monarchs built upon the precedents of preceding Iranian dynasties, including the Achaemenids, Seleucids, and Parthians, see Canepa 2018.

46 Hinz 1969, 191–198; Herrmann 1970, 168; Shahbazi 1988; Rose 1998, 42–43; Weber 2009, 613–615; Brosius 2010.

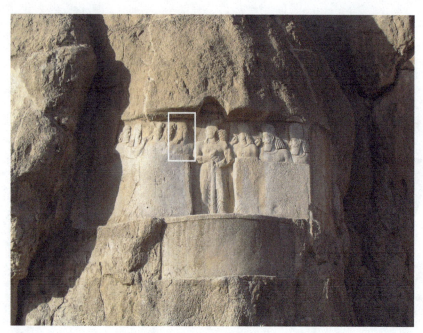

FIGURE 9.8 Warahrān II flanked by family and nobles. Naqsh-e Rustam II
IMAGE COURTESY OF LIVIUS.ORG

Tang-e Qandil (Figure 9.9),[47] Barm-e Delak I (Figure 9.10),[48] and Sar Mashhad (Figure 9.11),[49] as well as the medallion busts featuring the queen and crown

---

47 Although scholars generally agree that the relief at Tang-e Qandil dates to the reign of Warahrān II, opinion remains divided whether it was an official imperial commission, and whether a queen is depicted. For a recent summary of the literature on the relief, see Weber 2009, 621–624. For the view that the reliefs depict Warahrān II's queen, see Daems 2001, 55–56; Brosius 2010; Canepa 2018, 126. For the view that the relief may be unofficial, see de Waele 1978, 26; Herrmann 2000, 42–43; Haerinck and Overlaet 2009, 535. For the suggestion that the Tang e Qandil relief dates to the reign of Ardašīr I, one that has not gained popular acceptance, see Levit-Tawil 1993.

48 There is general scholarly consensus that the relief at Barm-e Delak I dates to the reign of Warahrān II, but as at Tang e Qandil some scholars question its official nature, and debate the identities of the figures depicted. For an overview of the opinions on the relief, see Weber 2009, 615–621. For the view that the relief was officially commissioned and depicts Warahrān II's queen, see Rose 1998, 42; Shahbazi 1998; Daems 2001, 55–56; Brosius 2010; Canepa 2018, 126. For the view that the relief may be unofficial and/or depict figures other than the king and queen, see de Waele 1978, 26; Shahbazi 1983; Vanden Berghe 1988; Shahbazi 1988; Herrmann 2000, 42–43; Haerinck and Overlaet 2009, 535. For the suggestion that the relief at Barm-e Delak I dates to the reign of Ardašīr I, one that has not gained popular acceptance, see Levit-Tawil 1993.

49 Herrmann 1970, 165–171; Harper and Meyers 1981, 38 and n50; Shahbazi 1988; Daems 2001, 56; Soudavar 2003, 78; Weber 2009, 601–605; Brosius 2010; Masia-Radford 2013, 924–925. The identification of the female figure in this relief as Anāhīd has not found general acceptance: Trümpelmann 1975.

LATE ANTIQUITY BETWEEN SASANIAN EAST AND ROMAN WEST 183

FIGURE 9.9 Relief dating to the reign of Warahrān II. King receiving a flower from female figure (queen?). Tang-e Qandil
IMAGE COURTESY OF LIVIUS.ORG

FIGURE 9.10 Relief dating to the reign of Warahrān II. Male figure (king?) presenting a flower to a female figure (queen?). Barm-e Delak 1
IMAGE COURTESY OF LIVIUS.ORG

FIGURE 9.11
Warahrān II defends his queen from a lion. Sar Mashhad
FREER GALLERY OF ART AND ARTHUR M. SACKLER GALLERY ARCHIVES, ERNST HERZFELD, FSA A.6 04.GN.2780

prince on a Sasanian silver cup found in Sargveshi, Georgia.[50] The latter object is precisely the type that written and visual sources attest was utilized for diplomatic exchange, and thus meant for circulation outside Sasanian territory.[51] While this precise example may have been a diplomatic gift that traveled north out of Sasanian territory, silver is among the items attested in Roman written sources as gifts from the Sasanian king, and a handled cup sporting a very similar shape to the Sargveshi cup appears among the gifts carried by Persians on the lowest register of Galerius' victory monument in Thessaloniki.[52]

Since Warahrān II rose to office after the short reigns of his two predecessors and was occupied during his reign putting down a serious coup led by a cousin, this king's experimentation with familial iconography adapted from the rival Roman realm has been understood as an attempt to project dynastic and successional stability in the face of real challenges to that position.[53] Regardless of the initial impetus for the imagery's adoption, given the attestation of Warahrān's family on both the traveling media of diplomatic silver and coinage, and the presence of dynastic coinage throughout Warahrān II's reign down to the early 290s, we can be fairly certain that the Roman court of the later third century was aware of the elevated role imperial women had taken in Sasanian ideology at the time.

Ironically, while Warahrān II was deploying the members of the royal house in his late 3rd century court propaganda to an extended degree, and was at least in part inspired to do so by ideas from the Roman west, the final

---

50   Art Museum of Georgia, Tbilissi. inv. nr. R 134. At the time of publication, the cup was in storage and not available for new photography. Harper 1974, 63–64, 70–71; Harper and Meyers 1981, 37–38, pl. 2; Shahbazi 1988; Rose 1998, 43; Brosius 2010. Weber 2009, 624–627 interprets the figures as Warahrān II, his queen, and the figure of the god Warahrān rather than the crown prince.

51   On gift exchange in Late Antiquity, see Harper and Meyers 1981, 15–23; Harper 1988, 154; Canepa 2009, 30–31, 156–166; Nechaeva 2014, 163–205.

52   Harper 1983, 1117–1118.

53   Alram and Gyselen 2012, 58.

decades of the third century in the Roman Empire saw the complete opposite. While the emperor Carus and his sons, whose reigns overlapped with the first part of Warahrān II's time in power, utilized imperial women to ideological effect in ways that were consistent with the traditions that had developed in the Roman Empire over the course of three centuries, Warahrān's last decade in power overlapped with the rise of the Tetrarchs, who consciously omitted imperial women from all manner of imperial propaganda, including coins, sculpture, inscriptions, and honorary titulature until the early fourth century. I have argued elsewhere that the absence of imperial women from the Roman ideological realm at this time should be understood as an intentional part of the Tetrarchic effort to distance themselves from their subjects, and that such a move fits well with the aims of other elements of their messaging, such as the striking non-naturalistic turn of their porphyry portraiture.[54] If one of the major functions of empresses in Roman imperial ideology in preceding generations was to foreground the humanity and procreative ability of the ruler as aided by his wife, Tetrarchic eschewal of ideological reference to royal women would have been an important way for the Roman co-emperors to compete with the status of a Sasanian ruler who they understood as claiming divine descent.[55] But equally, perhaps willingness to make such a radical break from a Roman tradition that had seen three centuries of unbroken ideological use of imperial women was in part driven by a desire to differentiate from trends in the Sasanian East, underway at the time of Diocletian's accession, that had begun to especially highlight the imperial consort.

Back in the east, Warahrān II was succeeded only briefly by the contested reign of his son Warahrān III, who was replaced within the year as a result of a coup that raised Narseh, Warahrān III's great uncle and a son of Šābuhr I, to the status of King of Kings. Securely dated to Narseh's reign is a rock relief (Figure 9.3) featuring the king mutually grasping a beribboned diadem with a standing female figure, who is presumed, based on the iconographic features already discussed, to represent Narseh's queen. The presence of a royal child in the midst of the scene's primary action,[56] along with the precedent

---

54   Chen 2018.
55   Debate continues as to how the Sasanians intended their imperial titulature to be understood, and specifically whether the king claimed divine descent. For a recent summary of the debate see Soudavar 2012, 30. However, the use of the Greek phrase ΕΚ ΓΕΝΟΥΣ ΘΕΩΝ in trilingual Sasanian inscriptions, together with the statement in the Tetrarchic *Pan. Lat.* II/10, 6 suggests the Romans of the time understood the Sasanian kings to claim divine descent.
56   Miri 2017, 71.

FIGURE 9.12 Silver bowl from the reign of Narseh. Metropolitan Museum accession no. 1970.5
PHOTO IN THE PUBLIC DOMAIN; CC0 1.0 UNIVERSAL (CC0 1.0)

for dynastic imagery set by Narseh's predecessor Warahrān II also weighs in favor of this understanding. A silver cup in the Metropolitan Museum of Art's collection may also feature Narseh's queen (Figure 9.12), to judge by the analogy with the Sargveshi cup, details such as the flying diadem ribbons that suggest royal iconography, the similarity of hairstyle to the Naqsh-e Rustam VIII relief (Figure 9.3), and stylistic details that place its execution in the late third century CE.[57]

What is striking then, is that Sasanian imperial women feature rather reliably in imperial propagandistic productions from the dawn of the Sasanian empire, right through the third century, and that from at least the reign of Warahrān II in the mid-270s, there is convincing evidence that the Sasanian court was particularly attuned to how imperial women were being utilized for ideological, particularly dynastic, effect within the Roman realm. But following Narseh's reign in the final part of the third century CE, imperial women

---

57 Metropolitan Museum accession no. 1970.5. Harper 1974, 79; Harper and Meyers 1981, 38, including n55, pl. 5; Rose 1998, 46–47; Masia-Radford 2013, 923.

LATE ANTIQUITY BETWEEN SASANIAN EAST AND ROMAN WEST   187

disappear from the Sasanian ideological realm until the final decades of Sasanian power in the seventh century CE, despite the fact that the media upon which imperial women's images once featured—monumental reliefs, silver plate, and coinage—all continue to be utilized by the Sasanian court for ideological purposes.[58] This pattern has neither been recognized previously, nor questioned. I believe, however, that the Romano-Persian competitive context that we have come to recognize over the last decade as an essential factor in the shape of Roman and Sasanian ideology in this period may again bear fruit in explaining the distribution of data related to the ideological use of imperial women.

4 Propagating the Capture of the Sasanian Imperial Family

Recall that Narseh's reign saw a decisive Roman Tetrarchic victory over Persian adversaries that allowed the Romans to reassert their superiority in the eyes of the two realms' mutual diplomatic contacts following the disaster under Valerian. Central to the Roman victory in 298 was the capture of Narseh's wives and children at Satala that we know of from its attestation in the written sources. But beyond the texts, there was also an insistent propagation of the event in extralinguistic visual terms, and evidence that Roman emperors attempted to call to mind the humiliating nature of this specific event even years after it took place.

As Canepa has recently shown, the same octopylon arch of Galerius from Thessaloniki, referenced earlier as commemorating the Romans' victory in 298, was particularly insistent upon the significance of the capture of Narseh's family.[59] Although only about half of the monument remains today, and what

---

58   Silver plate and coinage were produced more or less continuously through the Sasanian period in service to imperial propaganda. Imperial rock reliefs were central to imperial propaganda until the late fourth century when there is a hiatus in their popularity until the reign of Xosrow II at the end of the sixth century CE. On the return of the rock relief medium under Xosrow II, see Canepa 2009, 107; 2013. The figure of a Sasanian queen is known on a late-Sasanian silver dish of the sixth or seventh century: Walters Art Gallery, inv. no. 57.709; see Daems 2001, 56–57. A late-Sasanian or early-Islamic silver bust may depict a Sasanian royal woman associated with the family of Xosrow II; see Rousseau and Northover 2015. Coins depicting Boran, daughter of Xosrow II and one of two female late-Sasanian monarchs, were minted in the seventh century; see Malek and Curtis 1998. Brosius has suggested that the female figure in Xosrow II's relief at Taq-e Bustan is a Sasanian queen, but the suggestion has failed to gain acceptance, with most scholars instead preferring her traditional identification as the goddess Anāhīd. Recently identifying the figure as Anāhīd, see Brosius 2010; Canepa 2013.

59   Canepa 2009, 84–99.

FIGURE 9.13   Capture of the Persian Harem (A.I.2). Arch of Galerius, Thessaloniki
PHOTO BY AUTHOR

FIGURE 9.14
Transport of Persian prisoners (A.II.6). Arch of Galerius, Thessaloniki
PHOTO BY AUTHOR

remains is highly abraded, the surviving reliefs have been studied for decades, and pictures and drawings from an earlier era preserve details that are now more obscure.[60] Two panels on the arch's interior, one situated in the passage leading toward the rotunda building (Figure 9.13) and the other flanking the city's main thoroughfare (Figure 9.14), explicitly depicted the capture and

---

60   Kinch 1890; Laubscher 1975; Rothmann 1977; Meyer 1980; Canepa 2009, 84–99.

FIGURE 9.15
Mirrored scenes (top two panels; A.III.9–10) of Tetrarchs receiving a male Persian suppliant, while the captured Sasanian imperial family looks on. Personifications of Persian cities (third panel from top; A.III.11). Arch of Galerius, Thessaloniki
PHOTO BY AUTHOR

deportation of Narseh's wives. The former relief's current fragmentary condition is difficult to read, but analysis of the scene in a less weathered state identified the enthroned figure of a Sasanian queen in the midst of a chaotic battle scene, including male Persians dramatically defending a group of despairing women and children from the charge of Roman cavalry.[61] In the latter scene, Roman soldiers drive Persian captives away from the crenelated city gate. The two female Persians atop dromedaries at the right of the relief wear headdresses with domed profiles that either sit upon long hair or are accompanied by a draped veil; it is this attribute that has informed their identification as members of the Persian imperial family in the moment of their transport from the captured city.[62]

At least three other reliefs, this time on the monument's exterior, also made reference to the capture of Narseh's family. Moving through the octopylon to exit the city toward Adrianople or gain access to the adjacent hippodrome and palace, on the left external face of the monument the viewer saw two juxtaposed panels presenting mirrored compositions that include a seated Roman emperor receiving a male Persian suppliant, while a child and

---

61 Rothmann 1977 432; Meyer 1980, 387–393.
62 Meyer 1980, 383; Landskron 2005, 157.

FIGURE 9.16   *Pompa Triumphalis* with figures of Persian women and children aboard a cart (B.III.25). Arch of Galerius, Thessaloniki
PHOTO BY AUTHOR

a group of female figures in Eastern dress look on (Figure 9.15). This pair of scenes is interpreted as the Tetrarchic colleagues Diocletian and Galerius each hearing pleas for the safe release of the Persian king's family, who are shown in attendance.

Three additional scenes may also connect with the aftermath of the capture of the Persian imperial family. On the same external face of the arch, situated below the mirrored scenes just discussed, female figures holding cornucopias and scepters are understood as personifications of Persian cities or territories, perhaps the very geographic zones forfeited in exchange for the return of Narseh's family according to the terms of the Treaty of Nisibis (Figure 9.15).[63] Among the reliefs on the opposite pillar, Persian prisoners, including female and juvenile prisoners aboard a wheeled cart, are depicted as part of a *pompa triumphalis* (Figure 9.16).[64] Whether or not this scene was meant to specifically record the transportation and/or parade of Narseh's wives, or was of a more generic character familiar from Roman triumphal imagery of decades past, the imagery must have called to mind the specificity of the royal family's capture. Finally, present among the throng of gift-bearing Persians marching in the lowest register of the internal passageway that offered access to the city's palace and hippodrome, is a female figure supposed to be a Sasanian queen, based upon her tall headdress, which preserves traces of relief embellishment (Figure 9.17).[65]

Given her placement toward the background of the relief space, it is unclear whether this last figure's headdress included a veil. In all instances of their

---

63   Laubscher 1975, 42–43; Canepa 2009, 88.
64   Rothman 1977, 445–447; Canepa 2009, 91.
65   See Landskron 2005, 157 with previous literature.

FIGURE 9.17
Figure of Sasanian queen among a throng of gift-bearing Persians (B.1.18). Arch of Galerius, Thessaloniki
PHOTO BY AUTHOR

appearance on the monument, Narseh's wives are said to wear high tiaras draped with veils, similar to the headdresses depicted on elite women's statuary from Hatra and Palmyra in the third century.[66] Unfortunately, the monument's deteriorated state makes it difficult to read the precise details of the Sasanian imperial women's headgear as depicted on the arch, and specifically whether it integrated a draped veil as other scholars have suggested. Based on analogy with the better preserved medallion discussed below, it is possible that the imperial women on the arch are shown to wear domed hats placed upon long locks, an iconography that as we will see is much more analogous to the Sasanians' own depictions of royal women. Whether this headgear was placed upon long loosened hair or accompanied by a veil, it seems clear that the arch's artist made an effort at iconographically distinguishing these high-ranking Eastern women.

Taken all together, these scenes leave no doubt that the capture of Narseh's wives and children was prominently thematized on Galerius' victory monument as an event that allowed the Romans to propagandistically reassert military

---

66   Laubscher 1975, 40; Canepa, 2009 87–88.

FIGURE 9.18   Medallion minted in 298 at Siscia in honor of Galerius, from the Münzkabinett of the Staatliche Museen zu Berlin Collection (reg. no. 18200727)
IMAGE © 2004–2020 LECH STĘPNIEWSKI, HTTPS://WWW.FORUMANCIENTCOINS.COM/NOTINRIC/INDEX.HTML

strength and rectify their damaged international reputation.[67] Moreover, the situation of the octopylon within an imperial city, which among other functions stood as a monumental entrance to the city's Tetrarchic palace, virtually ensures that this imagery was confronted not only by city inhabitants, but also by ambassadors from the Persian Empire and elsewhere. The monument's highly trafficked and visible location made it a strategic place to forcefully commemorate the first Roman success against the Sasanians that was ideologically weighty enough to rival the enemy realm's capture of Valerian, and thus we can be assured that the Persians were aware that the Roman emperors were making pointed ideological use of this event.[68]

The theme of the abduction of Narseh's family is also recognizable on the reverse of a medallion inscribed VICTORIA PERSICA and minted in 298 at Siscia in honor of Galerius after his critical victory at Satala (Figure 9.18). Canepa has argued that the unusual combination of a kneeling Persian woman and child together with a standing male suppliant approaching the mounted emperor, with both male and female figures extending their arms in a pleading gesture, may be read as an allusion to the capture of Narseh's family and the subsequent negotiations for their return. The attestation of the subject on a

---

67   Canepa 2009, 96. On overlapping Roman and Sasanian international diplomatic contacts, see note 20.
68   Canepa 2009, 84–99.

FIGURE 9.19 Reverse of a Bronze sestersius from Rome issued by Lucius Verus, with a seated Parthian woman with Phrygian cap and coiffed hair tucked under the cap. ANS 1965.47.2
IMAGE IN THE PUBLIC DOMAIN: HTTP://NUMISMATICS.ORG/COLLECTION/1965.47.2?LANG=EN

transportable medium helps to further secure the idea that the Sasanian court was well aware the Romans had turned to propagating the memory of the imperial family's seizure in the aftermath of the Persian loss at Satala.[69]

Significantly, as on the arch of Galerius, but much more legible on the medallion, the dome-shaped headgear of the female suppliant is differentiated from the Phrygian-style caps worn by the other Persian figures. Roman iconography of Easterners was notoriously stereotyped during the imperial era, and made little attempt to integrate accurate elements of contemporary Persian dress into the visual shorthand they developed to signal the identity of the figures depicted. Thus, Parthians and Sasanians are generally indistinguishable in Roman iconography,[70] with both males and females typically donning the Phrygian cap to announce their Eastern identity, and women's hair is often

---

69   Garucci 1870, 112–118; Gnecchi 1912, v.2 pl.129; Dressel 1973, 1:306; Laubscher 1975, 135; Chrysos 1976, 16–17; Schoenebeck 1937, 370; Dignas and Winter 2007, 86; Canepa 2009, 98.
70   Landskron 2005, 208; Canepa 2009, 34–39.

coiffed and tucked under the head covering (Figure 9.19). But upon Galerius' medallion, the Persian woman's hat lacks the soft frontal fold of the Phrygian cap, sits atop long loosened ringlet locks that spill over her back, and no veil is visible. Given the similarity in subject matter and specific aspects of gesture shared between the figures on the Thessaloniki octopylon and the medallion, it seems most likely that the iconography distinguishing the Sasanian empresses is also parallel.

In turn, comparison with images of Sasanian empresses generated by the Persian court suggests that this distinctive and unprecedented feature of Roman iconography was an attempt to signal the imperial status of the captive figure and specifically call to mind the episode of the imperial family's capture. The foregoing survey of Sasanian empresses' imagery has shown that Persian court tradition depicted royal women with a few distinctive head coverings and hairstyles. Most commonly, imperial women were depicted with a cluster of bound curls gathered on top of the head (Figures 9.3, 9.9), wearing a headdress featuring an animal protome (Figure 9.6), or—more importantly for our purposes—wearing a high, rounded miter-style headdress over hair that falls in loose ringlets over her shoulders (Figures 9.4, 9.8, 9.11, and the Sargveshi cup[71]). It is this last miter-style head covering, adapted for use by Sasanian queens from a style used previously to mark Parthian royalty,[72] that most closely parallels the depiction of the female suppliant on Galerius' medallion. As the Sasanian imperial family was held captive for a period in the Roman west, it is conceivable that the integration of such a specific new element into Roman iconography at this time may have been based upon first-hand observation, or knowledge of Sasanian imagery. However the Romans came to adapt this detail, it should be understood as a discernible effort to visually signal the imperial station of the humbled figure, and as such, assert the ideological equivalency of this event with the Persians' capture of Valerian.

The reason for insisting upon the particulars of Sasanian imperial women's headgear as depicted in Tetrarchic iconography is that one further example may be connected to this novel Roman iconographic detail, and thus it may have been intended to evoke, if not specifically depict, the abduction of the Sasanian imperial family more than a decade after the Persian loss at Satala. Following historical precedent, the columnar bases on the Arch of Constantine in Rome, dedicated in 315 CE, are decorated with various groups of subjugated figures. This aspect of the imagery was intended to communicate the Roman

---

71   See Harper and Meyers 1981, 37–38, pl. 2.

72   Peck 1993.

emperor's claim to dominance over lands in both the eastern and western realms, and as the subjugated groups specifically comprise a male, a female, and a juvenile, there is an explicit intent to assert Roman hegemony that endures into the future.[73] Among these familial groups, located (appropriately) on the arch's eastern face, is a group whose costume—including the male figure's stereotypical Phyrgian style cap—indicates that the group should be understood to project Roman dominance in the East (Figure 9.20). The female figure, like the feminine Persianate figures on the preceding arch of Galerius and victory medallion, sports a distinct headdress. The overall profile of the head covering may be seen as broadly analogous to the Galerian examples.[74] Like those, it lacks the veil that was a critical component of contemporary elite women's headdresses from Hatra and Palmyra and is situated upon long loose hair, but differs in its novel insistence on the tiered or wrapped structure that is much more similar to headdresses worn by Parthian queens (Figure 9.21).[75] Perhaps in the years intervening since the seizure of the Sasanian imperial family, Roman iconography had come to conflate Parthian and Sasanian elite women's headgear as they had done with other details of Persian costume. Significantly, no other female captive depicted on the bases is marked out with details that allude to her high status. It is conceivable, given the preceding efforts to visually propagandize the capture of Narseh's family and the fact that this attribute is not common to Roman depictions of Persian women postdating the Arch of Constantine, that the symbolic statement about the breadth of Roman hegemony made with Constantine's arch imagery was shaded with subtle allusion to the most critical victory against the Persians in recent memory.

Returning, then, to consider the pattern of appearance of Sasanian imperial women in Persian propaganda, it is striking that at the same time the Romans heavy-handedly advertised the capture of King Narseh's wives and children as an essential part of the victory repaying the capture of Valerian decades prior, it appears the Sasanian court elected to discontinue its overt ideological use of female members of the royal house. Perhaps initially this was an effort not to call to mind the disastrous events of 298 so proudly publicized by Galerius and his colleagues. But why does this strategy persist for so long in the Persian

---

73   Kampen 1991, 235; Canepa 2009, 285 n47.

74   Landskron 2005, 161 identifies the headdress as a marker of elite status and recognizes the parallel with the imperial women's headdresses on the Arch of Galerius.

75   The headdress worn by Parthian queens is most clearly attested by coins that honor queen Musa, but a less elaborate, specifically undecorated, version of the crown may also be depicted crowning the queen of Gotarzes II on select coins. See Wroth 1903, pl. XXVII/18; Peck 1993.

FIGURE 9.20　Eastern captives from a column base on the Arch of Constantine's eastern face. Rome
IMAGE COURTESY OF THE MEDIA CENTER FOR ART HISTORY, DEPARTMENT OF ART HISTORY & ARCHAEOLOGY, © THE TRUSTEES OF COLUMBIA UNIVERSITY

FIGURE 9.21 Coin of Parthian king Phraataces and queen Musa
IMAGE COURTESY OF CLASSICAL NUMISMATIC GROUP, INC. HTTP://WWW
.CNGCOINS.COM, CC BY-SA 3.0

realm? This question must be left for future research, but what we can say is that whether in their emphasis or their strategic suppression in court ideology, imperial women were central to the ways that power was debated and represented between eastern and western empires at the dawn of Late Antiquity.

Acknowledgements

Alan Cameron's interests were vast, and his ability to make meaning from a panoply of ancient evidence—both written and visual—was remarkable. His example in questioning long-held assumptions treated as foundational to the field, and for blurring disciplinary boundaries has had an indelible impact on my work, for which—together with his generosity and good humor as a mentor—I am immensely grateful.

CHAPTER 10

Simony and the State

Politics and Religion in the Later Roman Empire

Michele Renee Salzman

A law of 469 issued by the emperors Leo and Anthemius to the praetorian prefect of the East and a slightly later law of 473 issued by the emperor Glycerius to the praetorian prefect of Italy are our earliest extant imperial laws against the sale of church offices, a practice known in English as simony.[1] There is no indication that there were earlier laws against this widespread custom. The sudden rush of imperial legislation in the late fifth century—one hundred and fifty years after Constantine had legalized the donation of money and property to the church—is the subject of this chapter. What made emperors legislate only now?

Scholars who discuss these laws against simony focus on the bishops and the church as their motivating force. Sabine Huebner, in an excellent 2009 article that focuses on the Eastern clergy, simply states that "it comes as little surprise that simony became an issue that church leaders denounced from ca. 400 on as the church and its clergy began to rise in power and gain imperial privileges."[2] She interprets attempts at controlling simony as a direct result of the growing wealth of the church which made becoming a bishop or a member of the clergy in an important church an increasingly viable financial investment. The assumption is that emperors were simply following the will of church leaders. While it is certainly true that emperors could respond to contemporary issues, it does not fully explain why they took the action they did in any particular instance. In fact, emperors had acted against the sale of secular office—i.e., office in the imperial bureaucracy—in laws from the fourth-century reign of Julian on, preserved in the Theodosian and Justinianic Codes.[3] Emperors could have acted earlier against the simony of church offices in support of the canon of the Ecumenical Council of 451. At that time, a number of bishops had

---

1   *Codex Iust.* ed. P. Krüger (1929), 3.30[31] for the Law of Leo and Anthemius. *Corpus Legum*, ed. Haenel 1857, 260, for the law of Glycerius.
2   Huebner 2009, 175.
3   *CTh* 8.4.9, 368 or 370 in reference to a lost law of Julian; 8.4.10; and for more on this, see Kelly 2004.

© THE TRUSTEES OF COLUMBIA UNIVERSITY IN THE CITY OF NEW YORK,
2021 | DOI:10.1163/9789004452794_011

SIMONY AND THE STATE 199

strongly condemned the sale of church offices, an issue that many bishops and clergy had raised earlier in homilies and letters from the late fourth century on.[4] In Rome, in the late fourth century the bishop Damasus (366–384) had written in his first decretal *ad Gallos* that church office should be bestowed based on merit, not due to favor or money, "the sin of Simon."[5] In essence, bishops and church leaders were policing their own clergy, and this led to Canon 2 in the Council of 451 which was reiterated, in the West, in several later Church Councils, notably the second Council of Arles, dated to 475–480.[6] There was no need for the state to intervene, from the perspective of the bishops. Indeed, state intervention could be—and was—seen as unwelcome.

Nonetheless, as this chapter will demonstrate, a number of late fifth-century emperors legislated on the sale of church offices and related financial practices with strongly stated moralizing rhetoric beginning in the late fifth century and continuing into the sixth century. As I will argue, state (i.e., imperial, senatorial, or royal) interventions in the form of law emerge as an effective avenue for weak rulers to assert their moral authority over a perceived problem—the venality of the clergy—that won them support from wealthy elites especially. By acting, as their imperial predecessors had not, the late fifth-century emperors Leo (in the East) and Anthemius and Glycerius (in the West) engaged in self-consciously Christian "moral" legislation to present themselves as defenders of the true faith in no small way to support their admittedly weak secular positions. These laws also appealed especially to the urban and senatorial elites in Constantinople and Rome, who were concerned that the sale of church offices and other corrupt financial practices in relation to church elections were jeopardizing the salvific value of their charity to the church. This was also the case in the sixth century, when the Senate, in 533, passed a resolution to control simony with the support of the Ostrogothic ruling family.[7]

State intervention against simony and related corrupt financial practices of the clergy also offended bishops who saw in such laws unwelcome secular interference. However, state intervention also forced bishops to not only discipline their clergy but also to assert their independence from state interference

---

4 Huebner 2009, 167–180; Lizzi Testa 2012b, 449–451 for discussion and lengthy bibliography. In addition to Damasus (note 5 below), the author of the *Apostolic Constitutions* also references the sin of Simon; see *Const. Apost.* VIII, 47, 29, ed. M. Metzger, *SC* 336, III, Paris 1987, 283.

5 Damas. *Ad Gallos* 10: "meritis enim et observandae legis ad istiusmodi dignitatis Artem ascedant, non Simonis pecunia vel gratia." For discussion of this, see Pietri 1976, 764–770.

6 See notes 10 and 13 below.

7 On this, see my discussion of Cassiodorus *Variae* 9.15 and 9.16 below; and also Lizzi Testa 2012b, 449–474.

at various key moments in the late fifth and early sixth centuries, the time that these imperial laws first appear. I focus here especially on the Western empire and the reactions of the late fifth- and early sixth-century bishops of Rome, beginning with Simplicius (468–483), Felix (483–492), and Gelasius (492–496), and then examine the sixth-century responses under the Ostrogothic kings, notably by Pope Symmachus (498–514). The bishops of Rome attest to several well-documented attempts to discipline the financial activities of their clergy revolving around money exchanged for office holding. These bishops acted, in part, in response to contemporary pressures from emperors, senators, and kings to remove venality—i.e. simony—from the church and its clergy. Indeed, in the absence of a Western emperor, a political situation that began with Pope Felix and continued through his successors, the bishops of Rome were free to claim even greater autonomy to handle simony and other disciplinary matters in the West.[8] The return of Justinianic control in the mid-sixth century changed the dynamics of state and church on the question of simony, as I will argue, but it did not prevent it.

To understand the contemporary actions that gave rise to state intervention against the simony of church office and to highlight the implications of these developments for the politics and religion of the late fifth- and sixth-century empire, I begin with the political and religious circumstances for the first laws against simony of church office by the Roman state. I then turn to the reactions of the bishops to state intervention and the financial abuses of the clergy by focusing on simony in relation in particular to the late fifth-century and early sixth-century papal elections. In the third section, I consider the implications of these late fifth-century interventions against simony as we see it unfold in the middle of the sixth century, at the Ostrogothic court of Athalaric and in Constantinople under Justinian. As I demonstrate, the late fifth- and early sixth-century Roman state had limited success in controlling the sale of church offices in the West, but weak rulers tended to use this issue to support their authority. It was both a stroke of brilliance and also the logical development of these failed state attempts to control simony that led Justianian, though explicitly disapproving of clerical venality, to essentially legitimize this practice in the church, just as earlier emperors had done for the sale of state offices. By passing laws that set limits for such transactions, now called consecration fees payable to the ordaining bishop and to the assisting clergy, Justinian claimed state authority to control simony in the church even as he reasserted the authority of the state over the church.[9] But to fully appreciate his actions,

---

8   For a summary of the papacy of Felix, see Salzman 2019b, 465–490.

9   Just. *Novel* 123.16, 546 CE.

SIMONY AND THE STATE

I argue, we need to look into the pattern of earlier imperial and royal precursors whose assertion of their right to legislate against venal clergy had developed out of the immediate problems they faced in the late fifth-century empire.

1 The Sale of Church Offices in the Late Fifth-Century Roman Empire

The English word, simony harkens back to Simon Magus, the venal sinner in Acts, whose attempt to buy the power to perform miracles led Peter to righteously denounce Simon: "May your money perish with you because you thought you could buy the gift of God with money" (Acts 8:18–20). The word simony in English conveys condemnation of the practice of selling church office. Church leaders and Councils had dealt with allegations of this kind of financial abuse for some time, with stipulations from the late fourth century on, but the practice of selling church office per se was only prohibited in canon law for the first time at the Council of Chalcedon in 451.[10] A particular scandal may have spurred this action: the sale of the office of bishop to Ibas of Emesa in 435.[11] The second canon of the Council of Chalcedon denounced any bishop or clergy who "put to sale a grace which cannot be sold," and ordered the removal from office of any found guilty of this "shameful and unlawful transaction."[12] Councils continued to prohibit this practice; at the Council in Constantinople in 459, and then in the Council of Arles, dated 475–480; and in the numerous Councils in Rome in 499, 501, and 502 in the context of the Laurentian schism, and again in the Council from Orleans in 533, bishops prohibited the sale of clerical office and continued to do so into the late sixth century.[13]

1.1 *Imperial Laws*
But it was not until 469, some eighteen years after the second canon of the Council of Chalcedon, that the emperors Anthemius and Leo passed a law condemning the sale of church offices as a threat to the security of the state:

---

10   For a good discussion of attempts by the church to prohibit simony, including the 451 Council of Chalcedon, see De Salvo 1995, 367–392.

11   De Salvo 1995, 367–392.

12   Percival 1900, 269, 871. See also the discussion by Jones 1964, 909–910.

13   For the Council of Constantinople in 459, see Mansi VII, 911–916; for the Council of Arles, see Canon 14, Munier 1963 *CCSL* 148.111–130; for Councils in Rome in 499, 501, and 502, see the *Acta Synhodorum habitarum Romae*, ed. Mommsen 1894, *MGH AA* 12, 399–455. In the sixth century, prohibitions continued in the West and East. In the West, see the Council of Orleans in 533, *Con. Aurel.* 2, Canons 3, 4, ed. Mansi; and the Council of Tours in 567, *Con. Tur*, II, Canon 27, ed. Mansi.

For surely what place can be safe and what circumstances can be excused if God's venerable temples are captured by money? What wall for integrity or what rampart for faith shall we provide if a cursed hunger for gold creeps into the venerable sanctuaries? What, finally can be protected or secure if uncorrupted sanctity is corrupted?[14]

Venality leads Leo to outline the parameters for selecting the right kind of bishop:

Let the profane ardor of avarice cease to threaten our altars, and let this disgraceful crime [sale of offices] be banished from our holy sanctuaries. Therefore, in our times, let chaste and humble bishops be chosen, so that, wherever they may go, they will purify everything with the morality of their own lives. A priest is ordained not with money but with prayers.[15]

The avarice of the clergy had offended these emperors.

The actual criminal charge was not new however, for the law asserted that the sale of offices constituted an attack on the emperor himself—*laesa maiestas* (injured majesty)—hence the offender should be "removed from the episcopate's rank ... after the fashion of a public accusation". Punishment, aside from loss of episcopal office after serving for a year, was to be condemned to "perpetual infamy." *Infamia* was, as Sarah Bond has shown, a term with widening religious force, for emperors condemned heretics, Jews, and pagans to this same state of *infamia*—entailing the loss of civic rights, dishonor, and social shaming, but not now exile as in earlier Roman law.[16] This was a serious offense, judging from the punishment.

I want to emphasize that neither in this law—nor in the Church canons—is the term simony used to decry the sale of episcopal or clerical offices. In reality, the practice of the sale of offices was widespread in late Roman society but it was called by a word other than simony, *suffragium*. As G. E. M. de St Croix has shown, originally this word meant the influence exercised by the

---

14   *Codex Iust.* 1.3.30[31]. 2: *Profecto enim quis locus tutus et quae causa esse poterit excusata, si veneranda dei templa pecuniis expugnantur ? quem murum integritati aut vallum fidei providebimus, si auri sacra fames penetralia veneranda proserpit ? quid denique cautum esse poterit aut securum, si sanctitas incorrupta corrumpitur?* Translation here adapted from Coleman and Norton 1966, 588.

15   *Codex Iust,* 1.3.30[31].3–4: 3. *Cesset altaribus imminere profanus ardor avaritiae et a sacris adytis repellatur piaculare flagitium. Ita castus et humilis nostris temporibus eligatur episcopus, ut, locorum quocumque pervenerit, omnia vitae propriae integritate purificet. 4. Non pretio, sed precibus ordinetur antistes ... D. viii id. Mart. Constantinopoli Zenone et Marciano Conss.*

16   Bond 2014, 1–30.

SIMONY AND THE STATE

powerful to secure a post. But by the late fourth century, *suffragium* had also come to mean (and often indistinguishably) the money paid by a candidate to secure a post, be it in civic government or in the ecclesiastical hierarchy.[17] Also used in Latin law was the term *ambitus*, or electioneering; this too was deemed a *crimen* in the law when it was aimed at influencing a voter through illegal payments.[18] It was the appropriation of such influence by private individuals that was the crime, since in civic practice, the appointment of an office holder was an honor that only an emperor could bestow according to imperial laws from Constantine on.[19] Hence, to appropriate this right by selling civic office was to appropriate the authority of the emperor, and so the punishment for "lese majesty" in the law of Leo and Anthemius made sense. Only in the late sixth-century Latin West does the adjectival form of the noun appear— *simoniacus*—not in law, but in a letter and in a treatise of Pope Gregory the Great, who talks about the payment of money as "*simoniaca haeresis*."[20] The noun *simonia* first appears in Latin only in the Carolingian period.[21] These shifts in vocabulary reflect the complex sets of conflicting interests and attitudes to this practice in the civic sphere where, as Kelly has shown, the sale of offices was a daily reality. Indeed, Kelly would see this shift in attitudes toward payment for offices, including fees paid upon retirement, as key to the development of late Roman bureaucracy, distinct from the early imperial government.[22] Given the complexity of reactions to the sale of offices in the civic sphere and the reactive nature of most imperial legislation, the imperial laws that erupt suddenly in the late fifth century suggest that these laws responded to specific contemporary problems. I turn now to explore the specific contexts of the 469 and 473 imperially imposed laws in an effort to contextualize developing ideas about simony and church offices.

1.2   The 469 Law of Leo and Anthemius

Leo (457–474) and his co-emperor Anthemius (467–472) were in need of support in the wake of the spectacular failure of their 468 attempted invasion of North Africa against the Arian Vandals; the loss of so many men, ships, and the cost of the failed expedition threatened the rule not just of Leo in the East, but of Anthemius in the West.[23] After 468, and more so than his predecessors, according to P. Wood, Leo engaged in self-conscious "Christian moral

---

17   de Ste Croix 1954, 48.

18   See OLD s.v. *ambitus*, s.v.6.

19   *CTh.*, 9.26.21 and 2.29.1; Just. *Nov.* 3.2; Lizzi Testa 2012b, 450.

20   Gregory Ep. 11.28; and Gregory Adv. Haeres. 1.23.2; 27.4.

21   Rosé 2018, 201–238.

22   Kelly 2004, 66–67; and 162–163 on *suffragium* in general as a term.

23   For discussion of this invasion and its failure, see especially Roberto 2014, 167–182.

legislation."[24] Exemplary of this religious turn are laws of 468 that banned trading on Sunday and public theatrical performances, and a law of 470 that mandated that no patriarch or steward could alienate any property owned by, given, sold, or bequeathed to the Constantinopolitan Church.[25]

In Constantinople, Leo also faced considerable opposition from the federate general Aspar, of Alanic and Gothic descent; he had been accused of having attempted an assassination of Leo's son-in-law Zeno in 469. In this period of intense political competition, Leo accentuated Aspar's Arianism, and employed stereotypical language to denigrate his followers and other "barbarian" groups.[26] Leo's increasing use of Christian moralizing language was intended to shore up support for his regime by emphasizing his religious purity. Thus Leo's law against simony, while following in outline the prohibition of the practice expressed by Canon 2 of the Council of Chalcedon in 451, takes a more vehement moral tone and considers the sale of church offices a crime against the emperor personally.[27] This rhetorical move was not an isolated attack on the venality of the bishops of the city. Leo's laws were part of a trend which continued in Constantinople under the emperor Zeno (476–491) that saw increased patronage of monasticism by imperial as well as senatorial elites as a reaction against perceived financial abuse by bishops and clergy.[28]

Leo's legislation against simony and the fiscal corruption of clerical elections in an effort to secure support for his rule was a lesson that was not lost on his co-ruler in the West, Anthemius. Although the 469 law of Leo and Anthemius discussed above was directed to the Eastern praetorian prefect and thus had as its primary audience the Eastern Empire and Constantinople, the issuing of it under both names evidences the ties between the two emperors. Indeed, an earlier *Novel* by Anthemius had already proclaimed that all laws of Leo applied in the Western empire under his control.[29] Leo had sent Anthemius to rule the West from Rome in 467, supporting him with money and military resources.[30]

Like Leo, Anthemius, intervened directly in the religious life of his capital, Rome. But Anthemius's views on religion and his support for it brought him into conflict with the then bishop of Rome, Hilary (November 461–February 29, 468). Anthemius, an Easterner, brought with him a more open attitude toward

---

24 Wood 2011, 298–314.

25 *Codex Iust.* 3.12.9 (469) for Sunday practices; 1.2.14. (ca. 470) on property alienation.

26 Wood 2011, 298–314.

27 Kelly, 2004, 161–163, on imperial control of the sale of secular office.

28 For example, the *Vita Danielis* presents Leo as the dominant patron of Daniel the monk, displacing bishops or clergy. See further, Wood 2011, 298–314.

29 *Nov. Anth.* 2 (468), ed. Haenel 1844, 346.

30 For the emperor Anthemius' career, see Anthemius 3, *PLRE* 2, 96–98.

SIMONY AND THE STATE

religion, and various Christian sects had been allowed to return or establish themselves in Rome. Anthemius brought a certain Philotheus, an adherent of what Pope Hilary decried as a heresy, to Rome and also allowed this Philotheus to bring a number of sects to hold new public assemblies (*conciliabuta nova*). When the pope protested, Anthemius restricted the meetings, but he did not exile the group. This example, one of a series that the later Pope Gelasius used, was intended to show the power of the papacy over the emperor, although the continued presence of this group in Rome undermines Gelasius's claim of the dominance of the church over the state.[31] On the contrary, Anthemius made the Neoplatonist, an alleged philhellene (pagan), Fl. Messius Phoebus Severus consul and urban prefect in 470.[32] Anthemius apparently had strained relationships with the bishops of Rome; Hilary's successor, Pope Simplicius (468–483), made no attempt to mediate the fighting that led, ultimately, to the demise of Anthemius in the civil war that broke out in 472 with the rebellion of the general Ricimer. Yet, we know that Anthemius had a number of senators who had supported him, and they had to be won over to support the emperor Glycerius who came to office after Anthemius' demise in March 473.[33]

1.3 The 473 Law of Glycerius

The general Ricimer turned to a Roman Christian, Glycerius, a former *comes domesticus*, to take up the position of Augustus. Glycerius passed a law against simony that has the dubious distinction of being the last law issued by a Western emperor. It is the sole law to survive from his fifteen-month rule; its importance to this emperor is suggested by its dating, passed just days after

---

31 Gelasius, *Ep.* 26.11 *ad Episcopos Dardaniae,* ed. Thiel 1868, 408: *Sanctae memoriae quoque papa Hilarius Anthemium imperatorem quum Philotheus Macedonianus eius familiaritate suffultus diversarum conciliabula nova sectarum in Urbem vellet inducere, apud beatum Petrum apostolum palam ne id fieret clara voce constrinxit, in tantum ut non ea facienda cum interpositione sacramenti idem promitteret imperator.* This information is part of Gelasius' assertion that emperors bowed to papal preeminence. He includes this case, along with Pope Simplicius' censure of the emperor Zeno, which famously did not prevent Zeno from advancing his *Henotikon.* For the limits of these assertions by Gelasius to control the bishops of the region of Dardania in the Balkans, a liminal area, see Demacopoulos 2013, 95–99. Here, too, with Philotheus, there is no evidence that Pope Hilary was able to bring about the removal of this man and his sect from the city.

32 For Severus, see Fl. Messius Phoebus Severus 19, *PLRE* 2, 1005–1006. For the allegation that Severus was planning a revival of Hellenism, see Dam. *Epit.* Phot. 108 = Phot. *Bibl.* 242 (p. 343b 6).

33 Senators supported the accession of Anthemius, and continued to support him even in the civil war. For his career, see *PLRE* 2, 96–98; for support during the civil war with Ricimer, see John of Ant., frag. 209.1 = Priscus, frag. 64.1, ed. Blockley, 372.

206 SALZMAN

taking office on March 11, 473. It was sent directly to the praetorian prefect of Italy and posted in Rome on April 29.[34]

Glycerius reiterated imperial restrictions on the sale of church offices, echoing the highly moralizing Christian rhetoric of the earlier law of Anthemius and Leo. Glycerius' righteous anger is largely at bishops (*antistites*) who follow them in this practice:

> From this practice it has developed that secular power is valued more than reverence for the clergy, and those who were called priests prefer to be tyrants over citizens (*tyrannopolitas*); and having neglected religion, the bishops chosen by the bribery of men, care more for public matters than divine ones, because they rejoice with impunity in their own delicts by this very privilege of perpetuity, and they, as if with the zeal that derives from certainty in its management, steal the church's resources which they, by covering the disgraceful deeds of their dastardly design, say are the riches of the poor, by giving rewards to some at court, by obligating themselves to others by financial bond, and by selling for the gain of the debtor what ought to be preserved for needy persons.[35]

This is a harsh attack on the bishops. Not only are bishops buying their offices, they are taking what does not rightfully belong to them. Thus, bishops live as tyrants who have usurped office to rule over citizens illicitly, for that is the meaning of bishops acting as *tyrannopolitas*, a strong statement indeed. This word occurs in only one other instance, a letter of Sidonius Apollinaris encouraging a fellow priest to continue to write biting satire as did, long before, the imperial official Ablabius about Constantine; if the analogy follows, the tyrannical authorities in Gaul, perhaps the Burgundians, are the subjects of particularly biting criticism underscored by this neologism in Sidonius.[36]

---

34   *Corpus Legum*, ed. Haenel 1857, 260, for the law of Glyerius sent to the praetorian prefect of Italy, Himelco. And a subsequent law indicates that it was posted in Rome on April 29; see Haenel 1857, 260–261.

35   Translation adapted from Coleman-Norton 1966, 905. For the Latin, see *Corpus Legum*, ed. Haenel 1857, 260: *Hinc natum est, ut antistitum reverentia magis potestas saeculi putaretur, et tyrannopolitas esse se malint, qui vocabantur antistites; ac religione neglecta, sub hominum patrociniis constituti, publica magis quam divina curarent, hoc ipso perpetuitatis privilegio delictorum suorum impunitate gaudentes, ecclesiarumque opes, quas mali propositi dedecora protegentes, pauperum dicunt esse divitias, studio veluti cuiusdam administrationis auferrent, aliis in praesenti dando praemia, nonnullis se chyrographis obligando, vendendoque in quaestum debitoris quod oportebat egentibus prorogari. Antistes* is best translated here as a bishop, as it is in other laws; see Lewis and Short 1975, s.v. *antistes*, 1.B, citing *Codex Iust.* 1.3; 1.18.

36   Sidonius Apollinaris, *Ep.* 5.8.3: *nam tua scripta nostrorum vitiis proficientibus tyrannopolitarum locupletabuntur.* I do not agree with Coleman-Norton 1966, 906n5, that

SIMONY AND THE STATE

Glycerius condemned the sale of church offices as *indecora cupiditas* (dishonorable greed).[37] But Glycerius's indignation has a more contemporary focus, for this law indicated that simony had brought on the divine anger that had led to the recent ills of the civil war:

> Wherefore we believe that it has happened that the Divinity has been offended which we recognize because we have experienced so many evils, and [the Divinity] has averted the favor of its Majesty and vexed the Roman people with such great misfortunes as have come to pass.[38]

By blaming the corrupt clerics for incurring divine anger, Glycerius diverted hostility away from the Arian military who had just fought against Anthemius in the recent civil war in Italy. Indeed, Glycerius, had been chosen by the Burgundian Arian successor to Ricimer, the general Gundobad. By passing this law against simony with such strong, moralizing language, Glycerius—like Leo—was asserting his fidelity to the faith against the corruption of venal clergy. This was a topic that all Christians—Arian or Chalcedonian—could unite behind. Thus, I do not see this law necessarily as a sign of Glycerius' support for Chalcedonian Christianity, as some scholars have argued, but rather as an attempt to bring together all Christians on a topic of shared agreement: the venality of ecclesiastical office.[39] And so, Glycerius concludes, this is an action that is "for the happiness of a better age"—*pro beatitudine saeculi melioris*—an appropriate wish given the recent, destructive civil war in Rome.[40] The

---

tryannopolitas refers to bishops as tyrant-ridden citizens, i.e., living under the tyranny of secular power. Rather, this case, as in Sidonius, is a reference to a tyrant, i.e., a usurper, who has come into power illicitly through his willingness to buy and sell offices. The bishops are thus acting as tyrants who usurp money that belongs to the poor and yet they "rejoice in their own delicts." Similarly, the Gallo-Romans are living under the tyranny of the Burgundians, who, in the view of Sidonius, have taken control unlawfully. This may also be an allusion to Gundobad who, as had Constantine (the object of satire noted at *Ep.* 5.8.2), killed his relatives to attain power unlawfully.

37   *Corpus Legum*, ed. Haenel 1857, 260.

38   *Corpus Legum*, ed. Haenel 1857, 260: *Unde factum credimus, ut offensa divinitas, quod tot malis probamus experti, favorem suae maiestatis avertere, et Romanam gentem tantis, quae transacta sunt, infortuniis fatigaret.* Here I agree with Roberto 2014, 167–182, that this is a reference to contemporary events and the recent civil war in particular.

39   Gusso 1992, 168–193, and at 180: "l'editto aveva, per il Nuovo imperatore, intenti di politica interna più che esterna, volto com'era ad ingraziarsi la Chiesa di Roma, per averla alleata contro i propri avversari."

40   Corpus Legum, ed. Haenel 1857, 260: Received at Rome: Datum III. Kal. Maii. Romae: *Quemadmodum Dominus noster invictissimus princeps Glycerius pro beatitudine saeculi melioris et suorum correctione mortalium, ne quid in supernae maiestatis deinceps ex sacerdotali ordinatione tentaretur iniuriam, ac....* (How our Lord the unconquered prince Glycerius for the happiness of a better age and the correction of its morals, lest someone

language echoes that of the contemporary restoration of the statue of Minerva in the Chalcidicum of the Roman senate by a senator who, like Glycerius, is looking forward to the return of peace and good government under this new emperor.[41]

Glycerius's law would also appeal to Roman senatorial aristocrats who were concerned about the corrupt and often violent elections that periodically disrupted civic life in Rome and in other cities. We know from a variety of sources that wealthy donors were concerned about clergy who used charitable donations for their own purposes. The sale of donated silver and gold for liturgical vessels, for instance, even to pay for the ransom of prisoners, was problematic. But the use of church monies to pay for clerical offices was a far less justifiable action. If the clergy alienated charitable gifts for whatever reason, donors feared for their salvation.[42] Given these concerns among wealthy elites, the law against simony would have been welcomed by affluent donors, many of whom were senators, whose support Glycerius courted as he tried to restore Rome and Italy after a divisive civil war.

How the bishops viewed Glycerius' law and his attempt to uphold a ban on the sale of church offices is not attested. Some bishops may have appreciated the emperor's moralizing law, as may be indicated by the fact that the law survived in a collection of Church canons from the Western empire.[43] That Glycerius' position spoke to real clerical concerns may help to explain the tradition which developed later that after he had stepped down from the emperorship, he had entered the church and was made bishop of Salona.[44] But state interference into the sale of church offices did spur late fifth-century

---

should attempt an injustice against divine majesty because of a priestly ordination then). Translation by author.

41 For the restoration of the statue, see *CIL* 6.526=1664 = *ILS* 3132: *simulacrum Minerbae/abolendo incendio/tumultus civilis igni/tecto cadente confratum/Anicius Acilius Aginatius Faustus v.c. et inl. Praef. Urbi/vic. sac. iud. in melius/integro proviso pro beatitudine temporis restituit.* 472? See Faustus 4, *PLRE* 2, 451.

42 See, for example, Ambrose, *De Off.* 2.15.70, and especially 2.28.136: *Melius est enim pro Misericordia causas praestare vel invidiam perpeti quam praetendere inclementiam, ut nos aliquando in invidiam incidimus, quod confregimus vasa mystica ut captivos redimeremus, quod arianis displicere potuerat.* Possidius, *Vit. Augustini* 24.15 calls them *vasa dominica.* For such concerns under Felix, Salzman 2019b, 465–490; see too *Concilia Galliae* a. 314–506, ed. Munier 1963, *CCSL* 148B, 12 and 42–51.

43 See *Corpus Legum*, ed. Haenel 1857, 260.

44 Ennodius *Carm.* 2.82, and *CIL* 5, 620n5. *PLRE* 2, 514, s.v. Glycerius, is dubious about this connection, but some scholars have accepted it, such as Gusso 1992, 168–193. The most we can say with confidence is that according to this later tradition that reworked the poems of Ennodius, the emperor Glycerius was associated with the bishop of the same name.

SIMONY AND THE STATE

bishops to try to police their own clergy all the more forcefully, especially after the demise of a Western emperor with the death of Nepos in 480. Not all bishops were pleased by imperial intervention in church finances, and some, like Gelasius, asserted their right to control church finances and to police clergy without state interference.

2   Papal Responses to State Control of Simoniacal Ordination

By and large, the bishops of Rome responded to imperial laws on simony and assertions of clerical financial abuse by taking direct action to control their clergy. Importantly, bishops claimed the authority to discipline their own clergy on this matter and resisted secular rulers and elites who tried to police the priesthood.

2.1   *Pope Simplicius*

Less than two years after Glycerius's law, in November 475, Pope Simplicius articulated, for the first time in the fifth-century church records of Rome, how the revenues to the church should be divided. In response to charges of fiscal abuse by an Italian bishop, Gaudentius, Simplicius set forth his four-fold division of funds: the monies in a church should be divided equally between bishop, clergy, ecclesiastical workers and for charity to strangers and the poor.[45] This was a clear attempt to restrict financial abuses by clergy and bishops, and it secured an income for those in the clergy. It had immediate implications for the sale of offices as well. Now all the priests would have to share their quarter of the pie—unlike in the East where priests were given set salaries.[46] Hence, if a bishop were to appoint a large number of priests, the funds for them would have to be further subdivided, an unwelcome reduction in salary. Yet there was incentive for bishops to appoint clergy, for they were needed.

---

45   Simplicius, *Ep.* 1.2, ed. Thiel: *Simul etiam de reditibus ecclesiae vel oblatione fidelium quid deceat nescienti, nihil licere permittat, sed sola ei ex his quarta portio remittatur. Duae ecclesiasticis fabricis et erogationi peregrinorum et pauperum profuturae, a Bonago presbytero sub periculo sui ordinis ministrentur; ultimam inter se clerici pro singulorum meritis dividant* (At the same time also about the rents of the church and the offering of the faithful, he should not permit anything which is not appropriate for one who does not know, but only a fourth portion should be given back to him from these. Two (portions), which will be of use for the ecclesiastical workers and for charity to strangers and the poor, should be administered by the priest from Bonagus under danger of his order; the last let the priests divide among themselves according to the merits of each individual). Translation by author.

46   On salaries for clergy in the East, see Huebner 2009, 167–180.

210 SALZMAN

But Simplicius' four-fold division of church property would have been welcomed by wealthy donors who were concerned about the misuse of their charity to the church. The *Scriptura* of 483, the testamentary will of Pope Simplicius, informs us about the arrangements made for the election of his successor. A number of clergy and secular leaders, including the praetorian prefect of Italy under Odoacer, Flavius Caecina Decius Maximus Basilius, came together in Rome in St. Peter's to ensure that the election take place without improper electioneering and without violence.[47] The document thus shows the bishop and the state working together to remove any suspicion of impropriety—i.e., bribery—in the selection of Simplicius' successor. As I have argued elsewhere, this document also includes Simplicius' willingness to work with secular elites who, along with the state, were concerned about allegations of improper conduct and simony in the election of a new bishop, a concern that was expressed openly by Glycerius' law.[48] Indeed, Simplicius' acceptance of secular voices in the choice of the bishop fits the precedent outlined by his predecessor Pope Leo, who urged that the wishes of the people be consulted in the choice of clergy.[49]

2.2 *Pope Gelasius (492–496)*

At the end of the fifth century, in a letter that had the force of a general decree or decretal, and in the face of an apparent shortage of clergy, Gelasius nonetheless refused to allow payments for church office. In his decretal, he connected this practice with the sin of Simon Magus explicitly:

> That if some from the ranks of the monks or the laity are chosen for the clergy, when no necessity compels it, the ancient determinations must be observed in their cases. If they are proved to have trafficked the holy rank for a price, they should be deposed from their office, for the crime of Simon Magus embraces the giver and recipient.[50]

---

47 *Acta syn. DII* [sic], ed. Mommsen 1894, *MGH AA* 12, 444–445, for the *Scriptura* of 483. For the praetorian prefect Basilius, see Basilius 12, *PLRE* 2, 217–218.

48 Salzman 2019b, 465–490.

49 Leo *Ep.* 10.4, 6; 40.

50 Gelasius, *Ep.* 14.24, trans. Neil and Allen 2014, 144–145, who note the allusion here to Acts 8:18–21. For the Latin see Gelasius, *Ep.* 14.24 *ad universos episcopos per Lucaniam, Brutios et Siciliam constitutos*, ed. Thiel 1868, 375: *De monachis laicisque copiosius in prima praeceptionis hujus parte digesta: quae vel quatenus pro rerum temporumque necessitate concessa sint, quemadmodum, ubi nullius necessitatis interesse probabitur, non nisi vetus institutio debeat custodiri. Quos vero constiterit indignos meritis sacram mercatos esse pretio dignitatem, convictos oportet arceri non sine periculo facinus tale patrantis: quia dantem pariter accipientque damnatio Simonis, quam sacra lectio testatur, involvit.*

SIMONY AND THE STATE

Moreover, Gelasius' assertion of his right to set this as general policy stands alongside scholarly discussion of his assertion of papal autonomy—if not papal primacy—in negotiation with the state, as was the case in his assertion of papal independence from imperial influence in the Acacian schism.[51]

2.3 Pope Symmachus and the Laurentian Schism

Charges of simony and the financial corruption of the election of Rome's bishop continued to be a problem in the West. Allegations of simony pervaded not just the contested election for Gelasius' successor Symmachus (498–514), but continued through his entire papacy. Symmachus had some senatorial backing, but he was opposed by the priest Laurentius with his supporters. Both had followers among lay aristocrats and clergy. The conflict, today known as the Laurentian Schism, revealed deep factionalism within the Roman church and society that erupted into fighting in the streets of Rome. The two contesting parties went to King Theoderic in Ravenna to resolve the matter. Even when Theoderic favored Symmachus based on priority of appointment, a hostile source attributed the outcome to bribery.[52]

At a synod in St. Peter's on March 1, 499, bishops from the suburbicarian churches and the priests and deacons of the Roman church met to hear the pope condemn simony, unlawful electioneering and bribery, and the fighting in the streets, all of which were attributed literally to the work of the Devil. The Council condemned these deeds:

Universi episcopi vel presbyteri dixerunt:	All the bishops and priests said:
Ut fiat rogamus.	We ask that it be done.
Dictum decies	Said ten times.
Ut scandala amputentur, rogamus.	We ask that the transgressions be removed.
Dictum novies	Said nine times.
Ut ambitus extinguatur, rogamus.	We ask that illegal vote-getting be ended.
Dictum duodecies.	Said twelve times.[53]

---

51   For discussion of Gelasius' "two powers" theory and the implications for papal authority, see the nuanced discussion by Neil and Allen 2014, 49–51; and the excellent revisionist reading by Demacopoulos 2013.

52   For the hostile source, see the so-called Laurentian Fragment, ed. Duchesne 1886, 46–48.

53   *Acta syn. DCCCXCVIIII, MGH AA 12*, 403–404, and 399–415 for the Council of 499.

The Council condemned the illegal canvassing for office using the traditional political and legal term *ambitus*, not simony. Indeed, *ambitus* for secular office had been condemned in the early empire, but state control over fees in the late empire had returned it to the authority of the state, as I noted earlier.[54] Here, the Council is using it for church offices, but it does not refer to the sin of Simon in this far less rhetorically crafted document. At the same time, the church asserted its right to make this determination.[55] Thus the first Council in St. Peter's confirmed Symmachus' stance on simony and rejected the intervention of the state or any secular authority in its internal workings. At the same time, the Council was aware that they might offend Theoderic, and so they arose and chanted in acclamation: "Hear O Christ! To Theoderic, Life! Said thirty times. We beg that thus he may be saved! Said twenty times."[56]

The reliance of Symmachus and the synod on Theoderic's support forestalled open conflict over who had authority over simony. Yet the Arian King was unwilling to act against the church in this matter, a sign of his politic position on religious matters in the early years of his rule.[57] Theoderic's visit to the city in 500 had offered further proof that the king would not take offense at this Council, and that he would have good relations with the new bishop of Rome. The Senate, pope, and people had joyfully greeted the Ostrogothic Arian King who abided by civic traditions, giving games and providing grain, though now to the poor outside St. Peter's as well as to the city at large.[58]

But allegations against Symmachus persisted, including charges of simony and adultery. The dispute turned violent. Theoderic ordered that another Council of bishops, dated to 501/2, question Symmachus about charges of corruption, including the misuse of church monies and the sale of church offices.[59] He was acquitted but the allegations of corruption continued. A third Council, in 502, was called in St. Peter's in which, in response to these charges and in anger at the intervention of the laity in church elections, the bishops

---

54   See also Kelly 2004, 66–67, 162–163.

55   *Acta syn. DII* [sic], ed Mommsen 1894, *MGH AA* 12, 447. For an excellent discussion and bibliography of the Laurentian Schism but with a focus on property not politics, see Sessa 2012, 212–245.

56   *Acta syn. DII* [sic], ed Mommsen 1894, *MGH AA* 12, 405: *Exaudi, Christe! Theoderico vitam! Dictum XXX. Ut ita servetur, rogamus. Dictum XX.* Moorhead 2015, 53 for discussion.

57   For more on Theoderic's policy toward Christians in his rule and his willingness in this early period to intervene in ecclesiastical matters only when asked, see Moorhead 2015, 50–58.

58   For Theoderic's visit to Rome, see the Anon. Val. 65, *MGH AA* 9, 324.

59   I follow here the dating of the councils as proposed by Moorhead 2015, 94n5, 52–56. His view seems most clear, based on the texts and evidence. For the councils, see the *Acta syn.* in *MGH AA* 12, ed. Mommsen 1894, 399–455.

SIMONY AND THE STATE

brought up the so-called *Testamentum* of Simplicius, his testamentary will, which had been used to set the precedent on this and several other issues.[60] Bishop Laurentius of Milan loudly proclaimed: *non licuit laico statuendi in ecclesia praeter papam Romanum habere aliquam potestatem* (No one of the laity has any power to decide such matters concerning the church except the Roman pope).[61] They also asserted again the right of the bishop to control the finances of the church, though it also stipulated that no pope could alienate church property in the country or houses in towns to the ownership of someone else.[62] This was a real restriction on the finances of the bishop of Rome and may have contributed to the desire to raise funds from appointing clergy to offices. Indeed, after the third synod of 502, Symmachus appointed some ninety-six priests and sixteen deacons over the remaining sixteen years of his papacy, a number far greater than three of his immediate predecessors whose combined rule led to seventy bishops in a fifteen-year period.[63] The pope allegedly resorted to taking money for his ordinations, one of the several avenues that he used to raise money.[64]

Theoderic did not intervene again to prevent financial abuses by Pope Symmachus. It seems that the Arian King was satisfied with Symmachus' papacy, especially the papacy's treatment of the Eastern emperor, Anastasius. Writing to the emperor after 506, Pope Symmachus made it clear that the emperor should keep his distance from church affairs in Italy.[65] In these years, Theoderic was increasingly secure in his control of Italy, and was famously praised by the church for his tolerance and noninterference in religious matters, a far different policy from the emperors in the East.[66] However, the Ostrogothic court did later take a strong moral stance against the sale of church offices, a willingness that can be directly correlated with the weakness of the rule of Theoderic's successor, Athalaric; his court was really under the control of his

---

60   Sessa 2012, 222–225; *Acta syn. DII* [sic], ed. Mommsen 1894, *MGH AA* 12, 444–448 for the *Testamentum* of Simplicius; 438–455 for this third Council.

61   *Acta syn. DII* [sic], ed. Mommsen 1894, *MGH AA* 12, 447.

62   *Acta syn. DII* [sic], ed. Mommsen 1894, *MGH AA* 12, 445–558. For financial limits on the pope, see also Moorhead 2015, 55.

63   For his ordinations, see *Liber Pont.* 53.12, ed, Duchesne 1886. I compare Symmachus's ordinations in the *Liber Pontificalis* with those recorded for his predecessors in the *Liber Pontificalis* at 50.5, 51.7, 52.3. See too the discussion by Moorhead 2015, 56.

64   For accepting funds, see Laur. Frag. 2, ed. Duchesne, 1886. For the argument on ordinations, see the previous note.

65   Symm. *Ep.* 10, ed. Thiel, 700–708; and cf. *LP* 53, ed. Duchesne, 1886, for strained relations with the Eastern emperor.

66   For Theoderic's religious tolerance, much discussed in the scholarship, see Arnold 2014, 73–74.

214 SALZMAN

mother Amalasuntha, and this set the stage once more for the intervention of the state in the church in an attempt to control simony in sixth-century Italy.[67]

3 The Sixth Century: The Ostrogothic Court and the Justinianic Turn

Two letters of Cassiodorus, written for King Athalaric in 533 revive the language of moral outrage that we saw in the laws of the late fifth-century emperors Leo and Anthemius, and Glycerius, discussed above. In 533, the Ostrogothic court was in a weakened position; Athalaric was a young ruler, and his mother, Amalasuntha, the acting regent, faced opposition from hostile Ostrogthic nobles.[68] Once again, violent fighting in the streets of Rome over a papal election and charges of simony occasioned the intervention of the state. With the death in 532 of Pope Boniface II, allegations of corruption circulated concerning the election of Pope John II (533–535). Cassiodorus' letter, written for Athalaric to Pope John II, discusses the charge that the sale of church property by clergy and men associated with the church took place in order to influence the election for one party or another. In the letter, Athalaric did not directly charge the pope with lying; it is not clear who is responsible, and so the guilt may lie with the rival party. Nonetheless, the king's letter evidences his strong condemnation of the practice of simoniacal ordination and shows how embedded this was in the church and in late Roman society. Athalaric also explained the motivations of those who reported on these violations, for they were rewarded for exposing the practice. Athalaric tells us quite explicitly the chain of allegations:

> Only recently a *defensor* of the church at Rome approached us with the tearful allegation that, when a bishop was sought for the apostolic seat, certain men exploited the difficulty of the time with an impious scheme and thus moved against the property of the poor with extorted promises so that, even to say it is abominable, sacred vessels were seen exposed for public auction. The deed was committed with as much crassness as the glory gained from the piety to eliminate it.[69]

---

67   Councils of Rome in 499, 501, and 502. *Acta Synhodorum habitarum Romae*, ed. Mommsen 1894, *MGH AA* 12, 399–455.

68   For more on the politics of the court in this moment, see especially Bjornlie 2014.

69   Cassiodorus, *Variae* 9.15.2 (c. 533), King Athalaric to Pope John. The translation here and throughout is from Bjornlie 2019, with adaptations as noted. Latin text from ed. T. Mommsen, MGH.AA 1894, 279: *nuper siquidem ad nos defensor ecclesiae Romanae flebili allegatione pervenit, cum apostolicae sedi peteretur antistes, quosdam nefaria machinatione necessitatem temporis aucupatos ita facultates pauperum extortis promissionibus*

SIMONY AND THE STATE 215

The desire to gain "glory" by acting against the guilty also prompted the king to act. His moral outrage, as articulated by Cassiodorus, emerges later in the letter:

> Let the just condemnation of Simon be recalled and dreaded, he who believed the source of all largesse could be bought.[70] Therefore, pray on our behalf, maintaining our edicts which you know agree with divine mysteries. But so that the will of the *Princeps* may become known more easily to those of every disposition, we have ordered this to be announced to the Senate and the people through the *Praefectus Urbis*, so that the public may recognize that we pursue those who, instead, are hostile to [divine] majesty (*maiestas*)—You, who rule by the grace of God, will also publish this to all the bishops, lest anyone would be free from blame who was able to acknowledge our ordinances.[71]

The resolution to this charge of simony required the intervention of the King/ *princeps*. Athalaric seeks the prayers of the pope, but he is clearly the one in charge. The hostility to majesty is likely a reference to the divine majesty of the church, as it is so used later in this letter and generally in the *Variae*, though it lacks the adjective divine in this case.[72] However, it is of interest that the *maiestas* offended by simony repeats the language used in Glycerius' earlier law, where "divine majesty" was similarly offended by this practice.[73]

This letter also gives precious information that there had also been an earlier law. Athalaric refers to a *Senatus consultum* or edict that had been passed

---

    ingravasse, ut, quod dictu nefas est, etiam sacra vasa emptioni publicae viderentur exposita. Hoc quantum fuit crudele committi, tanto gloriosum est adhibita pietate resecari.

70   For Simon Magus, see Acts 8:9–24.

71   Cassiodorus, *Variae* 9.15.11 (c. 533), King Athalaric to Pope John. Ed. T. Mommsen, MGH. AA 1894, 281: *recolatur et timeatur Simonis iusta damnatio, qui emendum credidit totius largitatis auctorem. orate ergo pro nobis edicta nostra custodientes, quae divinis noscitis convenire mysteriis. sed quo facilius principis votum universorum mentibus innotescat, hoc senatui, hoc populis per praefectum urbis praecipimus intimari, ut generalitas agnoscat nos illos persequi, qui maiestati potius videntur adversi. vos quoque hoc universis, quos deo propitio regitis, episcopis intimate, ne quia sit alienus a culpa qui potuit agnoscere constituta.*

72   See the previous note. In email correspondence of April 24, 2019, Shane Bjornlie observed that only twice does *maiestas* refer to an Amal in Mommsen's concordance, and one of these cases is to Eutharic, the son-in-law of Theoderic, who did not live long enough to rule. But the notion of the divine majesty of the church appears often, as in *Var.*5.40.6, and is repeated in this letter, 9.15.8 in reference to the church.

73   Glycerius' earlier law is explicitly stated as acting to protect "*supernae maiestatis*"; see note 40 above. Glycerius's law implies imperial majesty will be offended.

to control venal clergy after the death of Pope Boniface had led to such accusations and violence. Indeed, the Senate acted first, likely because the Amal court was at first hesitant to intervene. As Cassiodorus stated:

> When the fathers of the Senate, mindful of their own nobility, produced a resolution concerning the prohibition of such sales, if anyone is discovered to have promised anything for obtaining the episcopal office, either through his own actions or that of any other persons, that execrable contract will be deprived of all validity.[74]

The allusion to the willingness of the Senate to act—"mindful of their own nobility" (*nobilitatis suae memores*)—also highlights that senatorial elites demonstrated virtue by passing this law and were prompted to do so out of high-minded concern about the practice of simony at this moment, as they were in the late fifth century. Ending simoniacal ordination was an issue that united secular elite and the Amal court against the bishop of Rome and his clergy. In this letter, the carefully worded rhetoric of Cassiodorus reduced the potential for conflict between state and church. Athalaric emerges as a moral force in the maintenance of the Senate and its traditions, without openly attacking the bishop of Rome and his clergy. Faced with a critical Ostrogothic court and Senate, it is perhaps not surprising that the bishops of Rome soon turned to backing Justinian when he attacked Italy and Sicily in 535. Indeed, the imperial authorities were eager to secure the support of the Roman church through financial incentives, as they had by extending the time period allotted to claim lands by the church in a law of April 535.[75]

3.1 The Justinianic Turn

Given the consistently moralizing language of Roman emperors, Italian kings, and the popes against simony in the church that continued into the 530s, it comes as a surprise to discover that fourteen years after Athalaric's letter, the emperor Justinian in a law (*Novel* 123.16) dated to 546 turned away from this standard stance. Justinian prohibited: "payment to the person by whom he [a cleric] is appointed, or to other; all he is to pay are the customary perquisites to the appointer's staff and the usual recipient, not exceeding one year's wage."[76] According to the edict, candidates for bishoprics were expected to pay ordination fees, the amount of which depended on the income of their future church. Ordination fees ranged from several hundred solidi at the wealthiest sees to

---

74 Cassiodorus, *Variae* 9.15.3. For this senatorial edict, see Lizzi Testa 2012b, 449–474.
75 Just. *Nov.* 9.
76 Just. *Nov.* 123.16.

SIMONY AND THE STATE

fifty solidi at smaller ones. This law also stipulated amounts paid by bishops at their appointment, and by the archbishops and patriarchs, namely those of "the elder Rome," Constantinople, Alexandria, Theoupolis (Antioch), and Jerusalem. These were to pay no more than twenty pounds of gold.[77] The punishment for paying more was now a fine; for bishops it was triple the amount paid for the office.[78] Clerics below the episcopate were also allowed consecration fees, and Justinian also set upper limits.[79]

Justinian explained his motivation for setting limits even on the fees of bishops as follows: "We command that this is to be observed without fail, both so that churches do not become burdened with debts, and so that high priestly offices in them do not become venal."[80] The lofty morality of fifth-century emperors and of Cassiodorus' letter for Athalaric is gone; what we have instead is a flat statement and an acknowledgment of the system in which payments for church offices, like for secular offices, were now accepted and described as fees—not simony. In essence, the emperor was treating clerical office much as he had treated civic service. Justinian claimed that he was motivated in part to protect the church from debt. Thus, it is clear that in his eyes the maintenance of ordination fees was a financial resource which benefited the church. At the same time, by aiming to end the "venality" of clergy, Justinian also satisfied the desires of those who wanted to attain church office, for now there would be stated limits on the costs of ordination. Indeed, under Justinian, open competition for church offices, especially for that of bishop in major cities, increased among Eastern elites, as Huebner has shown.[81] I would add that the secular elites were similarly attracted to high office under Justinian in the West under these new economic and political conditions. The first securely dated bishops of Rome from aristocratic—i.e., wealthy—families, those who could afford to donate/pay for this high office, are attested first under Justinian, beginning with Vigilius (537–555), followed by Pelagius I (556–561) and John III (561–574).[82]

Finally, by regulating the payments of those who sought clerical office, Justinian cut out potential profits by middlemen who would have gained financially from this custom. Justinian's law aimed to control clerical ordination and thus remove a source of conflict in society. His action was in and of itself a reassertion of the right of the emperor to intervene in the church.

---

77   Just. *Nov.* 123.3.
78   Just. *Nov.* 123.3.
79   Just. *Nov.* 123.4
80   Just. *Nov.* 123.3.
81   Huebner 2009, 167–180.
82   Salzman 2019b, 465–489.

4   Conclusion

Emperors and kings issued sanctimonious prohibitions of the sale of church offices, starting in the late fifth century and continuing into the sixth century. As I have argued, this legislation emerged under weak secular rulers who adopted a moralizing stance against simony in part as a means of supporting their authority, and in part to gain the favor of secular elites who were similarly concerned about the venality of clergy. However, as I have also proposed, the assumption by secular rulers that they could legislate to control the financial affairs of late Roman bishops was in itself a potential source of tension, for the bishops saw it as their duty to control their clergy and their right to draw fees from ordinations. Simultaneously, imperial intervention to stamp down simony and venal clergy spurred bishops to more aggressively assert their control over the financial practices of their clergy, as discussion of the actions of a string of late fifth-century bishops demonstrates in the wake of Canon Two of the 451 Council of Chalcedon. In Italy, the arrival of the Arian rulers Odoacer and Theoderic produced an atmosphere of toleration that simultaneously freed Western bishops from the control of Eastern emperors and the patriarch. This political reality prompted fifth- and early sixth-century bishops in Italy from Felix through Symmachus to openly assert their independence from state control as they condemned simony among their clergy.

Nonetheless, the acceptance of payment for office permeated not just late Roman civic society, but also the church through the sixth century. In the midst of the Gothic War over control of Italy, Justinian's 546 law recognized the reality of this contemporary practice among the clergy. Justinian followed the policy of earlier rulers when he once more asserted that the state had the right to control venal clergy.[83] But the tone was radically different. By setting fees, Justinian could control costs. And this, as I have argued, was welcomed, especially by the secular elites. Indeed, in Rome, this is when aristocratic families entered the bishopric. It is deeply ironic that what began as a moral and political stand against simony by secular rulers ended by enabling wealthier Romans the opportunity to take up high church office.

Widespread discomfort over venal clergy and ordination continued even under Justinian's law. One of the best things that one could say about the unpopular Pope Pelagius I whose position was reliant on the Eastern emperor and his administrators was that: *Sacravit multos divina lege ministros/nil pretio faciens immaculata manus* (He ordained many priests but he did not do this

---

83   Just. *Nov.* 123.2–3; 16 (a. 546).

for money).[84] Clearly, many bishops and clergy did just that, and the general disdain for venal clergy continued to be a problem despite Justinian's *novel*. Moral outrage over payments for church office—even if called fees rather than simony—continued into the early Middle Ages to reemerge with particular force in the Reformation where the clergy would again have to confront extensive attempts by bishops and the state to control simony.[85]

Acknowledgements

I dedicate this paper to Alan Cameron. His joy in discussing Greek and Latin texts, his brilliant philological skills, and his determination to pursue evidence to make an argument are a continuing inspiration for me and for all those who encountered him. This chapter, which explores legal and papal documents to highlight the divide between religion and power, speaks to Alan's willingness to include in his study of antiquity all sorts of evidence. Though he is no longer with us, his passion for the truth inpsires me still to live up to the ideals of scholarship and friendship that he embodied. I also want to thank Shane Bjornlie for his helpful comments on this chapter. I delivered an earlier version of this in Rome in March of 2019 at the Swiss Institute; I thank the organizers of that event, notably Sarah Buehler and Sebastian Schmidt-Hofner, for the invitation.

---

84   *Liber Pontificalis*, ed. Duchesne 1886, 304 no. 7 ll. 13–14: *Sacravit multos divina lege ministros/nil pretio faciens immaculata manus* = *ICUR* ed. De Rossi 1888, vol. 2, 208. This epitaph, in St. Peter's, is described as "ante secretarium."

85   Rosé 2018, 201–238 has a good discussion of the later Middle Ages.

CHAPTER 11

Stenographers in Late Antiquity

Villains or Victims?

Raffaella Cribiore

Alan's wide, rich, and diverse interests are well known. In *The Last Pagans of Rome* he made some observations regarding stenographers in Late Antiquity, remarking that Jerome doubted their competence.[1] Jerome's rich friend Lucinius had sent a team of *notarii* from Spain to the Holy Land. Stenographers had a different function from copyists: their hands were not particularly skillful, and Jerome became especially anxious when he could not make use of a competent corrector. Alan did not express an opinion on the matter, but I would like to take up the challenge of evaluating, so far as is possible, stenographers' competence (or incompetence), their working methods, and the poor reputation they gained in antiquity.

Stenographers were employed in the Roman world from the time of the Republic, but they were not equally popular in the Greek world before Late Antiquity. They were called *exceptores* and *actuarii* in Latin. In Greek the terms *notarioi* and *exceptores* occur sporadically in papyri of the second and third centuries, though the quantity of evidence increases a great deal in Late Antiquity.[2] It appears that the second century saw a sporadic use of stenography. Itinerant sophists sometimes employed stenographers to record speeches they gave extemporaneously. Philostratus mentions them once with regard to the munificent Herodes Atticus, who gave the sophist Alexander ten shorthand writers and other great gifts.[3] The sources for Philostratus' sophists are mostly oral. One possible reason for this is that their speeches were not customarily recorded by stenographers. It appears that Galen used stenographers when friends and acquaintances unable to attend some of his medical demonstrations sent a team of tachygraphers, who occasionally asked the doctor to

---

1 Alan Cameron 2011a, 496.
2 Cf. Teitler 1985, 29–31. On the evidence of papyri, inscriptions, and the literary sources, see Boge 1974, 73–102.
3 Philostratus *VS* 574. Alexander was traveling and the tachygraphers had to record his performances. Cf. Heath 2004, 259–265.

© THE TRUSTEES OF COLUMBIA UNIVERSITY IN THE CITY OF NEW YORK,
2021 | DOI:10.1163/9789004452794_012

repeat the whole speech. Again, however, it does not seem that Galen often utilized this technique.[4]

It was in Late Antiquity that the use of stenography became widespread. In Arles stenographers even acquired their own saint and martyr, Saint Genesius, the patron of the city. The most ancient version of the saint's *Passio* dates from the fifth century. During the trial of some Christians, Genesius refused to write down their names and words, and threw his professional tablets to the ground.[5] In Late Antiquity stenographers became common figures who were indispensable in the production of records of Christological conferences and in the preservation of homilies.[6] This will be the main focus of my chapter, but first, I would like to present a general view of the conditions that facilitated the employment of tachygraphy. Some information regarding how people used personal writing and dictation may be useful.

1 Personal Writing and Dictation in Antiquity

It was always considered somewhat paradoxical that Christianity placed a high value on written texts even though most Christians could not read or write. The oral and the written, however, were not mutually exclusive. The illiterates were exposed to the written word and attained a close familiarity with the Christian scriptures through the catechetical process and homiletic rendition of texts in church.[7] Expert and nonexpert Christians—as Stanley Stowers called them—were not at opposite poles.[8] Most people did not need to understand complex doctrines and arguments.[9] In church the living voice of the preacher could reach everyone, though not with the same impact. While the oral dimension was paramount, stenographic signs could help. A stenographer confined the flow of words into small entities—which, ironically, presented many more difficulties of comprehension—but the signs were then "translated" into common language. What Augustine asserts in *De doctrina christiana* about stenographic signs indicates that some distrust surrounded

---

4 Boudon-Millot 2007, xciv–xcvi.
5 Cavallin 1945; Ronchey 2000.
6 It is time to reconsider stenographers and to review the evidence from various points of view. The excellent comprehensive works of Teitler are informative and irreplaceable but quite technical. See Teitler 1985, 1990, 2007.
7 Gamble 1995, 1–41.
8 Stowers 2016.
9 Of course, literate experts, such as Augustine, were the creative forces for the Christian movements in arguing against heresies and interpreting texts.

the work of stenographers. Illiterates must have regarded them with some suspicion. Augustine admitted the usefulness of letters, languages, and shorthand characters, declaring: *Ex eo genere sunt etiam notae, quas qui didicerunt proprie iam notarii appellantur. Utilia sunt ista nec discuntur illicite nec superstitione implicant* (signs are of this kind and those who have learned them properly are called *notarii*. There is nothing unlawful in learning the signs, nor do they involve one in superstition). Signs were related to magic.[10]

In Greek and Roman antiquity, an author could write and compose in his own hand or dictate to someone else. Quintilian maintained that dictation fatally harmed composition and recommended writing by night, when silence and privacy were conducive to concentration.[11] In Rome, the etiquette of correspondence demanded that a letter to a friend be written in a personal hand.[12] To be sure, authors who wrote in their own hand or those who composed their texts silently in their head, like Pliny, might have also dictated them to secretaries in the classical period.[13] In *Ad Fam.* 16.10, addressing his secretary and stenographer Tiro, Marcus Tullius Cicero wrote that in Tiro's absence his own compositions were silent, *sine te omnia mea muta esse.* In the second century Dio's strong predilection for dictation appears somewhat isolated. In *Oration* 18.18 he advised a young man he intended to train that he should not write personally, but instead dictate to a secretary. He declared that in expressing his thoughts aloud the person dictating was not a writer, but resembled someone addressing a live audience. Dio envisaged personal writing as something that happened very rarely.[14] While this was Dio's personal opinion at the time, there is no doubt that in the classical period literate people were rather familiar with personal writing.

---

10   *De doctrina christiana* 2.26.

11   Quint. 10.3.19–21 and 3.27. See Ker 2004.

12   Cf. the Roman rhetor Julius Victor, *Ars rhetorica* 27 who said that the ancients wrote in their own hand to those who were close to them. Fronto apologized because arthritis forced him to correct the text of a friend through a scribe, *Ep.* Volumnius Quadratus, ii.3 p. 187, van den Hout.

13   Gurd 2012, 9–11 on dictating and composing. Cf. Pliny, *Ep.* 9.36, who dictates repeatedly texts he has composed in his head (*cogito si quid in manibus*). At the time people penned their letters.

14   The young man he advises is allowed to write rhetorical exercises.

2   Stenographers in Late Antiquity

In Late Antiquity, however, the loud noise of voices dictating texts and letters, engaging in debates, and preaching in church is staggering. These were the voices that stenographers meant to capture and preserve. Without them, many texts would have been lost. In the classical period *dictare* meant "to dictate." In Late Antiquity *dictare* could mean "to say aloud and to dictate something to someone," but also took on the meaning of "to compose something, while saying it aloud at the same time."[15] The shift from the previous meaning is significant because it alludes to this less frequent personal and private writing. Jerome spelled out the whole possible gamut of literary activities: *hoc ipsum quod loquor, quod dicto, quod scribo, quod emendo, quod relego* (what I say, what I dictate, what I write, what I emend, and what I reread).[16] This passage shows him fully dictating and, after the text was written down, emending and rereading it a final time.

The writing habits of people and the characteristics of their letters and texts also contributed to making stenography slowly become a powerful and indispensable tool. The evidence of letters, documents, and texts in informal hands from Greek and Roman Egypt in Hellenistic and Roman times indicates that people wrote without being too self-conscious of their ability. A literate person might pen a letter in clumsy characters without turning to someone with a better hand. Things started to change in Egypt and the rest of the early Byzantine world when letters became long, elaborate, and full of artificial formulaic expressions. They were no longer vehicles for spontaneous messages, but now demanded knowledge of complex sentences in periodic style and requested proficient handwriting.[17] The change is already perceptible in the difference between the letters of the sophist Libanius and those of the Church Fathers.[18] The former were composed with artistry but were often quite short and spontaneous, while the latter were very long and somewhat repetitive. People began to refrain from writing, instead entrusting their thoughts to professionals. These developments became more accentuated in the early medieval

---

15   Arns 1953, 37–40 on the practice of Jerome, rightly considers *scribo* as a reference to a text being written by a secretary.

16   *Gal.* 3, 6, 10, *PL* 26. 433.

17   See Bagnall and Cribiore 2006, 16–18.

18   See Gruenbart 2005; Cribiore 2007, 8. More than 1500 letters of Libanius are preserved. On those concerning education, see Cribiore 2007.

period when dictation was the norm, writing techniques were intimidating, and their mastery became the exclusive task of specialized groups: monks and scribes.[19] These trends were already visible in Late Antiquity and contributed to reinforcing the power of scribes and stenographers. Shorthand writers had an advantage over the former since they had the ability to capture extensive texts that were delivered at speed. The stenographer stood at the center of the interplay of the oral and the written.

Allusions to personal writing in Late Antiquity are extremely rare. While this may be a sign that authors refrained from commenting on their personal writing skills, it is telling that they so often presented themselves in the act of dictating to stenographers or scribes. Augustine did not write even his marginal notes personally but had his secretary read aloud his text and jot down what he said.[20] Possidius reported that he wrote only one brief sixteen-page book in his own hand; the rest of his vast production was written by scribes.[21] The sophist Libanius, whose preserved corpus rivals those of some of the Christian fathers and who therefore left copious information on his writing habits, used both dictation and personal writing. He dictated his letters to secretaries, who then copied them into a copybook, and dictated his notes on declamations.[22] Yet, writing in his old age, he declared that he continued to compose and pen his works himself even though his hand was crippled with arthritis.[23] No doubt authors beyond Libanius put pen to paper, but the silence of the sources has some weight: dictation became irresistible.

In their books and treatises, late antique authors displayed a careful organization and an impeccable rhetorical style that was absent from their homilies. The extempore sermons recorded by shorthand writers were often repetitive, undeveloped, and redundant. One might cite the words of Pseudo-Plutarch about extempore delivery: "Those who speak offhand fall into a dreadful disregard of limit and into loquacity (*polylogia*)." As noted above, the underlying question of my chapter is how texts captured by stenographers could be trusted to correspond to what was dictated or delivered, and how they differed from those texts that were carefully emended. Did sermons, which were often colloquial and imperfect rhetorical pieces, correspond to what preachers

---

19   See Petrucci 1995; Clancy, 1993; Cribiore 1996, 156–158.

20   *Retract.* II.58, See Alan Cameron 2011a, 490.

21   Possidius, Indiculus 10³.15: *quaternio unus quem propria manu sanctus episcopus Augustinus initiavit.* He often penned part of his letters.

22   *Or.* 1.232, he said that his notes were too confused when they were produced in the "travails" of creation. His secretary copied them neatly.

23   He declared in *Or.* 11.1 that he had "more compositions than any man alive." See *Or.* 3.5 written after 387.

delivered, or did shorthand writers take some liberties with and make intrusions into a text? Furthermore, did stenographers who took down records at Christian conferences reproduce the dialogues faithfully, or were they guilty of omissions and additions?

3 Recording Christian Conferences

The proliferation of Christological controversies in the fourth, fifth, and sixth centuries, including theological splits, political rivalries, and passionate affirmations of faith, gave way to Councils that resulted in voluminous proceedings. When public documentation became the norm, stenographers were indispensable in producing records. Written texts were used to control debates and to smooth over difficult behaviors and resistance. The records taken down by shorthand writers were then "translated" and within a few days constituted the *Gesta*, the official versions of the conference. The compilation of records for the Carthage conference in 411 took only five days, from June 3 to 8, as the head stenographer had promised.[24] The stenographers' *notae* on tablets thus formed *schedae* that were signed by bishops from both parties. The language of all these proceedings is strongly tinged by polemics and oral expressions that give the flavor of the Latin spoken at the time, making the dialogues very vivid. The dialogues, which are sometimes very brief,[25] are entertaining to a certain extent. They document the theatrical behavior of the dissident bishops and testify to the antipathies, anxieties, and tactics of defiance of the weaker parties, which Brent Shaw has defined as "a pedagogy of the persecuted."[26] In all this, stenographers were caught in the middle. Accused (perhaps unjustly) of duplicitous behavior by dissident bishops, it is conceivable that they at times omitted records and shortened the written documents.

In 381 the evidence from the acts and commentary of the Council of Aquileia, which sealed the victory over Arianism, indicates that stenographers might have been assigned to the disputing parties in an imbalanced way. Like Augustine, Ambrose too saw the necessity of having them record the acts of the Council, but he apparently conducted the recording of the debates in a manner unfair to his opponent.[27] While normal practice would require that

---

24   Lancel 1972, 390.

25   Lancel 1972, 309: "Ces évêques avaient peu à dire, mais, ce peu, ils le disaient tous en employant les memes mots."

26   Shaw 2011, 564.

27   Grayson 1980. The marginal notes relating to the conference were preserved in a fifth-century manuscript with writings on the Arian controversy and part of the acts.

226 CRIBIORE

stenographers for both sides would take down the discussions in order to assure some objectivity, the acts of the conference testify to the continuous, fruitless requests of the Arian bishops Palladius and Secundianus of Illyricum to have their words recorded by their own shorthand writers. To a question from Ambrose, Palladius retorted, "I do not respond to you because you do not write down what I say. Only your words are written down and so I do not respond."[28] Palladius contested the fairness of the situation over and over, asking for a proper audience and for his side's own stenographers, and again refused to respond.[29] It is likely that the stenographers who reported on the Arians' interventions abridged them, since in Aquileia the whole business was conducted carelessly. Whatever the reality was, the Arian bishop Maximinus compiled passionate glosses half a century later, reporting repeatedly that what the Arians said was not written down because all the stenographers were on the Nicean side: *exceptores vestri sunt.*[30]

The same kinds of polemic resurface in the very voluminous proceedings of the Council of Chalcedon in 451, which again show the winning party controlling the agenda and the losers attempting to have their objections recorded.[31] The records were incomplete, and the stenographers, who again fell under suspicion, responded in various ways in attempts to exculpate themselves. A stenographer accused of taking down too-short records retorted that they had not been asked to write down the ordinary conversations and suggestions of the bishops.[32] Another *notarius* noticed the general tendency of extending consensus when only one speaker had expressed an opinion.[33] Here too the fight against the written word was extreme. Some bishops had brought their own notaries to ensure the veracity of the records. Juvenal of Jerusalem, in fact, sternly declared, "I had one notary of my own who kept a record alongside the other notaries."[34] And Theodore of Claudiopolis on a different occasion remarked, "Let him bring in his notaries and get his own to do the writing."[35] Discrepancies in the records and the fixation on comparing

---

Scholars have discussed the possibility that Ambrose was unfair to the other party, but Grayson 1980, 54–57 argued that such controversies about stenographers were not unusual.

28 Grayson 1980, 362, *Gesta* 43: *Non tibi respondeo, quia quaecumque ego dixi non sunt scripta. Vestra tantummodo scribuntur verba, non vobis respondeo.*

29 Grayson 1980, 368, *Gesta* e.g., 51.

30 Grayson 1980, 204–235, text 19. See *Gesta* e.g., 34 and 43.

31 Price and Gaddis 2005.

32 Price and Gaddis 2005, 1:261, *Gesta* 792.

33 Price and Gaddis 2005, 1:257, *Gesta* 767.

34 Price and Gaddis 2005, 1:153, *Gesta* 125.

35 Price and Gaddis 2005, 1:152, Gesta 122.

STENOGRAPHERS IN LATE ANTIQUITY

different written texts and finding validation pitted notary against notary. Faulty records could even be corrected against the private notes of an audience member who claimed that the official *notae* were wrong.[36] Ultimately conflicts exploded, and the records taken by stenographers were denounced by the weaker side. The Eastern bishops protested that they had been forced to sign "blank papers"[37] under constraint and threats: "We were threatened with exile. Soldiers with clubs and swords stood by and we took fright."[38]

The stenographic proceedings of the conference of Catholics and bishops in Carthage in 411 was intended to resolve the controversies between Catholics and Donatists. Speakers had to accept beforehand the rules of the presiding magistrate Marcellinus, who told them that their words were going to be recorded and that there would be jointly agreed-upon documents.[39] The unusual abundance of stenographers and the presence of those tasked with verifying the legitimacy of the records is proof of the significance of the event.[40] Distrust and suspicion were palpable from the beginning. In spite of Marcellinus' attempt to produce impeccable records by smoothing away difficulties, the *Gesta* testify to a continuous match between the parties, show the persistent suspicions some held concerning not being equally represented in writing, and reveal doubts about stenographers' partiality. Different testimonies might be read in turn by *exceptores* and *notarii* when there were worries about the former's trustworthiness.[41] At a certain point the Donatists requested that one of their own read the stenographers' acts. The polemic appeared futile, as a Catholic bishop remarked with some irony: "Note down that they have protested that records written by their own stenographers be read by their own stenographers," thus implying that in the climate of distrust every record should be checked by the other party.[42] But scorn could extend even to the reading skills of shorthand writers. When the presiding official Marcellinus (*tribunus et notarius*), who always attempted to be equitable, asked for both records to be read, an antagonistic Donatist bishop derided the reading skills of the stenographer Romulus, saying that he could not make out his words: "He does not know how to read,

---

36 Price and Gaddis 2005, 1:242, *Gesta* 644.

37 That is, papers that did not include their testimonies.

38 Price and Gaddis 2005, 1:140–141, *Gesta* 53 and 54.

39 Marcellinus was a fundamental key for the elaborate mechanism, see McLynn 2016.

40 Lancel 1972, 342–346, 390–391 remarks that every team worked for about six hours before being substituted. See Shaw 2011, 557–559.

41 Lancel 1975, 948–951, *Gesta* II 45–47: *Notarii ecclesiae recitent si de fide dubitant exceptorum.*

42 Lancel 1975, *Gesta* III 356.

228   CRIBIORE

he does not distinguish the phrases!"[43] Was the bishop hard of hearing? Was
the stenographer guilty of poor reading skills, like an incompetent schoolboy?
It is difficult to know for certain, but one suspects that this shorthand writer
may have been wrongly abused and ridiculed, as others had been.

4 Noisy Schoolrooms: The Sermons

Let us now consider sermons. The competence of stenographers in recording the words of speakers in councils and writing down preachers' sermons is
not always easy to assess. Both at conferences and in churches stenographers
received spoken words tinged with everyday language that they were unable
or unwilling to correct. They were transcribing texts pronounced in the heat
of discussion, when rhetoric was far from the minds of speakers. In churches,
the speakers' struggle to overcome the audience's noise and the clamor of
acclamations that were repeated over and over may have impeded the writing of *notae*.[44] Were churches like classrooms, one wonders? Educational texts
(Quintilian, Libanius) show that clamor, sometimes boisterous, accompanied
lectures. The audience of a preacher was probably less intentionally mischie-
vous, but reacted negatively to boredom, fatigue, and lack of understanding.[45]
Loud comments, chants, shouts, public communications with other parish-
ioners, and applause interfered with the preacher's attempts to be heard.[46] A
preacher needed to reach a multiform, restless public. Like a teacher of rhetoric, a bishop must have felt that his seed was scattered around haphazardly
and at risk of getting lost. Brent Shaw, who pointed to the difficulty preachers
encountered because of this, nevertheless called bishops' sermons "gems of
their rhetorical talent."[47] But there were gems and gems. If a physical link had
to be established between a preacher and the audience, sermons necessarily had to follow a simpler canvas. Extempore rhetoric was not always conducive to brilliant results, and there could be notable disparities between
formal treatises and what Possidius called "improvised sermons" (*repentinis*

---

43   Lancel 1975, 1192, *Gesta* III 54 and 255: *non legit, non distinguit sensus*. Thus, according to
      bishop Emeritus he did not pause between words and his reading was confused.

44   See Augustine *Ep.* 213 of 426 CE to Theodosius and Valentinianus. In the Church of Peace
      stenographers were also recording the acclamations: "The people shouted thirty-six
      times, To God be thanks! To Christ be praise! Oh Christ, hear us; may Augustine live long!
      was said thirteen times. You, our father! You, our bishop! was said eight times. He is wor-
      thy and just, was said twenty times," and the list goes on.

45   On six new sermons of Augustine, see Schiller et al. 2008.

46   On the reactions of preachers and audiences, see Pontet 1946, 38–47.

47   Shaw 2011, 414–416. Augustine's sermons were unrevised but those of Ambrose were
      emended with the exception of two: *De sacramentis* and *De mysteriis*.

STENOGRAPHERS IN LATE ANTIQUITY 229

sermonibus).[48] The vast majority of sermons, in fact, appear disappointing in spite of recent attempts to reevaluate them by considering specific frameworks of time, space, and audience. Besides the suffocating abundance of exegesis and dogma, most of them show rudimentary rhetorical skills, are unadorned, and use a familiar style. Were stenographers responsible for this?

Most of the sermons that are extant do not seem to have been edited, but rather represent the versions that stenographers wrote down during delivery (including informal admonitions and requests for silence). Scribes then reproduced the texts in regular letters. Though emendations would have improved the text, most preachers were not willing to take this second step. Augustine left the majority of his sermons unrevised:[49] he was interested in collecting them, but not with an eye toward publication.[50] In the fourth century the bishop of Brescia, Gaudentius, circulated his twenty-one sermons (which he called *tractatus*), but only after emending them.[51] He reminds one of writers like Diodorus Siculus, who declared that he was disowning books of his that had been disseminated without his permission and corrections.[52] Likewise, Gaudentius stated that sermons recorded by some *notarii* could not be considered his unless he corrected them: "They have nothing to do with me and are not mine" (*nihil ad me attinet; mea iam non sunt*).[53] Did this statement derive from a general distrust in stenographers? It does not seem so. Rita Lizzi Testa pointed rightly to "religious solicitudes, in a period of heated debate with the Arians."[54] Gaudentius' testimony of how those sermons were written down is in fact revealing. Some people had tried to collect them by hiding *notarii* in church (*latenter appositis*) as he preached.

Emending a sermon recorded by a stenographer consisted not only of correcting mistakes but especially of making a text shorter and more compact. Different recensions of a few sermons of Augustine reveal texts that were written by stenographers and then emended.[55] When two texts of a sermon appear in the manuscripts, with one shorter and one more extensive but differing from

---

48   Possidius *Vita Aug.* 7.1l, Shaw 2011, 411; on the difference between written and oral sermons, Müller 2012, 299–300.

49   In *Ep.* 265 to Seleuciana, a religious woman, Augustine shows that he doubted the full competence of a particular *notarius*, but this is an isolated episode. Seleuciana, moreover, may have misinterpreted his words.

50   Houghton 2008, 28–31 and note 17.

51   See Olivar 1991, 915–918.

52   Diod. Sic. *Library of History* 40.8.

53   PL 20, cols. 831–832.

54   Lizzi Testa, forthcoming.

55   Lambot 1969. See also Lambot in the introduction of sermon 37, *CCSL* vol. 41, 444, where he says that the tradition reveals two archetypes, one of which was found in the library of Augustine. They derived from the texts of two different stenographers.

the other in only a few respects, it is possible to identify the latter as the version that a stenographer took down. Sometimes one may reach certainty. Studying two versions of Augustine x *Tractatus in Ioannis epistulam*, M. Comeau noticed a more complete version in A, while B showed many omissions such as repetitions, questions, exclamations, and superfluous information.[56] Comeau concluded that A was closer to the sermon given by Augustine. This editor did not, in any case, comment upon the few stenographic signs in the margins of version A, and yet these seem a confirmation that A represented the text transcribed from the tablet of a stenographer.

I suggest that the extant evidence shows that stenographers transmitted an extempore text mechanically with limited intrusions.[57] The simple fact that they reproduced so many repetitions in a homily should indicate that they did not edit but rather followed a preacher blindly. Few homilies show their direct textual interventions,[58] which might suggest that stenographers dutifully conformed to what was delivered in church without adding much. In a text of John Chrysostom, Alexandre Olivar showed a few insignificant words that might have been introduced in this way, but also pointed toward an interesting example that confirms the utter dependence of a tachygrapher on a preacher: he in fact dutifully reproduced a mistake by John Chrysostom without being able or willing to correct it.[59] The few examples of stenographers' intrusions in a homily allow us to evaluate the reasons for which they did so.

A stenographer could be justified in occasionally omitting a well-known prayer that usually came at the beginning and end of all sermons given by Augustine, since the audience would have known it by heart. When he filled up empty pauses in a preacher's homily, however, he improvised but did so with prudence.[60] In the year 426 Augustine preached a series of sermons over several consecutive days: 320, 321, 322, 323, 324 and 124. The sequence contains several texts: a homily of Augustine, a booklet (read in church) with the story of a mother and her sick children, one of whom was cured by St. Stephen, a

---

56 Comeau 1932. The writer of B, moreover, attempted to clean up the text by eliminating popular words and substituting classical terminology.

57 Lambot 1969, 83–84: "attentifs à no manquer aucun mot, des tachygraphes prenaient fébrilement des notes, avec autant d'exactitude que d'agilité."

58 It is unlikely that the scribes who "translated" stenographers' texts got rid of their insertions in order to write down a preacher's *ipsissima verba*.

59 Olivar 1991, 908, 909.

60 Deferrari 1922, 214–216. Prayers could be omitted or shortened, since people could supply them by memory.

STENOGRAPHERS IN LATE ANTIQUITY   231

sermon on the events, and two further homilies about two other miracles.[61] During an emotional speech, it was announced that the sister of the youth cured by St. Stephen had been healed too. Augustine, who had begun to talk about a different miracle, was interrupted by the crowd going wild with cries of joy and tears. The stenographer filled the period of interruption caused by the crowd's reactions as follows:

> And while Augustine was saying this, the people around the shrine of Saint Stephen began to shout: "God be thanked! Christ be praised!" In the midst of this continuous clamor, the young woman who had just been cured was led into the apse. When they saw her, the people prolonged their shouting for some time with great joy and weeping, not uttering any words, but just making noise. When silence was eventually obtained, Augustine said ...[62]

It is clear that in these few lines the stenographer became a narrator who spoke in his own voice.

A similar situation emerges from the homily *In illud, quando ipsi subiciet omnia* that was traditionally attributed to John Chrysostom but was later shown to be by Severianus of Gabala, who was active in Constantinople when Chrysostom was bishop.[63] This homily too was delivered extemporaneously.[64] In the words of the stenographer, "when a small child afflicted by a disease was in the crowd, (the preacher said)." This is an explanation of what comes next and introduces a digression by the preacher. At the end of the sermon the stenographer added a few more words to explain the appearance of three men who were sick. It is clear that these were the words of a witness and not of the preacher. Another direct intervention on the part of a shorthand writer is visible in a sermon of Augustine. The heading of a section consists of explanatory words clarifying that after the sermon, people had asked Augustine not to

---

61   See Meyers 2006.

62   Sermon 323.4. The translation was adapted from Hill 1990.

63   Voicu 1980. Goodall 1979, 78–62 considered the homily I Corinthians 15.28 as written by Chrysostom and explained its loose style by the fact that it had been taken down by a stenographer. Haidacher 1907 commented on the stenographer's intervention in this supposed Chrysostom sermon. Wikenhauser 1907 repeated Haidacher's text.

64   Severus was active at the end of the fourth and the beginning of the fifth centuries. On the similarity of his sermons to classical diatribe, see Uthemann 1998.

depart before the birthday of the blessed Cyprian. A stenographer had added the explanation that was followed by a short sermon on that subject.[65]

These examples show that shorthand writers left the body of a sermon intact. Their personal interventions into texts were minimal. They did not impinge upon a sermon's substance, and they dutifully followed a preacher's words. But why did they encroach at all, even if insignificantly? The stenographers who were active recording the sermons I discussed above had a certain degree of culture and cared for the smooth appearance of their discourses. They were interested in building a solid frame so that the discourse could continue smoothly. There are very few examples of extraneous occurrences that took place during a sermon of Augustine, and none in those of John Chrysostom. When disturbances due to a crowd's vocal enthusiasm occurred and caused a preacher to be silent for some time, a stenographer made some cosmetic additions that would tie the different parts of a discourse together. One might suggest, humorously, that these writers did not like to be idle and continued in a frenzy of fast writing. Inevitably, reconstructing what we do not know from a few cases in antiquity is very difficult. It is impossible to measure the competence of all shorthand writers. In a 1855 letter to W. D. Fox, Darwin wrote, "I have no faith in anything short of actual measurement"—a striking statement that rarely applies to antiquity. Based on what I have been able to "measure," I suggest that stenographers were not villains, but they might have been victims of prejudice and false expectations.

---

65   Sermon 163B.6. The stenographer wrote "people asked them," that is, not only Augustine. The plural pronoun perhaps indicated that Augustine was surrounded by others, such as secretaries. Houghton 2008, 30 reported also in homily 20.5 that the stenographer added that an exhortation to pay attention happened after the sermon.

CHAPTER 12

Three Questions about the Ancient Hospital

W. V. Harris

The origins of the hospital are a popular historical subject, but notwithstanding expert work by such scholars as Georg Harig and Vivian Nutton, there is considerably more to say. What follows is not an attempt to re-write the early history of the hospital,[1] but merely a clarification of some of the issues, in the form of three key questions, questions as it happens of progressively increasing difficulty. The underlying problem is how to fit the history of the late antique hospital into larger patterns of social, cultural, and religious change. And it is quite crucial to ask, as to my great surprise no scholar has yet asked, what the effects of hospitalization were in ancient times, and what ancient peoples expected them to be. Contagion and control must both be taken into account.

1 Were there Roman Hospitals Prior to the Fourth Century CE?

The answer is of course yes.[2] Ample evidence shows that by the first century CE the Roman state organized military *valetudinaria*, that large-scale Roman slave-holders commonly organized *valetudinaria* to care for their slaves, and that these institutions, the military ones especially, were 'hospitals' by any reasonable definition.

It is not to my purpose here to determine which marshal or emperor first instituted military *valetudinaria*. It was obviously in the interests of commanders to care attentively for the sick and wounded of all ranks, and Velleius lauds Tiberius for having done so during his German and Pannonian campaigns

---

1 A longer, revised version of this chapter will appear in Harris, forthcoming. I wish to thank Anne Hunnell Chen and Noel Lenski for critiquing an earlier version, and Alan Bowman and Vivian Nutton for important items of information.

2 Seriously misleading accounts of this matter abound, even in what appear to be works of scholarship. Crislip 2005 will serve as an example. As to pre-Christian antiquity, he puts forward (101–102) three defining characteristics of a hospital that they supposedly did not possess: (1) 'inpatient facilities'—which are in reality richly attested; (2) professional medical care—which is amply attested as far as military hospitals are concerned; and (3) they have to be charities—unlike the vast majority of modern hospitals! As to how a hospital should be defined, see below.

© THE TRUSTEES OF COLUMBIA UNIVERSITY IN THE CITY OF NEW YORK,
2021 | DOI:10.1163/9789004452794_013

(2.114.1–2). There already seems to have been a relatively simple *valetudinarium* at Haltern on the River Lippe while Augustus was still alive.[3] An army document from Egypt that has been dated palaeographically to the early first century CE mentions a legionary *valetudinarium*.[4] It has been claimed that Hod Hill camp in Dorset includes an early (Claudian) *valetudinarium*,[5] but I shall not enter here into the problem of identifying *valetudinaria* archaeologically. They became highly elaborate structures, by ancient standards. Ido Israelowich in a recent publication lists seventeen such sites,[6] and there are other probable cases. We also have a certain amount of epigraphical evidence.[7] In short, the phenomenon is attested from Syria and Egypt via Rome itself to northern Britain, and from the Julio-Claudians to the Severans (but not securely, as far as I know, thereafter).[8] Pseudo-Hyginus' second-century handbook on the fortification of camps tells (chs. 4 and 35) how the *valetudinarium* should be sited.[9] Auxiliary units as well as legions possessed them. Doctors and other medical personnel were normally in attendance.[10] A military historian concludes, with these hospitals in mind, that 'the army provided outstanding medical care'.[11] By the standards of the time, of course.

---

3   So Nutton 1992, 52. Baker 2002 and 2004 over-reacted against archaeologists' over-facile identifications of military *valetudinaria*, and many of their identifications remain valid, including in all likelihood this one. See further Künzl 2005.

4   *PSI* XIII.1307 = Fink 1971, no. 51 (Trismegistos 62947). The date is Fink's. An Egyptian document of 138, *BGU* VII.1564 (Trismegistos 9473), refers in a military context to a ὑγιαστή-ριον, which was certainly a *valetudinarium*, but it is not clear whether it was in Egypt or Cappadocia.

5   The chronology is clear enough (Richmond 1968, 117–123) but although Richmond indicated no doubt about the building that he identified as a *valetudinarium* the uncertainty of Wilmanns seems justified (1995, 109–110: 'recht unsicher'). This was an auxiliary fort.

6   Israelowich 2016, 216.

7   *ILS* 2117, 2437, 2438, 2458, 9174; *CIL* VI.175 and XIII.8099; *AÉ* 1933 no. 120, 1937 no. 181 (which misled a recent writer into supposing that there was a military *valetudinarium* at Praeneste) and 1995 nos. 1259d and e; for Syria, Jarry 1985, 114–115 (whence *AÉ* 1987 no. 952); *T.Vindol.* II.155. I have not attempted to make an exhaustive list; see further Ricci 2015, 358–359.

8   They seem to have been forgotten by the time of Vegetius. The HA writer was apparently unaware of them when he wrote *Hadrian* 10 and *Severus Alexander* 47, but he was no military expert. Crislip 2005, 127, incidentally, has both the chronology and the geography of the military *valetudinarium* badly wrong.

9   Cf. Gourevitch 2011, 111–113. For another mention see *Dig.* 50.6.7 (6) (Tarruntenus Paternus 1 *milit.*).

10   Nutton 2012, 185

11   Rankov 2007, 69.

THREE QUESTIONS ABOUT THE ANCIENT HOSPITAL

In fact the worst fighting very often took place, as Nutton has pointed out,[12] far from legionary hospitals: most of the seriously wounded would have died of their wounds or of peritonitis or gangrene far from any medical institution.[13] Yet Nutton may have been right to regard the availability of *valetudinaria* as a 'perk' of military service.[14]

Equally incontrovertible evidence shows that at one time wealthy Roman slave-holders also maintained *valetudinaria* for their slaves. Once again, it seems impossible to say when this began: the earliest literary reference is in Seneca, but some of the epigraphical evidence goes back to the lifetime of Livia (ob. 29 CE).[15] For Seneca, the house of a man of wealth might routinely contain a *valetudinarium* attended by a doctor (*De ira* 1.16.4—the patients are implicitly urban household slaves). There was routinely a *valetudinarium* for the slaves on a country estate in Columella's time; the *vilicus* and his wife were in charge, and there is no mention of doctors (11.1.18, 12.3.7–8), but Varro (*RR* 1.16.4) shows that it was normal for landowners to think about the availability of doctors (it was better (sc. more economical) to summon one from a nearby settlement but wealthy people maintained their own).

Whether there were other kinds of *valetudinaria* depends partly on how we take Celsus' reference to 'large hospitals' (*ampla valetudinaria*, 1 pr. 65). They are staffed, in his account, by over-worked doctors. Is he referring to military or slave hospitals or both, or to some other institution?[16] Seneca can imagine himself as a patient in a *valetudinarium* (*Ep.* 27.1), which is similarly ambiguous.[17]

'"Hospitals" the *valetudinaria* were not', claims John Scarborough,[18] not explaining himself but presumably taking over the substance of the book he was reviewing, which established nothing of the kind. Those who maintain this opinion are quite misguided (they are almost certainly right, as we shall see later, to maintain that the late antique hospital did not derive from these

---

12 Nutton 2012, 184.

13 But some known *valetudinaria* were certainly in battle zones, e.g. Fendoch and Inchtuthil.

14 Nutton 2012, 185.

15 *CIL* VI.9084 and 9085. Other epigraphical references: *CIL* VI 4475, 8639, 9602, and 33917. The only such reference outside the capital is *CIL* X.703 (Surrentum). Nutton 1992, 50–51 suggested that the institution was a reaction to the supposedly increased value of slaves now that foreign wars were less frequent.

16 As Ricci observes, however, the passage of Seneca, *De ira*, just cited seems to presuppose a simple typology of *valetudinaria*: they were either military or in the houses of the wealthy (2015, 361).

17 For further discussion of these passages, see Harig 1971, 191–192. Yet other ambiguous references are to be found in Seneca, *Quaest.Nat.* I pr.5 and Tacitus, *Dial.* 21.1 (the latter appears to be the latest literary reference to a civilian *valetudinarium*).

18 Scarborough 2006, 614.

high-imperial institutions, but that is another matter entirely). If you demand that an ancient hospital must be very much like a modern hospital to count as a hospital at all, error is inevitable. One might as well deny that the ancients had schools—for assuredly no ancient school was at all like a modern one (the physical structures were relatively small and makeshift, the organizational structures were entirely different).

Whether other ancient institutions should be deemed to have been hospitals depends partly on definition. What is a hospital? The renowned Karl Sudhoff offered the following: 'buildings of any kind in which sick people are accepted for the care and recovery of their health'.[19] The *OED* gives the following as 'the current sense' (as it is also the current meaning of *Krankenhaus, hôpital, ospedale* and so on): 'an institution or establishment for the care of the sick or wounded, or of those who require medical treatment'. The dictionary recognizes that until the eighteenth century the English term sometimes referred to a hostel for pilgrims or the indigent.[20] But when Harig suggested that Sudhoff's definition needed to be improved by reference to the length of the patient's stay and the 'manner of treatment',[21] he may have been going too far.

We may agree that an institution is not a hospital, but rather a 'surgery' or a 'clinic' or an 'aid-post', if it does not accommodate patients overnight or is very small, and that is an issue relevant to the term *iatreion* (see below) but of no wider significance for the historical problem at hand. 'Manner of treatment' is a much thornier matter. Two questions are involved (both highly relevant to the early Christian hospital as well as to earlier times): (1) were doctors present? (2) are we or are we not willing to refer to institutions that offered primarily religious cures, Asklepieia in particular, as hospitals? There can be no hospital without the at least occasional presence of doctors, that is obvious.[22] The question of the Asklepieia and similar institutions is much more difficult. We can leave aside the occasional advice possibly given by real doctors at

---

19 'Baulichkeiten irgendwelcher Art, in welchen kranke Menschen zur Pflege und zur Wiederherstellung ihrer Gesundheit Aufnahme fanden', Sudhoff 1913, 1. He excludes poorhouses and the like.

20 Hence the complication that historians speak of 'foundling hospitals', whereas such an institution in the contemporary world would be referred to as an orphanage or by some euphemism. In my view, it causes only confusion if one defines a hospital as 'a pauper enclosure' (Horden 2004/5, 364; cf. 2012, 719), since that is not by any means how the word is used in modern English. M. A. Anderson 2012, 12, misrepresents contemporary usage and invents a definition of his own (21), with unfortunate consequences.

21 Harig 1971, 180.

22 Some will maintain that there was no clear line in antiquity between doctors and other medical practitioners, but that is I think substantially false; Harris 2016b, 29–33.

THREE QUESTIONS ABOUT THE ANCIENT HOSPITAL

Asklepieia.[23] It can be urged that in antiquity it was, for most sick people, just as sensible to pray to Asklepios as to obtain treatment from a physician, if not more so. As a compromise we can think of healing shrines that in any sense accommodated the sick for any length of time—as some Asklepieia did[24]—as 'proto-hospitals'. As a possible model for late antique hospitals they must not be forgotten.

Other classical practices also require consideration.[25] As for the *iatreion* ('a doctor's workplace'), it was a consulting and surgical space.[26] There is no clear evidence that patients overnighted there, but one wonders whether doctors who performed excruciating and debilitating surgery always sent their patients home on the same day. At some date in the second century BCE Cos honored a certain doctor named Onasandros because, among other good deeds, he had 'opened an *iatreion*' there (*SEG* 41 [1991], no.680, line 24),[27] where 'opened' obviously suggests an institution not merely a private residence. A well-to-do doctor like the proprietor of the House of the Surgeon at Rimini certainly had space enough to allow patients to stay.[28] Some scholars hold that public physicians (see below) commonly received the cost of an *iatreion* from the city.[29] And ancient doctors did not perform surgery unaccompanied, so that the scene in an *iatreion* must often have been very different from the discrete modern consulting room. It appears furthermore from Plautus' *Menaechmi* (948–956) that in the Hellenistic world (as in the nineteenth century) doctors

23 Those who have claimed that real doctors sometimes practised medicine at Asklepieia have yet to produce any cogent evidence to that effect. Cf. Edelstein and Edelstein 1945, 2:158; Demand 1994, 94; Harris 2016b, 23. There seems to be no clear evidence of an *iatros* practising medicine in an Egyptian temple, though that would scarcely be surprising; see further Hirt Raj 2006, 297.

24 According to Harig 1971, 181, it is a mistake to see any Asklepieia as 'krankenhausähnliche Institutionen' because there were no lodgings for sick people inside the shrine at Epidaurus but only just outside. This is a quibble. The sick could not be allowed to lodge inside the shrine for the obvious reason that deaths (and births) were not supposed to take place there (Pausanias 2.27.6). It was presumably the great Asclepian cult centers—Pergamum and Cos as well as Epidaurus—that most attracted prolonged visits. For Asclepian cures that took days or even months see Harig, ibid.; Girone 1998, 44n23. Vitruvius 1.2.7 evidently takes it for granted that those who visit *fana* of such gods as Aesculapius and Salus for cures will stay for some time.

25 The claim of Garzya 1997, 351 that the late antique hospital was 'the heir of the Roman *hospitium*' was simply erroneous.

26 Harig 1971, 183; Samama 2003, 37.

27 Samama 2003, no. 137.

28 See De Carolis 2009.

29 Samama 2003, 41, citing a Delian inscription of 179 BCE (her no. 109), which is not enough to establish a general pattern.

sometimes took in resident patients, but there is little other evidence for such a practice.[30]

Whether a large *iatreion* was much different from a small hospital is a question insistently raised by the site of Allianoi (Paşa Ilıcası), an ancient spa near Pergamum (a site that has very regrettably been inundated by 30 metres of reservoir water).[31] A substantial second-century building there has been described as a hospital, and it was evidently the scene of fairly intense surgical activity. Architecturally the building bore some—but in truth not very much—resemblance to a military *valetudinarium*. According to Nutton, the most likely interpretation is that 'this was an ἰατρεῖον of a size and complexity not previously encountered in the archaeological record'.[32] But serious uncertainty remains: on the one hand it seems quite possible that a building at Allianoi deserved the name of hospital, on the other hand it probably did not continue to function into the fourth century.

2　Why Were There Not More Hospitals for Civilians, Other Than Slaves, Prior to the Fourth Century CE?

This was a world of ostentatious philanthropy, and yet there were no all-purpose hospitals. The Greek tradition, going back in some cases to the sixth century BCE and spreading in due course widely and to some places in the West, was for cities to appoint salaried public physicians (one or more) who treated their patients either in the doctor's own *iatreion* or in the patient's home.[33] This is not the place for a discussion of the historical problems involved, such as in particular the willingness of public doctors to treat the poor. In theory, a good doctor of the second century CE was meant to cure the wealthy and the destitute alike.[34] This expectation was enshrined in a law of 368 (*C.Th.* 13.3.8).[35] All this may make the nonexistence of all-purpose hospitals more remarkable.

30　In this case the physician proposes to treat his insane patient for twenty days. See further Harig 1971, 186; Nutton 2012, 404n85. It is intriguing that Epictetus (*Discourses* 3.22.62) imagines a situation in which a sick man might be invited to stay in the house of a friend in order to be nursed (*nosokomêthênai*).

31　Baykan 2012 (with a plan on 194 and an English summary). This report was criticized in detail by Nutton 2014, 382–389. Further discussion is needed.

32　Nutton 2014, 386.

33　Samama 2003, 38–45, Nutton 2014, 87, 151, 249, etc. For the imbalance between the East and the West, see Gourevitch 2011, 114.

34　See Samama 2003, no. 022 from Athens, the epigram of Sarapion, which describes the doctor's duties (*SEG* 28 [1978], no. 225). See especially Gourevitch 1984, 278–288.

35　'As many *archiatri* shall be appointed as there are districts of the city [of Rome] … Such physicians, knowing that their subsistence allowances are paid from the taxes of

THREE QUESTIONS ABOUT THE ANCIENT HOSPITAL

The great advantage of the *valetudinarium* was that it regimented those who, in the eyes of the military authorities or the slave-holders, as the case might be, needed to be controlled and accounted for.[36] Columella makes this clear (12.3.7–8): farm slaves are often injured on the job, and the overseers must see that they are taken care of properly; they must also be on the lookout for malingerers. The case of the soldiers is different—emperors needed to cajole them as well as discipline them. In both cases the inmates and their health were valuable, and also in different ways dangerous. It is also highly relevant that both the government and the large slave-holders possessed the capital that permitted them to build substantial structures.

In theory, individual philanthropists might have stepped into the breach to create other kinds of hospitals, as indeed eventually began to happen in the second half of the fourth century CE. One reason why they did not do so in high imperial times was no doubt the very limited idea of social welfare that prevailed, in different forms, throughout the western world until the nineteenth century. Yet the possessing classes did take modest steps to alleviate famines.[37]

There was, I suggest, another, stronger reason. All educated Greeks and Romans knew (from Thucydides' time, if not earlier, in the case of the Greeks; by the last generation of the Republic, if not earlier, in the case of Rome) that some diseases were highly contagious. Isocrates as well as Thucydides provide evidence, as do many later Greek writers; from Sallust onwards the Latins do as well.[38] The paradox that almost all ancient medical writers ignored contagiousness has been noted by a number of scholars;[39] Vivian Nutton has canvassed possible explanations in some detail,[40] and I shall offer a different explanation in a forthcoming book—here it is sufficient to recognize the fact itself. Most educated Greeks and Romans knew that to herd seriously ill people together in a confined space was to put them in harm's way.[41] That was justified, so it was evidently thought, in the case of soldiers and slaves, where discipline was paramount (and in fact both soldiers and slaves were more likely than most sick people to be suffering from injuries or wounds not infectious diseases).

---

the people, shall prefer to minister to the poor honorably rather than to serve the rich shamefully.'

36   Cf. Majno 1975, 393.
37   Garnsey 1988; Giovannini 1991.
38   For details and discussion see Harris, forthcoming.
39   See especially Leven 1993; Nutton 2000.
40   Ibid.
41   Caelius Aurelianus, quite probably agreeing with the thinking of Soranus (whose relevant work is of course lost), expressed the community's dilemma: send the contagious patients away for the good of the rest, or obey the laws of humane medicine and risk other lives by taking care of them (*Chron.* 4.13).

240   HARRIS

It so happens that a rare piece of evidence suggests the human cost of ancient hospitalization. A duty roster from the fort at Vindolanda (*T.Vindol.* II.154), probably of 90 CE and in any case certainly of that period, lists thirty-one soldiers as medically unfit, no fewer than ten of them because they were *lippientes*,[42] suffering from a serious eye condition that we cannot certainly identify. The most likely suspect, as Danielle Gourevitch has pointed out, is conjunctivitis,[43] which is extremely contagious, all the more so when no proper precautions are taken. It is a reasonable conjecture that conjunctivitis continued to spread inside the Vindolanda *valetudinarium.*

Any educated person to whom it occurred to institute a hospital for miscellaneous sick people is likely to have performed a calculus different from those of the military commanders and the slave-holders: since such an institution inevitably housed a number of highly infectious patients, morbidity and mortality could be expected to be dire, as they always were in hospitals everywhere in the premodern world.[44] (This problem is still surprisingly severe, at least in the United States). The third-century bishop Dionysius of Alexandria seems to have known as much about contagion as almost anyone else in antiquity (and bishop Cyprian of Carthage may have been aware too);[45] such awareness may indeed have caused them *not* to found the first Christian hospitals (there were other inhibiting factors as well).

3   What Led the Christians of the Fourth and Fifth Centuries to Found Hospitals?

This is a more complicated question, and I will limit myself to a series of observations. The motives of philanthropists are seldom simple, and in this instance philanthropy may not in any case be the most appropriate concept.

In the first place, there was probably no continuity with the Roman *valetudinarium.*[46] We are more aware now than we used to be that there were

---

42   The reading of the first four letters of 'lippientes' may seem uncertain in the published version, but the co-editor Professor Bowman kindly informs me that the letters 'li' are 'very clear' and that he has 'no doubts' about the reading as a whole.

43   Gourevitch 2011, 111n11. Infectious conjunctivitis might help to explain the extraordinary number of oculists' stamps that have been found in the north-west provinces (cf. *RIB* II.2446). Trachoma is also contagious.

44   See Risse 1992, 182, etc.

45   Cf. Leven 1993, 47–48. For Dionysius see Eusebius, *HE* 7.22. The evidence about Cyprian, viz. Pontius, *Vita Cypriani* 9, is less clear.

46   Wilmanns 1995, 136–137, appears to be unique in claiming otherwise (but she seems to retreat from this claim, 138). She mistakenly supposes that the existence of military

THREE QUESTIONS ABOUT THE ANCIENT HOSPITAL

still large slave households in the fourth century[47] and some of them may have included *valetudinaria*, but there is not a shred of evidence to that effect. As for the military *valetudinarium*, there is no sign of it in Vegetius or any other fourth-century writer, which is not surprising now that the military unit's base was much less likely to be elaborate or long-lasting. Thus, we can say that the Christians invented the hospital, though they were not the first to do so. And what they invented was probably less like a modern hospital than the military *valetudinarium* had been (because it was more like a rest home).

Secondly, we face a problem of terminology. The specific Greek word for a hospital was νοσοκομεῖον, but it is not attested until 400 (Jerome, *Ep.* 77). Scholars have recklessly assumed that *xenodocheia* (hostels) and even *ptôcheia* (poorhouses) were, in part at least, hospitals, even though there is no reason to think that doctors were ever in attendance at such places in the fourth or fifth century. But matters are not so simple, for as we shall see we have at least one piece of evidence (in Epiphanius) that a fourth-century *ptôchotropheion* harbored invalids—who may, however, have been disabled people and 'incurables' who were not considered to be likely to benefit from the attention of doctors. And by 390 it could be assumed that the *xenodocheion* of Antioch contained people who were sick (John Chrysostom, *Homm. In Matt.* 66.3 = *PG* 58.630).[48]

It is clear in any case, as Glen Bowersock has observed, that the fourth-century Christian churches were more interested in helping the indigent than in healing the sick.[49] Which, it must be said, was a more realistic policy.

But a further point of major importance is that the chief fortress of traditional religious belief in the fourth century was the vast network of old healing cults, above all—but not only—the Asklepieia, large and small, that covered the Hellenized and semi-Hellenized world.[50] The first important sanctuary that the Christians destroyed or at least heavily damaged was the Asklepieion

---

    doctors is evidence that there were still military *valetudinaria* in the fourth century. Her statement (137n317) that Vegetius knew of the latter is incorrect. Her most interesting claim, which has been supported in the past by archaeologists who have worked on the site, is that the *valetudinarium* in the legionary camp at Lauriacum (Lorch) was still in use at least into the fourth century. But Baker 2002, 71, doubts that we can identify a *valetudinarium* at Lauriacum at all.

47   See Harper 2011 passim, e.g. 190–191.

48   For the chronology, see J. N. D. Kelly 1995, 90. Cf., probably somewhat earlier, the assumption that a *xenôn* housed some people who were ill (John Chrysostom, *Ad Stagirium* 3.13 (*PG* 47.490)).

49   Bowersock 2010, 46: 'The indigent were naturally often sick, but it was their poverty, not their health, that first inspired Christian charity.'

50   For their diffusion, see Riethmüller 2005, chapter 2; Panagiotidou 2016, 86–92. Riethmüller registers more than 900 sites.

at Aegae in Cilicia in 331.[51] Christian apologists had long been denigrating Asklepios 'with singular bitterness';[52] according to Eusebius, Asklepios draws souls away from the 'true saviour' (*Vita Const.* 3.56). By the end of the fourth century—the reign of Theodosius was crucial—almost all the major sanctuaries of the health god had been destroyed or closed down.[53] In some cases at least the sites were Christianized, but whether particular sites were promptly converted is a side issue.[54] What mattered was establishing the claim that in some sense Christ was a better healer, and in order to do this a few Christian leaders realized that new institutions were needed that were similar in function to the old ones. Thus, the Christian hospital was, in its earliest phase, a religiously motivated attempt to displace the traditional religious centers of pseudohealing.[55]

Let us come now to the specific evidence about fourth- and fifth-century Christian initiatives that modern scholars have referred to as hospitals. The results are somewhat meagre in the context of a still enormous empire.

(1) It seems to have been prior to 360 (when his patron Macedonius was deposed as bishop of Constantinople) that one Marathonius 'superintended buildings (*sunoikias*) of the sick and destitute' in the eastern capital (Sozomen 4.27.4).[56] It is intriguing that he had previously been an army officer (and as such had greatly enriched himself, according to Sozomen); intriguing also that he superintended them (*epemeleito*), he did not found them. How long had they been in existence? There is no mention of doctors.

(2) The heretic-hunter Epiphanius tells us (*Adversus Haer.* 75) that Bishop Eustathius of Sebasteia (in Pontus), at some date which must be prior to 377,

---

51 Eusebius claims (*Vita Const.* 3.56) that this was the work of soldiers under the orders of Constantine, but presumably there was some local initiative. Other sources include Sozomen, *HE* 2.5, Libanius, *Or.* 30.39, Zonaras 13.12, *IG* IV².438. See further Averil Cameron and Hall 1999, 303; Renberg 2017, 1:209.

52 As observed by Edelstein and Edelstein 1945,2:132. They mention *inter alia* Justin, *Apol.* 54.10 and *Dial.* 69.3, Tertullian, *Ad nat.* 2.14 and Origen, *Contra Cels.* 3.25. This did not prevent Christian image-makers from stealing the god's iconography: Dinkler 1980.

53 See Nutton 2012, 311. Athens appears to have been an exception: the Asklepieion is considered to have gone on functioning until the mid-fifth century, the key evidence being Marinus, *Vita Procli* 29, where the exceptional character of this survival is recognized.

54 For Pergamum, see Feissel 1999, 267. The general question of the Christian re-use of the sites of Asklepieia is too complex to be entered into here; cf. Gregory 1986, 238. How and when the important healing cult of Isis at Menouthis outside Alexandria was brought to an end also seems to need further investigation.

55 Wickkiser 2006, 37n43, rightly points out a significant difference: a visit to an Asklepieion was not cost-free (but she underestimates the accessibility of such shrines in many regions). She is mistaken, however, in claiming that Asklepieia only tried to heal incurable conditions (as her own tables show, 27–28).

56 Cf. Crislip 2005, 130–131.

founded a *ptôchotropheion* which was also intended to house τοὺς λελωβη-μένους καὶ ἀδυνάτους, that is to say 'the maimed and disabled'.[57] A hospice not a hospital, apparently. We should not suppose that Eustathius' action was unique.

(3) We turn to the famous foundation of Basil of Caesarea outside that city. In the first place there is his own letter (94) of 372 to '(H)elias', the governor of the province, who was evidently a Christian too. Basil seems very defensive, and the governor has heard accusers. Basil admits that he has constructed *katagôgia* (lodgings) for travelers and for those who need *therapeia* 'because of weakness', and he has supplied these people with 'nurses' (*nosokomountas*), medical men (*iatreuontas*), porters, and attendants. In another letter (176) he refers to it as a *ptôchotropheion*.[58] Seven years later Basil was dead, and in due course Gregory of Nazianzus composed a lengthy eulogy (*Or.* 43). From the flood of pious verbosity it emerges that Basil had taken the lead in founding a leper colony outside Caesarea (sect. 63).[59] His achievement was to remove the lepers from the city, but what he did for them we are not specifically told (there is no mention of doctors):[60] 'To Basil belonged the sick, and the relief of their wounds, and the imitation of Christ, as he cleansed leprosy (*lepra*), not by a word, but in deed.' Caelius Aurelianus, on the other hand, discussing *elephantiasis* (a form of leprosy) and the opinion of some people that the urban victims of the disease should be isolated, their purpose being 'to protect the rest of the citizens from injury through contact [*contagione*] with the disease' (*Chron.* 4.13), maintains that isolating patients in this way is contrary to the principles of medicine. We in any case have two divergent accounts of what Basil did, neither of them altogether objective. The *katagôgia* are likely to have been real, however: the provincial governor could easily verify the claim.

(4) Shortly before he died in 373 the holy man Ephrem assisted at Edessa in Mesopotamia 'those who were sick as a result of a famine by setting up 300 beds in public porticoes (*embolois*)' (Sozomen, *HE* 3.16.15). That may well have been 'the first refuge specifically for the care and support of the sick',[61] but it was not a hospital.

---

57 This expression does not mean quite 'crippled with disease' (Nutton 2012, 314), still less 'lepers and other sick people' (Van Minnen 1995, 197). The root of λελωβημέν- was occasionally used to refer to lepers, but on the three other occasions when Epiphanius uses the word it refers to the maimed.

58 Cf. Kislinger 1984, 176.

59 As to how well *lepra* corresponded to Hansen's disease, we can avoid the question.

60 Basil himself had at least a measure of medical expertise (sect. 23).

61 Bowersock 2010, 48.

244 HARRIS

(5) In a letter of 400 Jerome says of Fabiola, a wealthy woman from the old capital, that she was the first person to found a νοσοκομεῖον,[62] presumably in Rome. The rhetorical details that Jerome offers need be no more exact than his claim that she was descended from Fabius Cunctator. But the claim that she was the first tells us that by 400 there were other *nosokomeia*, not necessarily in Rome itself. (It seems to be many centuries before we have further evidence of a hospital in the city).[63]

(6) John Chrysostom found a *nosokomeion* already in being at Constantinople (was this one of the establishments there that was apparently in existence forty years earlier (see above)?), presumably in 398, and established several more, according to Palladius (*Dial.* p.32). He appointed doctors to serve them. But Palladius heroized his subject, and it may be that his new foundations amounted to his not completed project of constructing a leper colony in the city's outskirts.[64]

(7) *CIG* 9256 = Samama 2003, no. 328, is the fifth-century epitaph of a man who was apparently (the text is a little uncertain) the doctor of a *nosokomeion*. He is in fact the only epigraphically attested hospital doctor before 500 CE. The provenance—Euchaïta in the Pontus region—is intriguing, for Euchaïta was already becoming an important pilgrimage center, based on the cult of St Theodore the Recruit, just in the late fourth century.[65] Cumont suggested that the *nosokomeion* in question was a dependency of the local monastery.[66]

---

62 Jerome *Ep.* 77.6: *et prima omnium* νοσοκομεῖον *instituit, in quo aegrotantes colligeret de plateis, et consumpta languoribus atque inedia miserorum membra foveret. Describam ego nunc diversas hominum calamitates, truncas nares, effossos oculos, semiustos pedes, luridas manus, tumentes alvos, exile femur, crura turgentia, et de exesis ac putridis carnibus vermiculos bullientes? Quoties morbo regio, et pedore confectos humeris suis ipsa portavit? quoties lavit purulentam vulnerum saniem quam alius aspicere non valebat? Praebebat cibos propria manu, et spirans cadaver sorbitiunculis irrigabat.* Fabiola died in the period 397–400. It may be relevant that she had spent some time in eastern parts of the empire.

63 Crislip 2005, 103 seems to claim that the *xenodochium* built by a Roman senator at Portus (Jerome, *Ep.* 66 and 77) was a hospital. Meiggs 1973, 403 correctly describes it as a 'rest-house'.

64 Concerning this project see J. N. D. Kelly 1995, 120. Nutton 2012, 416n144, cites Nilus of Ancyra, *Letters* 3.33, for the familiar existence of *nosokomeia* within Nilus' lifetime, which ended ca. 430, but this is very uncertain evidence because the letters attributed to Nilus are crammed with anachronisms; see Alan Cameron 1976.

65 See Haldon 2018, esp. 213. But he was mistaken to say that the presence of this doctor 'impl[ies]... the existence of a hospital' (219); the hospital is explicitly mentioned. Gregory of Nyssa, about 380, had credited the saint with among other things an *iatreion* 'for all sorts of illnesses' (*De sancto Theodoro* 70 (*PG* 46.745)).

66 In J. G. C. Anderson et al. 1910, 217.

(8) *S. Danielis Stylitae Vita Antiquior* 87 mentions an incident in which an anonymous pilgrim spent time in a *nosokomeion* at Ancyra. The hagiography was written after Daniel's death in 493, but probably not long afterwards. It was at least a plausible detail.

Thus the haul is very limited geographically: Caesarea, Euchaïta, Constantinople, and Rome. This in a period of relatively abundant sources. It can be presumed that there were other *nosokomeia*, unattested, for example in Alexandria, but the vision of a late Roman Empire promptly sprouting hospitals, dear to some scholars, turns out to be a mirage.[67]

These texts implicitly require us to ask who the patients or inmates really were. I will leave further discussion of this question for another occasion, simply noting for the moment Carlo Cipolla's description of the hospital at Prato in 1621:

> At that time, hospitals took in sick people only incidentally. In normal times the hospital took in above all the very poor who had nothing to eat and nowhere to sleep. In one of the Podestà of Prato's reports we read that the 32 patients in the hospital in mid-February 'are not very ill and their illness is caused rather by deprivation than anything else, as it is easy to see that they are famished'.[68]

4   Concluding Observations

Two final points. It is sometimes claimed that what made the new Christian hospital remarkable was that it was open to everyone.[69] No scholar familiar with the writings of the fourth-century Christians will find it easy to believe that the Christian authorities were so open-minded. Epiphanius is the anti-hero of religious intolerance, but he was merely an extreme case. Such indications as we have suggest that the Christians looked after the welfare of Christians, and right-thinking Christians at that (Arian or Nicene as the case

---

67   Ferngren and Amundsen 1996, 2975, for example, wrote that 'Hospitals quickly expanded throughout the eastern Empire in the late fourth and fifth centuries ... They spread to the West as well.' For hospitals in the eastern Mediterranean in the sixth and seventh centuries, see Kislinger 1984, 179.

68   Cipolla 1992, 69.

69   Thus Van Minnen 1995, 158n17. So too Marcone in Marcone and Andorlini 2006, 16: 'L'assistenza predicata dai cristiani rappresenta una novità radicale rispetto alla tradizione antica in primo luogo perché è esercitata verso tutti gli appartenenti a una comunità, rispetto alla quale non ci sono stranieri [e] non ci sono esclusi.'

might be).[70] A text that points in the opposite direction is Julian's *Letter* 84.[71] Writing in 362 to one Arsacius, 'chief priest' of Galatia, the emperor tells him that it has been the virtues of the Christians that have won them converts: among other things, they support not only their own poor but 'ours' as well (430d). Elsewhere, more vaguely, the emperor tells the Antiochenes that the charity of the Christian women of Antioch to the needy creates admiration for 'atheism' (i.e. Christianity) (*Misopogon* 363a). But *Letter* 84 is probably a forgery, as Peter Van Nuffelen has shown, on grounds unrelated to the oddity remarked on here.[72] The letter does not in fact appear in the MSS of Julian's letters but is 'preserved' by the historian Sozomen (5.16.5–15). Whether he (or someone else) invented it to exalt the Christians or edited a real letter need not concern us.

Late antique medical writers, whose works are of daunting dimensions, ignore the hospital altogether, which naturally puzzles those who think that it soon produced a 'major revolution' in healthcare.[73] But the reasons are more or less obvious. Such hospitals had nothing to do with high-level healthcare: they were of no interest to sick people with funds—the sort of people who would be the patients of Oribasius or Theodorus Priscianus or Caelius Aurelianus. And such institutions did nothing whatsoever to improve health outcomes. Which was perhaps of no great concern to those Christians who thought that death was a transition into life (cf. Augustine, *CD* 13.4, etc.).

---

70   Cf. Harris 2016c, 289. It can of course easily be argued that intolerance served the Christian churches very well. On selectivity in fourth-century Christian charity, with particular respect to Basil, see Horden 2012, 718.

71   22 Wright.

72   Van Nuffelen 2002, with arguments of varying strength. The counterarguments of Bouffartigue 2005 amount to very little.

73   Such as Van Minnen 1995, 153.

CHAPTER 13

Celebrity and Power

Circus Factions *Forty Years On*

Charlotte Roueché

Alan Cameron first engaged with the *Greek Anthology* as a purely literary work; he described his interest as originating at his much loved alma mater, St Paul's School.[1] As well as being stimulated by the epigrams, he was delighted to learn that the Palatine manuscript of the *Anthology* was owned for a time by John Clement, who was one of the earliest scholars of St Paul's School.[2] Clement went to live with Thomas More, who appointed him tutor to his children; he even features in the conversation that prefaces *Utopia*. After excelling in literary skills, he travelled to the Low Countries and Italy to train in medicine. When he returned to England, in 1525, he married More's adopted daughter Margaret Giggs.[3] Religious upheavals meant that they moved several times, and eventually went to live in Belgium. During his lifetime he acquired a significant collection of Greek and Latin manuscripts, including a volume described (in 1551 by Stephanus) as a *'vetus codex epigrammatum'* and in the inventory of his books of 572, an *'epigrammatum liber magnus et perantiquus'*.[4] It was apparently this connection with the school of which he was so proud that first piqued Alan's interest in the *Anthology*, on which he began a study in the 1960s.

The *Anthology*, as we know, included texts that had been used for inscriptions. The boom in epigraphic discoveries during the nineteenth century turned up more and more examples of texts found both in the *Anthology* and on stone. One of these was a monument for the charioteer, Porphyrius, identified in 1845 standing in the forecourt of the Church of St Irene in Constantinople, and published fully by Mordtmann in 1880.[5] Mordtmann's illustrations (plate 16) did not really bring home what an astonishing monument this was. The most important aspect of this discovery for scholars of the time was that it was inscribed with two epigrams from the Planudean Anthology, 340 and 342.

---

1 Alan Cameron 1993a, vii.
2 Wallis 2008.
3 Bowker 2008.
4 The story is set out in Alan Cameron 1993a, 178–186.
5 Mordtmann 1880.

© THE TRUSTEES OF COLUMBIA UNIVERSITY IN THE CITY OF NEW YORK,
2021 | DOI:10.1163/9789004452794_014

The monument seems to have formed part of a collection of antiquities brought at some time into the grounds of the Topkapi palace. In 1962 a team of archaeologists led by Nezih Fıratlı working in the grounds of the palace found, among other architectural elements, a new statue base for Porphyrius.[6] Fıratlı had already worked closely with Louis Robert, and included some comments from him in his 1964 publication,[7] identifying four further epigrams from the *Anthology* (*Anth. Plan.* 351, 352, 353, and 35). It was therefore natural that he entrusted the publication of the monument and its inscriptions to Robert. When Alan, working on the *Anthology*, heard about the new discoveries, he wrote to Robert, who invited him to publish the monument.

The exciting thing about archaeology and epigraphy is that, at any moment, we can be confronted with an aspect of the world that we study for which we were not prepared. For Alan, this confrontation meant not one book, but two: *Porphyrius the Charioteer*, published in 1973, and *Circus Factions* completed in 1975.

What the Porphyrius monuments make clear is quite how important the charioteers were. These are spectacular sculptural structures, erected at a period when statuary was becoming increasingly rare; this situation is clearer than ever thanks to the work of the Last Statues of Antiquity team.[8] Alan recognized this, and was drawn into confronting more seriously than anyone had done before the question of the factions. He brought two particularly important skills. First of these, of course, was an excellent philological toolset, which he was to use all his life. But secondly, he brought a deep understanding of Roman history and culture to the study of Byzantium and its institutions, which enabled him to look clearly at the New Rome in terms of its past, and its self-understanding, rather than its future: thus the subtitle of *Circus Factions* is *Blues and Greens at Rome and Byzantium*. His analysis, therefore, was of a process of evolution, of both language and structures.[9]

He was also influenced, as we all are, by his contemporary experience. For decades, serious-minded scholars had wrestled with the question of why such matters should be of such importance; commitment to the colours must surely represent some political or religious affiliation. Alan was able to draw on contemporary developments: in *Circus Factions* (completed in 1975) he cited very recent work in modern sociology, such as Cohen 1972, and current historiography, such as Hobsbawm 1973. New approaches to social violence made good

---

6 Fıratlı and Rollas 1964, 196; whence Melink 1965, 149; Robert 1964, 368; Robert and Robert 1965, no. 248.
7 Fıratlı and Rollas 1964, 196n10.
8 Smith and Ward-Perkins 2016.
9 For a summary, see Alan Cameron 1976c, 1–3.

CELEBRITY AND POWER

sense given the increasing prominence of football-related violence. It was this approach that enabled him to clear away a lot of misconceptions. It was not necessary to attribute serious political or religious motivations to rioting groups, even if they sometimes acquired such significance. Typically, Alan cleared away a lot of dead wood and lazy thinking. Work since then may have developed a more complex picture, but Alan's groundwork made progress possible. Analysis of this kind now seems obvious to us and can be applied more widely.[10]

In his review of *Porphyrius* Jean Gascou suggested the need to look more closely at the practicalities.[11] In fact, Alan was engaging with these questions. In the later *Circus Factions*, by starting his enquiry with Roman institutions, he took the question back to its roots in the practical challenges of providing large public entertainments. While his demonstrations were perhaps a bit too tidy—for example, the suggestion that the imperial authorities imposed an amalgamation of circus and theatre organizations[12]—he raised issues that would continue to be addressed. Where his analysis was weakest, as Gascou showed, was in considering the financial aspects. The papyri make it clear that the costs of entertainments could fall on local communities. In Egypt, for instance, we can see the Apions contributing to those costs.[13] The idea of central imperial organization is thus further undermined.

One thing that has happened in the last decades is far more study of the mechanisms of public entertainments in the Roman period in the provinces. The information is primarily epigraphic, and keeps on changing. In 2006 Georg Petzl published an inscription from Alexandria Troas recording rulings provided by Hadrian to the association of actors—the Technitai of Dionysus—over various aspects of their work;[14] a colloquium at the Fondation Hardt in 2011 used this text to open a discussion on the organization of shows/spectacles.[15] The study of the circus factions in Late Antiquity must be set within this background. There is a great deal more still to be understood about the relationship of the chariot organizations to the organizations that provided other forms of entertainment and for which, by the sixth century, they were apparently responsible.

The Porphyrius monuments illustrate the arbitrariness of the distinction that we choose to make between literary and inscribed texts, between words

---

10   See, for example, Hatlie 2006.
11   Gascou 1976, written before the publications of *Circus Factions*, but informed by Alan Cameron 1974b, 1974c.
12   Alan Cameron 1976c, 244–249.
13   So Jones, 2012, 315.
14   Petzl and Schwertheim 2006; with Jones 2007; Ascough et al. 2012, no. 6786.
15   Coleman and Nelis-Clément 2012.

transmitted on parchment and those transmitted on stone—or on papyrus. Alan found himself having to deal with a considerable quantity of inscriptions. I had first visited Aphrodisias with Joyce Reynolds in 1970, charged with recording late antique or Byzantine inscriptions, and I rapidly found myself recording references to the factions. We learned that Alan was writing about late antique chariot racing, and I was able to pass three of the inscriptions to him in time for inclusion in the addenda to *Porphyrius*.[16] In *Circus Factions* he took this approach further; he built on work by Aikaterine Christophilopoulou (1966) to make a collection of references to the circus colours in the Greek East, outside Constantinople (published as Appendix B). There have been a lot of discoveries and publications since then; while the list of literary texts remains much the same, there is more epigraphic material. For the purposes of this chapter I have been creating a small corpus of inscriptions to enhance that list; I was able to build on the recent work by Adam Łajtar.[17] I propose to publish the materials as a corpus as soon as possible; here I provide a list (Table 13.1) in order to provide some general indications.

I have collected about seventy-eight items: about, because it depends, in a couple of cases, on an assumed reading, and also on how texts are grouped together. Since *Circus Factions*, some clusters of inscriptions have been published from Alexandria, Aphrodisias, Ephesus, and Tyre. Alan was aware of many, but not all of these. There have been some re-datings (Thessalonika) and some scattered new finds (Germia, Rhodiapolis). The materials we have can be presented under various headings.

1 Geographical Distribution

We have thirty locations. Of these Alexandria,[18] Gortyn,[19] Oxyrhynchus,[20] Thessalonika,[21] and Tyre[22] had functioning hippodromes in Late Antiquity. At both Gerasa[23] and Scythopolis, there had been a hippodrome, but in both cases this had been converted for amphitheater spectacles probably during the fourth century.

---

16   Alan Cameron 1973, 276.
17   Łajtar and Młynarczyk 2017.
18   Humphrey 1986, 505–512.
19   Humphrey 1986, 523–524.
20   Humphrey 1986, 516–519.
21   Humphrey 1986, 625–631.
22   Humphrey 1986, 461–473.
23   Humphrey 1986, 495–504.

CELEBRITY AND POWER   251

2   Types of Text

Almost all the inscriptions refer to Blues or Greens; there are two known references to Reds, at Aphrodisias (49) and apparently at Reimea (63).

By far the most common kind of text is a victory acclamation, of the form Νικᾷ ἡ τύχη, 'The fortune of the Blues/Greens triumphs (Nika)'; there are thirty-nine examples, with one variant: 'May the fortune of the Greens be bad!' (no.40, and cf. 74) A significant number of acclamations associate the good fortune of the factions with that of someone else: with the emperor/emperors (nos. 7, 8, 9,?11, 14, 15); with the city (35, 38, 55) or a village (51); with a group (butchers, 42; Jews, 46); or of individuals (4, 26, 27, 70, 75 and cf. 18). The second most common group is of place (*topos*) texts. The phrase 'place of the Blues/ Greens' is common: unsurprisingly, many of these are on the seats in auditoria (Aphrodisias, Miletus), but others, such as those on columns, are more difficult to interpret (nos. 58, 59, 60, 76).

3   Personal

Some of the recorded texts appear to be private. Three are on funerary monuments (3, 22, 52); one is on a comb (75); a couple are on bricks or tiles (1, 68) or a pithos (61); some graffiti are also likely to be private (18, 30, 70 (with a mention of 'he who wrote this'), 77), and perhaps others, although the borderline is not always clear.

4   Official Buildings

There are official texts on mosaic floors of what have been identified as clubhouses at Gerasa (62) and Tyre (55, 56); a mosaic text at Scythopolis may survive from a similar building (67). What are more difficult to interpret are *topos* texts, 'place of Greens/Blues', which are found on building elements such as those on columns at Tyre (58, 59, 60) and Oxyrhynchus (76).

5   Performance Spaces

The acclamations on the façade of the theatre building at Nysa (31, 32) perhaps indicate the role of the factions in performances. At Aphrodisias we also have a room, at the back of the stage, reserved for the Mimes of the Green faction (36).

There are plenty of references to the factions on the seats of auditoria: in the theatre at Miletus (24, 25), and in the theatre, odeon, and stadium at Aphrodisias (39–48). These can reasonably be associated with the support of performers in those buildings. There are also references to the factions on the seats of the small auditorium at Kom el-Dikka (72–74). Here the focus is very clearly on the chariot races, with named charioteers, and images of the races; there is no clear indication that their presence in what may well have been a lecture theatre can be related to performances in that space.[24]

6   Main Streets/Street Monuments

Many, if not all, of the factional inscriptions in auditoria appear to be informal, private work. There are also texts on paving, or on steps that are presumably informal: for example, texts accompanying a gameboard (20, perhaps 29). But some may fall into the category of texts on paving intended to direct ceremonial activity,[25] for which see in particular the inscriptions on the paving of the assembly area of the Sanctuary of Artemis at Magnesia on the Maeander.[26]

There are also more imposing examples in public spaces, and in positions that would not always be easy to reach. The hand may appear informal to an epigrapher used to the script of earlier periods, and the formulae are almost all acclamations; but these texts seem clearly to have a public function. The most imposing series is at Ephesus (7–16);[27] it is clear from these that such texts cannot always be dismissed as informal graffiti, and that their status should be assessed in each case. There are similar public texts at Aphrodisias (33–35), and perhaps at Didyma (26, 27) and Rhodiapolis (53).

A slightly problematical example is to be found at Oxyrhynchus where, in 1912, Professor Pistelli, searching for papyri, reported finding a columnar monument constructed of several sections: two squared, then one octagonal made up of several blocks, and above that a cornice supporting what may have been a cylindrical base. On the west side of the octagonal section he recorded a *topos* inscription for the Blues (76), and on the west side of the cylindrical base an acclamation for the emperor Phocas (77). Pistelli assumed that this was to support a column, but it seems more likely that it is a statue base.[28] The hands of the texts were similar, and the whole was published the same year as an

---

24   Derda et al. 2007.
25   See Roueché 2014, 140.
26   Bingöl 2007, 85–87.
27   For a detailed discussion see Roueché 1999.
28   Compare the description of a composite column, ὁ σύνθετος κίων, erected by Phocas in Constantinople. Gehn 2012.

CELEBRITY AND POWER 253

ensemble.[29] The texts were seen by Petrie's expedition in 1922;[30] by then the lower text (76) appears to have been less readable. The monument has become known as the Column of Phocas. It has recently been carefully examined by the current excavator, Professor Josep Padro Parcerisa, of Barcelona, and his team, to whom I would like to express my sincere thanks. Professor Padró has confirmed to me by letter that in spring 2019 no traces of lettering could be determined; presumably the soft stone has been eroded. It seems to me uncertain whether the two texts—one a utilitarian *topos* text, and the other an acclamation—should necessarily be closely associated, even though, since Pareti's publication, they have regularly been discussed together.

7 Buildings/Doorways

A further (and rather unexpected) category is inscriptions on doorways. Those on monumental entrances (at Ephesus, 7, 8, 11, and perhaps 13) can be associated with other prominent texts in the street. There are other examples, however, where the texts seem to be associated with the entrance into a building. It is perhaps not surprising that several of these are from Syria, where inscriptions on lintels are very common (63–66); but the description of no.4, from Gortyn, and no.50, from Stratonicaea, suggest that these too may have been over doorways. Louis Robert commented on the '*épigraphie des linteaux*', observing its frequency in Syria.[31] These texts are clearly protective and apotropaic: thus Theophanes (*Chron.*, 178) relates how the citizens of Antioch inscribed prayers on their lintels to protect themselves from an earthquake. The use of factional acclamations in such a context must therefore raise questions about how we should understand some of these texts. More surprising still, is that no. 65, at Umm el-Jimal, is over a doorway into a church; no. 23, at Priene, is also inscribed in a church.

8 Conclusions

This collection of texts, therefore, shows references to the circus colours used in various ways. There is simple professional membership: a charioteer (3); stage performers (22, 36, and perhaps Helladia, the owner of the comb, 75); or the ownership of buildings (55, 56, 62). There are acclamations closely

---

29 Pareti 1912.
30 Petrie 1925, 13 with a rather careless transcription.
31 See Robert 1960, 354, 360–361; 1964, 265–266; e.g. *IGLS* 877, 1406, 1559, 1705.

associated with performance, in auditoria, and there are others that appear to be associated with ceremonial activities in streets and public spaces. There are the practical, if enigmatic, *topos* inscriptions. But there are others that may not necessarily be directly associated with factional activity; rather, they seem to be invocations.

Perhaps the significance of the most common phrase—the Νικᾷ ἡ τύχη formula—is not just a concern for the faction and its activities, whether in entertainment or ceremonial, but the invocation of good fortune. Victory is a constant theme in circus performances, with the images of victories displayed;[32] the colours are constantly engaging with victory. Perhaps to acclaim them, and to write that acclamation on a jar (61) or a tile (68) or the lintel of a house, is not a simple expression of partisanship but rather an attempt to share in their good fortune, and their power to win. It may be for this reason that the acclamation is found next to a graffito gameboard (20, and also perhaps 29). Such a prayer was apparently even appropriate in a church (23, 65).

When Christophilopoulou and Alan Cameron worked on assembling these texts, they were looking for evidence for the factions and their organization in the eastern provinces. As so often, assembling a body of data can provide new and different insights. The material collected here suggests that the presence of acclamation of the colours is not necessarily evidence of an organization in that place; instead, it may tell us far more, and indicate new areas of research. What is the understanding of Tyche in Late Antiquity, and what does it mean to invoke her?[33] More broadly, what are the benefits of invoking/depicting competitors, victors, and victory? Does an acclamation for a faction convey some kind of invocation of a victorious entity, rather than anything more formal, just as the wearing of a Manchester United shirt does not indicate formal membership, but rather an association with victory and success? The text from Rhodiapolis (53) refers to warding off *phthonos*; a graffito at Ephesus may imply similar concerns (18).[34] Here we return to Alan's work.[35] It was he who established clearly that the NIKA of the acclamations represents most often— although not always—not the imperative, νίκα, 'win!' (as might be expected from a crowd of fans) but the indicative, νικᾷ, 'is victorious'. Those using the phrase may not always have been thinking precisely about the syntax; but such a statement can assert the power of fortune to aid and protect. Yet again, careful scholarship has cleared away old assumptions, and left us with new complexities to interpret.

---

32 See the circus programmes; Roueché 2007a, 62.
33 On this see questions raised by Dunbabin 2017, particularly 158–159, 169–170.
34 Roueché 2007b.
35 Alan Cameron 1973, 75–78.

TABLE 13.1 Eastern Empire: inscriptions mentioning the factions (as at winter 2019)

	Place	Reference	Support	Type
1.	Thebes (Pthiotis)	https://epigraphy.packhum.org/text/333526	A brick	Nika
2.	Thessalonika	https://epigraphy.packhum.org/text/137201	Panel/letter	?
3.	Thessalonika	https://epigraphy.packhum.org/text/138030.	Sarcophagus	Affiliation
4.	Gortyn	https://epigraphy.packhum.org/text/200963	Block—?lintel	Nika
5.	Myriophyton	*SEG* 48.887, 155	Reused ?block	Nika
6.	Smyrna	*I. Smyrna* 886	A block	?
7.	Ephesus	*I. Ephesos* 2090	Street: doorway	Acclamation
8.	Ephesus	*I. Ephesos* 1196	Street: doorway	Acclamation
9.	Ephesus	*I. Ephesos* 1191.a	Street: column	Acclamation
10.	Ephesus	*SEG* 57.1119.c	Street: column	Nika
11.	Ephesus	*SEG* 39.1187	Street: gateway	Acclamation
12.	Ephesus	*Unpublished*	Column	Acclamation
13.	Ephesus	https://epigraphy.packhum.org/text/250868	Gateway	Nika
14.	Ephesus	*I. Ephesos* 1191.b	Column	Invocation
15.	Ephesus	*I. Ephesos* 1192.1	Street: column capital	Acclamation
16.	Ephesus	*SEG* 49 1448	Street: column capital	Nika
17.	Ephesus	https://epigraphy.packhum.org/text/250870	Step	Nika
18.	Ephesus	*SEG* 57.1119.a, b	Base, on the side	Invocation
19.	Ephesus	https://epigraphy.packhum.org/text/250869	Paving stone	Nika
20.	Ephesus	*I. Ephesos* 1194	Step	Nika

TABLE 13.1 Eastern Empire: inscriptions mentioning the factions (as at winter 2019) (*cont.*)

Place	Reference	Support	Type
21. Ephesus	*I. Ephesos 1193*	Paving stone	Nika
22. Ephesus	https://epigraphy.packhum.org/text/250529	Gravestone	Affiliation
23. Priene	https://epigraphy.packhum.org/text/254043	Church, base of altar	Nika
24. Miletus, Theatre	https://epigraphy.packhum.org/text/351669	Theatre seats	Topos
25. Miletus, Theatre	https://epigraphy.packhum.org/text/351676	Theatre seats	Topos
26. Didyma	https://epigraphy.packhum.org/text/247688	Column	Acclamation
27. Didyma	https://epigraphy.packhum.org/text/247689	Column	Acclamation
28. Didyma	https://epigraphy.packhum.org/text/247685	Plaque	Nika
29. Didyma	https://epigraphy.packhum.org/text/247690	On a step	Nika
30. Didyma	https://epigraphy.packhum.org/text/247691	On a relief	?
31. Nysa	*SEG* 59.1241	Theatre façade	Nika
32. Nysa	*SEG* 59.1242	Theatre façade	Nika
33. Aphrodisias	http://insaph.kcl.ac.uk/iaph2007/iAph010403.html	Street: column	Nika
34. Aphrodisias	http://insaph.kcl.ac.uk/iaph2007/iAph010404.html	Street: panel of Tetrapylon	Nika
35. Aphrodisias	http://insaph.kcl.ac.uk/iaph2007/iAph040013.html	Public portico	Nika/Auxi
36. Aphrodisias	http://insaph.kcl.ac.uk/iaph2007/iAph080104.html	Theatre stage: room	Nika
37. Aphrodisias	http://insaph.kcl.ac.uk/iaph2007/iAph080105.html	Theatre stage: step	Nika
38. Aphrodisias	http://insaph.kcl.ac.uk/iaph2007/iAph080106.html	Theatre stage: façade	Nika
39. Aphrodisias	http://insaph.kcl.ac.uk/iaph2007/iAph080054.html	Theatre seats	Nika
40. Aphrodisias	http://insaph.kcl.ac.uk/iaph2007/iAph080055.html	Theatre seats	Kaka

TABLE 13.1 Eastern Empire: inscriptions mentioning the factions (as at winter 2019) (*cont.*)

Place	Reference	Support	Type
41. Aphrodisias	http://insaph.kcl.ac.uk/iaph2007/iAph080057.html	Theatre seats	Nika
42. Aphrodisias	http://insaph.kcl.ac.uk/iaph2007/iAph080061.html	Theatre seats	Topos/Nika
43. Aphrodisias	http://insaph.kcl.ac.uk/iaph2007/iAph080064.html	Theatre seats	Topos
44. Aphrodisias	http://insaph.kcl.ac.uk/iaph2007/iAph080107.html	Theatre seats	Nika
45. Aphrodisias	http://insaph.kcl.ac.uk/iaph2007/iAph020008.html	Odeon seats	Topos
46. Aphrodisias	http://insaph.kcl.ac.uk/iaph2007/iAph020018.html	Odeon seats	Topos
47. Aphrodisias	http://insaph.kcl.ac.uk/iaph2007/iAph100003.html	Stadium seats	?Topos
48. Aphrodisias	http://insaph.kcl.ac.uk/iaph2007/iAph100004.html	Stadium seats	?Topos
49. Aphrodisias	*SEG* 61.847	Paving stone (Reds)	Nika
50. Stratonicaea	I. *Stratonikeia* 1020	Epistyle/lintel	Nika
51. Büyükyaka	https://epigraphy.packhum.org/text/281236	?Block	Invocation
52. Germia	*SEG* 63.1199	Gravestone	Affiliation
53. Rhodiapolis	*SEG* 60.1557	Loose, ?from the north wall	Acclamation
54. Heliopolis/Baalbek	https://epigraphy.packhum.org/text/245122	Temple, column	Nika
55. Tyre	*SEG* 52.1601	Floor: clubhouse	Nika
56. Tyre	*SEG* 52.1602	Floor: ?clubhouse	Building text
57. Tyre	*SEG* 52.1605	Hippodrome: column	Nika

TABLE 13.1   Eastern Empire: inscriptions mentioning the factions (as at winter 2019) (*cont.*)

Place	Reference	Support	Type
58. Tyre	*SEG* 52.1606	Hippodrome: column	Topos
59. Tyre	*SEG* 52.1607	Hippodrome: column	Topos
60. Tyre	*SEG* 52.1608	Hippodrome: column	Topos
61. Hippos	*EtTrav* 30 (2017), 289–302	Pithos	Nika
62. Gerasa	*SEG* 37.1548	Floor: ?clubhouse	Building text
63. Reimea	*IGLS* XV (2014) 381	Lintel of a house	Nika
64. Taff	*IGLS* XV (2014) 51	Lintel of a house	Nika
65. Umm al-Jimal	https://epigraphy.packhum.org/text/341673	Lintel of a church	Nika
66. Umm al-Jimal	https://epigraphy.packhum.org/text/341674	Lintel of a house	Nika
67. Scythopolis	*SEG* 54.1678	Floor: ?clubhouse	Nika
68. Umm ar-Rasas	*SEG* 47.2083	Tile	Prayer (assoc.)
69. Jerusalem	https://epigraphy.packhum.org/text/319457	?Block	Nika
70. Alexandria	https://epigraphy.packhum.org/text/217101	?Block/stele	Nika
71. Kom el-Dikka	*SEG* 56.1975	Slabs in baths	?Topos
72. Kom el-Dikka	https://epigraphy.packhum.org/text/223649	Auditorium seat	Nika/imprecation
73. Kom el-Dikka	https://epigraphy.packhum.org/text/223650	Auditorium seat	Nika
74. Kom el-Dikka	https://epigraphy.packhum.org/text/223651	Auditorium seat	Nika/imprecation

TABLE 13.1 Eastern Empire: inscriptions mentioning the factions (as at winter 2019) (*cont.*)

Place	Reference	Support	Type
75. Antinoe	https://www.louvre.fr/en/oeuvre-notices/comb	Comb	Nika
76. Oxyrhynchus	https://epigraphy.packhum.org/text/222092	Column	Topos
77. Oxyrhynchus	https://epigraphy.packhum.org/text/222093	Column	Acclamation
78. Valley of the Kings	https://epigraphy.packhum.org/text/225941	Painted text in a tomb	?

CHAPTER 14

Alan Cameron and Byzantium

Averil Cameron

Rereading Alan's books and articles for this chapter was a moving experience. It reminded me forcibly of his vigorous and confident style, evident from the very beginning, and of those early years of discovery, before the invention of Late Antiquity, when even the later Roman Empire was something new for Oxford classicists like us, and Byzantium seemingly a world away.

In order to look back at the development of Alan's work we have to think ourselves back to that long-ago world of the 1960s when all this was new, and when invigorating possibilities lay ahead for anyone eager to move beyond the then narrow world of Oxford ancient history. Alan and I met and became engaged while we were both undergraduates at Oxford and married as soon as I took finals in 1962; he was a year ahead of me and by then already a lecturer in the Classics department at the University of Glasgow. Like Jasper Griffin and Miriam Dressler, and Martin West and Stephanie Pickard, we were one of the couples who attended the famous seminar held by Eduard Fraenkel in Corpus Christi College; the first two pairs married in 1960. Alan has written of being influenced by reading Gibbon while on holiday, and I remember that well. It was on a holiday that we took together in the Black Forest, staying improbably in youth hostels, in I think 1961, when, again improbably from today's perspective,[1] Gibbon's *Decline and Fall*, and Gibbon's inimitable prose, were our companions. How much Alan's ideas about Byzantium were influenced by Gibbon is an interesting question, but several of his books range over a long chronological span reaching well into the middle Byzantine period, and he had no hesitation in linking what we would now call Late Antiquity with later Byzantine developments. He was not bothered by the problems about periodization that have loomed large in recent scholarship, and he did not hesitate to pursue a topic into the then unknown territory of later centuries if that was where the argument led. Whether he was very interested in Byzantium as such, or in the broader historical questions about it, I rather doubt; in the same way he wrote powerfully on late antique material objects without being much interested

---

1   See now Whittow 2018.

© THE TRUSTEES OF COLUMBIA UNIVERSITY IN THE CITY OF NEW YORK,
2021 | DOI:10.1163/9789004452794_015

ALAN CAMERON AND BYZANTIUM

in art history in the traditional sense of stylistic evaluation, and indeed being rather disparaging of it.[2]

While we agonize today about when Byzantium began and when Late Antiquity finished, Alan did not mind much about terminology, just as he did not involve himself in the current wave of companions or handbooks requiring syntheses rather than original argument. So his 'wandering poets', many of them from the fifth century, came from 'Byzantine Egypt'; the 'empress and the poet' belonged to 'Byzantine times',[3] and Daniel the Stylite was 'an early Byzantine holy man',[4] while his devastating demolition of Anthony Kaldellis' thesis about covert Neoplatonism in the sixth-century historians is called 'Paganism in sixth-century Byzantium'[5] and John the Lydian was 'the perfect Byzantine civil servant'.[6] In *Greek Mythography*, with an important chapter on scholia (164–183) and a major contribution to the history of book culture, Gregory of Nazianzus is as Byzantine as anyone.[7] Alan's stream of major articles about ivory diptychs and late antique silver also belongs in this border area, though perhaps they are more late antique than Byzantine (or in his own language late Roman).[8] So does his work on consuls,[9] in relation to which again he tended to prefer the term 'late Roman'. I do not discuss here his *Claudian* (1970), his work on Synesius,[10] or *The Last Pagans of Rome* (2011), all dealing with the late fourth century (and demonstrating his deep familiarity with late antique literature from both East and West); nor indeed *Callimachus and his Critics* (1995), testimony to his engagement with Greek epigrams since his schooldays, or his extraordinary *Greek Mythography in the Roman World*

---

2   Alan Cameron, forthcoming. The term 'art-historical papers' was how he referred to them, but his papers are not art historical in the traditional sense; they deal with questions of prosopography, ownership and patronage, supposed pagan implications, and the nature and interpretation of ivory diptychs (the latter intended as preliminary to a catalogue of late antique consular ivories he had planned with Anthony Cutler). He was particularly concerned to argue against the many erroneous assumptions (as he saw it) made by scholars about the employment of Christian and pagan iconography.

3   Alan Cameron 2016b, 47.

4   Alan Cameron 2016b, 51.

5   Alan Cameron 2016b, 255–286.

6   Alan Cameron 2016b, 10.

7   Alan Cameron 2004, 222.

8   Alan Cameron, forthcoming. I am grateful to Jaś Elsner for sharing his introduction in advance of publication.

9   Bagnall et al. 1987.

10   Alan Cameron 1993b, a book that grew out of a graduate seminar he held in the late 1980s, following up his strong reaction in 1983 to a draft of an article by Timothy Barnes (ix); but he had announced his interest in Synesius already in *Claudian*, as he explains in his preface, and the book that eventually resulted developed differently from his original plan.

(2004).[11] Instead I have preferred to assess a different topic, his contribution to Byzantine studies, and in particular to underline the breadth of his knowledge and his persistence in following an argument wherever it might take him, both of which tell us much about his typical methods of working. He often commented himself in remarks in his prefaces and elsewhere on the genesis of his ideas and the processes by which his eventual publications came into being, and it is fascinating to observe his characteristic approach and way of working, as well as the sometimes complex shifts and turns in the evolution of his books, at times over a substantial period. Roger Bagnall puts it well when he comments that 'One book led to another, growing at an oblique angle, without formalized projects.'[12] This did not extend to systematic discussion of Late Antiquity or Byzantium, but rather was evidence of a constant and fearless intellectual questioning centred always on solving problems avoided or not noticed by other scholars; often too his starting point was the need for rebuttal of an argument he found wrong-headed.

Passing references to later Byzantine material turn up in unexpected places, for instance a reference to the tenth-century *Vita Basilii* in his wonderful article in the *Journal of Roman Studies* on the young Achilles.[13] In *Callimachus and his Critics*, he cites Paul Magdalino's book on the emperor Manuel I Comnenus, and goes to it again for the locations for oral performance—a theme currently central among Byzantine literary scholars.[14] But he also sometimes used the term 'Byzantinists' disparagingly.[15] He did refer to 'late antiquity': for instance his paper originally published in an edited book by Roger Bagnall on Byzantine Egypt uses 'Byzantine' in the title but 'late antiquity' in the opening lines.[16] He also liked dropping debunking or informal language into serious discussions:

---

11   Characteristically he declares in the latter's preface 'Like most of my books, this is not the one I had planned to write' (Alan Cameron 2004, xi; see Bagnall 2018, 242); also typical of him is that he turned aside to write it while engaged on his 'major project,' the book that was to become *The Last Pagans of Rome*, and that he began writing it independently of several existing publications that might have been of substantial help (xi). Nor is it the 'systematic history of Graeco-Roman mythography' that might have been expected (x); instead his 'point of departure into this murky field of study' (viii) was a reading of the highly obscure *Narrationes*, a set of summaries of the stories in Ovid's *Metamorphoses*, to which, as he says, few scholars had paid any attention at all hitherto, or if they had, had dismissed as 'late' or medieval and 'utterly lacking in value'. Not Alan of course.

12   Bagnall 2018, 243.

13   Alan Cameron 2009, 13–14.

14   Magdalino 1993; cf. Alan Cameron 1995, 352, 345.

15   Alan Cameron 1995, 5, cf. 13.

16   Alan Cameron 2016b, 147–162; cf. Bagnall 2007, 21–46. Alan Cameron 2016b contains a selection of key articles previously published elsewhere, some of which are revised or even completely rewritten; this is explained in notes or short prefaces to each paper, but it

witness 'dull Byzantine debs',[17] 'Byzantine hack',[18] or 'some Byzantine collector' (of epigrams),[19] and his reference to the tenth-century anthologist Cephalas as 'an assistant teacher'.[20] Similarly, the poetic description of the Church of the Holy Apostles dedicated to the tenth-century emperor Constantine VII Porphyrogenitus by his contemporary Constantine the Rhodian, is described as 'dreary but not unimportant', and another of Constantine's poems as 'silly',[21] while Alan's impressive discussion of the early tenth-century scholar Arethas is hardly more sympathetic.[22]

Alan's work is eminently quotable and one could continue in this vein much longer.[23] But to return to my main theme, I am struck first by his sheer range and as ever by his extraordinary tenacity in following a problem or an argument (often a highly technical argument) as far as it went, and frequently far into periods and material well outside the range of the average late Roman or late antique specialist. The same tenacity lay behind his habit of sometimes letting things wait for years before final publication (something of which he was perversely proud, as he was also of the fact that he had never done a PhD[24])—while in the meantime new puzzles had occurred to him that he needed to follow up. I remember even in those early years that he would often comment on how striking it was that an argument was so often transformed by a reference or an idea that he came across unexpectedly, or that occurred to him at the very last minute, and this certainly continued. *The Last Pagans of Rome*, published in 2011, is in this regard revelatory about the way in which his original ideas developed and were refined over a very long period, something on which he often reflected himself.

---

means that future users of Cameron's work need to be watchful about which version they are citing.

17   Alan Cameron 2016b, 69.

18   Alan Cameron 2004, vii.

19   Alan Cameron 2016b, 99.

20   Alan Cameron 1993a, 110.

21   Alan Cameron 1993a, 300, 301. On Constantine the Rhodian see James with Vassis 2012; Bernard 2020; a sympathetic view from the viewpoint of narrativity, very different from Alan's approach, can be found in Veikou 2018, 21–22.

22   Alan Cameron, 1993a, 283–292.

23   As demonstrated in Peter Wiseman's brilliant contribution to the memorial event held in London in March 2018, which identified a treasury of quotable remarks in Alan's works, many of them asides made with breathtaking confidence.

24   Though hardly thinkable now, and a frequent source of surprised comment among Alan's American colleagues, this was common at the time among Oxford classicists who went on to become well-known scholars, Alan's near-contemporary Jasper Griffin being a case in point, but Martin West, his friend since schooldays, being an exception (Fowler 2018, 97: 'a time [1959] when doctoral students were quite rare birds').

Although Alan's focus remained on what we now call Late Antiquity (including the sixth century), and he was not a Byzantinist as such, there is in fact a good deal to say about Alan and Byzantium.[25] I will begin from those early years and the genesis as I see it of the work that came out of them.

Claudian, Porphyrius and *Circus Factions* were published in quick succession,[26] underpinned by a series of magisterial articles in the general field of late Roman literary culture in both Latin and Greek.[27] He had at the time already written the prosopographical articles on late Roman literary figures for *PLRE* I (published in 1971),[28] which gave him the prosopographical skills for his later work on *subscriptiones*, consuls, and late Roman silver and ivory diptychs; they are also on display in his later article on the house of Anastasius.[29] There were a number of pointers forward: the *Parastaseis*, seemingly of the eighth century, features in both *Porphyrius* (disparagingly, 109 f.), where he argues for a sixth-century anthology of charioteer epigrams taken from monuments (116), and *Circus Factions*. We were both at the time in touch with Robert Browning, who had suggested Agathias to me as a topic when I was still at Oxford, and the fact that I was myself working on Agathias and necessarily also Procopius was certainly a factor;[30] we wrote a joint article on the sixth-century epigrams of Agathias' *Cycle*,[31] and this led Alan naturally to *Porphyrius*, and from there to chariot racing and to his discovery of the potential for debunking the various religious and sociological theories then in vogue about Blue and Greek violence (he preferred to see it as 'soccer hooliganism'; he was similarly out of sympathy with sociological or even political explanations of the Columbia student unrest we both witnessed in New York in 1968, on which see below). I was also

---

25   This chapter deals with his literary and historical work; for his work on late antique silver and ivory, see Elsner forthcoming.

26   Alan Cameron 1970, 1973, 1976.

27   Especially Alan Cameron 1964a and 1966, but also others including Alan Cameron 1965 on late antique Greek poets (the paper that gave its name to Alan Cameron 2016b) and 1969 on the 'last days' of the Academy at Athens (rewritten but with the same title in Alan Cameron 2016b, 205–245).

28   Jones et al. 1971.

29   Alan Cameron 1978.

30   Agathias was the subject of my PhD (1966), and see Averil Cameron 1970.

31   A relatively neglected topic at the time, though Barry Baldwin and R. C. McCail were interlocutors; Viansino 1967 appeared in the year after our *JHS* article, but Schulte 2006 only after another forty years. See now the work of Arianna Gullo (whose PhD Alan examined at Pisa), including Gullo, forthcoming b, and for different approaches focusing on the content, Garland 2011 and Herrin 2017; for a gendered approach, Smith 2019, with 112–118 on the hippodrome poems. Alan's interest in the *Greek Anthology* had begun at St Paul's School at an early age, and it would be hard in general to overestimate the impact of his school years on his development as a classical scholar.

ALAN CAMERON AND BYZANTIUM   265

soon working on Corippus' panegyrical Latin poem on Justin II, which opened
up the theme of imperial ceremony in Constantinople in the sixth century.[32]
Alan was pursuing all these directions at the same time, as well as writing his
fundamental papers on Ammianus, Macrobius and the *Historia Augusta*[33] and
much more. A puzzling question, or something he had read that he thought
self-evidently wrong, always set him off. Moreover, working on Claudian, a
Latin poet but with an Alexandrian background,[34] required him to consider
both late Latin and late Greek poetry, unlike many other scholars, so it is not
surprising that his classic article, 'Wandering Poets: A Literary Movement in
Byzantine Egypt', also belongs to this period (it was published in 1965).[35]

Porphyrius the Charioteer arose out of this early interest in late Greek epigrams; he explains in the preface that he had written to Louis Robert, who had
identified the epigrams on a new statue base in Istanbul discovered in 1963
relating to Porphyrius, the famous late fifth-century and early sixth-century
charioteer, whereupon Robert had unexpectedly invited him to publish them
for the first time.[36] An earlier such base for a statue of Porphyrius had been
discovered in the nineteenth century, and Alan used the opportunity to produce a brilliant exposition of the epigrams, as well as of both bases and other
known charioteer statues, and about the rage for chariot racing in fifth- and
sixth-century Byzantium. Porphyrius was the rock star of his day and this
appealed to Alan very much. The subject suited him perfectly. He amply ful-
filled, and indeed no doubt exceeded, the expectations of the great (and exact-
ing) Louis Robert, as the latter indeed recognized. The first sentence of the
book's preface reads 'This is a complex book, with a history no less complex',
and it proceeded to describe the book's genesis and the development of Alan's
ideas from an early interest in epigrams in the *Greek Anthology* to the phenomenon of chariot racing, the commemoration of charioteers, and the part played
by the factions who were their patrons. This was a real discovery: as he wrote
in his inimitable style, 'There is a whole literature on the ascetic saint [not a
topic that interested him], yet not so much as a single good article devoted to

---

32   Averil Cameron 1976.
33   Alan Cameron 1964b.
34   Alan Cameron 1970.
35   It stands as chapter 1 in Alan Cameron 2016b (for which it also provided the volume's
      title), but this version has been 'largely rewritten, with much additional material'.
36   Alan Cameron 1973, v; for discussion of these bases, which once held statues see http://
      laststatues.classics.ox.ac.uk, nos. 349 and 361. Eighteen such monuments to charioteers
      are known from Constantinople but the Porphyrius bases are the only two to survive: see
      Smith and Ward-Perkins 2016, 140. See Chapter 13, this volume.

the fame of the charioteer.'[37] He took his brief in the widest possible sense. He demonstrated the chronology of the statues set up to the famous charioteer Porphyrius and identified the (missing) statue from the new base as the second of four set up within a few years of each other. He not only published the new inscriptions, which include acclamations in prose, but also identified epigrams from the *Greek Anthology* which must once have occupied missing panels on the Porphyrius base known earlier (which he recognized as actually being later in date), commented on the iconography of the bases, identified three new manuscripts of Planudes, and discussed the date at which the epigrams were copied from the stone and the nature of the collection of which they formed part (topics central to his later book on the *Greek Anthology*). It is an example of scholarship in the round, and a sparkling display of Alan's energy and curiosity. Writing *Porphyrius* led him to consider material evidence and to develop for the first time what later became his characteristic manner of combining material and textual evidence:[38] in the present case he was able to combine the evidence of epigrams in the Planudean Anthology with that of the surviving bases, and to comment on the steadily rising level of competition among the patrons of these charioteers. Most of their statues had been of bronze, including the first statues set up in honour of Porphyrius, but Porphyrius's fourth statue, the third set up by the Blues, used gold (i.e. gilding) as well as bronze; the Blues used bronze again for his fourth while the Greens later honoured him first in bronze, and then in silver and bronze, but only used 'the supreme compliment' of gold alone for a statue in honour of his rival, Uranius.[39] Already at that time Alan was alive to the characteristics of *ekphrasis*, now a major subject among Byzantinists (though he considered it 'monotonously stylized' in Byzantine texts; 1973, 195–200), and he ingeniously deduced from later iambic poems describing paintings of Porphyrius and other charioteers that they referred to a single painting on the ceiling of the gallery in the *Kathisma* or imperial box in the hippodrome contemporary with the charioteers themselves (188–206). Although he was otherwise not particularly given to investigations on the ground, working on the book took Alan to Istanbul to see the bases themselves. He also set the evidence of the new base in the wider context both of public entertainments and of the role played by the Blues and Greens; his conclusion (232–244) lists examples of factional violence and clearly points forward to the discussion that would follow three

---

37   Alan Cameron 1973, 3.

38   The importance of this development in his work is also emphasized by Elsner, forthcoming.

39   Alan Cameron 1973, 221–222.

years later in *Circus Factions*. Written while he was still only in his early thirties, and very different from his first book on Claudian published only three years earlier, *Porphyrius the Charioteer* is a brilliant achievement. It presents us with a bravura combination of scholarship and ingenuity—even more so than in the better-known *Circus Factions*, which grew out of it, and for which it provided the indispensable foundation.

In the preface to *Porphyrius* Alan wrote that he intended to write a book on 'Early Byzantine Epigrams in the Greek Anthology'.[40] That book never appeared, but it found expression instead in 1993 in a rather different work, *The Greek Anthology: from Meleager to Planudes*, a book with an extraordinarily bold chronological sweep. He was already working on *The Greek Anthology* in the 1970s and it is a pioneering book. He had become interested in how epigrams, especially on monuments, found themselves collected into anthologies, and specifically into what we call the *Greek Anthology*, a collection known from the tenth-century Palatine MS and the later thirteenth-century anthology made by Maximos Planudes, which exists in a signed MS of 1301 in Venice.[41] Alan did not discuss the historical context of Planudes, but he was very interested in the Palatine MS and the (lost) tenth-century collection made by Constantine Cephalas (the 'assistant teacher' mentioned earlier), and established that the two anonymous scribes, labeled J and C, were both scholars themselves.[42] Already in *Porphyrius* (109) he had identified a role for Gregory Magister, the teacher of Cephalas, in transcribing epigrams from monuments. Here he argues that Arethas had a copy of the anthology of Cephalas, connects Constantine Porphyrogenitus's collection 'On epigrams' with Cephalas, and further identifies J, the tenth-century redactor of the collection, with the well-known poet and writer Constantine the Rhodian, the subject of Alan's uncomplimentary remarks mentioned earlier.[43] This was an important discovery, and though questions have been raised, it has been accepted by later specialists, including Marc Lauxtermann. Foteini Spingou says of this discovery that it has tremendous implications for the book and literary culture of

---

40   Alan Cameron 1973, v.

41   This interest extended to the *Garlands* of Meleager (first century BC) and Philip (which Alan dated (Alan Cameron 1980a) to the end of the reign of Claudius or under Nero), discussed in Alan Cameron 1993a, and see Alan Cameron 1968a; his work on epigram also led him to Callimachus, and to the book on the latter published soon after *The Greek Anthology* (Alan Cameron 1995).

42   Alan Cameron 1993a, 97–120.

43   Spingou 2019, 390 describes Cephalas as a 'genius, who managed to collect and justify the preservation of more than 4,000 epigrams' in an anthology that was 'complete, organized and adaptive'.

Byzantium: 'Alan's book was groundbreaking'.[44] *The Greek Anthology* exemplifies the tendency towards long gestation in Alan's work mentioned earlier: it was not published until 1993. As Alan says in his preface, he had done the bulk of the work for *The Greek Anthology* in the 1970s and he sent the text to Oxford University Press in 1980—but typically he allowed it to rest there for more than a decade, only turning occasionally to the necessary copy-editing.[45] He did not have the advantage of Lauxtermann's book of 2003 or of papers by him on Cephalas and the first edition of the Planudean Anthology, or of recent work by another scholar on the so-called *syllogae minores*, and on the principles of selection in poetic anthologies,[46] and I am not sure that he would have been very interested in the more recent and striking upsurge of publications on Byzantine poetry, especially of the eleventh and twelfth centuries, much of it on very different sorts of questions than his.[47] A broader view of Byzantine anthologies is now possible, encompassing more examples than Alan covers in his book,[48] and as Spingou points out, it was a kind of poetic anthologizing that gained speed from the mid-eleventh century onwards and that continued into the Palaeologan period. *The Greek Anthology* stands less as a complete study of Byzantine poetic anthologies than as a key example of Alan pursuing his initial interest in the sixth-century *Cycle* of Agathias to its logical conclusion in the middle and late Byzantine periods. Its publication was a landmark, and the fact that it belongs essentially to the 1970s makes it even more remarkable.

Alan's references to tenth-century literary production in Constantinople include a number of remarks about the so-called Macedonian renaissance then in vogue, on which unsurprisingly he was not keen;[49] he was also critical of the claims about Hellenism made by Kurt Weitzmann and Paul Lemerle and expressed approval of Cyril Mango's more acerbic approach.[50] His earlier remark in *The Greek Anthology* when writing about Agathias' sixth-century *Cycle* that 'the classicizing Indian summer was rapidly followed by a Christian winter' (48) lets us know his own sympathies.

---

44   Spingou, personal communication, and see Spingou 2019; Lauxtermann 2003 and personal communication; see Orsini 2000, with Lauxtermann 2007, especially 196 n5.

45   Bagnall 2018, 239; the book's preface is dated April 1991. Admittedly procedures at the Press were extremely lax at that time.

46   Maltomini 2008, with Maltomini 2011; see also Demoen 2012.

47   E.g. Bernard and Demoen 2012; Bernard 2014.

48   Spingou 2019, with the lists of collections and anthologies at Appendix 1, 398–399.

49   He contributed to a volume on alleged 'renaissances', but with reference to late-fourth-century Rome: Alan Cameron 1984b, an early precursor of *LPR*.

50   Alan Cameron 1993a, 327–328 n61.

ALAN CAMERON AND BYZANTIUM   269

The projected history of early Byzantine epigrams was therefore transformed into something different. But the conclusion to *The Greek Anthology* (329–343) gives us an idea of what that history might have covered, with comments on the immediate success of Cephalas' anthology and a list of Byzantine epigrammatists, including John Geometres and later writers. His vision was narrower than that of Lauxtermann, and very different from the concerns of most recent specialists on Byzantine poetry, and his bibliographical base betrays its origin in the 1970s.[51] But *The Greek Anthology* remains a major *tour de force* and despite important new work by others on inscribed and book epigrams and on anthologies its principal arguments still stand.[52]

As I have already mentioned, *Porphyrius* looked ahead to the curious and still-puzzling work known as the *Parastaseis*, or 'Short Notes', and that was no doubt the origin of the idea for the seminar Alan and I ran together in 1974–76 at King's College London, where I was Reader in Ancient History and where he had become Professor of Latin two years earlier. Recent critics have dated it to different points in the eighth century or argued that some of it is later and belonged to a different collection; they have wondered whether the *Parastaseis* was meant as a kind of guidebook to Constantinople, or if not, what it was: perhaps an example of Byzantine encyclopaedism or the habit of collecting snippets, or a collection of unrelated excerpts, or perhaps a kind of parody, an indication of the low level of knowledge of the urban past in eighth-century Constantinople and the fascination of an urban landscape that included many remains no longer understood, some of which also aroused fear and suspicion among contemporaries, or a key stage in the evolution of patriographic texts dealing with the history of the city, or a telling indicator of Byzantine attitudes to statuary and images.[53] Clearly there is still no agreement, and there was little helpful context for the work we did on the text in the 1970s, nearly five decades ago now: Gilbert Dagron's *Constantinople imaginaire*, with reference to the *Parastaseis*,[54] did not appear until 1984, and earlier works on the monuments of Constantinople were uncertain guides. With its references to 'philosophers' and its frequently expressed suspicion that late antique statues were likely to be prophetic or inhabited by demons, the *Parastaseis* also belongs within the tradition of magic and the occult explored by Paul Magdalino and others.[55]

---

51   Though see his list of late Addenda at 400–403.
52   See Rhoby 2014 and Spingou 2019; Rhoby 2014, 636–638 discusses an epigram from a sarcophagus, for which see Alan Cameron 1993, 319; I owe this point to Foteini Spingou.
53   James 1996; Anderson 2011; Odorico 2014; Berger 2016; most recently Chatterjee 2017 (a reference I owe to Jaś Elsner).
54   See Dagron 1984b, 29–48.
55   E.g. Magdalino 2013.

The publication of a translation and commentary in the Columbia series edited by William Harris and others including Alan himself did not take place until 1984,[56] and Alan was not an active contributor to the preparation of the text after he had left to take up his post at Columbia in 1977, although we were able to take advantage of a lengthy unpublished paper written by him during these years on Constantine and the foundation of Constantinople, on which see below. The volume assumes that the *Parastaseis* is in some sense a unified text, and the idea, which now seems somewhat over-literal, that this was the work of a group of lesser bureaucrats trying to make sense of the statuary and urban environment of Constantinople hardly understood in their day is owed to Alan. Crucially, the preoccupation in the text with earlier monuments appealed to his interests at the time, and he had seen its potential when working on *Porphyrius*. Given his sensitivity to fiction and fantasy, had he returned later to the *Parastaseis* he might well have been able to sort out some of its contradictions and its wilder guesses more satisfactorily. But while much has been written on the text in recent years to revise the positions taken in the 1984 volume, many of the questions exposed in it remain; this is still the basic translation and commentary and the publication brought deserved attention to the importance of this puzzling and hitherto neglected text.

Many of the sections in the *Parastaseis* contain garbled references to Constantine and the early history of Constantinople, and this was a subject that also appealed to Alan. He spoke at the 1983 Byzantine Studies Conference on Constantine and the foundation of Constantinople, a subject wreathed in obscurity and mythology as well as what he considered to be obfuscation in recent scholarship, and one just right for his critical eye, and in 1987 another BSC abstract had the title 'Rome and Constantinople: Growth of a Mystique'.[57] These papers were not published, but the volume on the *Parastaseis* draws on the first, and he had planned a book dealing with the Foundation ceremonies of Constantinople.[58] In his lengthy unpublished paper on 'The Foundation of

---

56 Averil Cameron and Herrin et al., 1984; see viii on the members of the seminar (Alan and myself, Robin Cormack, Liam Gallagher, Judith Herrin, Geoffrey House, Lucy-Anne Hunt, Marlia Mundell Mango, Charlotte Roueché, and Caro Wilson) and the gestation of the publication. The editorial work was begun in 1978 by Charlotte Roueché and continued by Robin Cormack and Judith Herrin and myself; the final version was the work of myself and Judith Herrin.

57 See also Alan Cameron 1982.

58 Carla Asher and Javier Arce, personal communications; a contents list corresponding well with the divisions in his 1980s paper as well as an annotated text survive on Alan's laptop, and it seems he had revisited the file quite recently. Tim Barnes's *Constantine and Eusebius* was published in 1981, but Alan had little sympathy with Barnes's insistence on Constantine's Christianity or indeed with Eusebius. The *Parastaseis* on the other hand

ALAN CAMERON AND BYZANTIUM 271

Constantinople' from the early 1980s he was at pains not only to dispel the legends that quickly grew up round the event but also to argue against the 'massive additions' made to them in recent scholarship, his starting points being the Italian historians Santo Mazzarino and Lellia Cracco Ruggini, with whom he also engaged in other publications. He argued against the idea that there were pagan elements in the foundation ceremonies, and that Constantine represented himself in the guise of the sun god Helios in the statue placed on top of his column in the city—an interpretation that has become popular again in recent years among the voluminous list of publications on Constantine that have come out since the anniversaries of the Battle of the Milvian Bridge and the Edict of Milan. Alan's paper, some ninety-five typescript pages in length, is a tour de force consisting of ten sections each aimed at rebutting a theory or theories he considered misguided: they are headed: 1. Introduction, 2. *Etrusca disciplina*, 3. *Tyche*, 4. Flora, 5. Helios, 6. Praetextatus and Sopater, 7. The Trojan connection, 8. The palladium, 9. *Consecratio* and the God of the martyrs, and 10. 324 and 328; there is a further section, also numbered as 10, headed 'New Rome'. The subject as a whole was perfect for him, given his sharp eye for both late antique and Byzantine accretions and modern errors. It gave him an opportunity, for example, to debunk the claim made by John the Lydian in the sixth century[59] of a connection with the foundation ceremonies by the Neoplatonist Sopater and 'Praetextatus the hierophant' (not in any case, as Alan argues against Cracco Ruggini, the Roman grandee Vettius Agorius Praetextatus, who was to feature at some length in *The Last Pagans of Rome*). His book on the subject would have been important, and very different in approach from Gilbert Dagron's books on Constantinople and the *Patria*, published in 1974 and 1984,[60] just as Dagron's later book on the hippodrome[61] differs fundamentally from Alan's *Circus Factions* (below). He was less attracted than Dagron by the process of the emergence of legend or by later Byzantine beliefs about Constantine. On full display in his unpublished paper however are not only his astonishing grasp of late antique and early Byzantine texts in both Latin and

---

had clearly stimulated his interest; it contains several confused and confusing entries on Constantine's statue and on the foundation of the city, and Alan's paper, 'The Foundation of Constantinople', is cited several times in the commentary as forthcoming: Averil Cameron and Herrin 1984, 36n95, 217, 243, 264. My knowledge of it derives from an early typescript copy without footnotes and undated, which must be the one we used for the volume; it dates back to the days before computers when Greek had to be handwritten and footnotes written separately; in recent years Alan became proficient at using technology (principally *Nota Bene*), even to the point of preparing camera-ready copy.

59   John the Lydian, *De Mens.* IV.2.
60   Dagron 1974 (1984a), 1984b.
61   Dagron 2011.

Greek and differing widely in date and type, but also many of the characteristic questions and themes that feature in his other publications.

Let me go back to the 1970s and turn to *Circus Factions*, published in 1976 while Alan was Professor of Latin at King's College London, where he gave his inaugural lecture in 1974 on 'Bread and Circuses: The Roman Emperor and his People'. I do not remember exactly when the idea of *Circus Factions* took shape, but it complemented *Porphyrius* and expanded the conclusions to that book; indeed, Alan himself says that it 'continued and completed' the investigation he had undertaken in *Porphyrius*.[62] He also pursued the technical aspects of chariot racing, relevant to both books. The film of *Ben Hur* with Charlton Heston as the charioteer Ben Hur had been released in 1959 and Alan sent Charlton Heston a copy of his inaugural lecture; he was thrilled to receive a personal reply as well as a collection of stills from the film and learned that Heston had trained for several months for filming of the chariot race, but the meeting with Heston that he had hoped for did not materialize. *Circus Factions* was also stimulated by reading what Alan considered misguided theories about the significance of the factions under Justinian and the reasons for factional violence. Barry Baldwin referred to Alan's 'customary learning and verve', and to the book as a 'masterly work of demolition',[63] and I well remember the vituperation Alan directed at the time at the unfortunate Jacques Jarry, for example, and to anyone who ascribed religious or social agendas to the Blues and Greens.[64] We had spent the momentous year 1967–68 both teaching in the graduate school at Columbia, and Alan wrote the piece mentioned above about the student protests at Columbia for the *Oxford Magazine* on our return to London in the early summer of 1968, playing down their seriousness.[65] An article on demes

---

62   Alan Cameron 1976, Appendix H, 344. The writing of *Circus Factions* delayed the completion of the book on epigrams announced in the preface to *Porphyrius*, though not for long: *The Greek Anthology* went to press in 1980 although it was not published until 1993.

63   Baldwin 1984b.

64   See Alan Cameron 1980b. It is worth mentioning here the antipathy towards Christianity that runs through a number of his publications, including *The Last Pagans of Rome*, and that breathes through many of his remarks elsewhere; at the same time, as Elsner points out, many of his art-historical papers are aimed, like *LPR*, at demolishing the assumption that Christians could not themselves be patrons or owners of supposedly 'pagan', i.e. classicizing, art. The central argument of *LPR* is that the late Roman elite was fully Christianized by the late fourth century; it follows Alan's opposition, expressed already in the 1960s, to the persistent modern attempts to argue for a 'pagan resistance' to Christianity in the late fourth century.

65   Alan Cameron 1968b; this seems all the more surprising given the events in Paris in May of the same year and recent student protests at the LSE in London, and indeed in the light of our actual experiences in New York.

ALAN CAMERON AND BYZANTIUM   273

and factions in 1974 begins 'There is surely no subject in all Byzantine history on which more sheer fantasy and nonsense has been written than the so-called "demes" and factions of the circus.'[66] Serious motivations are also played down in the role of the factions in the fall of the emperor Phocas in the early seventh century. Alan had been taught at New College by the Marxist ancient historian Geoffrey de Ste Croix, who made a great impression on him, as he did on all his pupils, but he had no time for Marxist or structuralist explanations, arguing explicitly against 'the fragile Marxist analysis' of the factions; according to him 'Marxist historians' had only succeeded in producing a 'refined version' of the thesis of the hapless G. Manojlović, published in the 1930s.[67] In the introduction he says that he 'particularly' wished to combat the Marxist view that the factions somehow represented a rise in popular sovereignty, and even more vehemently the notion that, as one scholar claimed, they marked a 'direct line from the hippodrome of Constantinople to the Russian Revolution'.

Perhaps he went too far in his refusal to allow the Blue and Green supporters any deeper motives, to evaluate the reign of Justinian,[68] or to relate the sixth-century events to urban conditions in early Byzantine cities (this was before the later spate of writing about such topics).[69] But he demonstrates to the full his extraordinary chronological range, and expressed his dissatisfaction with earlier scholarship on the factions that focused only on the early empire or the later Byzantine period: he thought a longer view was needed that took in the real changes over many centuries.[70] Alan was driven, as usual, by the detailed problems of the evidence, and came up with a typically ingenious and far-reaching proposal about the reorganization of funding for public entertainments in which he found an answer to some of his questions. He also connected the role played by the factions with the theatre claques and their organized chanting identified in fourth-century Antioch by J. H. W. G. Liebeschuetz, and with acclamations,[71] and he was naturally much taken by the contemporary accounts of the Nika riots of AD 532 in Procopius and John Malalas, though he argued that Paul Maas was right to dissociate from them

---

66   Alan Cameron 1974b.
67   Alan Cameron 1976, 82, 39, 3, 72, 74, 98; see Manojlović, 1936.
68   He would not have been in sympathy with Bell 2013, for example.
69   I wrote a short plea for social context myself: Averil Cameron 1984, and for urban violence in fifth- and sixth-century eastern cities see Averil Cameron 2011.
70   Bagnall 2018, 237.
71   Alan Cameron 1976, 234–249. See Liebeschuetz 1972; Roueché 1989, 1993; Roueché 1993 discusses acclamations and the connection that Alan makes between the factions and theatre claques.

the famous dialogue reported by Theophanes.[72] His work on the factions, like his book on Porphyrius, also took him again into the field of material evidence, especially the factional inscriptions and graffiti that form a major subject in Charlotte Roueché's later publications on Aphrodisias. These were still early days in late antique archaeology, but Alan drew on inscriptions from Ephesus,[73] mentioned as yet unpublished material from Miletus, Aphrodisias, and Alexandria,[74] and included an appendix listing evidence for Blues and Greens in the eastern provinces that draws on the epigraphic evidence then available (Appendix B); no surprise to find the name of Louis Robert recurring here. Another appendix contains addenda and corrigenda to *Porphyrius* and also draws on epigraphic evidence. This seems to me important as an early example of his coverage and his openness to material evidence. In *Porphyrius* he had included an important discussion of the physical arrangement of the hippodrome and the statuary on the *spina* that has been central in more recent discussions,[75] and here he corrects one of his earlier claims.

Circus Factions came with a total of eight appendices (numbered alphabetically) on a wide range of questions. They also include a discussion of Byzantine factions and Islamic *futuwwa*, stimulated by a paper by Speros Vryonis.[76] Alan saw both of these, as well as the Hellenistic and early imperial *neoi*, as typical young men's groups, the sort of thing one finds in any society and could see no direct connection between them.

The last chapter of *Circus Factions* and the book's Epilogue take him into later Byzantine territory. Again, he starts with a demolition, this time of the theory that a later unspecified emperor stripped the factions of their powers and reduced them to a ceremonial role; according to him they had never possessed such powers and their ceremonial role actually became more, not less, important as time went on. The last chapter presents a rapid run-through of Byzantine history up to the tenth century, with some acute remarks about the tenth-century *Book of Ceremonies*, positing that there was some kind of ceremonial book already in existence in the sixth century, and doing an efficient demolition job along the way. The Blues and Greens had never had a political role and did not go into 'decline'; instead, their supposed 'decline' was actually 'an ascent to respectability'. 'Hooliganism' occurred often according to him, for example in the late Byzantine period, but Vryonis was wrong to imagine

---

72 Maas 1912; Alan Cameron 1976, Appendix C, 318–351, typically also expressing reservations on Maas's claim that the dialogue was metrical.

73 Alan Cameron 1976, 146–149.

74 Alan Cameron 1976, 196.

75 E.g. Bassett 2004.

76 Appendix G, 341–343.

ALAN CAMERON AND BYZANTIUM 275

that the guilds that he claimed played a part in insurrections in the eleventh century were reviving the role played by the factions in the sixth. Alan concludes: the circus factions 'deserve no prominent mention in any history of popular expression', and their one 'original, important and lasting contribution to Byzantine life and institutions' was their role in ceremonial, which, however, did not survive the imperial move from the Great Palace to Blachernae in the twelfth century. Since 2011 we have had a very different study of their role by Gilbert Dagron which explores its symbolism and its quasi-religious aura, neither of them topics of interest to Alan.[77] By the time Dagron's book on the hippodrome came out in 2011 Alan was preoccupied with ivory diptychs and with the late-fourth-century subject matter of *The Last Pagans of Rome*; I wonder what he made of it. *Circus Factions* is reductionist. It is also pugnacious throughout. And irrespective of the merits of its argument it displays to the full the breadth of Alan's range and his energetic determination to pursue problems wherever they led.

How then is Alan's overall contribution to Byzantine studies regarded? His body of work covers so many different fields that the Byzantine element tends to be drowned out except in specialist areas like epigram, or indeed in studies of early Byzantine or late antique silver and ivories. At the time of writing it is the reaction to *The Last Pagans of Rome* that dominates the discussion; it is his biggest book and it touches live concerns, especially among Italian scholars, some of whom feel bruised by its arguments.[78] A broader survey of his work shows that Alan's mind was that of a fertile scholar who habitually pursued multiple leads simultaneously, and who formed and sometimes announced plans for future work, not all of which came to anything because he discovered other possibilities in the meantime. So to conclude, my main impressions from the present exploration are firstly of his very wide scholarly reach and complete lack of inhibition about any supposed disciplinary boundaries, and secondly, his pursuit of the parts of Byzantine studies that happened to be of interest to him, without ever feeling that he needed to take a holistic view or necessarily bring the pieces together. For that reason Byzantinists may find him hard to deal with. He was a problem-solver, not a synthesizer, and least of all a theorist, and the problems he wanted to solve had nothing to do with the current agendas or academic fashions that drive others. And what a problem-solver he was.

---

77   Dagron 2011.
78   He does not pull his punches; for immediate reactions, at times pained or even indignant, see Lizzi Testa 2013a. See also, e.g. on the *Historia Augusta*, Alan Cameron 2011a, 627–629, 635–636.

Few others have had or are likely to have his penetrating energy as a scholar, and still fewer his sheer confidence and panache.

Acknowledgements

I am very grateful to Carla Asher for sharing some materials with me and for her comments on an earlier draft, to Jaś Elsner for valuable comments and corrections, and to Marc Lauxtermann and Foteini Spingou for their help in relation to the *Greek Anthology* and to Foteini Spingou for advance sight of her important paper (2019). Roger Bagnall's *Memoir* of Alan Cameron was published by the British Academy in *Biographical Memoirs of Fellows of the British Academy* 17, 229–246 (2018), available online. A more systematic trawl through Alan's articles than I have been able to do here, with attention to their dates of publication, would tell us much about the genesis of his books. His characteristic ways of working are also described by Jás Elsner, "Introduction", in Alan Cameron, *Historical Studies in Late Roman Art and Archaeology* (Leuven: Peeters, forthcoming) and Lellia Cracco Ruggini and Rita Lizzi Testa, "Cameron, Alan", in C. Ando and M. Formisano, eds., *The New Late Antiquity* (Heidelberg: Universitäts Verlag; forthcoming).

References

For reprints of Alan Cameron's articles, see the List of Publications.

Adams, J. N. 1982. *The Latin Sexual Vocabulary*. London.

Agosti, G. 1997. "P.Oxy. 3537r: etopea acrostica su Esiodo," *ZPE* 119, 1–5.

Agosti, G. 2001. "L'epica biblica nella tarda antichità greca. Autori e lettori nel IV e V secolo," in F. Stella (ed.), *La scrittura infinita. Bibbia e poesia in età medievale e umanistica*. Florence, 67–104.

Agosti, G. 2004. "Due note sulla convenienza di Omero," in A. Marcone (ed.), *Società e cultura in età tardoantica*. Florence, 38–57.

Agosti, G. 2005. "L'etopea nella poesia greca tardoantica," in E. Amato and J. Schamp (eds.), *ΗΘΟΠΟΙΙΑ. La représentation de caractères entre fiction scolaire et réalité vivante à l'époque impériale et tardive*. Salerno, 34–60.

Agosti, G. 2006–2007. "Cultura greca negli epigrammi epigrafici di età tardoantica," *Incontri triestini di filologia classica* 6, 3–18.

Agosti, G. 2008. "Literariness and Levels of Style in Epigraphical Poetry of Late Antiquity," *Ramus* 37, 191–213.

Agosti, G. 2009. "Niveaux de Style, lettérarité, poétiques: pour une histoire du système de la poésie classicisante au VIᵉ siècle," in P. Odorico, P. A. Agapitos, and M. Hinterberger (eds.), *"Doux remède …". Poésie et poétique à Byzance*. Paris, 99–119.

Agosti, G. 2010a. "*Paideia* classica e fede religiosa: annotazioni sul linguaggio dei carmi epigrafici tardoantichi," *Cahiers du Centre Gustave Glotz* 21, 329–353.

Agosti, G. 2010b. "*Saxa loquuntur?* Epigrammi epigrafici e diffusione della *paideia* nell'Oriente tardoantico," *AT* 18, 163–180.

Agosti, G. 2010c. "Libro della poesia e poesia del libro nella Tarda Antichità," *Cento Pagine* 4, 11–26.

Agosti, G. 2011a. "Usurper, imiter, communiquer: le dialogue interculturel dans la poésie grecque chrétienne de l'antiquité tardive," in N. Belayche and J. D. Dubois (eds.), *L'oiseau et le poisson. Cohabitations religieuses dans les mondes grec et romain*. Paris, 275–299.

Agosti, G. 2011b. "Le brume di Omero. Sofronio dinanzi alla *paideia* classica," in L. Cristante and S. Ravalico (eds.), *Il calamo della memoria. Riuso di testi e mestiere letterario nella tarda antichità* IV. Trieste, 33–50.

Agosti, G. 2013. "Classicism, *paideia*, Religion," in R. Lizzi Testa (ed.), *The Strange Death of Pagan Rome: Reflexions on a Historiographical Controversy*. Turnhout, 123–140.

Agosti, G. 2015a. "*Paideia* greca e religione in iscrizioni dell'età di Giuliano," in A. Marcone (ed.), *L'imperatore Giuliano: realtà storica e rappresentazioni*. Florence, 223–239.

Agosti, G. 2015b. "La mise en page come elemento significante nell'epigrafia greca tardoantica," in M. Maniaci and P. Orsini (eds.), *Scrittura epigrafica e scrittura libraria: fra Oriente e Occidente*. Cassino, 45–86.

Agosti, G. 2016a. "Epigrafia metrica tardoantica e democratizzazione della cultura," in L. Cristante and V. Veronesi (eds.), *Forme di accesso al sapere in età tardoantica e altomedievale* VI. Trieste, 131–147.

Agosti, G. 2016b. "Les langues de l'épigramme épigraphique grecque: regard sur l'identité culturelle chrétienne dans l'antiquité tardive," in E. Santin and L. Foschia (eds.), *L'épigramme dans tous ses états: épigraphiques, littéraires, historiques*. Online at: https://books.openedition.org/enseditions/5621).

Agosti, G. 2016c. "Praising the God(s). Homeric Hymns in Late Antiquity," in A. Faulkner, A. Vergados, and A. Schwab (eds.), *The Reception of the Homeric Hymns*. Oxford, 221–240.

Agosti, G. 2017. "Présence d'Homère dans les épigrammes épigraphiques tardives," in Y. Durbec and F. Trajber (eds.), *Traditions épiques et poésie épigrammatique*. Leuven, 225–244.

Agosti, G., and Gonnelli, F. 1995. "Materiali per la storia dell'esametro nei poeti cristiani greci," in M. Fantuzzi and R. Pretagostini (eds.), *Struttura e storia dell'esametro greco* I. Pisa and Rome, 289–434.

Alföldi, A. 1937. *A Festival of Isis in Rome under the Christian Emperors of the IVth Century*. Budapest.

Alföldi, A. 1942–1943. *Die Kontorniaten: ein Verkanntes Propagandamittel der Stadtrömischen heidnischen Aristokratie in ihrem Kampfe gegen das christliche Kaisertum*, 2 vols. Budapest.

Alföldi, A. 1952. *A Conflict of Ideas in the Later Roman Empire: The Clash Between the Senate and Valentinian I*. Oxford.

Alföldi, A. 1967. *Studien zur Geschichte der Weltkrise des 3. Jahrhunderts nach Christus*. Darmstadt.

Alram, M. 2008. "Early Sasanian Coinage," in S. Stewart and V. S. Curtis (eds.), *The Sasanian Era*. London, 17–30.

Alram, M. 2015. "The Cultural Impact of Sasanian Persia along the Silk Road—Aspects of Continuity," *E-Sasanika* 14, 1–25.

Alram, M., and Gyselen, R. 2012. *Sylloge Nummorum Sasanidarum, Ohrmazd I.–Ohrmazd II*. Vol. 2. Vienna.

Amato, E., and Schamp, J. (eds.). 2005. *ΗΘΟΠΟΙΙΑ. La représentation de caractères entre fiction scolaire et réalité vivante à l'époque impériale et tardive*. Salerno.

Amato, E., and Ventrella, G. 2005. "L'éthopée dans la pratique scolaire et littéraire. Répertoire complet," in E. Amato and J. Schamp (eds.), *ΗΘΟΠΟΙΙΑ. La représentation de caractères entre fiction scolaire et réalité vivante à l'époque impériale et tardive*. Salerno, 213–231.

REFERENCES

Amirav, H., and Romeny, B. ter Haar (eds). 2007. *From Rome to Constantinople: Studies in Honour of Averil Cameron*. Leuven.

Ammirati, S. 2007. "Intorno al Festo Farnesiano (Neap. IV A 3) e ad alcuni codici di argomento profano conservati presso la Biblioteca Apostolica Vaticana," *Miscellanea Bibliothecae Apostolicae Vaticanae* 14, 7–93.

Ammirati, S. 2020. "Produzione e circolazione libraria nella Roma del IX secolo. Nuove possibili attribuzioni?," in S. Ammirati, A. Ballardini, and G. Bordi (eds.), *"Grata più delle stelle." Pasquale I (817–824) e la Roma del suo tempo*. Rome.

Anastasius Bibliotecarius. 1602. *Anastasii, S. R. E. Bibliothecarii Historia, De Vitis Romanorum Pontificum a B. Petro Apostolo usque ad Nicolaum I ... Deinde vita Hadriani II et Stephani VI*. Mainz.

Anderson, B. 2011. "Classified Knowledge: The Epistemology of Statuary in the *Parastaseis Syntomoi Chronikai*," *Byzantine and Modern Greek Studies* 35, 1–19.

Anderson, J. G. C., Cumont, F., and Grégoire, H. (eds.). 1910. *Recueil des inscriptions grecques et latines du Pont et de l'Arménie*. (Studia Pontica III). Brussels.

Anderson, M. A. 2012. "Hospitals, Hospices and Shelters for the Poor in Late Antiquity." Ph.D. Dissertation, Yale University.

Arnaldi, G. 1961. "Anastasio Bibliotecario," in *Dizionario Biografico degli Italiani*. Vol 3. Rome.

Arnheim, M. T. W. 1972. *The Senatorial Aristocracy in the Later Roman Empire*. Oxford.

Arnold, J. 2014. *Theoderic and the Roman Imperial Restoration*. New York.

Arns, P. E. 1953. *La technique du livre d'après saint Jérôme*. Paris.

Ascough, R. A., Harland, P. A., and Kloppenborg, J. S. (eds.). 2012. *Associations in the Greco-Roman World: A Sourcebook*. Waco, TX.

Athanassakis, A. 1976. "The Etymology and Meaning of ὁμοίιος," *Rheinisches Museum für Philologie* 119, 4–7.

Bagnall, R. S. (ed.). 2007. *Egypt in the Byzantine World*. Cambridge.

Bagnall, R. S. 2018. "Alan Douglas Edward Cameron," *Biographical Memoirs of Fellows of the British Academy* 17, 229–246.

Bagnall, R. S., and Bransbourg, G. 2019. "The Constantian Monetary Revolution," *ISAW Papers* 14. Online at: http://isaw.nyu.edu/publications/isaw-papers.

Bagnall, R. S., Cameron, A., Schwartz, S. R., and Worp, K. A. (eds.). 1987. *Consuls of the Later Roman Empire*. Atlanta.

Bagnall, R. S., and Cribiore, R. 2000. *Women's Letters from Ancient Egypt, 300 BC–AD 800*. Ann Arbor.

Baker, P. A. 2002. "The Roman Military *valetudinaria*: Fact or Fiction?," in R. Arnott (ed.), *The Archaeology of Medicine*. Oxford, 69–79.

Baker, P. A. 2004. *Medical Care for the Roman Army on the Rhine, Danube and British Frontiers*. Oxford.

Baldini, A. 1999. "Un'ipotesi su una tradizione occidentale post-flavianea," in F. Paschoud (ed.), *Historiae Augustae Colloquium VII: Colloquium Genevense*. Bari, 9–31.

Baldini, A. 2002. "Ancora sulla *devotio* di Claudio Gotico: Aurelio Vittore fonte diretta della *Historia Augusta* e di Nicomaco Flaviano," in G. Bonamente and F. Paschoud (eds.), *Historiae Augustae Colloquium VIII: Colloquium Perusinum*. Bari, 11–31.

Baldwin, B. 1984a. "Dioscorus of Aphrodito: the Worst Poet of Antiquity?," in *Atti del XVII Congresso Internazionale di Papirologia (Napoli, 19–26 maggio 1983)*. Naples, 327–331.

Baldwin, B. 1984b. "The Sports Fans of Rome and Byzantium," *Liverpool Classical Monthly* 9 (2), 28–30.

Ballou, S. H. 1914. *The Manuscript Tradition of the Historia Augusta*. Leipzig.

Banaji, J. 2007. *Agrarian Change in Late Antiquity: Gold, Labour, and Aristocratic Dominance*. New ed. Oxford.

Barnes, T. D. 1976. "The *Epitome de Caesaribus* and its Sources," *CPh* 71, 258–268.

Barnes, T. D. 1987. "Regional Prefectures," in J. Straub (ed.), *Bonner Historia Augusta Colloquium 1984/1985*. Bonn, 13–23.

Barnes, T. D. 1991. "Jerome and the *Historia Augusta*," in G. Bonamente and N. Duval (eds.), *Historiae Augustae Colloquium I: Colloquium Parisinum*. Macerata, 19–28.

Barnes, T. D. 1997. "Was heisst Fälschung?," *Archiv für Kulturgeschichte* 79 (2), 259–267.

Barnes, T. D. 1999. "The *Historia Augusta* and Christian Hagiography," in F. Paschoud (ed.), *Historiae Augustae Colloquium VII: Colloquium Genevense*. Bari, 33–41.

Barnes, T. D. 2010. *Early Christian Hagiography and Roman History*. Tübingen.

Bassett, S. 2004. *The Urban Image of Late Antique Constantinople*. Cambridge.

Bastien, P. 1994. *Le buste monétaire des empereurs romains*. Wetteren.

Baykan, D. 2012. *Allianoi Tıp Alatleri*. Istanbul.

Baynes, N. 1926. *The Historia Augusta: Its Date and Purpose*. Oxford.

Beckby, H. (ed.). 1967–1968. *Anthologia Graeca*, I–IV. Munich.

Bell, H. I., and Crum, W. E. 1925. "A Greek-Coptic Glossary," *Aegyptus* 6, 177–226.

Bell, P. N. 2013. *Social Conflict in the Age of Justinian*. Oxford.

Benario, H. W. 1980. *A Commentary on the* Vita Hadriani *in the* Historia Augusta. Chico, CA.

Béranger, J. 1985. "Le *privatus* dans l'Histoire Auguste et dans la tradition historique," in J. Straub (ed.), *Bonner Historia Augusta Colloquium 1982/1983*. Bonn, 21–55.

Berger, A. 2016. "Magical Constantinople Statues, Legends, and the End of Time," *Scandinavian Journal of Byzantine and Modern Greek Studies* 2, 9–30.

Bergmann, M. 1977. *Studien zum Römischen Porträt des 3. Jahrhunderts n. Chr.* Bonn.

Bernard, F. 2014. *Writing and Reading Byzantine Secular Poetry, 1025–1081*. Oxford.

Bernard, F. 2020. "Constantine the Rhodian's *Ekphrasis* in its Contemporary Milieu," in M. Mullett and R. Ousterhout (eds.), *The Holy Apostles: a Lost Monument, a Forgotten Project, and the Presentness of the Past*. Washington, D.C., 145–156.

REFERENCES   281

Bernard, F., and Demoen, K. 2012. *Poetry and its Contexts in Eleventh-Century Byzantium.* Farnham.

Bertotti, T. 1969. "Rutiliana," in A. Traina (ed.), *Contributi a tre poeti latini (Valerio Flacco, Rutilio Namaziano, Pascoli).* Bologna, 93–134.

Bertrand-Dagenbach, C. (ed.). 1993. *Histoire Auguste,* Tome III, 2: *Vie d'Alexandre Sévère.* Paris.

Bertrand-Dagenbach, C., and Chausson, F. (eds.). 2014. *Historiae Augustae Colloquium XII: Colloquium Nanceiense.* Bari.

Bianchini, F. 1718–1735. *Anastasii Bibliothecarii De vitis Romanorum Pontificum, cum Praefatione, Prolegomenis, Variantibus lectionibus, et Notis historicis, atque Chronologicis Francisci Bianchini, et aliorum notis historicis.* 4 v. Rome.

Bilotta, M. A. 2011. *I libri dei papi. La curia, il Laterano e la produzione manoscritta ad uso del Papato nel medioeveo (secoli VI–XIII) (Studi e testi 465).* Vatican City.

Bing, P., and Bruss, J. S. (eds.). 2007. *Brill's Companion to Hellenistic Epigram.* Leiden.

Bingöl, O. 2007. *Magnesia on the Meander: Magnesia ad Maeandrum.* Istanbul.

Birley, A. R. 1996. "Fiction in the *Epitome*?," in G. Bonamente and M. Mayer (eds.), *Historiae Augustae Colloquium IV: Colloquium Barcinonense.* Bari, 68–82.

Birley, A. R. 2003. "The *Historia Augusta* and Pagan Historiography," in G. Marasco (ed.), *Greek and Roman Historiography in Late Antiquity, Fourth to Sixth Century A.D.* Leiden, 127–149.

Bischoff, B. 1990. *Latin Paleography: Antiquity and the Middle Ages* (trans. D. Ó. Cróinín and D. Ganz). Cambridge.

Bischoff, B. 1994. *Manuscripts and Libraries in the Age of Charlemagne* (trans. and ed. M. Gorman). Cambridge.

Bjornlie, M. S. 2013. *Politics and Tradition between Rome, Ravenna and Constantinople: A Study of Cassiodorus and the* Variae, *527–554.* Cambridge.

Bjornlie, M. S. 2019. *Cassiodorus' "Variae": A New Complete Translation.* Berkeley.

Bleckmann, B. 1992. *Die Reichskrise des III. Jahrhunderts in der spätantiken und byzantinischen Geschichtsschreibung. Untersuchungen zu den nachdionischen Quellen der Chronik des Johannes Zonaras.* Munich.

Bleckmann, B. 1996. "Überlegungen zur Enmannschen Kaisergeschichte und zur Formung historischer Traditionen in tetrarchischer und konstantinischer Zeit," in G. Bonamente and M. Mayer (eds.), *Historiae Augustae Colloquium IV: Colloquium Barcinonense.* Bari, 11–37.

Bleckmann, B. 1999. "Von Theopomp zur *Historia Augusta*: zu einer Technik historiographischer Fälschung," in F. Paschoud (ed.), *Historiae Augustae Colloquium VII: Colloquium Genevense.* Bari, 43–57.

Bleckmann, B., and Brandt, H. (eds.). 2017. *Historiae Augustae Colloquium XIII: Colloquium Dusseldorpiense.* Bari.

Blockley, R. C. 1983. *The Fragmentary Classicising Historians of the Later Roman Empire II: Text, Translation and Historiographical Notes.* Liverpool.

Boge, H. 1974. *Griechische Tachygraphie und Tironische Noten*. Berlin.

Bolgia, C., McKitterick, R., and Osborne, J. (eds.). 2011. *Rome Across Time and Space, c. 500–1400: Cultural Transmissions and the Exchange of Ideas*. Cambridge.

Bolmarcich, S. 2002. "Hellenistic Sepulchral Epigrams on Homer," in M. A. Harder, R. F. Regtuit, and G. C. Wakker (eds.), *Hellenistic Epigrams*. Leuven, 67–83.

Bonamente, G., and Brandt, H. (eds.). 2007. *Historiae Augustae Colloquium X: Colloquium Bambergense*. Bari.

Bonamente, G., and Duval, N. (eds.). 1991. *Historiae Augustae Colloquium I: Colloquium Parisinum*. Macerata.

Bonamente, G., Heim, F., and Callu, J.-P. (eds.). 1998. *Historiae Augustae Colloquium VI: Colloquium Argentoratense*. Bari.

Bonamente, G., and Mayer, M. (eds.). 1996. *Historiae Augustae Colloquium IV: Colloquium Barcinonense*. Bari.

Bonamente, G., and Paschoud, F. (eds.). 2002. *Historiae Augustae Colloquium VIII: Colloquium Perusinum*. Bari.

Bond, S. 2014. "Altering Infamy: Status, Violence, and Civic Exclusion in Late Antiquity," *Classical Antiquity* 33 (1), 1–30.

Boudon-Millot, V. (ed.). 2007. *Galien, Tome I*. Paris.

Bouffartigue, J. 2005. "L'authenticité de la letter 84 de l'empereur Julien," *Revue de Philologie* 79, 231–242.

Bougard, F. 2009. "Composition, diffusion et reception des parties tardives du *Liber pontificalis* romain (VIII\ᵉ–IX\ᵉ siècles)," in F. Bougard and M. Sot (eds.), *Liber, Gesta, histoire. Ecrire l'histoire des évêques et des papes, de l'Antiquité au XXI\ᵉ siècle*. Turnhout, 127–152.

Bowersock, G. W. 2010. "*Parabalani*: A Terrorist Charity in Late Antiquity," *Anabases* 12, 45–54.

Bowker, M. 2008. "Clement [Clements; *née* Giggs], Margaret (1508–1570)," *Oxford Dictionary of National Biography*. Online at: https://doi.org/10.1093/ref:odnb/5604.

Boyce, M., Chaumont, M. L., and Bier, C. 1989. "Anāhīd," in *Encyclopaedia Iranica* 1. London, 1003–1011.

Brandt, H. 1996. *Kommentar zur Historia Augusta, Band 2: Vita Maximi et Balbini*. Bonn.

Brandt, H. 2010. "Hermann Dessau, Otto Hirschfeld, Otto Seeck, Theodor Mommsen und die *Historia Augusta*," in L. Galli Milić and N. Hecquet-Noti (eds.), *Historiae Augustae Colloquium Genevense in honorem F. Paschoud septuagenarii*. Bari, 93–103.

Brocca, N. 2003–2004. "Memoria poetica e attualità politica nel panegirico per Avito di Sidonio Apollinare," *Incontri triestini di filologia classica* 3, 279–295.

Brocca, N. 2005. "Il *proditor Stilicho* e la distruzione dei *Libri Sibyllini*," in I. Gualandri, F. Conca, and R. Passerella (eds.), *Nuovo e antico nella cultura greco-latina di IV–VI secolo*. Milan, 137–184.

REFERENCES

Brosius, M. 2010. "Women in Pre-Islamic Persia," in *Encyclopaedia Iranica*. Online at: http://www.iranicaonline.org/articles/women-i.

Brown, P. 1992. *Power and Persuasion in Late Antiquity*. Madison, WI.

Brown, P. 2011a. "Back to the Future: Pagans and Christians at the Warburg Institute in 1958," in P. Brown and R. Lizzi Testa, *Pagans and Christians in the Roman Empire: The Breaking of a Dialogue IVth–VIth Century A.D.* Münster, 17–24.

Brown, P. 2011b. "Paganism: What We Owe the Christians," *New York Review of Books* 58 (6) (April 7), 68–72.

Brown, P. 2012. *Through the Eye of a Needle: Wealth, the Fall of Rome, and the Making of Christianity in the West, 350–550 AD*. Princeton, NJ.

Brown, P. 2015. *The Ransom of the Soul: Afterlife and Wealth in Early Western Christianity*. Cambridge.

Browning, R. 1992. "The Byzantines and Homer," in R. Lamberton and J. J. Keaney (eds.), *Homer's Ancient Readers. The Hermeneutics of Greek Epic's Earliest Exegetes*. Princeton, NJ, 134–148.

Bruggisser, P. 1991. "Le char du préfet. Echos païens et chrétiens d'une polémique dans l'*Histoire Auguste* et chez Quodvultdeus," in G. Bonamente and N. Duval (eds.), *Historiae Augustae Colloquium I: Colloquium Parisinum*. Macerata, 93–100.

Bruggisser, P. 1996. "*Privatus* dans l'oeuvre de Symmaque: une incidence de la lexicographie sur la datation de l'*Histoire Auguste*," in G. Bonamente and M. Mayer (eds.), *Historiae Augustae Colloquium IV: Colloquium Barcinonense*. Bari, 111–132.

Budge, E. A. Wallis (ed.). 1893–1894. *The Discourses of Philoxenus, Bishop of Mabbôgh, A.D. 485–519*, 2 vols. London.

Burgess, R. W., and Kulikowski, M. 2013. *Mosaics of Time: The Latin Chronicle Traditions from the First Century BC to the Sixth Century AD, Volume I: A Historical Introduction to the Chronicle Genre from its Origins to the High Middle Ages*. Turnhout.

Calafato, S. 1958. *La proprietà privata in S. Ambrogio*. Turin.

Caldwell, C. H. 2018. "The Roman Emperor as Persian Prisoner of War: Remembering Shapur's Capture of Valerian," in J. H. Clark and B. Turner (eds.), *Brill's Companion to Military Defeat in Ancient Mediterranean Society*. Leiden, 335–358.

Callu, J.-P. 1985. "La première diffusion de l'Histoire Auguste (VIe–IXe S.)," in J. Straub (ed.), *Bonner Historia Augusta Colloquium 1982/1983*. Bonn, 89–129.

Callu, J.-P. 1992. *Histoire Auguste*, Tome 1, 1: *Vies d'Hadrien, Aelius, Antonin*. Paris.

Cameron, Alan. 1964a. "The Roman Friends of Ammianus," *JRS* 54, 15–28.

Cameron, Alan. 1964b. "Literary Allusions in the *Historia Augusta*," *Hermes* 92, 363–377.

Cameron, Alan 1965. "Wandering Poets: A Literary Movement in Byzantine Egypt," *Historia* 14, 470–509.

Cameron, Alan. 1966. "The Date and Identity of Macrobius," *JRS* 56, 25–38.

Cameron, Alan. 1967a. "Macrobius, Avienus and Avianus," *CQ* 17, 385–395.

Cameron, Alan. 1967b. "Rutilius Namatianus, St. Augustine, and the date of the *De reditu*," *JRS* 57, 31–39.

Cameron, Alan. 1967c. "Two Notes on The Greek Anthology (Anth. Pal. ix. 474, 395 and 458)," *BICS* 14, 58–61.

Cameron, Alan. 1968a. "The *Garlands* of Meleager and Philip of Thessalonica," *GRBS* 9, 323–349.

Cameron, Alan. 1968b. "Student Rebellion at Columbia," *Oxford Magazine* (Trinity Term no. 8), 403–404.

Cameron, Alan. 1969. "The Last Days of the Academy at Athens," *Proceedings of the Cambridge Philological Society* n.s. 15, 7–29.

Cameron, Alan. 1970. *Claudian: Poetry and Propaganda at the Court of Honorius*. Oxford.

Cameron, Alan. 1973. *Porphyrius the Charioteer*. Oxford.

Cameron, Alan. 1974a. "Claudian," in J. W. Binns (ed.), *Latin Literature of the Fourth Century*. London, 134–159.

Cameron, Alan. 1974b. "Demes and Factions," *BZ* 44, 74–91.

Cameron, Alan. 1974c. "Heresies and Factions," *Byzantion* 44, 92–120.

Cameron, Alan. 1976a. "Paganism and Literature in Fourth Century Rome," *EFH* 23, 1–30.

Cameron, Alan. 1976b. "The Authenticity of the Correspondence of St. Nilus of Ancyra," *GRBS* 17, 181–196.

Cameron, Alan. 1976c. *Circus Factions: Blues and Greens at Rome and Byzantium*. Oxford.

Cameron, Alan. 1978. "The House of Anastasius," *GRBS* 19, 259–276.

Cameron, Alan. 1980a. "The *Garland* of Philip," *GRBS* 21, 43–62.

Cameron, Alan. 1980b. "Circus Factions and Religious Parties: A Rejoinder," *Byzantion* 50, 336–337.

Cameron, Alan. 1982. "Anthusa: Notes on the Iconography of Constantinople," in *Eighth Annual Byzantine Studies Conference: Abstracts of Papers*. N.p. 41.

Cameron, Alan. 1984a. "A New Late Antique Ivory," *AJA* 88, 397–402.

Cameron, Alan. 1984b. "The Latin Revival of the Fourth Century," in W. Treadgold (ed.), *Renaissances before the Renaissance*. Stanford, 42–58, 182–184.

Cameron, Alan. 1985. *Literature and Society in the Early Byzantine World*. London.

Cameron, Alan. 1986. "Pagan Ivories," in F. Paschoud, G. Fry, and Y. Rütsche (eds.), *Symmaque. Colloque génévois à l'occasion du mille six centième anniversaire du conflit de l'autel de la Victoire*. Paris, 41–64.

Cameron, Alan. 1993a. *The Greek Anthology: From Meleager to Planudes*. Oxford.

Cameron, Alan (with J. Long and with a contribution by L. Sherry). 1993b. *Barbarians and Politics at the Court of Arcadius*. Berkeley.

Cameron, Alan. 1995. *Callimachus and his Critics*. Princeton, NJ.

REFERENCES 285

Cameron, Alan. 1996. "Orfitus and Constantius: A Note on Roman Gold-Glasses," *JRA* 9, 295–301.

Cameron, Alan. 1998. "Consular Diptychs in their Social Context: New Eastern Evidence," *JRA* 11, 385–403.

Cameron, Alan. 1999a. "The Antiquity of the Symmachi," *Historia* 48, 477–505.

Cameron, Alan. 1999b. "The Last Pagans of Rome," in W. V. Harris (ed.), *The Transformations of Urbs Roma in Late Antiquity*. Portsmouth, RI, 109–121.

Cameron, Alan. 2000. "Claudian Revisited," in F. E. Consolino (ed.), *Letteratura e propaganda nell'Occidente latino da Augusto ai regni romanobarbarici*. Rome, 127–144.

Cameron, Alan. 2004. *Greek Mythography in the Roman World*. Oxford.

Cameron, Alan. 2007a. "The Probus Diptych and Christian Apologetic," in H. Amirav, and R. B. ter Haar Romeny (eds), *From Rome to Constantinople: Studies in Honour of Averil Cameron*. Leuven, 191–202.

Cameron, Alan. 2007b. "Poets and Pagans in Byzantine Egypt," in R. S. Bagnall (ed.), *Egypt in the Byzantine World*. Cambridge, 21–46.

Cameron, Alan. 2009. "Young Achilles in the Roman World," *JRA* 99, 1–22.

Cameron, Alan. 2011a. *The Last Pagans of Rome*. New York.

Cameron, Alan. 2011b. "*Antiquus error/novus error*: the *HA*, Nicomachus Flavianus, and the 'Pagan Resistance,'" *JRA* 24, 835–846.

Cameron, Alan. 2013. "The Origin, Function, and Context of Consular Diptychs," *JRS* 103, 174–207.

Cameron, Alan. 2015. "City Personification and Consular Diptychs," *JRS* 105, 250–287.

Cameron, Alan. 2016a. *Studies in Late Roman Literature and History*. Bari.

Cameron, Alan. 2016b. *Wandering Poets and Other Essays on Late Greek Literature and Philosophy*. Oxford.

Cameron, Alan. 2016c. "Were Pagans Afraid to Speak Their Minds in a Christian World? The Correspondence of Symmachus," in M. Salzman, M. Sághy, and R. Lizzi Testa (eds.), *Pagans and Christians in Late Antique Rome*. Cambridge, 64–111.

Cameron, Alan. 2016d. "The Status of Serena and the Stilicho Ditpych," *JRA* 29, 509–516.

Cameron, Alan. 2017. "Presentation Diptychs or Fancy Stationery?," *JLA* 10 (2), 300–324.

Cameron, Alan. 2020. "Jerome and the *Historia Augusta*," *HSCPh* 111.

Cameron, Alan. Forthcoming. *Historical Studies in Late Roman Art and Archaeology*. Leuven.

Cameron, Averil. 1970. *Agathias*. Oxford.

Cameron, Averil. 1976. *Corippus, In laudem Iustini minoris libri quattuor*. London.

Cameron, Averil. 1984. "'Sports Fans' of Rome and Byzantium," *Liverpool Classical Monthly* 9 (4), 50–51.

Cameron, Averil. 2006. "New Themes and Styles in Greek Literature, a Title Revisited," in S. F. Johnson (ed.), *Greek Literature in Late Antiquity: Dynamism, Didacticism, Classicism*. London, 11–28.

Cameron, Averil. 2011. *The Mediterranean World in Late Antiquity, AD 395–700.* Second ed. London.

Cameron, Averil and Cameron, Alan. 1964. "Christianity and Tradition in the Historiography of the Late Empire," *CQ* 14, 316–328.

Cameron, Averil and Cameron, Alan. 1966. "The *Cycle* of Agathias," *JHS* 86, 6–25.

Cameron, Averil, and Hall, S. G. (trans. and comm.). 1999. *Eusebius: Life of Constantine.* Oxford.

Cameron, Averil, and Herrin, J., in conjunction with Alan Cameron, R. Cormack, and C. Roueché (eds.). 1984. *Constantinople in the Eighth Century. The* Parastaseis Suntomai Chronikai. *Introduction, Translation and Commentary* (Columbia Studies in the Classical Tradition 10). Leiden.

Canepa, M. P. 2009. *The Two Eyes of the Earth.* Berkeley.

Canepa, M. P. 2010. "Theorizing Cross-Cultural Interaction in the Ancient and Early Medieval Worlds," *Ars Orientalis* 38, 7–29.

Canepa, M. P. 2013. "Sasanian Rock Reliefs," in D. T. Potts (ed.), *The Oxford Handbook of Ancient Iran.* Oxford, 856–877.

Canepa, M. P. 2018. *The Iranian Expanse: Transforming Royal Identity through Architecture, Landscape, and the Built Environment, 550 BCE–642 CE.* Oakland.

Carcopino, J. 1928. "Chronologie et histoire littéraire. A propos du poème de Rutilius Namatianus," *RÉL* 6, 180–200; expanded and altered as "La date et le sens du voyage de Rutilius Namatianus," in *Rencontres de l'histoire et de la littérature romaines* (Paris, 1963), 233–270.

Carlà, F. 2009. *L'oro nella tarda antichità: aspetti economici e sociali.* Turin.

Cascón, A. 1996. "El humor en la *Historia Augusta.* Características literarias y función crítica," in G. Bonamente and M. Mayer (eds.), *Historiae Augustae Colloquium IV: Colloquium Barcinonense.* Bari, 148–163.

Castorina, E. 1967. *Claudius Rutilius Namatianus, De Reditu.* Florence.

Cavallin, S. 1945. "Saint Génès le notaire," *Eranos* 4, 150–176.

Chastagnol, A. 1960. *La préfecture urbaine à Rome sous le Bas-Empire.* Paris.

Chastagnol, A. 1962. *Les fastes de la préfecture de Rome au Bas-Empire.* Paris.

Chastagnol, A. 1976. "*Carinus effeminatus* (Car. 16.1–5)," in J. Straub (ed.), *Bonner Historia Augusta Colloquium 1972/1974.* Bonn, 84–90.

Chastagnol, A. 1994. *Histoire Auguste: Les empereurs romains des IIᵉ et IIIᵉ siècles.* Paris.

Chatterjee, P. 2017. "Viewing the Unknown in Eighth-century Constantinople," *Gesta* 56, 137–149.

Chausson, F. 1997. "*Severus*, XVII, 5–XIX, 4: une identification?," in G. Bonamente and K. Rosen (eds.), *Historiae Augustae Colloquium V: Colloquium Bonnense.* Bari, 97–113.

Chen, A. Hunnell. 2016. "Rival Powers, Rival Images: Diocletian's Palace at Split in Light of Sasanian Palace Design," in D. Slootjes and M. Peachin (eds.), *Rome and the Worlds beyond its Frontiers.* Leiden, 213–242.

REFERENCES 287

Chen, A. Hunnell. 2018. "Omitted Empresses: The (Non-)Role of Imperial Women in Tetrarchic Propaganda," *JLA* 11(1), 42–82.

Chin, C. M., and Schroeder, C. T. 2017. *Melania: Early Christianity through the Life of One Family*. Berkeley.

Choksy, J. K. 1989. "A Sasanian Monarch, his Queen, Crown Prince, and Deities: The Coinage of Wahram II," *American Journal of Numismatics* 1, 117–135.

Christol, M. 1998. "Auréolus et l'*Histoire Auguste*," in G. Bonamente, F. Heim, and J.-P. Callu (eds.), *Historiae Augustae Colloquium VI: Colloquium Argentoratense*. Bari, 115–135.

Christol, M. 2014. "Gallien, Claude et Aurélien," in C. Bertrand-Dagenbach, and F. Chausson (eds.), *Historiae Augustae Colloquium XII: Colloquium Nanceiense*. Bari, 159–183.

Christophilopoulou, A. 1966, "Οἱ ἔκτος τῆς Κωνσταντινουπόλεως βυζαντινοὶ δῆμοι," in Χαριστήριον εἰς A. K. Ὀρλάνδον. Athens, 11, 329–332.

Chrysos, E. 1976. "Some Aspects of Roman-Persian Legal Relations," *Kleronomia* 8, 1–60.

Cipolla, C. 1992. *Miasmas and Disease: Public Health and the Environment in the Pre-Industrial Age*. New Haven, CT.

Clancy, M. T. 1993. *From Memory to Written Records: England 1066–1307*. London.

Clark, E. A. 1984. *The Life of Melania the Younger: Introduction, Translation, and Commentary*. New York.

Clemente, G. 2013. "Introduction," in R. Lizzi Testa (ed.), *The Strange Death of Pagan Rome: Reflexions on a Historiographical Controversy*. Turnhout, 13–29.

Clemente, G. 2019. "The Power and the Doctrine from Gelasius to Vigile," in R. Lizzi Testa and G. Marconi (eds.), *The* Collectio Avellana *and Its Revivals*. Newcastle upon Tyne, 2–12.

Cohen, S. 1972. *Folk Devils and Moral Panics*. London.

Coleman, K., and Nelis-Clément, J. (eds.). 2012. *L'organisation des spectacles dans le monde romain* (EFH 58). Geneva.

Coleman-Norton, P. R. 1966. *Roman State and Christian Church: A Collection of Legal Documents to 535 A.D.* 3 vols. London.

Combes, I. A. H. 1998. *The Metaphor of Slavery in the Writings of the Early Church: From the New Testament to the Beginning of the Fifth Century*. Sheffield.

Comeau, M. 1932. "Sur la transmission des sermons de Saint Augustin," *RÉL* 10, 408–422.

Consolino, F. E. 2013. "Macrobius' *Saturnalia* and the *Carmen contra paganos*," in R. Lizzi Testa (ed.), *The Strange Death of Pagan Rome: Reflexions on a Historiographical Controversy*. Turnhout, 85–107.

Corsaro, F. 1981. *Studi rutiliani*. Bologna.

Courcelle, P. 1958. "Le colle et le clou de l'âme dans la tradition néo-platonicienne et chrétienne," *Revue Belge de Philologie et d'Histoire* 36, 72–95.

Cracco Ruggini, L. 1976. "Ambrogio di fronte alla compagine sociale del suo tempo," in G. Lazzati (ed.), *Ambrosius episcopus*. Vol. 1. Milan, 230–265.

Cracco Ruggini, L. 1977. "Apoteosi e politica senatoria nel IV s. d. C.: il dittico dei Symmachi al British Museum," *Rivista Storica Italiana* 89, 425–489.

Cracco Ruggini, L. 1995 [1961]. *Economia e società nell' 'Italia Annonaria': Rapporti fra agricoltura e commercio dal IV al VI secolo d. C.* Second ed. Bari.

Cracco Ruggini, L. 2010. "Archeologia e storia: i dittici tardoantichi," *Atti dell'Accademia Nazionale dei Lincei. Memorie. Classe di Scienze morali, storiche e filologiche* 9, 26 (3), 715–730.

Cracco Ruggini, L., and Lizzi Testa, R. Forthcoming. "Alan Cameron," in C. Ando and M. Formisano (eds.), *The New Late Antiquity*.

Cribiore, R. 1994. "A Homeric Writing Exercise and Reading Homer in School," *Tyche* 9, 1–8.

Cribiore, R. 1996. *Writing, Teachers, and Students in Graeco-Roman Egypt*. Atlanta.

Cribiore, R. 2001. *Gymnastics of the Mind. Greek Education in Hellenistic and Roman Egypt*. Princeton, NJ.

Cribiore, R. 2007. *The School of Libanius in Late Antique Antioch*. Princeton, NJ.

Crislip, A. T. 2005. *From Monastery to Hospital: Christian Monasticism and the Transformation of Health Care in Late Antiquity*. Ann Arbor, MI.

Cuq, E. 1903. "Les préfets du prétoire régionaux," in *Mélanges Boissier*. Paris, 147–155.

Daems, A. 2001. "The Iconography of Pre-Islamic Women in Iran," *Iranica Antiqua* 36, 1–150.

Dagron, G. 1974. *Naissance d'une capitale: Constantinople et ses institutions de 330 à 451*. Paris.

Dagron, G. 1984a. *Naissance d'une capitale: Constantinople et ses institutions de 330 à 451*. 2nd ed. Paris.

Dagron, G. 1984b. *Constantinople imaginaire: études sur le recueil des Patria*. Paris.

Dagron, G. 2011. *L'hippodrome de Constantinople: jeux, peuple et politique*. Paris.

Daryaee, T. 2009. *Sasanian Persia: The Rise and Fall of an Empire*. New York.

Davidson, I. J. 2001. *Ambrose. De Officiis*. Oxford.

Davis, R. 1989. *The Book of Pontiffs (Liber pontificalis): The Ancient Biographies of the First Ninety Roman Bishops to AD 715*. Liverpool.

Davison, J. A. 1956. "The Study of Homer in Graeco-Roman Egypt," in *Akten des VIII. Internationalen Kongresses für Papyrologie*. Vienna, 51–58.

De Carolis, S. (ed.). 2009. *Ars medica. I ferri del mestiere. La domus "del Chirurgo" di Rimini e la chirurgia nell'antica Roma*. Rimini.

Deferrari, R. J. 1922. "St. Augustine's Method of Composing and Delivering Sermons," *AJPh* 43, 97–123, 193–219.

Demacopoulos, G. E. 2013. *The Invention of Peter: Apostolic Discourse and Papal Authority in Late Antiquity*. Philadelphia.

REFERENCES 289

Demand, N. 1994. *Birth, Death, and Motherhood in Classical Greece*. Baltimore.

Demoen, K. 2012. "Flee from Love who Shoots with the Bow! The *Anthologia Palatina* and the Classical Epigrammatic Tradition in Byzantium," in J. Nelis (ed.), *Receptions of Antiquity*. Gent, 57–67.

Den Hengst, D. 1991. "The Author's Literary Culture," in G. Bonamente and N. Duval (eds.), *Historiae Augustae Colloquium I: Colloquium Parisinum*. Macerata, 161–169.

Den Hengst, D. 2002. "The Discussion of Authorship," in G. Bonamente and F. Paschoud (eds.), *Historiae Augustae Colloquium VIII: Colloquium Perusinum*. Bari, 187–195.

Den Hengst, D. 2007. "Die Kausalkonjunktionen *quod, quia,* und *quoniam* in der *Historia Augusta*," in G. Bonamente and H. Brandt (eds.), *Historiae Augustae Colloquium X: Colloquium Bambergense*. Bari, 165–173.

Derda, T., Markiewicz, T., and Wipszycka, E. (eds.). 2007. *Alexandria: Auditoria of Kom el-Dikka and Late Antique Education (Journal of Juristic Papyrology* Supplement 8). Warsaw.

De Rossi, G. B. 1886. "Commentatio de origine, historia, indicibus scrinii et bibliothecae Sedis Apostolicae," in H. Stevenson, *Codices Palatini Latini Bibliothecae Vaticanae* I. Rome. i–cxxxii.

De Rossi, G. B. (ed.). 1888. *Inscriptiones Christianae Urbis Romae* II. Rome.

De Salvo, L. 1995. "Simonie e malversazioni nell'organizzazione ecclesiastica IV–V secolo," in R. Soraci (ed.), *Corruzione, repressione e rivolta morale nella tarda antichità*. Catania, 367–392.

Dessau, H. 1889. "Über Zeit und Persönlichkeit der Scriptores Historiae Augustae," *Hermes* 24, 337–392.

Dessau, H. 1892. "Über die Scriptores Historiae Augustae," *Hermes* 27, 561–605.

Dessau, H. 1894. "Die Überlieferung der Scriptores Historiae Augustae," *Hermes* 29, 393–416.

De Waele, E. 1978. "Sur Le Bas-Relief Sassanide de Tang-e Qandil et La 'Bas-Relief au Couple' de Barm-i Dilak," *Revue des Archéologues et Historiens d'art de Louvain* 11, 9–32.

Díaz Lavado, J. M. 2007. "Homero y la escuela," in J. A. Fernández Delgado, F. Pordomingo and A. Stramaglia (eds), *Escuela y literatura en Grecia antigua*. Cassino, 207–224.

Dignas, B., and Winter, E. 2007. *Rome and Persia in Late Antiquity: Neighbours and Rivals*. Cambridge.

Dinkler, E. 1980. *Christus und Asklepios*. Heidelberg.

Doblhofer, E. 1970. "Drei spätantike Reiseschilderungen," in D. von Ableitinger and H. Gugle (eds.), *Festschrift Karl Vretska zum 70. Geburtstag überreicht von seinem Freunden und Schülern*. Heidelberg, 1–22.

Doblhofer, E. 1972. *Rutilius Claudius Namatianus: De reditu suo sive Iter Gallicum*, 2 vols. Heidelberg.

REFERENCES

Doblhofer, E. 1983. "Bellerophon und Kirke zwischen Heiden und Christen," in P. and W. Meid (eds.), *Festschrift Robert Muth*. Innsbruck, 73–87.

Dodgeon, M. H., and Lieu, S. N. C. 1991. *The Roman Eastern Frontier and the Persian Wars (A.D. 226–363): A Documentary History*. London.

Dressel, H. 1973. *Die römischen Medaillione des Münzkabinetts der staatlichen Museen zu Berlin*. 2 vols. Zurich.

Drijvers, J. W. 2009. "Rome and the Sasanid Empire: Confrontation and Coexistence," in P. Rousseau (ed.), *A Companion to Late Antiquity*. Chichester, 441–454.

DuBois, P. 2003. *Slaves and Other Objects*. Chicago.

Du Cange, C. 1710. *Caroli Du Fresne, domini Du Cange, Glossarium ad scriptores mediae et infimae latinitatis*. 3 vols. Frankfurt.

Duchesne, L. (ed.). (1886–1892, 1957) 1981. *Le "Liber pontificalis": Texte, introduction et commentaire*. 3 vols. Vol. 3 edited by C. Vogel. Paris.

Dufourcq, A. 1905. "Rutilius Namatianus contre Saint Augustin," *Revue d'histoire et de littérature religieuses* 10, 488–492.

Dunbabin, K. 2017. "Athletes, Acclamations and Imagery from the End of Antiquity," *JRA* 30, 151–174.

Durbec, Y., and Trajber, F. (eds.). 2017. *Traditions épiques et poésie épigrammatique*. Leuven.

Duval, Y. 1968. "Recherches sur la langue et la littérature latines: Bellérophon et les ascètes chrétiens: 'Melancholia' ou 'otium,'" *Caesarodunum* 3, 183–190.

Dyck, A. R. 1987. "The Glossographoi," *HSCPh* 91, 119–160.

Edelstein, E. J., and Edelstein, L. 1945. *Asclepius*. 2 vols. Baltimore.

Edwell, P. 2013. "Sasanian Interactions with Rome and Byzantium," in D. T. Potts (ed.), *The Oxford Handbook of Ancient Iran*. Oxford, 840–855.

Ekbom, M. 2013. *The* Sortes Vergilianae*: A Philological Study*. Uppsala.

Elsner, J. Forthcoming. "Introduction," in Alan Cameron, *Historical Studies in Late Roman Art and Archaeology*. Leuven.

Enmann, A. 1884. "Eine verlorene Geschichte der römischen Kaiser und das Buch *De viris illustribus urbis Romae*," *Philologus*, Supplementband 4, 335–501.

Erbse, H. 1953. "Homerscholien und hellenistische Glossare bei Apollonios Rhodios," *Hermes* 81, 163–196.

Estiot, S. 2012. "The Later Third Century," in W. Metcalf (ed.), *The Oxford Handbook of Greek and Roman Coinage*. Oxford, 548–550.

Fantuzzi, M. 2010. "Typologies of Variation on a Theme in Archaic and Classical Metrical Inscriptions," in M. Baumbach, A. Petrovic, and I. Petrovic (eds.), *Archaic and Classical Greek Epigram*. Cambridge, 289–310.

Feissel, D. 1999. "Le Roufinion de Pergame au 6e siècle d'après un sceau nouvellement publié," *Revue des Études Byzantines* 57, 263–269.

REFERENCES 291

Felten, J. 1913. *Nicolai progymnasmata (Rhetores Graeci* 11). Leipzig.

Ferngren, G. B., and Amundsen, D. W. 1996. "Medicine and Christianity in the Roman Empire: Compatibilities and Tensions," in W. Haase (ed.), *Aufstieg und Niedergang der Römischen Welt* 11, 37, 3. Berlin, 2957–2980.

Ferrari, M. 1973. "Spigolature bobbiesi," *Italia medioevale e umanistica* 16, 1–41.

Festy, M. 1998. "En éditant l'*Epitome de Caesaribus*," in G. Bonamente, F. Heim, and J.-P. Callu (eds.), *Historiae Augustae Colloquium VI: Colloquium Argentoratense*. Bari, 153–166.

Festy, M. 1999a. *Pseudo-Aurélius Victor: Abrégé des Césars*. Paris.

Festy, M. 1999b. "Aurélius Victor, source de l'*Histoire Auguste* et de Nicomaque Flavien," in F. Paschoud (ed.), *Historiae Augustae Colloquium VII: Colloquium Genevense*. Bari, 121–133.

Festy, M. 2007. "L'*Histoire Auguste* et les Nicomaques," in G. Bonamente and H. Brandt (eds.), *Historiae Augustae Colloquium X: Colloquium Bambergense*. Bari, 183–195.

Fielding, I. 2017. *Transformations of Ovid in Late Antiquity*. Cambridge.

Fink, R. O. 1971. *Roman Military Records on Papyrus*. Cleveland.

Fıratlı, N., and Rollas, A. N. 1964. "Les nouvelles trouvailles de Topkapi Saray," *Istanbul Arkeoloji Müzeleri yilligi: Annual of the Archaeological Museums of Istanbul* 11–12, 96–103, 199–206.

Fischer, G. 1986. "Rutilius and the Fifth Lepidus," *Museum Philologicum Londiniense* 7, 31–36.

Fo, A. 1992. *Rutilio Namaziano, Il Ritorno*. Turin.

Fo, A. 2004. "Crittografie per amici e nemici in Rutilio Namaziano: la questione del 'quinto Lepido' e il *cognomen* di Rufio Volusiano," *Paideia* 59, 169–195.

Fournet, J.-L. 1992. "Une éthopée de Caïn dans le Codex des Visions de la Fondation Bodmer," *ZPE* 92, 253–266.

Fournet, J.-L. 1995. "L'homérisme à l'époque protobyzantine: l'exemple de Dioscore d'Aphrodité," *Ktèma* 20, 301–315.

Fournet, J.-L. 1999. *Hellénisme dans l'Égypte du VIe siècle. La bibliothèque et l'œuvre de Dioscore d'Aphrodité* (Mémoires de l'Institut français d'archéologie orientale 115), 2 vols. Cairo.

Fournet, J.-L. 2003. "Théodore, un poète chrétien alexandrin oublié. L'hexamètre au service de la cause chrétienne," in D. Accorinti and P. Chuvin (eds.), *Des Géants à Dionysios. Mélanges offerts à F. Vian*. Alexandria, 521–539.

Fournet, J.-L. 2009. "Rapport des conférences en papyrologie grecque," in *Livret-Annuaire de l'École Pratique des Hautes Études, Section des sciences historiques et philologiques*, 140e année, 2007–2008. Paris. 117–120.

Fournet, J.-L. 2010. "Sur les premiers documents juridiques coptes," in A. Boud'hors and C. Louis (eds.), *Études coptes XI. Troisième journée d'études (Marseille, 7–9 juin 2007)*. Paris, 125–137.

Fournet, J.-L. 2012. "Homère dans les papyrus non littéraires: le Poète dans le contexte de ses lecteurs," in G. Bastianini and A. Casanova (eds.), *I papiri omerici*. Florence, 125–157.

Fournet, J.-L. 2019. "Dioscore et l'école," in G. Agosti and D. Bianconi (eds.), *Pratiche didattiche tra centro e periferia nel Mediterraneo tardoantico*. Spoleto, 193–216.

Fournet, J.-L. 2020. "L'éthopée entre culture profane et christianisme," in P. Chiron and B. Sans (eds.), *Les* progymnasmata *en pratique de l'Antiquité à nos jours—Practicing the* Progymnasmata, *from Ancient Times to Present Days*. Paris, 77–90.

Fowler, R. 2018. "Martin Litchfield West," *Biographical Memoirs of Fellows of the British Academy* 17, 89–120.

Franklin, C. V. 2013. "History and Rhetoric in the *Liber Pontificalis* of the Twelfth Century," *Journal of Medieval Latin* 23, 1–33.

Franklin, C. V. 2017. "Reading the Popes: The *Liber pontificalis* and its Editors," *Speculum* 92 (3), 607–629.

Franklin, C. V. 2018. "Theodor Mommsen, Louis Duchesne and the *Liber Pontificalis*: Philology between Objectivity and Engagement," in C. Kraus and M. Formisano (eds.), *Marginality, Canonicity, Passion*. Oxford, 99–140.

Franklin, C. V. 2019. "Frankish Redaction or Roman Exemplar? Revisions and Interpolations in the Text of the *Liber pontificalis*," in Y. Fox and E. Buchberger (eds.), *Inclusion and Exclusion in Mediterranean Christianities, 400–800*. Turnhout, 17–46.

Frye, D. 1993. "Is Cl. Postumus Dardanus the Lepidus of "De Reditu Suo" 1.307?" *Hermes* 12, 382–383.

Frye, R. N. 1972. *Gestures of Deference to Royalty in Ancient Iran*. Leiden.

Frye, R. N. 1983. "The Political History of Iran under the Sasanians," in E. Yarshater (ed.), *The Cambridge History of Iran*, Vol. 3. Cambridge, 116–180.

Fündling, J. 2006. *Kommentar zur Historia Augusta*, Vol 4: *Vita Hadriani*. Bonn.

Fynn-Paul, J. 2009. "Empire, Monotheism, and Slavery in the Greater Mediterranean Region from Antiquity through the Early Modern Era," *Past & Present* 205, 3–40.

Gamble, H. Y. 1995. *Books and Readers in the Early Church: A History of Early Christian Texts*. New Haven, CT.

Gantner, C. 2013. "The Lombard Recension of the *Liber pontificalis*," *Rivista di storia del cristianesimo* 10 (1), 67–114.

Gantner, C. 2014. *Freunde Roms und Völker der Finsternis: die päpstliche Konstruktion von Anderen im 8. und 9. Jahrhundert*. Vienna.

Ganz, P. F. (ed.). 1990. *Tironische Noten*. Wiesbaden.

Garland, L. 2011. "Public Lavatories, Mosquito Nets and Agathias' Cat: the Sixth-century Epigram in its Justinianic Context," in N. G. and L. Garland (eds.), *Basileia: Essays on Imperium and Culture in Honour of E. M. and M. J. Jeffreys*. Virginia, Queensland, 141–158.

REFERENCES 293

Garnsey, P. 1988. *Famine and Food Supply in the Graeco-Roman World: Responses to Risk and Crisis.* Cambridge.

Garnsey, P. 1996. *Ideas of Slavery from Aristotle to Augustine.* Cambridge.

Garucci, R. 1870. "Brass Medallion Representing the Persian Victory of Maximianus Galerius," *Numismatic Chronicle and Journal of the Royal Numismatic Society* 10, 112–118.

Garulli, V. 2017. "Les dérivés du nom d'Homère dans la tradition épigrammatique," in Y. Durbec and F. Trajber (eds.), *Traditions épiques et poésie épigrammatique.* Leuven, 141–156.

Garzya, A. 1997. "Science et conscience dans la pratique médicale de l'antiquité tardive et byzantine," *EFH* 43, 337–359.

Gascou, J. 1976. "Les institutions de l'hippodrome en Égypte byzantine," *Bulletin de l'Institut français d'archéologie orientale* 76, 185–212.

Gaskell, R. 2004. "Printing House and Engraving Shop: A Mysterious Collaboration," *The Book Collector* 53, 213–251.

Gehn, U. 2012. "LSA-2775," in http://laststatues.classics.ox.ac.uk.

Gentili, B., and Prato, C. (eds.). 1988. *Poetarum elegiacorum testimonia et fragmenta, Pars prior.* 2nd ed. Leipzig.

Ghirshman, R. 1962. *Iran: Parthes et Sassanides.* Paris.

Giardina, A. 1988. "Carità eversiva: le donazioni di Melania la Giovane e gli equilibri della società tardoromana," *Studi storici* 29, 127–142.

Giardina, A., Cecconi, G. A., and Tantillo, I. (eds.). 2016. *Flavio, Magno Aurelio Cassiodoro Senatore, Varie* IV. Rome.

Gibson, C. A. (ed. and trans.). 2008. *Libanius's* Progymnasmata*: Model Exercises in Greek Prose Composition and Rhetoric.* Atlanta.

Gilliam, J. F. 1980. "Rostovtzeff's Obituary of Enmann," in Straub 1980, 120–133.

Giorgi, I. 1897. "Appunti intorno ad alcuni manoscritti del *Liber pontificalis*," *Archivio della Società Romana di storia patria* 20, 247–312.

Giovannini, A. (ed.). 1991. *Nourrir la plèbe.* Geneva.

Girone, M. 1998. Ἰάματα: *guarigioni miracolose di Asclepio in testi epigrafici.* Bari.

Glancy, J. A. 2002. *Slavery in Early Christianity.* Oxford.

Gnecchi, F. 1912. *I medaglioni romani.* 3 vols. Milan.

Göbl, R. 1952. "Sasanidische Münzstudien II: Römische und sasanidische Büstengruppen," *Mitteilungen der österreichischen Numismatischen Gesellschaft* 7/10, 133–135.

Göbl, R. 1971. *Sasanian Numismatics.* Brunswick.

Goodall, B. 1979. *The Homilies of St. John Chrysostom on the Letters of St. Paul to Titus and Philemo.* Berkeley.

Gorce, D. (ed.). 1962. *Vie de Sainte Mélanie* (SC 90). Paris.

294 REFERENCES

Gourevitch, D. 1984. *Le triangle hippocratique dans le monde gréco-romain: le malade, sa maladie et son médecin*. Rome.

Gourevitch, D. 2011. *Pour une archéologie de la médecine romaine*. Paris.

Gray, C. (ed.). 2015. *Jerome, Vita Malchi: Introduction, Text, Translation, and Commentary*. Oxford.

Grayson, R. 1980. *Scolies ariennes sur le Concile d'Aquilée*. Paris.

Gregory, T. E. 1986. "The Survival of Paganism in Christian Greece: A Critical Essay," *AJPh* 107, 229–242.

Gruenbart, M. 2005. *Formen der Anrede im byzantinischen Brief von 6. bis zum 12. Jahrhundert*. Vienna.

Gullo, A. Forthcoming a. "Nonnian Poets (?): The Case of Julian the Egyptian," in B. Verhelst (ed.), *Nonnus in Context IV (Ghent 19–21 April 2018)*. Leuven.

Gullo, A. Forthcoming b. *Antologia Palatina. Epigrammi funerari (Libro VII). Introduzione e commento*. Pisa.

Gurd, S. A. 2012. *Work in Progress: Literary Revision as Social Performance in Ancient Rome*. Oxford.

Gusso, M. 1992. "Sull' Imperatore Glycerio (473–474 d.C)," *Studia et Documenta Historiae et Iuris* 58, 168–193.

Guttilla, G. 1994–5. "Presenze di Ausonio e di Paolino da Nola nel *De Reditu Suo* di Rutilio Namatiano," *Annali del Liceo Classico "G. Garibaldi" di Palermo* 31–32, 161–196.

Gutzwiller, K. 2017. "Homeric Allusions in Meleager," in Y. Durbec and F. Trajber (eds.), *Traditions épiques et poésie épigrammatique*. Leuven, 193–204.

Gyselen, R. 2010. "Romans and Sasanians in the Third Century: Propaganda Warfare and Ambiguous Imagery," in H. Börm and J. Wiesehöfer (eds.), *Commutatio et Contentio: Studies in the Late Roman, Sasanian, and Early Islamic Near East in Memory of Zeev Rubin*. Düsseldorf, 71–87.

Haenel, G. (ed.) 1844. *Novellae Constitutiones imperatorum Theodosii II., Valentiniani III., Maximi, Maioriani, Severi, Anthemii*. Bonn.

Haenel, G. (ed.). 1857. *Corpus Legum ab Imperatoribus Romanis ante Iustinianum latarum quae extra Constitutionum Codices supersunt*. Leipzig.

Haerinck, E., and Overlaet, B. 2009. "The Sasanian Rock Relief of Bahram II at Guyum Fars, Iran." *Iranica Antiqua* 44, 531–538.

Haidacher, S. 1907. "Drei unedierte Chrysostomus-Texte einer Baseler Handschrift," *Zeitschrift für katholische Theologie* 31 (1), 141–171.

Haldon, J. 2018. "Euchaïta: from Late Roman and Byzantine Town to Ottoman Village," in J. Haldon, H. Elton, and J. Newhard (eds.), *Archaeology and Urban Settlement in Late Roman and Byzantine Anatolia: Euchaïta—Avkat—Beyözü and its Environment*. Cambridge, 210–254.

Harder, A. 2007. "Epigram and the Heritage of Epic," in P. Bing and J. S. Bruss (eds.), *Brill's Companion to Hellenistic Epigram*. Leiden, 409–428.

REFERENCES 295

Harder, A. 2017. "Big Heroes in a Small Format," in Y. Durbec and F. Trajber (eds.), *Traditions épiques et poésie épigrammatique*. Leuven, 87–98.

Harig, G. 1971. "Zum Problem "Krankenhaus" in der Antike," *Klio* 53, 179–195.

Harl, K. 1996. *Coinage in the Roman Economy, 300 BC to AD 700*. Baltimore.

Harper, K. 2011. *Slavery in the Late Roman World, AD 275–425*. Cambridge.

Harper, P. O. 1974. "Sasanian Medallion Bowls with Human Busts," in D. Kouymijan (ed.), *Near Eastern Numismatics, Iconography, Epigraphy and History: Studies in Honor of George C. Miles*. Beirut, 61–80.

Harper, P. O. 1983. "Sasanian Silver," in E. Yarshater (ed.), *The Cambridge History of Iran* III. Cambridge, 1113–1129.

Harper, P. O. 1988. "Sasanian Silver: Internal Developments and Foreign Influences," in *Argenterie Romaine et Byzantine: Actes de La Table Ronde, Paris 11–13 Oct. 1983*. Paris, 331–345.

Harper, P. O., and Meyers, P. 1981. *Silver Vessels of the Sasanian Period*. New York.

Harrill, J. A. 2006. *Slaves in the New Testament: Literary, Social, and Moral Dimensions*. Minneapolis.

Harris, W. V. 2016a. "Religion on the Battlefield. From the *Saxa Rubra* to the *Frigidus*," in V. Gasparini (ed.), *Miscellanea di studi storico-religiosi in onore di Filippo Coarelli nel suo 80° anniversario*. Stuttgart, 437–450.

Harris, W. V. 2016b. "Popular Medicine in the Classical World," in W. V. Harris (ed.), *Popular Medicine in Graeco-Roman Antiquity: Explorations* (Columbia Studies in the Classical Tradition 42). Leiden, 1–64.

Harris, W. V. (ed.). 2016c. *Popular Medicine in Graeco-Roman Antiquity: Explorations* (Columbia Studies in the Classical Tradition 42). Leiden.

Harris, W. V. 2016d. *Roman Power: A Thousand Years of Empire*. Cambridge.

Harris, W. V. Forthcoming. *Desperate Remedies: A Social History of Ancient Healthcare*.

Hartke, W. 1940. *Geschichte und Politik im spätantiken Rome*. Leipzig.

Hartke, W. 1951. *Römische Kinderkaiser*. Berlin.

Harvey, P. B. 2005. "Jerome Dedicates his 'Vita Hilarionis,'" *Vigiliae Christianae* 59, 286–297.

Hatlie, P. 2006. "Monks and Circus Factions in Early Byzantine Political Life," in M. Kaplan (ed.), *Monastères, images, pouvoirs et société à Byzance*. Paris, 13–25.

Heath, M. 2004. *Menander, a Rhetor in Context*. Oxford.

Heath, M. 2008. "Aristotle on Natural Slavery," *Phronesis* 53, 243–270.

Heather, P., and Moncur, D. (eds.). 2001. *Politics, Philosophy, and Empire: Select Orations of Themistius*. Liverpool.

Hedrick, C. W. 2000. *History and Silence: Purge and Rehabilitation of Memory in Late Antiquity*. Austin, TX.

Heitsch, E. 1963. *Die griechischen Dichterfragmente der römischen Kaiserzeit* (Abhandlungen der Akademie der Wissenschaften in Göttingen, Phil.-hist. Klasse, Dritte Folge, Nr. 49), I. Second ed. Göttingen.

Heitsch, E. 1964. *Die griechischen Dichterfragmente der römischen Kaiserzeit* (Abhandlungen der Akademie der Wissenschaften in Göttingen, Phil.-hist. Klasse, Dritte Folge, Nr. 58), II. Göttingen.

Hendry, M. 1996–97. "Juvenalia," *Museum Criticum* 30–31, 253–266.

Herbers, K. 2009. "Agir et écrir: les actes des papes du IXᵉ siècle et le *Liber pontificalis*," in F. Bougard and M. Sot (eds.), *Liber, Gesta, histoire. Ecrire l'histoire des évêques et des papes, de l'Antiquité au XXIᵉ siècle*. Turnhout, 109–126.

Herrin, J. 2017. "Tantalus Ever in Tears: The Greek Anthology as a Source of Emotions in Late Antiquity," in M. Alexiou (ed.), *Greek Laughter and Tears: Antiquity and After*. Edinburgh, 75–86.

Herrmann, G. 1970. "The Sculpture of Bahram II," *Journal of the Royal Asiatic Society of Great Britain and Ireland* 2, 165–171.

Herrmann, G. 2000. "The Rock Reliefs of Sasanian Iran," in J. Curtis (ed.), *Mesopotamia and Iran in the Parthian and Sasanian Periods. Rejection and Revival c. 238 BC–AD 642*. London, 35–45.

Hezser, C. 2005. *Jewish Slavery in Antiquity*. Oxford.

Hill, E. 1990. *The Works of Saint Augustine: A Translation for the 21st Century*. Brooklyn.

Hillgruber, M. 2000. "Homer im Dienste des Mimus. Zur künstlerischen Eigenart der Homeristen," *ZPE* 132, 63–72.

Hillgruber, M. 2001. "Corrigendum und Addendum zu ZPE 132 (2000), 63–72," *ZPE* 134, 42.

Hinz, W. 1969. *Altiranische Funde und Forschungen*. Berlin.

Hirschfeld, O. 1913. *Kleine Schriften*. Berlin.

Hirt Raj, M. 2006. *Médecins et malades de l'Égypte romaine*. Leiden.

Hobsbawm, E. J. 1973. *Primitive Rebels: Studies in Archaic Forms of Social Movement in the Nineteenth and Twentieth Centuries*. Manchester.

Hock, R. 2001. "Homer in Greco-Roman Education," in D. MacDonald (ed.), *Mimesis and Intertextuality in Antiquity and Christianity*. Harrisburg, PA, 56–77.

Hohl, E. 1911. "Vopiscus und die Biographie des Kaisers Tacitus," *Klio* 11, 178–229, 294–324.

Hohl, E. 1912. "Vopiscus und Pollio," *Klio* 12, 474–482.

Hohl, E. 1914. "Das Problem der Historia Augusta," *Neue Jahrbücher für das klassische Altertum* 23, 698–712.

Hohl, E. 1916. "Zur Historia Augusta," *RhM* 68, 316–319.

Hohl, E. 1920. "Über den Ursprung der Historia Augusta," *Hermes* 55, 296–310.

Holste [Holstenius], L., and Boissonade, J. F. (1817). *Lucæ Holstenii Epistolæ ad diversos, quas ex editis et ineditis codicibus collegit atque illustravit Jo. Franc. Boissonade. Accedit editoris commentatio in inscriptionem græcam*. Paris.

Honoré, T. 1998. "L'*Histoire Auguste* à la lumière des constitutions impériales," in G. Bonamente, F. Heim, and J.-P. Callu (eds.), *Historiae Augustae Colloquium VI: Colloquium Argentoratense*. Bari, 191–212.

REFERENCES

Hopkinson, N. (ed.). 1994. *Studies in the Dionysiaca of Nonnus*. Cambridge.

Horden, P. 2004–2005. "The Earliest Hospitals in Byzantium, Western Europe, and Islam," *Journal of Interdisciplinary History* 35 (3), 361–389.

Houghton, H. A. G. 2008. *Augustine's Text of John; Patristic Citations and Latin Gospel Manuscripts*. Oxford.

Huebner, S. 2009. "Currencies of Power: The Venality of Offices in the Later Roman Empire," in A. Cain and N. Lenski (eds.), *The Power of Religion in Late Antiquity*. Burlington, VT, 167–180.

Huff, D. 1986. "Archaeology IV: Sasanian," in *Encyclopaedia Iranica* II. London, 302–308.

Humbach, H., and Skjærvø, P.O. 1983. *The Sassanian Inscription of Paikuli*. Wiesbaden.

Hunter, R. L. 2005. "Speaking in *Glossai*: Dialect Choice and Cultural Politics in Hellenistic Poetry," in W. M. Bloomer (ed.), *The Contest of Language. Before and Beyond Nationalism*. Notre Dame, IN, 187–206.

Hunter, R. L. 2018. *The Measure of Homer: The Ancient Reception of the "Iliad" and the "Odyssey"*. Cambridge.

Husson, G. 1993. "Les homéristes," *Journal of Juristic Papyrology* 23, 93–99.

Huyse, P. 1999. *Die Dreisprachige Inschrift Šabuhrs I. an Der Ka'ba-i Zardušt*. Corpus Inscriptionum Iranicarum 3. London.

Ibrahim, M. H. 1976–1977. "The Study of Homer in Graeco-Roman Education," *Athena* 76, 187–195.

Israelowich, I. 2016. "Medical Care in the Roman Army during the High Empire," in W. V. Harris (ed.), *Popular Medicine in Graeco-Roman Antiquity: Explorations* (Columbia Studies in the Classical Tradition 42). Leiden, 215–230.

James, L. 1996. "'Pray not to fall into temptation and be your own guard': Pagan Statues in Christian Constantinople," *Gesta* 35, 12–20.

James, L. (ed.), with Vassis, I. 2012. *Constantine of Rhodes, On Constantinople and the Church of the Holy Apostles*. Farnham.

Jarcho, V. 1999. "P.Oxy. 3537: A True Ethopoea?," *Eikasmos* 10, 185–199.

Jarry, J. 1985. "Nouveaux documents grecs et latins de Syrie du Nord et de Palmyrène," *ZPE* 60, 109–115.

Jenal, G. 1995. *Italia ascetica atque monastica. Das Asketen- und Mönchtum in Italien von den Anfängen bis zur Zeit der Langobarden (c. 150/250–604)*. 2 vols. Stuttgart.

Johne, K.-P. 1976. *Kaiserbiographie und Senatsaristokratie. Untersuchungen zur Datierung und sozialen Herkunft der Historia Augusta*. Berlin.

Jones, A. H. M., Martindale, J. R., and Morris, J. (eds.). 1971. *The Prosopography of the Later Roman Empire* I. *A.D. 260–395*. Cambridge.

Jones, B. C. 2016. "Scribes Avoiding Imperfections in their Writing Materials," *Archiv für Papyrusforschung und verwandte Gebiete* 62, 371–383.

Jones, C. P. 2007. "Three New Letters of the Emperor Hadrian," *ZPE* 161, 145–156.

Kampen, N. B. 1991. "Between Public and Private: Women as Historical Subjects in Roman Art," in S. B. Pomeroy (ed.). *Women's History and Ancient History*. Chapel Hill, 218–248.

Kaniecka, M. S. (ed. and trans.). 1928. *Vita Sancti Ambrosii, Mediolanensis Episcopi, a Paulino eius notario ad beatum Augustinum conscripta*. Washington, D.C.

Kelly, C. 2004. *Ruling the Later Roman Empire*. Oxford.

Kelly, G. 2008. *Ammianus Marcellinus: The Allusive Historian*. Cambridge.

Kelly, J. N. D. 1995. *Golden Mouth: The Story of John Chrysostom, Ascetic, Preacher, Bishop*. London.

Kent, J. P. C. 1967. "FEL. TEMP. REPARATIO," *Numismatic Chronicle*, 7th series, 7, 83–90.

Ker, J. 2004. "Nocturnal Writers in Imperial Rome: The Culture of *lucubrate*," *CPh* 99, 209–242.

Kinch, K.-F. 1890. *L'arc de Triomphe de Salonique*. Paris.

Kinney, D. 2008. "First-Generation Diptychs in the Discourse of Visual Culture," in G. Bühl, A. Cutler, and A. Effenberger (eds.), *Spätantike und byzantinische Elfenbeinbildwerke im Diskurs*. Wiesbaden, 149–166.

Kinney, D., and Cutler, A. 1994. "A Late Antique Ivory Plaque and Modern Response," *AJA* 98 (3), 457–472.

Kislinger, E. 1984. "Kaiser Julian und die (christliche) Xenodocheia," in W. Hörandner et al. (eds.), *ΒΥΖΑΝΤΙΟΣ. Festschrift für Herbert Hunger*. Vienna, 171–184.

Klein, R. 1988. *Die Sklaverei in der Sicht der Bischöfe Ambrosius und Augustinus*. Stuttgart.

Kleiner, D. E. E. 1992. *Roman Sculpture*. New Haven, CT.

Klingshirn, W. 1985. "Charity and Power: Caesarius of Arles and the Ransoming of Captives in Sub-Roman Gaul," *JRS* 75, 183–203.

Knudsen, R. A., 2014. *Homeric Speech and the Origins of Rhetoric*. Baltimore.

Kolb, F. 1972. *Literarische Beziehungen zwischen Cassius Dio, Herodian, und der Historia Augusta*. Bonn.

Kolb, F. 1998. "Andreas Alföldi und die Historia-Augusta-Forschung," in G. Bonamente, F. Heim, and J.-P. Callu (eds.), *Historiae Augustae Colloquium VI: Colloquium Argentoratense*. Bari, 213–222.

Kulikowski, M. 2007. *Rome's Gothic Wars from the Third Century to Alaric*. Cambridge.

Kulikowski, M. 2017a. "Urban Prefects in Bronze," *JLA* 10, 3–41.

Kulikowski, M. 2017b. "Malalas in the Archives," in L. Carrara, M. Meier, and C. Radtki (eds.), *Die Weltchronik des Johannes Malalas—Quellenfragen*. Stuttgart, 203–215.

Kulikowski, M. Forthcoming. "Andreas Alföldi and Late Antiquity," in C. Ando and M. Formisano (eds.), *The New Late Antiquity*.

Künzl, E. 2005. "Aesculapius im Valetudinarium," *Archäologisches Korrispondenzblatt* 35, 55–64.

Labriolle, P. 1928. "Rutilius Claudius Namatianus et les moines," *RÉL* 6, 30–41.

REFERENCES

299

Łajtar, A., and Młynarczyk, J. 2017. "A Faction Acclamation Incised on a Pithos Found Near the North-West Church at Hippos (Sussita)," *Études et Travaux* 30, 289–302.

Lambot, D. C. 1969. "Les sermons de Saint Augustin pour les fêtes de martyrs," *Revue Bénédictine* 79, 82–97.

Lana, I. 1961. *Rutilio Namaziano*. Turin.

Lancel, S. (ed.). 1972. *Actes de la conférence de Carthage en 411*. Vol. 1. Paris.

Lancel, S. (ed.). 1975. *Actes de la conférence de Carthage en 411*. Vols. 2 and 3. Paris.

Landskron, A. 2005. *Parther und Sasaniden: das Bild der Orientalen in der Römischen Kaiserzeit*. Vienna.

Lapidge, M. 2017. *The Roman Martyrs: Introduction, Translations and Commentary.* Oxford.

Laubscher, H. P. 1975. *Der Reliefschmuck des Galeriusbogens in Thessaloniki*. Berlin.

Laurence, P. 2002. *Gérontius: La vie latine de sainte Mélanie. Edition critique, traduction et commentaire*. Jerusalem.

Lauritzen, D. (ed.). 2015. *Jean de Gaza, Description du tableau cosmique*. Paris.

Lauxtermann, M. 2003. *Byzantine Poetry from Pisides to Geometres*. Vienna.

Lauxtermann, M. 2007. "The Anthology of Cephalas," in M. Hinterberger and E. Schiffer (eds.), *Byzantinische Sprachkunst. Studien zur byzantinischen Literatur gewidmet Wolfram Hörandner zum 65. Geburtstag*, Byzantinisches Archiv 20, 194–208.

Leclerc, P., Martín Morales, E., and de Vogüé, A. (eds.). 2007. *Jérôme: Trois vies de moines (Paul, Malchus, Hilarion)*. Paris.

Lehmann, P. 1965 [1909]. "Anhang: Die lateinischen Handschriften in alter Capitalis und in Uncialis auf Grund von L. Traubes Aufzeichnungen," in L. Traube, *Vorlesungen und Abhandlungen*, Vol. 1. Munich, 159–261.

Lenski, N. 2011. "Captivity and Romano-Barbarian Interchange," in R. W. Mathisen and D. Shanzer (eds.), *Romans, Barbarians and the Transformation of the Roman World: Cultural Interaction and the Creation of Identity in Late Antiquity*. Farnham, 185–198.

Lenski, N. 2014. "Captivity among the Barbarians and its Impact on the Fate of the Roman Empire," in M. Maas (ed.), *The Cambridge Companion to the Age of Attila*. New York, 230–246.

Lenski, N. 2016. "Imperial Legislation and the Donatist Controversy: From Constantine to Honorius," in R. Miles (ed.), *The Donatist Schism: Controversy and Contexts*. Liverpool, 166–219.

Lenski, N. 2017. "Peasant and Slave in Late Antique North Africa, c. 100–600 CE," in R. Lizzi Testa (ed.), *Late Antiquity in Contemporary Perspective*. Cambridge, 113–155.

Lenski, N. 2018. "Framing the Question: What Is a Slave Society?," in N. Lenski and C. M. Cameron (eds.), *What Is a Slave Society? The Practice of Slavery in Global Perspective*. Cambridge, 15–57.

Lenski, N. 2019. "Searching for Slave Teachers in Late Antiquity," in C. Sogno (ed.), Ποιμένι λαῶν: *Studies in Honor of Robert J. Penella (Revue des Études Tardo-antiques, Supplément 7)*. Wetteren, 127–191.

Leonardi, C. 1967. "Anastasio Bibliotecario e l'ottavo concilio ecumenico," *Studi medievali*, 3rd series, 8, 59–172.

Leven, K.-H. 1993. "Miasma und Metadosis—antike Vorstellungen von Ansteckung," *Medizin, Gesellschaft und Geschichte* 11, 44–73.

Levison, W. 1911. "Die Papstgeschichte des Pseudo-Liutprand und der Codex Farnesianus des Liber Pontificalis," *Neues Archiv* 36, 415–438.

Levit-Tawil, D. 1993. "Re-Dating the Sasanian Reliefs at Tang-e Qandil and Barm-e Dilak," *Iranica Antiqua* 28, 141–168.

Lewis, C. T., and Short, C. 1969 [1879]. *A Latin Dictionary*. Oxford.

Lewis, D. 2018. *Greek Slave Systems in Their Eastern Mediterranean Context, c. 800–146 BC*. Cambridge.

Liebeschuetz, J. H. W. G. 1972. *Antioch: City and Administration in the Later Roman Empire*. Oxford.

Liebeschuetz, J. H. W. G. 2005. *Ambrose of Milan: Political Letters and Speeches*. Liverpool.

Liebs, D. 1980. "Alexander Severus und das Strafrecht," in J. Straub (ed.), *Bonner Historia Augusta Colloquium 1977/1978*. Bonn, 115–147.

Liebs, D. 1983. "Strafrechtliches in der Tacitusvita," in J. Straub (ed.), *Bonner Historia Augusta Colloquium 1979/1981*. Bonn, 157–171.

Lippold, A. 1991. *Kommentar zur Historia Augusta*, Vol. 1: *Maximini Duo*. Bonn.

Lippold, A. 1999. "Geschichte und Gegenwart: Deutung der römischen Geschichte und die Darstellung der neuesten Zeit bei Vopiscus," in F. Paschoud (ed.), *Historiae Augustae Colloquium VII: Colloquium Genevense*. Bari, 153–177.

Lippold, A. 2002. "*Claudius, Constantius, Constantinus*: die *V. Claudii* der *HA*. Ein Beitrag zur Legitimierung der Herrschaft Konstantins aus stadtrömischer Sicht," in G. Bonamente and F. Paschoud (eds.), *Historiae Augustae Colloquium VIII: Colloquium Perusinum*. Bari, 309–331.

Livrea, E. 1972. "Una 'tecnica allusiva' apolloniana alla luce dell'esegesi omerica alessandrina," *Studi italiani di filologia classica* n.s. 44, 231–243.

Livrea, E. 2001. "Una *crux* dioscorea," *ZPE* 137, 22–23.

Lizzi, R. 1989. *Vescovi e strutture ecclesiastiche nella città tardoantica (l'Italia annonaria nel IV–V secolo d.C.)*. Como.

Lizzi Testa, R. 2004. *Senatori, popolo, papi. Il governo di Roma al tempo dei Valentiniani*. Bari.

Lizzi Testa, R. 2007. "Christian Emperor, Vestal Virgins, and Priestly Colleges: Reconsidering the End of Roman Paganism," *AT* 15, 251–262.

Lizzi Testa, R. 2009. "Alle origini della tradizione pagana su Costantino e il senato romano (Amm. 21, 10, 8 e Zos. 2, 32, 1)," in P. Rousseau and M. Papoutsakis (eds.), *Transformations of Late Antiquity: Essays for Peter Brown*. Farnham, 85–128.

REFERENCES 301

Lizzi Testa, R. 2012a. "Il sacco di Roma e l'aristocrazia romana, tra crisi politica e turbamento religioso," in A. Di Berardino, G. Pilara, and L. Spera (eds.), *Roma e il Sacco del 410: realtà, interpretazione, mito*. Rome, 81–112.

Lizzi Testa, R. 2012b. "La vendita delle cariche ecclesiastiche: interdizioni canoniche e provvedimenti legislative dal IV al VI secolo," *Cristianesimo nella storia* 33, 449–474.

Lizzi Testa, R. (ed.). 2013a. *The Strange Death of Pagan Rome: Reflexions on a Historiographical Controversy*. Turnhout.

Lizzi Testa, R. 2013b. "Costantino e il Senato romano," in *Costantino I. Enciclopedia Costantiniana sulla figura e l'immagine dell'imperatore del cosiddetto Editto di Milano 313–2013*, Vol. 1. Rome, 351–367.

Lizzi Testa, R. 2015. "The Famous 'Altar of Victory Controversy' in Rome: The Impact of Christianity at the End of the Fourth Century," in J. Wienand (ed.), *Contested Monarchy: Integrating the Roman Empire in the Fourth Century AD*. Oxford, 405–419.

Lizzi Testa, R. 2019. "L'autorità del concilio di Serdica in Occidente: testimonianze ambrosiane (epp. 30, 2–3; 72, 10)," *Cristianesimo nella storia* 40, 35–58.

Lizzi Testa, R. Forthcoming. "Gaudentius of Brixia," in *Brill Encyclopedia of Early Christianity*.

Lizzi Testa, R., and Marconi, G. (eds.). 2019. *The* Collectio Avellana *and Its Revivals*. Newcastle upon Tyne.

López, A. G. 2013. *Shenoute of Atripe and the Uses of Poverty: Rural Patronage, Religious Conflict and Monasticism in Late Antique Egypt*. Berkeley.

Lucchesi, E. 1977. *L'usage de Philon dans l'œuvre exégétique de Saint Ambroise: une 'Quellenforschung' relative aux commentaires d'Ambroise sur La Genèse*. Leiden.

Lukonin, V. G. 1969. *Kul'tura Sasanidskogo Irana. Iran v III–V vv*. Moscow.

Luschey, H. 1986. "Ardašir II. Rock Reliefs," in *Encyclopaedia Iranica* II. London, 377–380.

Maas, P. 1912. "Metrische Akklamationen der Byzantiner," *BZ* 21, 28–51.

Maas, P. 1958. *Textual Criticism*. Oxford.

MacCoull, L. S. B. 1988. *Dioscorus of Aphrodito: His Work and his World*. Berkeley.

Madec, G. 1974. *Saint Ambroise et la philosophie*. Paris.

Magdalino, P. 1993. *The Empire of Manuel I Komnenos, 1143–1180*. New York.

Magdalino, P. 2013. "Generic Subversion? The Political Ideology of Urban Myth and Apocalyptic Prophecy," in D. Angelov and M. Saxby (eds.), *Power and Subversion in Byzantium*. Farnham, 207–220.

Magnelli, E. 2004. "App. Anth. II 400 C: Oppiano come Erinna?," *Prometheus* 30, 269–274.

Malek, H. M., and Curtis, V. S. 1998. "History and Coinage of the Sasanian Queen Bōrān (AD 629–631)," *Numismatic Chronicle* 158, 113–129.

Mallan, C., and Davenport, C. 2015. "Dexippus and the Gothic Invasions: Interpreting the New Vienna Fragment (*Codex Vindobonensis Hist. gr.* 73, ff. 192v–193r)," *JRS* 105, 203–226.

Maltomini, F. 2008. *Tradizione Antologica dell'epigramma greco: le sillogi minori di età bizantina e umanistica*. Rome.

Maltomini, F. 2011. "Selezione e organizzazione della poesia epigrammatica fra IX e X secolo—la perduta antologia di Constantino Cefala e l'*Antologia Palatina*," in P. Van Deun and C. Macé (eds.), *Encyclopedic Trends in Byzantium?* Leuven, 109–124.

Manojlović, G. 1936. "Le peuple de Constantinople, de 400 à 800 après J.-C.," *Byzantion* 11, 617–716.

Mansi, G. D. (ed.). 1759–1798. *Sacrorum Conciliorum Nova et Amplissima Collectio*. Florence.

Marcone, A. 2008–2009. "L'ultima aristocrazia pagana di Roma e le ragioni della politica," *Incontri triestini di filologia classica* 8, 99–111.

Marcone, A., and Andorlini, I. 2006. "Salute, malattia e "prassi ospedaliera" nell' Egitto tardoantico," in R. Marino, C. Molè and A. Pinzone (eds.), *Ammalato poveri e poveri ammalati*. Catania, 15–35.

Marriot, I. 1979. "The Authorship of the *Historia Augusta*: Two Computer Studies," *JRS* 69, 65–77.

Marshall, P. K. 1983. "*Scriptores Historiae Augustae*," in L.D. Reynolds (ed.), *Texts and Transmissions*. Oxford, 354–356.

Martin, G. 2017. "Die Struktur von Dexipps *Skythika* und die *Historia Augusta*," in B. Bleckmann and H. Brandt (eds.), *Historiae Augustae Colloquium XIII: Colloquium Dusseldorpiense*. Bari, 97–114.

Martin, G., and Grusková, J. 2014a. "'Scythica Vindobonensia' by Dexippus (?): New Fragments on Decius' Gothic Wars," *GRBS* 54, 728–754.

Martin, G., and Grusková, J. 2014b. "'Dexippus Vindobonensis (?)': Ein neues Handschriftenfragment zum sog. Herulereinfall der Jahre 267/268," *Wiener Studien* 127, 101–120.

Martin, G., and Grusková, J. 2014c. "Ein neues Textstück aus den 'Scythica Vindobonensia' zu den Ereignissen nach der Eroberung von Philippopolis," *Tyche* 29, 29–43.

Masia-Radford, K. 2013. "Luxury Silver Vessels of the Sasanian Period," in D. T. Potts (ed.), *The Oxford Handbook of Ancient Iran*. Oxford, 920–994.

Maspero, J. 1916. *Papyrus grecs d'époque byzantine* (Catalogue général des antiquités du Musée du Caire, vol. 3). Cairo.

Matthews, J. 1975. *Western Aristocracies and Imperial Court, A.D. 364–425*. Oxford.

Mattingly, H. 1933. "FEL. TEMP. REPARATIO," *Numismatic Chronicle*, 5th series, 13, 182–202.

Mazzarino, S. 1989. *Storia sociale del vescovo Ambrogio*. Rome.

REFERENCES 303

McKitterick, R., Osborne, J., Richardson, C. M., and Story, J. (eds.). 2013. *Old Saint Peter's, Rome*. Cambridge.

McLynn, N. B. 1994. *Ambrose of Milan: Church and Court in a Christian Capital*. Berkeley.

McLynn, N. 2016. "The Conference of Carthage Reconsidered," in R. Miles (ed.), *The Donatist Schism: Controversy and Contexts*. Liverpool, 220–248.

Meiggs, R. 1973. *Roman Ostia*. 2nd ed. Oxford.

Meissner, B. 1996. "Computergestützte Untersuchungen zur stilischen Einheitlichkeit der *Historia Augusta*," in G. Bonamente and M. Mayer (eds.), *Historiae Augustae Colloquium IV: Colloquium Barcinonense*. Bari, 175–215.

Menci, G. 2012. "Un epigramma del Certamen Homeri et Hesiodi (309–312 Allen) in P. Duk. inv. 665," *ZPE* 180, 43–47.

Meyer, H. 1980. "Die Frieszyklen am Sogenannten Triumphbogen des Galerius in Thessaloniki," *Jahrbuch des Deutschen Archäologischen Instituts* 95, 374–444.

Meyers, J. (ed.). 2006. *Les miracles de saint Étienne. Recherches sur le recueil pseudo-augustinien* (BHL7860–7861) *avec édition critique, traduction et commentaire*. Turnhout.

Miles, R. (ed.). 2016. *The Donatist Schism: Controversy and Contexts*. Liverpool.

Miri, N. 2017. "Representation of Children in Sasanian Rock Reliefs," *International Journal of Humanities* 24, 67–80.

Mombritius, B. 1910. *Sanctuarium, seu vitae sanctorum; novam hanc editionem curaverunt duo monachi Solesmenses*. 2 vols. Paris.

Momigliano, A. 1954. "An Unsolved Problem of Historical Forgery: the *Scriptores Historiae Augustae*," *Journal of the Warburg and Courtauld Institutes* 17, 22–46.

Momigliano, A. 1974. "The Lonely Historian Ammianus Marcellinus," *Annali della Scuola Normale Superiore di Pisa* 3rd series, 4, 1393–1407.

Mommsen, T. 1890. "Die Scriptores Historiae Augustae," *Hermes* 25, 228–292.

Mommsen, T. (ed.). 1894. *Acta Synhodorum habitarum Romae*, in *MGH Auctores Antiquissimi* 12. Berlin, 399–455.

Mommsen, T. (ed.). 1898. *Libri pontificalis Pars prior. Gesta pontificum romanorum I. Monumenta Germaniae Historica*. Berlin.

Moorhead, J. 2015. *The Popes and the Church of Rome in Late Antiquity*. London.

Morales, H. 2005. *Vision and Narrative in Achilles Tatius'* Leucippe *and* Clitophon. Cambridge.

Mordtmann, J. H. 1880. "Das Denkmal des Porphyrius," *Mitteilungen des Deutschen Archäologischen Instituts—Athenische Abteilung* 5, 295–308.

Mousavi, A., and Darayee, T. 2012. "The Sasanian Empire: An Archaeological Survey," in D. Potts (ed.), *A Companion to the Archaeology of the Ancient Near East*. Chichester, 1076–1094.

Müller, H. 2012. "Preacher: Augustine and His Congregation," in V. Mark and S. Reid (eds.), *A Companion to Augustine*. Malden, MA, 297–309.

Munier, C. (ed.). 1963. *Concilia Galliae a. 314–506*. Turnhout.

Musavi Haji, R. S., and Mehrafarin, R. 2009. "The Lady Represented in Narseh's Relief: Shapurdokhtak or Anahita?," *International Journal of Humanities* 16 (2), 75–85.

Nardelli, J.-F. 2016. "Historia Augusta contra Christianos II: nouvelles considérations sur la paideia païenne et sur l'ambiance antichrétienne dans l'Histoire Auguste," *AT* 24, 257–284.

Nautain, P. 1980. "La liste des oeuvres de Saint Jérôme dans le 'De viris illustribus,'" *Orpheus* n.s. 1, 52–75.

Nechaeva, E. 2014. *Embassies—Negotiations—Gifts: Systems of East Roman Diplomacy in Late Antiquity*. Stuttgart.

Neil, B., and Allen, P. (eds. and trans.). 2014. *The Letters of Gelasius I (492–496)*. Turnhout.

Nixon, C. E. V., and Rogers, B. S. (eds.). 1994. *In Praise of Later Roman Emperors: The Panegyrici Latini*. Berkeley.

Nutton, V. 1992. "Healers in the Medical Market Place: Towards a Social History of Graeco-Roman Medicine," in A. Wear (ed.), *Medicine in Society: Historical Essays*. Cambridge, 15–58.

Nutton, V. 2000. "Did the Greeks Have a Word for it? Contagion and Contagion Theory in Classical Antiquity," in L. I. Conrad and D. Wujastyk (eds.), *Contagion: Perspectives from Pre-Modern Societies*. Aldershot, 137–162.

Nutton, V. 2012. *Ancient Medicine*. 2nd ed. London.

Nutton, V. 2014. "Rhodiapolis and Allianoi: Two Missing Links in the History of the Hospital?," *Early Christianity* 5, 371–389.

Odorico, P. 2014. "Du recueil à l'invention du texte: le cas des *Parastaseis Suntomoi Chronikai*," *BZ* 107, 755–784.

Olivar, A. 1991. *La predicación cristiana antigua*. Barcelona.

Oppedisano, F., and La Rocca, A. 2016. *Il senato romano nell'Italia ostrogota*. Rome.

Orsini, P. 2000. "Lo scriba J dell'Anthologia Palatina e Costantino Rodio," *Bollettino della Badia Greca di Grottaferrata* n.s. 54, 425–435.

Osborne, J. 1990. "The Use of Painted Initials by Greek and Latin Scriptoria in Carolingian Rome," *Gesta* 29 (1), 76–85.

Osborne, J. 2011. "Rome and Constantinople in the Ninth Century," in C. Bolgia, R. McKitterick, and J. Osborne (eds.), *Rome Across Time and Space, c. 500–1400: Cultural Transmissions and the Exchange of Ideas*. Cambridge, 222–236.

Overlaet, B. 2013. "And Man Created God? Kings, Priests and Gods on Sasanian Investiture Reliefs," *Iranica Antiqua* 48, 313–354.

Page, D. L. (ed.). 1967. *Poetae melici Graeci*. 2nd ed. Oxford.

Palanque, J.-R. 1933a. *Saint Ambroise et l'empire romain: Contribution à l'histoire des rapports de l'église et de l'état à la fin du quatrième siècle*. Paris.

Palanque, J.-R. 1933b. "Famines à Rome à la fin du IVe siècle," *Revue des Études Anciennes* 31, 346–356.

REFERENCES   305

Panagiotidou, O. 2016. "Asclepius: a Divine Doctor, a Popular Healer," in W. V. Harris (ed.), *Popular Medicine in Graeco-Roman Antiquity: Explorations* (Columbia Studies in the Classical Tradition 42). Leiden, 106–124.

Pareti, L. 1912. "Verdi e azzuri ai tempi di Foca e due iscrizioni inedite di Oxyrhynchos," *Studi Italiani di filologia classica* 19, 305–315.

Paschoud, F. 1965. "Réflexions sur l'idéal religieux de Symmaque," *Historia* 14, 215–235.

Paschoud, F. 1967. Roma Aeterna. *Études sur le patriotisme romain dans l'Occident latin à l'époque des grandes invasions.* Neuchâtel.

Paschoud, F. (ed.). 1971–1989. *Zosime: Histoire Nouvelle.* 3 v. in 5. Paris.

Paschoud, F. 1978. "Une relecture poétique de Rutilius Namatianus," *Museum Helveticum* 35, 319–328.

Paschoud, F. 1991. "L'*Histoire Auguste* et Dexippe," in G. Bonamente and N. Duval (eds.), *Historiae Augustae Colloquium I: Colloquium Parisinum.* Macerata, 217–269.

Paschoud, F. 1994. "Nicomaque Flavien et la connexion byzantine (Pierre le Patrice et Zonaras): à propos du livre récent de Bruno Bleckmann," *AT* 2, 71–82.

Paschoud, F. (ed.). 1996. *Histoire Auguste*, Vol. v, 1: *Vies d'Aurélien et de Tacite.* Paris.

Paschoud, F. (ed.). 1999a. *Historiae Augustae Colloquium VII: Colloquium Genevense.* Bari.

Paschoud, F. 1999b. "Propos sceptiques et iconoclastes sur Marius Maximus," in F. Paschoud (ed.), *Historiae Augustae Colloquium VII: Colloquium Genevense.* Bari, 241–254.

Paschoud, F. (ed.). 2001. *Histoire Auguste*, Vol. v, 2: *Vies de Probus, Firmus, Saturnin, Proculus et Bonose, Carus, Numérien et Carin.* Paris.

Paschoud, F. 2006. *Eunape, Olympiodore, Zosime. Scripta Minora.* Bari.

Paschoud, F. (ed.). 2011. *Histoire Auguste*, Vol. iv, 3: *Vies des Trente Tyrans et de Claude.* Paris.

Paschoud, F. 2014. "Casaubon et Saumaise commentateurs de l'*Histoire Auguste*," in C. Bertrand-Dagenbach and F. Chausson (eds.), *Historiae Augustae Colloquium XII: Colloquium Nanceiense.* Bari, 405–418.

Paschoud, F. 2017. Review of S. C. Zinsli *Kommentar zur Historia Augusta*, Vol. 5: *Heliogabalus, AT* 25, 495–499.

Paschoud, F. (ed.). 2018. *Histoire Auguste*, Vol. iv, 1: *Vies des deux Maximins, des trois Gordiens, de Maxime et Balbin.* Paris.

Paschoud, F., Fry, G., and Rütsche, Y. (eds.). 1986. *Symmaque. Colloque génévois à l'occasion du mille six centième anniversaire du conflit de l'autel de la Victoire.* Paris.

Patzig, E. 1904. "Die römischen Quellen des salmasischen Johannes Antiochenus I Eutrop und Ammian, mit einem Anhang zur Textkritik der Scriptores Hist. Aug.," *BZ* 13, 13–50.

Peck, E. 1993. "Crown: From the Seleucids to the Islamic Conquest," in *Encyclopaedia Iranica* vi. London, 408–418.

Peek, W. (ed.). 1968–1975. *Lexikon zu den Dionysiaka des Nonnos*, 4 vols. Hildesheim.

Pépin, J. 1964. *Théologie cosmique et théologie chrétienne: Ambroise, Exam. I 1, 1–4*. Paris.

Pepper, T. W. 2010. "A Patron and a Companion: Two Animal Epitaphs for Zenon of Caunos (*P. Cair. Zen.* IV 59532 = SH 977)," in T. Gagos (ed.), *Proceedings of the 25th International Congress of Papyrology*. Ann Arbor, 605–622.

Percival, H. R. (ed.). 1900. *The Seven Ecumenical Councils of the Undivided Church and their Canons and Dogmatic Decrees*, Vol. 14. New York.

Peter, H. 1892. *Die Scriptores Historiae Augustae: Sechs literargeschichtliche Untersuchungen*. Leipzig.

Peter, H. 1911. *Wahrheit und Kunst. Geschichtschreibung und Plagiat im klassischen Altertum*. Leipzig.

Petrie, W. M. Flinders. 1925. *Tombs of the Courtiers and Oxyrhynkhos*, London.

Petrovic, I. 2017. "The Cult of Homer in Alexandria and Epigram SH 979," in Y. Durbec and F. Trajber (eds.), *Traditions épiques et poésie épigrammatique*. Leuven, 115–119.

Petrucci, A. 1971. "L'onciale romana. Origini, sviluppo e diffusione di una stilizzazione grafica altomedievale (sec. VI–IX)," *Studi medievali*, 3rd series, 12, 75–132.

Petrucci, A. 1995. *Writers and Readers in Medieval Italy*. London.

Petzl, G., and Schwertheim, E. 2006. *Hadrian und die dionysischen Künstler. Drei in Alexandria Troas neugefundene Briefe des Kaisers an die Künstler-Vereinigung*. Bonn.

Pietri, C. 1976. *Roma Christiana*. Rome.

Polara, G. 1974. "Il nonno di Simmaco," *Parola del Passato* 157, 261–266.

Pontet, M. 1946. *L'exégèse de Saint-Augustin prédicateur*. Paris.

Portmann, W. 1988. *Geschichte in der spätantiken Panegyrik*. Frankfurt.

Potts, D. T. (ed.). 2013. *The Oxford Handbook of Ancient Iran*. Oxford.

Pralon, D. 2017. "Homère dans les épigrammes grecques," in Y. Durbec and F. Trajber (eds.), *Traditions épiques et poésie épigrammatique*. Leuven, 283–311.

Price, R., and Gaddis, M. (eds.). 2005. *The Acts of the Council of Chalcedon*. 3 vols. Liverpool.

Rabe, H. (ed.). 1913. *Hermogenis opera*. Leipzig.

Ramelli, I. 2016. *Social Justice and the Legitimacy of Slavery: The Role of Philosophical Asceticism from Ancient Judaism to Late Antiquity*. Oxford.

Ramsey, B. 1997. *Ambrose*. London.

Rankov, B. 2007. "Military Forces," in P. Sabin, H. Van Wees, and M. Whitby (eds.), *The Cambridge History of Greek and Roman Warfare*, Vol. 2. Cambridge, 30–75.

Ratti, S. (ed.). 2000. *Histoire Auguste*, Vol. IV, 2: *Vies des deux Valériens et des deux Galliens*. Paris.

Ratti, S. 2007. "Nicomaque Flavien *senior* auteur de l'*Histoire Auguste*," in G. Bonamente and H. Brandt (eds.), *Historiae Augustae Colloquium X: Colloquium Bambergense*. Bari, 305–317.

REFERENCES

Ratti, S. 2010. *Antiquus Error: les ultimes feux de la résistance païenne. Scripta varia augmentées de cinq études inédites.* Turnhout.

Ratti, S. 2012a. *Polémiques entre païens et chrétiens.* Paris.

Ratti, S. 2012b. "Rutilius Namatianus: Jérôme Carcopino avait raison!," *Anabases* 16, 237–240.

Ratti, S. 2016a. *L'Histoire Auguste. Les païens et les chrétiens dans l'Antiquité tardive.* Paris.

Ratti, S. 2016b. "Jeu de l'allusion dans l'*Histoire Auguste* ou vide de l'interprétation? À propos de David Rohrbacher, *The Play of Allusion in the Historia Augusta*," *AT* 24, 501–511.

Rees, R. 2018. "Panegyric," in S. McGill and E. Watts (eds.), *A Companion to Late Antique Literature.* New York, 209–220.

Reeve, M. 2011. "Rome, Reservoir of Ancient Texts?," in C. Bolgia, R. McKitterick, and J. Osborne (eds.), *Rome Across Time and Space, c. 500–1400: Cultural Transmissions and the Exchange of Ideas.* Cambridge, 52–59.

Renaud, J.-M. 2003. "Le catastérisme chez Homère. Le cas d'Orion," *Gaia* 7, 205–214.

Renberg, G. 2017. *Where Dreams May Come: Incubation Sanctuaries in the Greco-Roman World.* 2 vols. Leiden.

Rengakos, A. 1992. "Homerische Wörter bei Kallimachos," *ZPE* 94, 21–47.

Rengakos, A. 1993. *Der Homertext und die Hellenistischen Dichter.* Stuttgart.

Rengakos, A. 1994. *Apollonios Rhodios und die antike Homererklärung.* Munich.

Reynolds, L. D., and Wilson, N. G. 2013. *Scribes and Scholars: A Guide to the Transmission of Greek and Latin Literature.* 4th ed. Oxford.

Rhoby, A. 2014. *Byzantinische Epigramme auf Stein nebst Addenda zu Bänden 1 und 2.* Vienna.

Ricci, C. 2015. "*Pro bona valetudine*: considerazioni sul personale addetto all'infermeria e sui *valetudinaria* di Roma." *Humanitas: rivista bimestrale di cultura* 70 (3), 353–366.

Richmond, I. A. 1968. *Hod Hill,* II. *Excavations Carried out between 1951 and 1958 for the Trustees of the British Museum.* London.

Riethmüller, J. W. 2005. *Asklepios: Heiligtümer und Kulte.* 2 vols. Heidelberg.

Risse, G. B. 1992. "Medicine in the Age of Enlightenment," in A. Wear (ed.), *Medicine in Society: Historical Essays.* Cambridge, 149–195.

Robert, F. 2015. "La présence d'Homère dans les *progymnasmata* d'époque impériale," in S. Dubel, A.-M. Favreau-Linder and E. Oudot (eds.), *A l'école d'Homère.* Paris, 73–86.

Robert, J., and Robert, L. 1965. "Bulletin épigraphique," *Revue des Études Grecques* 78, 70–204.

Robert, L. 1948. *Hellenica. Recueil d'épigraphie, de numismatique et d'antiquités grecques,* IV. Paris.

Robert, L. 1964. "Rapport sur les cours au Collège de France et les missions," *Annuaire du Collège de France* 64ᵉ année, 358–370.

Roberto, U. 2014. "Il senato di Roma tra Antemio e Glicerio. Per una rilettura di CIL. VI 526 = 1664 = ILS 3132," in M. L. Caldelli and G. Gregori (eds.), *Epigrafia e ordine senatorio, 30 anni dopo*. Rome, 167–182.

Rohrbacher, D. 2015. *The Play of Allusion in the Historia Augusta*. Madison, WI.

Ronchey, S. 2000. "Les procès-verbaux des martyres chrétiens dans les *Acta Martyrum* et leur fortune," *Mélanges de l'École Française de Rome—Antiquité* 112 (2), 723–752.

Rosé, I. 2018. "Simon le Magicien, hérésiarque? L'invention de la Simoniaca heresis par Grégoire le Grand," in F. Mercier and I. Rosé (eds.), *Aux marges de l'hérésie. Inventions, formes et usages polémiques de l'accusation d'hérésie au Moyen Âge*. Rennes, 201–238.

Rose, J. 1998. "Three Queens, Two Wives, One Goddess: The Roles and Images of Women in Sasanian Iran," in G. Hambly (ed.), *Women in the Medieval Islamic World: Power, Patronage and Piety*. New York, 29–54.

Rothman, M. S. Pond. 1977. "The Thematic Organization of the Panel Reliefs on the Arch of Galerius," *AJA* 81, 427–454.

Rotman, Y. 2009. *Byzantine Slavery and the Mediterranean World* (trans. J. M. Todd). Cambridge, MA.

Roueché, C. 1999. "Looking for Late Antique Ceremonial: Ephesos and Aphrodisias," in H. Friesinger and F. Krinzinger (eds.), *100 Jahre Österreichische Forschungen in Ephesos*. Vienna, 161–168.

Roueché, C. 2007a. "Spectacles in Late Antiquity: Some Observations," *AT* 16, 59–64.

Roueché, C. 2007b. "Interpreting the Signs: Anonymity and Concealment in Late Antique Inscriptions," in H. Amirav and B. ter Haar Romeny (eds.), *From Rome to Constantinople: Studies in Honour of Averil Cameron*. Leuven, 221–234.

Roueché, C. 2014. "Using Civic Space: Identifying the Evidence," in W. Eck and P. Funke (eds.), *Öffentlichkeit—Monument—Text*. Berlin, 135–158.

Rougé, J. 1961. "Une émeute à Rome au IVᵉ siècle. Ammien Marcellin, XXVII, 3, 3–4: essai d'interprétation," *Revue des Études Anciennes* 63, 59–77.

Rousseau, V., and Northover, P. 2015. "Style and Substance: A Bust of a Sasanian Royal Woman as a Symbol of Late Antique Legitimacy," *JLA* 8 (1), 3–31.

Rubin, Z. 2001. "The Sasanid Monarchy," *CAH* XIV, 638–661.

Rücker, N. 2012. *Ausonius an Paulinus von Nola. Textgeschichte und literarische Form der Briefgedichte 21 und 22 des Decimus Magnus Ausonius*. Göttingen.

Runia, D. T. 1990. *Exegesis and Philosophy: Studies on Philo of Alexandria*. Aldershot.

Runia, D. T. 1993. *Philo in Early Christian Literature: A Survey*. Minneapolis.

Russo, A. 2019. "Rutilio Namaziano, Paolo Diacono e gli *Epigrammata Bobiensia*," *Italia medioevale e umanistica* 60, 33–59.

REFERENCES 309

Sabbah, G. 1984. "De la rhétorique à la communication politique: Les Panégyriques latins," *Bulletin de l'Association G. Budé* 43, 363–388.

Sajdak, J. (ed.). 1931. *Ioannis Kyriotis Geometrae Hymni in SS. Deiparam*. Poznan.

Salzman, M. R. 2018. "Symmachus' Varro: Latin Letters in Late Antiquity," *BICS* 61 (2), 92–105.

Salzman, M. R. 2019a. "Contestations between Elites: Italo-Roman Senatorial Aristocrats and the Senate in the *Collectio Avellana*," in R. Lizzi Testa and G. Marconi (eds.), *The* Collectio Avellana *and Its Revivals*. Newcastle upon Tyne, 138–158.

Salzman, M. R. 2019b. "Lay Aristocrats and Ecclesiastical Politics: A New View of the Papacy of Felix III (483–492 C.E.) and the Acacian Schism," *Journal of Early Christian Studies* 27 (3), 465–490.

Samama, É. 2003. *Les médecins dans le monde grec: sources épigraphiques sur la naissance d'un corps médical*. Geneva.

Sandnes, K. 2009. *The Challenge of Homer: School, Pagan Poets and Early Christianity*. London.

Sansone, D. 1990. "The Computer and the *Historia Augusta*: A Note on Marriot," *JRS* 80, 174–177.

Sarre, F., and Herzfeld, E. 1910. *Iranische Felsreliefs: Aufnahmen und Untersuchungen von Denkmälern aus alt- und mittelpersischer Zeit*. Berlin.

Savino, E. 2017. *Ricerche sull'Historia Augusta*. Naples.

Scarborough, J. 2006. Review of P. A. Baker *Medical Care for the Roman Army on the Rhine, Danube and British Frontiers*. *JRA* 19, 610–614.

Schelstrate, E. 1692. *Antiquitas Ecclesiae Dissertationibus Monimentis Ac Notis Illustrata*. Rome.

Schiller, I., Weber, D., and Weidmann, D. 2008. "Sechs neue Augustinuspredigten," *Wiener Studien* 121, 227–284.

Schindel, N. 2013. "Sasanian Coinage," in D. T. Potts (ed.), *The Oxford Handbook of Ancient Iran*. Oxford, 814–839.

Schindel, N. 2014. *Sylloge Nummorum Sasanidarum—Schaaf Collection*. Vienna.

Schissel, O. 1929–1930. "Theodoros von Kynopolis," *Byzantinisch-neugriechische Jahrbücher* 8, 331–349.

Schlumberger, J. 1985. "Die verlorenen Annalen des Nicomachus Flavianus: ein Werk über Geschichte der römischen Republik oder Kaiserzeit?," in J. Straub (ed.), *Bonner Historia Augusta Colloquium 1982/1983*. Bonn, 305–329.

Schlumberger, J. 1998. "Zu Komposition und Quellen der *Vita Probi*," in G. Bonamente, F. Heim, and J.-P. Callu (eds.), *Historiae Augustae Colloquium VI: Colloquium Argentoratense*. Bari, 313–323.

Schmeidler, J. 1927. "Die SHA und der heilige Hieronymus," *Philologische Wochenschrift* 47, 955–960.

Schoenebeck, H. von. 1937. "Die Zyklische Ordnung der Triumphalreliefs am Galeriusbogen in Saloniki," *BZ* 37 (2), 361–371.

Schofield, M. 1990. "Ideology and Philosophy in Aristotle's Theory of Slavery," in G. Patzig (ed.), *Aristoteles "Politik": Akten des XI. symposium aristotelicum*. Göttingen, 1–27.

Schulte, H. 2006. *Paralipomena Cycli: Epigramme aus der Sammlung des Agathias*. Trier.

Schütrumpf, E. 1993. "Aristotle's Theory of Slavery—A Platonic Dilemma," *Ancient Philosophy* 13, 111–123.

Schütrumpf, E. 2003. "Slaves in Plato's Political Dialogues and the Significance of Plato's Psychology for the Aristotelian Theory of Slavery," in W. Detel, A. Becker, and P. Scholz (eds.), *Ideal and Culture of Knowledge in Plato*. Stuttgart, 245–260.

Schwartz, J. 1987. "Noms apocryphes dans l'Histoire Auguste," in J. Straub (ed.), *Bonner Historia Augusta Colloquium 1984/1985*. Bonn, 197–202.

Scipioni, S. 2013. "Un codice heinsiano di Ovidio: Farnesianus e Parmensis?," in M. Palma and C. Vismara (eds.), *Per Gabriella: Studi in ricordo di Gabriella Braga* IV. Cassino, 1689–1701.

Seeck, O. (ed.). 1883. *Q. Aurelii Symmachi quae supersunt*. Monumenta Germaniae Historica. Auctores Antiquissimi VI, 1. Berlin.

Seeck, O. 1890. "Studien zur Geschichte Diocletians und Constantins, III: Die Entstehungszeit der Historia Augusta," *Jahrbücher für klassische Philologie* 36, 609–639.

Seeck, O. 1894. "Zur Echtheitsfrage der Scriptores Historiae Augustae," *RhM* 49, 208–224.

Seeck, O. 1919. *Regesten der Kaiser und Päpste für die Jahre 311 bis 476 n. Chr. Vorarbeit zu einer Prosopographie der christlichen Kaiserzeit*. Stuttgart.

Seeck, O. 1931. "Symmachus 18," in *RE* IV A. Stuttgart, cols. 1141–1161.

Sessa, K. 2012. *The Formation of Papal Authority in Late Antiquity: Roman Bishops and the Domestic Sphere*. Cambridge.

Shahbazi, A. S. 1983. "Studies in Sasanian Prosopography I: Narse's Relief at Naqš-i Rustam," *Archäologische Mitteilungen aus Iran* 16, 255–268.

Shahbazi, A. S. 1988. "Bahrām I / Bahrām II," in *Encyclopaedia Iranica* III. London, 514–522.

Shaw, B. D. 2011. *Sacred Violence: African Christians and Sectarian Hatred in the Age of Augustine*. Cambridge.

Shayegan, R. M. 2004. "Hormozd I," in *Encyclopaedia Iranica*, XII. London, 462–464.

Sigalas, A. 1937. *Des Chrysippos von Jerusalem Enkomion auf den hl. Johannes den Täufer*. Athens.

Sistakou, E. 2007. "Glossing Homer: Homeric Exegesis in Early Third Century Epigram," in P. Bing and J. S. Bruss (eds.), *Brill's Companion to Hellenistic Epigram*. Leiden, 391–408.

Sistakou, E. 2011. "Mock Epic in the *Greek Anthology*," in B. Acosta-Hughes, C. Cusset, Y. Durbec, and D. Pralon (eds.), *Homère revisité: parodie et humour dans les réécritures homériques*. Besançon, 193–209.

REFERENCES

Sivan, H. S. 1986. "Rutilius Namatianus, Constantius III and the Return to Gaul in Light of New Evidence," *Mediaeval Studies* 48, 522–532.

Skiadas, A. D. 1965. *Homer im griechischen Epigramm*. Athens.

Smith, R. R. R., and Ward-Perkins, B. 2016. *The Last Statues of Antiquity*. Oxford.

Smith, S. D. 2019. *Greek Epigram and Byzantine Culture: Gender, Desire and Denial in the Age of Justinian*. Cambridge.

Snodgrass, A. M. 1967. *Arms and Armour of the Greeks*. London.

Sordi, M. 2008. *Sant'Ambrogio e la tradizione di Roma*. Rome.

Soudavar, A. 2003. *The Aura of Kings: Legitimacy and Divine Sanction in Iranian Kingship*. Costa Mesa, CA.

Soudavar, A. 2009. "The Vocabulary and Syntax of Iconography in Sasanian Iran," *Iranica Antica* 44, 417–460.

Soudavar, A. 2012. "Looking through the Two Eyes of the Earth: A Reassessment of Sasanian Rock Reliefs," *Iranian Studies* 45 (1), 29–58.

Spallone, M. 1982. "Il Par. Lat. 10318 (Salmasiano): dal manoscritto alto-medievale ad una raccolta enciclopedica tardo-antica," *Italia Medioevale e Umanistica* 25, 1–71.

Spingou, F. 2019. "Byzantine Collections and Anthologies of Poetry," in W. Hörandner, A. Rhoby, and N. Zagklas (eds.), *A Companion to Byzantine Poetry*. Leiden, 381–403.

Stathakopoulos, D. C. 2004. *Famine and Pestilence in the Late Roman and Early Byzantine Empire: A Systematic Survey of Subsistence Crises and Epidemics*. Burlington, VT.

Stern, H. 1953. *Date et destinataire de l'*Histoire Auguste. Paris.

Stover, J. 2020. "New Light on the *Historia Augusta*," *JRS* 110, 167–198.

Stover, J., and Kestemont, M. 2016. "The Authorship of the *Historia Augusta*: Two New Computational Studies," *BICS* 59, 140–157.

Stowers, S. K. 2016. "Why Expert Versus Nonexpert is Not Elite Versus Popular Religion: The Case of the Third Century," in N. P. DesRosiers and L. C. Vuong (eds.), *Religious Competition in the Greco-Roman World*. Atlanta, 139–153.

Straub, J. 1939. *Vom Herrscherideal in der Spätantike*. Stuttgart.

Straub, J. 1952. *Studien zur Historia Augusta*. Bern.

Straub, J. 1963. *Heidnische Geschichtsapologetik in der christlichen Spätantike*. Bonn.

Straub, J. 1972. *Regeneratio Imperii. Aufsätze über Roms Kaisertum und Reich im Spiegel der heidnischen und christlichen Publizistik*. Darmstadt.

Straub, J. (ed.). 1980. *Bonner Historia Augusta Colloquium 1977/1978*. Bonn.

Straub, J. (ed.). 1985. *Bonner Historia Augusta Colloquium 1982/1983*. Bonn.

Straub, J. (ed.). 1987. *Bonner Historia Augusta Colloquium 1984/1985*. Bonn.

Sudhoff, K. 1913. "Aus der Geschichte des Krankenhauswesens im früheren Mittelalter in Morgenland und Abendland," *Ergebnisse und Fortschritte des Krankenhauswesens* 2, 1–30.

Sundermann, W. 1964. "Zur Proskynesis in sasanidischen Iran," *Mitteilungen des Instituts für Orientforschung* 10, 275–286.

Supino Martini, P. 1987. *Roma e l'area grafica romanesca (secoli X–XII)*. Alessandria.

Supino Martini, P. 2012. *Scritti "romani": Scrittura, libri e cultura a Roma in età medievale.* Rome.

Swift, L. J. 1979. "*Iustitia* and *Ius Privatum*: Ambrose on Private Property," *AJPh* 100, 176–187.

Syme, R. 1968. *Ammianus and the Historia Augusta.* Oxford.

Syme, R. 1971a. *Emperors and Biography: Studies in the Historia Augusta.* Oxford.

Syme, R. 1971b. *The Historia Augusta: A Call for Clarity.* Bonn.

Syme, R. 1983. *Historia Augusta Papers.* Oxford.

Tedesco, P. 2018. "'The Missing Factor': Economy and Labor in Late Roman North Africa," *JLA* 11, 396–431.

Teitler, H. C. 1985. *Notarii and exceptores: An Inquiry into Role and Significance of Shorthand Writers in the Imperial and Ecclesiastical Bureaucracy of the Roman Empire (From the Early Principate to c. 450 A.D.).* Amsterdam.

Teitler, H. C. 1990. "Notae et notarii. Tachygraphie und Tachygraphen im 5. und 6. Jahrhundert," in P. F. Ganz (ed.), *Tironische Noten.* Wiesbaden, 3–15.

Teitler, H. C. 2007. "Kurzschrift," *RAC* 22, 518–545.

Thiel, A. (ed.). 1868. *Epistolae Romanorum pontificum genuinae et quae ad eos scriptae sunt a s. Hilaro usque ad Pelagium II.* Braunsberg.

Thomas, R. F. 1986. "Virgil's *Georgics* and the Art of Reference," *HSCPh* 90, 171–198.

Thomson, M. 2012. *Studies in the Historia Augusta.* Brussels.

Tissol, G. 2002. "Ovid and the Exilic Journey of Rutilius Namatianus," *Arethusa* 35, 435–446.

Tissoni, F. 2000. *Cristodoro di Copto. Un'introduzione e un commento.* Alessandria.

Trajber, F. 2017. "Remarques sur les 'épigrammes' de l'*Iliade*," in Y. Durbec and F. Trajber (eds.), *Traditions épiques et poésie épigrammatique.* Leuven, 1–12.

Trout, D. E. 1999. *Paulinus of Nola: Life, Letters, and Poems.* Berkeley.

Trümpelmann, L. 1975. *Das Sasanidische Felsrelief von Sar Mašhad.* Berlin.

Tsagalis, C. 2008. *Inscribing Sorrow: Fourth-Century Attic Funerary Epigrams.* Berlin.

Tsagalis, C. 2017. "Three Modes of Intertextuality: Homeric Resonances in Hellenistic Epigram," in Y. Durbec and F. Trajber (eds.), *Traditions épiques et poésie épigrammatique.* Leuven, 141–156.

Tse, E. K., Tweedie, F. J., and Frischer, B. D. 1998. "Unravelling the Purple Thread: Function Word Variability and the *Scriptores Historiae Augustae*," *Literary and Linguistic Computing* 13, 141–149.

Turcan, R. 1993. *Histoire Auguste*, Vol. III, 1: *Vies de Macrin, Diaduménien, Héliogabale.* Paris.

Ureña Bracero, J. 1999. "Homero en la formación retórico-escolar griega: etopeyas con tema del ciclo troyano," *Emerita* 67, 315–339.

Ureña Bracero, J. 2007. "Algunas consideraciones sobre la autoría de los *progymnasmata* atribuidos a Libanio," in J. A. Fernández Delgado, F. Pordomingo, and A. Stramaglia (eds.), *Escuela y literatura en Grecia antigua.* Cassino, 645–689.

REFERENCES   313

Uthemann, K.-H. 1998. "Forms of Communication in the Homilies of Severian of Gabala: A Contribution to the Reception of the Diatribe as a Method of Exposition," in M. B. Cunningham and P. Allen (eds.), *Preacher and Audience: Studies in Early Christian and Byzantine Homiletics.* Leiden, 155–177.

Vanden Berghe, L. 1966. *Archéologie de l'Iran Ancien.* Leiden.

Vanden Berghe, L. 1988. "Barm-e Delak," in *Encyclopaedia Iranica* III. London, 805–807.

Vanderspoel, J. 1995. *Themistius and the Imperial Court.* Ann Arbor, MI.

van der Valk, M. 1949. *Textual Criticism of the Odyssey.* Leiden.

van der Valk, M. 1963. *Researches on the Text and* scholia *of the Iliad*, I–II. Leiden.

Van Minnen, P. 1995. "Medical Care in Late Antiquity," in P. J. van der Eijk, H. F. J. Horstmanshoff, and P. H. Schrijvers (eds.), *Ancient Medicine in its Socio-Cultural Context*, Vol. 1. Amsterdam, 153–169.

Van Nuffelen, P. 2002. "Deux fausses lettres de Julien l'Apostat (la lettre aux juifs, Ep. 51 [Wright], et la lettre à Arsacius, Ep. 84 [Bidez])," *Vigiliae Christianae* 56, 131–150.

Van Nuffelen, P. 2017. "The Highs and Lows of Biography," in B. Bleckmann, and H. Brandt (eds.), *Historiae Augustae Colloquium XIII: Colloquium Dusseldorpiense.* Bari, 175–187.

van Opstall, E. M. (ed. and comm.). 2008. *Jean Géométrès, Poèmes en hexamètres et en distiques élégiaques.* Leiden.

Vasey, V. R. 1982. *The Social Ideas in the Works of St. Ambrose: A Study on De Nabuthe.* Rome.

Veikou, M. 2018. "Telling Spaces in Byzantium," in C. Messis, M. Mullett, and I. Nilsson (eds.), *Storytelling in Byzantium: Narratological Approaches to Byzantine Texts and Images.* Uppsala, 1–32.

Velaza, J. 1996. "El texto de Virigilio en la *H.A.*," in G. Bonamente and M. Mayer (eds.), *Historiae Augustae Colloquium IV: Colloquium Barcinonense.* Bari, 297–305.

Vera, D. 1981. *Commento storico alle* Relationes *di Quinto Aurelio Simmaco.* Pisa.

Vera, D. 1983. "Strutture agrarie e strutture patrimoniali nella tarda antichità: l'aristocrazia romana fra agricoltura e commercio," *Opus* 2, 489–533.

Vera, D. 1986. "Simmaco e le sue proprietà: struttura e funzionamento di un patrimonio aristocratico del quarto secolo d. C.," in F. Paschoud, G. Fry, and Y. Rütsche (eds.), *Symmaque. Colloque génévois à l'occasion du mille six centième anniversaire du conflit de l'autel de la Victoire.* Paris, 231–276.

Vera, D. 1992–93. "Schiavitù rurale e colonato nell'Italia imperiale," *Scienze dell'Antichità: Storia Archeologia Antropologia* 6–7, 185–224.

Vera, D. 1995. "Dalla 'villa perfecta' alla villa di Palladio: sulle trasformazioni del sistema agrario in Italia fra principato e dominato," *Athenaeum* 83, 189–211, 331–356.

Vera, D. 1999. "Silenzi di Palladio e l'Italia: Osservazioni sull'ultimo agronomo romano," *AT* 7, 283–297.

Vera, D. 2012. "Questioni di storia agraria tardoromana: Schiavi, coloni, villae," *AT* 20, 115–122.

Vera, D. 2020. *I doni di Cerere. Storie della terra nella tarda Antichità (strutture, società, economia)*. Turnhout.

Verbaal, W. 2006. "A Man and his Gods: Religion in the De reditu suo of Rutilius Claudius Namatianus," *Wiener Studien* 119, 157–171.

Verdenius, W. J. 1970. *Homer, the Educator of the Greeks* (Mededelingen der Koninklijke Nederlandse Akademie van Wetenschapen, AFD Letterkunde, nieuwe Reeks 33, 5). Amsterdam.

Vessereau, J. 1904. *Claudius Rutilius Namatianus*. Paris.

Vian, P. 2001. "Un bibliotecario al lavoro: Holste, la Barberiniana, la Vaticana e la Biblioteca della regina Cristina di Svezia," *Studi e testi* 402, 445–492.

Viansino, G. 1967. *Epigrammi di Agazia Scolastico*. Milan.

Viljamaa, T. 1968. *Studies in Greek Encomiastic Poetry of the Early Byzantine Period* (Commentationes Humanarum Litterarum, Societas Scientiarum Fennica 42, 4). Helsinki.

Visser, C. E. 1938. *Götter und Kulte im ptolemäischen Alexandrien*. Amsterdam.

Vogler, C. 1979. *Constance II et l'administration impériale*. Strasbourg.

Voicu, S. J. 1980–1982. "Un'omelia di Severiano di Gabala: *In illud, quando ipsi subiciet omnia (CPG 4761)*," *Rivista di studi bizantini e neoellenici* 17–19, 5–11.

Vuolanto, V. 2003. "Selling a Freeborn Child: Rhetoric and Social Realities in the Late Roman World," *Ancient World* 33, 169–207.

Wacht, M. 1982. "Privateigentum bei Cicero und Ambrosius," *Jahrbuch für Antike und Christentum* 25, 28–64.

Wallis, P. 2008. "Clement, John (d.1572)," *Oxford Dictionary of National Biography*. Online at: https://doi.org/10.1093/ref:odnb/5603.

Waltz, P. 1931. "L'inspiration païenne et le sentiment chrétien dans les épigrammes funéraires du VIᵉ siècle," *L'Acropole* 6, 3–21.

Warmington, B. 2012. "Aspects of Constantinian Propaganda in the Panegyrici Latini," in R. Rees (ed.), *Latin Panegyric*. Oxford, 335–348.

Watts, E. 2015. *The Final Pagan Generation*. Oakland.

Wear, A. (ed.). 1992. *Medicine in Society: Historical Essays*. Cambridge.

Webb, R. 2010. "Between Poetry and Rhetoric: Libanios' Use of Homeric Subjects in his *progymnasmata*," *Quaderni Urbinati di Cultura Classica* 95 (2), 131–152.

Weber, U. 2009. "Wahrām II, König der Könige von Ērān und Anērān," *Iranica Antiqua* 44, 559–643.

Wegner, M., Bracker, J., and Real, W. 1979. *Gordianus III. bis Carinus*. Berlin.

West, M. L. 1972. *Iambi et Elegi Graeci*, II. Oxford.

West, M. L. 1973. *Textual Criticism and Editorial Technique*. Stuttgart.

Whitby, M. 1994. "From Moschus to Nonnus: The Evolution of the Nonnian Style," in N. Hopkinson (ed.), *Studies in the Dionysiaca of Nonnus*. Cambridge, 99–155.

REFERENCES 315

Whittow, M. 2018. "Do Byzantine Historians Still Read Gibbon?," in K. O'Brien (ed.), *The Cambridge Companion to Edward Gibbon*. Cambridge, 78–92.

Wickkiser, B. 2006. "Chronicles of Chronic Cases and Tools of the Trade at Asklepieia," *Archiv für Religionsgeschichte* 8, 25–40.

Wifstrand, A. 1933. *Von Kallimachos zu Nonnos*. Lund.

Wikenhauser, A. 1907. "Mitteilungen," *Archiv für Stenographie* 58, 268–272.

Wilmanns, J. C. 1995. *Der Sanitätsdienst im Römischen Reich*. Hildesheim.

Wolff, E., with S. Lancel and J. Soler. 2007. *Rutilius Namatianus, sur son retour*. Paris.

Wood, P. 2011. "Multiple Voices in Chronicle Narratives: The Reign of Leo I (457–474) in Book Fourteen of Malalas," *JLA* 4 (2), 298–314.

Wood, S. 1986. *Roman Portrait Sculpture, 217–260 A.D.: The Transformation of an Artistic Tradition* (Columbia Studies in the Classical Tradition 12). Leiden.

Wroth, W. W. 1903. *Catalogue of the Coins of Parthia*. London.

York, J. M. 1972. "The Image of Philip the Arab," *Historia* 21, 320–332.

Zecchini, G. 2017. "Il nuovo Dexippo e l'*Historia Augusta*," in B. Bleckmann, and H. Brandt (eds.), *Historiae Augustae Colloquium XIII: Colloquium Dusseldorpiense*. Bari, 189–196.

Zilliacus, H. 1967. *Zur Abundanz der spätgriechischen Gebrauchssprache*. Helsinki.

Zinsli, S. C. 2014. *Kommentar zur Historia Augusta*, Vol. 5: *Heliogabalus*. Bonn.

Zonghetti, A. 2005. "Il codice di Gioveniano," *Arte medievale* 4 (1), 21–36.

Zumpt, A. W. 1837. *Observationes in Rutilii Claudii Namatiani carmen De reditu suo*. Berlin.

Index

Abraham 54
Achilles 262
Aemilii Lepidi: *see* Lepidi
Agathias 88–93, 264, 268
Agimundus, Homiliary of 152–153, 159, 161
Ajax 88
Aksum, kingdom of 173 n.
Alexander Severus 28
Alexandria 245, 250; Alexandrian
    poetry 85
Alexandria Troas 249
Alföldi, A. 2, 3, 27, 30
Allianoi (near Pergamum) 238
Amalasuntha (ruler of Italy) 213–214
Amato, E. 126
ambitus 203, 212
Ambrose 8, 41–65, 225–226
Ammianus Marcellinus 2, 3, 7, 31, 35, 265
Anāhīd (Persian deity) 173, 176, 182 n., 187 n.
Anastasius Bibliothecarius 137 n., 166
Ancyra 12, 245
Anicii 3
Anthemius (emperor) 198, 199, 201–202,
    203–205
Anthologia Palatina: *see Palatine Anthology*
Antinoopolis 127
Antioch 170, 246, 253, 273
anti-semitism 50, 58, 68, 73; *and see*
    synagogue at Callinicum
Antoninus Pius 17
Aphrodisias 250–252
Apion family 249
Apollonius of Rhodes 92
Apollonius the Sophist 94
Ardašīr I 177–178
Arethas (Byzantine scholar) 267
Arian Christians 63, 204, 207, 212, 218
Aristarchus 94–95, 100–102
Aristotle 44–45, 47, 50, 64; *Problems* 76
Armenia 173 n.
army, Roman 233–234
Arusianus Messius 3
Asklepieia 236–237, 241–242
Aspar (*cos.* 434) 204
Athalaric, King 214–216

Augustine 224, 229, 230–231, 246
Augustus 234
Aurelius Victor 26, 31
Ausonius 74–75
'Avianus' (fabulist) 3

Baldwin, B. 272
Basil of Caesarea 47, 49–51, 56–58, 64–65,
    243
Basilius, Fl. Caecina Decius Maximus
    (*cos.* 480) 210
Baynes, N. 26–27
Bellerophon 73–75
Ben Hur 272
betacism 156
Bianchini, Francesco 138–146, 151, 153–155,
    157, 165, 167
bilingualism, Greek-Latin 4
Birt, T. 1
Bishapur 176
bishops Chapter 10 *passim*
black bile 71, 76, 79
Bleckmann, B. 4, 36–37
Bond, S. 202
Book of Ceremonies 274
Bowersock, G. W. 241
bribery: *see ambitus*, simony, *suffragium*
Browning, R. 264
Byzantines, Byzantium 165, 260–275
'Byzantinists', disparaging use of term 262

Caelius Aurelianus 243
Callimachus 92
Cameron, Alan: 32, 33, 34, 35, 66–67, 96,
    103, 104, 134, 168–169, 197; challenges
    current opinions 2; and circus
    factions 247–259; and *Greek
    Anthology* 134, 247–259, 264 n., 267;
    and prosopography 2; scholarly
    development of 1–2, Chapter 14
    passim; *Last Pagans of Rome* 2, 3,
    4, 6–7, 8, 9, 24, 33, 67, 68, 83–84, 220,
    263, 275
Canaan (grandson of Noah) 58
Capraria (Capraia), monks of 67, 70–77

INDEX

Caracalla 27
Carcopino, J. 67
Carolingians 138, 165
Carus 170, 185
Cassiodorus 214–216
Celsus (medical writer) 235
Charlemagne 138–139
Chastagnol, A. 3, 25
Chi-Rho 18
Christ as healer 242
Christianity and paganism, conflict
   between 3, 241–242
Christianity and slavery Chapter 4 *passim*
Christianization of culture 129
Christodorus of Coptos 85, 93, 96–97,
   99–100, 102
Christophilopoulou, A. 250, 254
Cicero 33, 56, 64–65, 75, 222
Cipolla, C. 245
circus factions 247–259, 264–267, 272–275
Claudian 1, 3
Clement, John (16th c. scholar) 247
Codex Theodosianus 28, 238
Columbia University 270, 272
Columella 235, 239
Comeau, M. 230
communism, primitive 56–61, 65
Constans 17
Constantine 25, 26, 271
Constantine Cephalas (anthologist) 267
Constantine the Rhodian (poet) 263
Constantinople 13, 93, 97, 242, 269–271
Constantius II 12–21
contagious diseases 239–240
Coptic 105–106, 132
Cos 237
Councils of the Church 201, 225–228;
      Aquileia (381 CE) 225–226;
      Arles (475–480 CE) 199, 201;
      Carthage (411 CE) 227–228;
      Chalcedon (451 CE) 198–199,
      201, 226–227; Constantinople (459
      CE) 201; Orleans (533 CE) 201;
      Rome 201, 211–212
Cracco Ruggini, L. 9, 10, 271
Cumont, F. 244

Dagron, G. 269, 271, 275
Daniel the Stylite 245

Dardanus, Cl. Postumus (PPO *Galliarum*)
   70
Darwin 232
David (king of Israel) 53
debt 59–63
Dessau, H. 25
De Ste Croix, G. E. M. 202–203, 273
Dexippus 37–38
dictation 222, 224
Didyma 252, 256
Dio Chrysostom 54, 101–102, 222
Diocletian 16, 170, 173–175, 177, 185, 187, 190
Dionysius of Alexandria 240
Dioscoros of Aphrodite 104–133
doctors 234–238, 241, 242, 244; public 238
Donatists 227–228
Dressler, M. [Griffin] 260
Duchesne, L. 135, 144–148

Edessa 243
Egypt 249
ekphrasis 86, 93, 96–97, 266
Elagabalus 18
Elsner, J. 276
Enmann's *Kaisergeschichte* 26, 31
Ensslin, W. 2
Ephesus 250, 252–256
Ephrem (holy man) 243
epigrams 85–102
Epiphanius 242, 245
Erbse, H. 95
Essenes 57–58
ethopoia, Chapter 7 *passim*; defined, 120–121
Euchaïta (Pontus) 244
'Eugenia' (fictitious saint) 79–80
Eugenius I (pope) 139, 153–154, 156–157
Eusebius 242
Eustathius (Homer commentator) 98
Eustathius of Sebasteia (bishop) 242–243
Eutropius 26, 31, 37
Eve 58

Fabiola (wealthy philanthropist) 244
famine 61, 65
Felix (pope) 200
FEL TEMP REPARATIO (coin legend)
   11–22
Ferrari, M. 67
Festus, Postumius Rufus, *signo* Avienius 3

Finley, M. I. 44
Fıratlı, N. 248
Flavianus, Virius Nicomachus senior 4, 24, 31, 36–37
Flinders Petrie, W. M. 253
Fo, A. 69, 70
Fraenkel, E. 260
futuwwa, Islamic 274

Galen 220–221
Galerius 192, 194; Arch of: *see* Thessalonica
Garnsey, P. 45, 48–49
Gascou, J. 249
Gaudentius of Brescia 229
Gelasius (pope) 200, 205, 209, 210–211
Genesius ('saint') 221
Gerasa 250–251, 258
Germia (Galatia) 250, 257
Gerontius (biographer) 77, 80–82
Gibbon 1 n., 260
Giggs, M. 247
Glycerius (emperor) 198, 199, 205–208
God, Christian 42–43, 45–46, 53–56, 59–61, 64–65
Gordian III 169
Gorgo (Gorgona), hermit of 68, 70, 72
Gortyn 250, 253, 255
Goths 65
Gourevitch, D. 240
Gratian 61
Greek Anthology 86, 96, 103, 134, 247–248, 264–268, 276
Gregorius II (pope) 148–149, 165
Gregory the Great 166, 203
Gregory Magister 267
Gregory of Nazianzus 85, 93, 95–96, 102, 243
Griffin, J. 260, 263 n.

Ḥaḍramawt, rulers of 173 n.
Hadrian 249
Hadrian II (pope) 166
Haltern 234
hapax legomena 86, 88–93
Harig, G. 233, 236
Harper, K. 44 n.
Harris, W. V. 270
Hartke, W. 31

Hatra 191, 195
healing miracle 231
Hercules 178
Hermogenes of Tarsus 128
Herodes Atticus 220
Herodian 29
Hesiod 121
Heston, Charlton 272
Hilarius (pope) 204–205
Hirschfeld, O. 26, 27
Historia Augusta 4, 23–39, 265;
anachronisms in 25–28; date
of 30–36; sources of 28–30
Hod Hill (Dorset) 234
Hohl, E. 26
Holste (Holstenius), L. 137–138, 144–146, 154, 167
Homer 73–76, Chapter 6 *passim*, Chapter 7 *passim*
Homeric Hymns 93, 97
'Homeromania' 130–132
homilies 224–225, 228–232
Hormizd I 171 n., 179, 184
Huebner, S. 198, 217
Hyginus, Ps.- 234

iatreion (doctor's workplace) 237–238
infamia 202
infrared photos of papyri 105–106
initials, decorated (in illuminated
manuscripts) 156–165
Isaac 45, 48, 51
Ishmael (son of Abraham and Hagar) 51
Israelowich, I. 234
Istanbul 248, 265

Jacob and Esau (sons of Isaac) 45–46, 48–51, 53–55, 65
Jarry, J. 272
Jerome 34, 223, 244; *Life of Hilarion* 24, 32–36, 220
Jesus 53, 55
John II (pope) 214
John Chrysostom 230, 231, 244
John the Deacon 166
John the Lydian 271
Jordanes 37–38
Joseph (son of Jacob) 52–55, 65

INDEX   319

Julian   173 n., 246
Justinian   148, 200–201, 216–218
Juvenal   90
Juvenal (bishop of Jerusalem)   226
Juvenianus Codex   152, 157, 161

Kaldellis, A.   261
Kelly, C.   203
Kitzinger, E.   9
Kom el-Dikka   252, 258
Klein, R.   49

Lachmann method   135
Lactantius   172–173
Łajtar, A.   250
Lana, I.   67
Last Statues of Antiquity team   248
Laurentian Schism   211–214
Lauxtermann, M.   267–269, 276
Lehmann, P.   145–146
Lemerle, P.   268
Leo (emperor)   198, 199, 201–202, 203–204
lepers, leprosy   243, 244
Lepidi   69–70
Lepidus, Cl. (*comes rei privatae*)   70
Levison, W.   154
lexicon, Greek, in late antiquity   131
Libanius   54, 128, 223, 224
Liber pontificalis   134–167
Liebeschuetz, J. H. W. G.   273

Maas, P.   273
Mabillon, Jean   139
MacCoull, L. S. B.   105
Macedonian renaissance, so-called   268
Macrobius   3, 4
Magdalino, P.   262, 269
Magnesia on the Maeander   252
Manchester United   254
Mango, C.   268
Manojlović, G.   273
Marathonius (hospital supervisor?)   242
Marcellinus (*tribunus et notarius*)   227–228
Marius Maximus   29
Marxism   273
Maspero, J.   105
Maximinus (Arian bishop)   226
Maximos Planudes   266

Mazzarino, S.   271
McLynn, N.   41
melancholy: *see* black bile
Melania the Younger   77–83
Messius Phoebus Severus: *see* Severus
Milan   59, 61–62, 271
Miletus   251–252, 256, 274
military medical care   233–235, 239
Momigliano, A.   2
Mommsen   26, 135, 144–145, 147–148
monetary system, Roman   16–17
monks: *see* Capraria, Gorgo
Mordtmann, J. H.   247
More, Thomas   247
Mosaic Law   51

Naqsh-e Rajab (Iran)   178, 179
Naqsh-e Rustam, inscription of Šābuhr
    [Sapor] I at   170 n., 176, 179, 181, 185–187
Narseh (Sasanian king)   176, 185–187
Narses (Byzantine general)   148
Neoplatonism   261
New Testament   44
Nicholas I (pope)   166
Nicolaos (rhetorician)   128
Nicomachi Flaviani   8, 9–10; *and see*
    Flavianus
Nika riots   273–274
Nilus of Ancyra   244 n.
Nisibis, treaty of   170
Noah   54, 58
Nonnos   87, 91, 108–109, 112–114, 120
nosokomeion   244
Nutton, V.   233, 235, 238, 239
Nysa   251, 256

Odysseus   101
Ohrmazd (Iranian god)   178
Old Testament   51–53, 58
Olivar, A.   230
Olybrius   3
Olympiodorus   5–6
Orfitus, Memmius Vitrasius   6–7
Ostrogoths   38
Ovid   69, 74
Oxford   260
Oxyrhynchos   122, 250–252, 259

320   INDEX

Pack, R. A. 2
'paganism' 4–5
paganism and Christianity: *see* Christianity
    and paganism
Palatine Anthology 128
Palladius (Arian bishop) 226
Palladius (author of the *Lausiac History*)
    81–82, 244
Palmyra 191, 195
Pandulphus Romanus (12th c. cardinal)
    147–149
panegyric 11–16, 19–21
Parastaseis 264, 269–270
Parcerisa, J. P. 253
Pareti, L. 253
Parma 139, 153
Parthians 193–195, 197
Paschoud, F. 4, 23, 31
Paul I (pope) 139, 157, 162
Paul the Silentiary 113, 118
Paul of Tarsus 46–47, 50–51, 53–56, 59,
    64–65
Paulinus 74–75
paying for ecclesiastical office: *see* simony
Pelagius I (pope) 218–219
Pepin (king of the Franks) 139
Persian empire: *see* Parthians, Sasanian
    Empire
Peter (apostle) 157
Peter, H. 26
Petronius Probus: *see* Probus
Petzl, G. 249
Philip the Arab 169, 180–181
Philo Chapter 4 *passim*
philosophers 13–15
Phocas 252
Pickard [West], S. 260
Pighi, G. B. 2
Pinianus (husband of Melania) 78–79
Pistelli, E. 252
Planudes, Planudean Anthology 247, 266,
    267, 268
Plato, Platonizing 49–50, 51
Plautus 237–238
Pliny the younger 7
Polara, G. 5
Porphyrius 247–250, 264–266, 274
Potiphar 52
Praetextatus, Vettius Agorius 2, 4, 7, 271
Priene 253, 256

Priscillian 76
Probinus, Anicius (*cos.* 395) 3
Probus, Sex. Claudius Petronius
    (*PPO Italiae*) 7, 27, 28
προγυμνάσματα 125–126
Prosopographia Imperii Romani 25
ptôcheia, ptôchotropheia 241, 243
Ptolemaic rulers 180

Queen Christina 137
Quintilian 222
Quintus of Smyrna 91, 96

ransoming of prisoners 62–65
Ratti, S. 8, 23, 31, 67 n.
Reimea (Roman Arabia) 251, 258
Reynolds, J. 250
Rhodiapolis 250, 252, 254, 257
Ricimer 205
Rimini, House of the Surgeon 237
Robert, L. 248, 253, 265, 274
Rome 44, Chapter 8 *passim*; Altar of
    Victory 63; Arch of Constantine
    194–196; *and see* senate
Roueché, C. 274
Rufius Festus Avienius: *see* Festus
Rushdie, Salman 39
Rutilius Namatianus 3, 66–84

Šābuhr I 169–173, 176, 179
Šābuhr II 20–21
Salmasianus Codex 152, 157, 160–164
Sar Mashhad (Iran) 182, 184
'Saraceni', raid of 150
Sargveshi cup 184, 186, 194
Sasanian Empire 20–21, 168–197
Satala (Armenia) 170, 187, 192–194
Scarborough, J. 235
Schelstrate, Emmanuel 138
Schütrumpf, E. 50
scripts: minuscule 151, 167; uncial 134, 136,
    139, 145, 151–157, 166–167
Scythopolis (Judaea) 250–251, 258
Seeck, O. 1, 26
Seleucids 177, 180, 181
senate of Rome 6, 205, 208, 215–216
Seneca 235
Sergius II (pope) 146, 149–150, 152
sermons: *see* homilies
Severianus of Gabala (bishop) 231

INDEX

Severus, Fl. Messius Phoebus (*cos.* 470)   205
Shaw, B.   225
Sidonius Apollinaris   66 n., 206
Simon Magus   201, 210
simonia, simoniacus   203
simony   198–219
Simplicius (pope)   200, 205, 209–210,
    212–213
sin   54–56, 58–60, 65
slavery, slaves   41–65, 235, 239, 240–241
Socrates (historian)   129
Sozomen   246
sortes Vergilianae   26
Spingou, F.   267, 268, 276
stenographers   220–232
Stephen v (pope)   135, 165
Stilicho   3, 68, 70
Stoicism, Stoics   45, 47–56, 64–65
Stowers, S.   221
St. Paul's School   247, 264 n.
Stratonicaea (*provincia Asia*)   253, 257
Straub, J.   3, 4, 27, 31
Sudhoff, K.   236
subscriptiones   3
suffragium   202–203
Supino Martini, P.   166–167
Syme, R.   25 n., 27 n., 29, 32, 34–35
Symmachi   3, 5, 6, 9–10
Symmachus, Q. Aurelius (*cos.* 391)   1, 2, 6–8,
    61, 68
Symmachus, Aurelius Valerius Tullianus
    (*cos.* 330)   5
Symmachus (pope)   200, 211–214
synagogue at Callinicum, destruction of
    61–62
Synesius   101–102
Syria   170, 253

Tang-e Chowgan (Iran)   176
Tang-e Qandil (Iran)   182 n.
Technitai of Dionysus   249
Tetrarchy   16, 173–175, 177, 185, 187–195
Themistius   11–22
Theocritus   100–102
Theodore of Cynopolis   121
Theodore the Recruit, St.   244
Theoderic (king of the Ostrogoths)   211–213
Theodosius senior   9

Theodosius i   15 n., 61–62, 65
Thessalonica, Thessaloniki   62, 250, 255;
    Arch of Galerius   173–175, 184, 187–195
Thompson, E. A.   2
Tiberius   233–234
Traube, L.   145
Tyche   254
Tyre   250–251, 257–258

Umm el-Jimal (Jordan)   253, 258
Umm ar-Rasas (Jordan)   258

valetudinaria   Chapter 12 *passim*
Valentinian ii   61
Valerian   169–170, 172, 187, 192, 194, 195
van der Valk, M.   95
Van Nuffelen, P.   246
variatio, poetic   124
Varro   235
Vatican Library   Chapter 8 *passim*
Ventrella, G.   126
Vera, D.   6
Victory: on coin types   18, 192; Altar of, 63;
    victory acclamations   254; *and see*
    Thessalonica, Arch of Galerius
Vigilius (pope)   217
Vindolanda   240
Vitrasius: *see* Orfitus
Volusianus   5, 66 n., 68–69, 80
Vryonis, S.   274

Warahrān i   178, 179
Warahrān ii   170, 180–185
Warahrān iii   185
Weitzmann, K.   268
West, M. L.   9 n., 260, 263 n.
women, imperial Roman   148, 168–169, 177,
    185
Wood, P.   203–204
writing   Chapter 11 *passim*

xenodocheion   241

Zeno (philosopher)   45, 56
Zeno (emperor)   204
Zonaras   36, 37
Zosimus   24
Zumpt, A. W.   70

Printed in the United States
by Baker & Taylor Publisher Services